SAMENESS AND SUBSTANCE RENEWED

In this book, which thoroughly revises and greatly expands his classic work *Sameness and Substance* (1980), David Wiggins retrieves and refurbishes in the light of twentieth-century logic and logical theory certain conceptions of identity, of substance and of persistence through change that philosophy inherits from its past. In this new version, he vindicates the absoluteness, necessity, determinateness and all or nothing character of identity against rival conceptions. He defends a form of essentialism that he calls individuative essentialism, and then a form of realism that he calls conceptualist realism, a position he seeks to place in relation to one surviving insight of idealism. In a final chapter, he advocates a human being based conception of the identity and individuation of persons, arguing that any satisfactory account of personal memory must enforce and follow through all the normative requirements that flow from its logically inalienable aspiration to furnish direct knowledge of the rememberer's own past. This important book will appeal to a wide range of readers in metaphysics, philosophical logic, and analytic philosophy.

DAVID WIGGINS is Wykeham Professor of Logic Emeritus in the University of Oxford, Fellow of the British Academy, and Foreign Honorary Member of the American Academy of Arts and Sciences. His publications include *Needs, Values, Truth: Essays in the Philosophy of Value* (1987) and many journal articles.

SAMENESS AND SUBSTANCE RENEWED

DAVID WIGGINS

Wykeham Professor of Logic Emeritus in the University of Oxford

PUBLISHED BY THE PRESS SYNDICATE OF THE UNIVERSITY OF CAMBRIDGE
The Pitt Building, Trumpington Street, Cambridge, United Kingdom

CAMBRIDGE UNIVERSITY PRESS
The Edinburgh Building, Cambridge CB2 2RU, UK
40 West 20th Street, New York, NY 10011–4211, USA
10 Stamford Road, Oakleigh, VIC 3166, Australia
Ruiz de Alarcón 13, 28014 Madrid, Spain
Dock House, The Waterfront, Cape Town 8001, South Africa

http://www.cambridge.org

First published 2001

Printed in the United Kingdom at the University Press, Cambridge

Typeface Baskerville MT 11/12.5 pt.   *System* QuarkXPress™   [SE]

A catalogue record for this book is available from the British Library

Library of Congress Cataloguing in Publication data
Wiggins, David.
Sameness and substance renewed / David Wiggins.
p. cm.
Rev. edn of *Sameness and substance*. Oxford: Blackwell, 1980.
Includes bibliographical references and index.
ISBN 0 521 45411 5 (hardback) – ISBN 0 521 45619 3 (paperback)
1. Identity.   2. Individuation (Philosophy).   3. Essence (Philosophy).   4. Conceptualism.   5. Substance (Philosophy).   I. Wiggins, David. Sameness and substance.   II. Title.
BD236.W53   2001
110–dc21   00–065152

ISBN 0 521 45411 5 hardback
ISBN 0 521 45619 3 paperback

Contents

Preface

When *Sameness and Substance* (Blackwell, 1980) went out of print, Cambridge University Press agreed to take over the book. They suggested that the Longer Notes be dropped and certain smaller matters be attended to in recognition of what has happened since 1979. They urged that the chapter about personal identity be superseded. In the process of my discovering how just and sensible these proposals were, then forming the resolve to follow the substance theory through more single-mindedly and to a greater distance, there came into being the version I have called *Sameness and Substance Renewed*.

Whether *Sameness and Substance Renewed* is the same book as *Sameness and Substance* is not a question of importance – the matter of a joke that will fail nobody who wants to make it, or else of an exercise for the reader (not to be attempted before reading the new Chapter Six or without regard to the sort of ambiguities set out in Chapter One, §§6–7). The present text seeks to correct all the things in the 1980 version that I know to be plain wrong. Then, in the same dialect of mid twentieth-century English, it extends that version at some of the places where more was needed. Most conspicuously, there is a new chapter about identity, vagueness and supervenience; and, as requested, the old chapter on personal identity is entirely replaced. Those who interest themselves closely in the annals of disputes about these subjects will have to retrieve the old pages 149–89 from the same dust-heap of history as harbours most of the theses and questions once explored in the Longer Notes of the 1980 version.

In the text from 1980 that survived all these decisions, there has been rewriting and abbreviation. Neither of these processes could be carried far enough. But the reader may be assured that the present version does not set out to transcribe everything that still seems to me to be true from *Sameness and Substance* (1980) or from the book that *Sameness and Substance* itself consolidated. That earlier book was called *Identity and Spatio-Temporal*

Continuity, was published in 1967 and ran to seventy-eight pages of text. By chance or good luck, the present preface is addressed from the same place as was the 1967 preface. But neither chance nor luck, nor yet an inflexible will to abandon absolutely everything save that which is central, could have restored the same brevity or the same simplicity of purpose that was possible in 1967, given the wider range of well formed questions now wanting attention.

This is not the book that I should have written if I had been starting afresh or I had been able to train a freer fancy or a more impartial attention upon the logical and philosophical literature of identity produced in the twenty-one years since *Sameness and Substance* was given to the publisher. But I have tried to update whatever has been allowed to remain – or else to test it off the page against alternative options made newly visible. It has been a great help that Sabina Lovibond's and Stephen Williams's collection *Identity, Truth and Value: Essays for David Wiggins* (Blackwell, 1996), henceforth their (1996), recently obliged me to review everything I was committed to. *Sameness and Substance Renewed* follows through the implications of the commentary I offered in *Identity, Truth and Value* upon the essays presented there by Timothy Williamson, Harold Noonan and Paul Snowdon. Not only that. It follows through the reactions to which I was moved or provoked by the numerous other items that I happened upon in composing replies to these three scholars. For everything Williamson, Noonan and Snowdon did directly and indirectly to provoke these reactions I am extremely grateful. In the case of some of the other démarches in the field, however, it has seemed that the best reaction is to take note but remain silent. Some will disappear without the ministrations of comment or criticism. Others will not disappear, but will seem misguided to anyone I can convince of the correctness of the approach to identity that is exemplified in this book. Yet others of more recent provenance must wait their turn to be read until this book is given to the new publisher, who has waited long enough.

Acknowledgements to Noonan and Snowdon apart, as to Williamson (who did me a further favour by accepting the publisher's invitation to review the whole draft), there are newer debts of gratitude, to William Child, Stephen Williams, Christopher Peacocke, Naci Mehmet and Ian Rumfitt, for instance, each of whom read some version of some chapter or section or extract. I am grateful to New College and the Sub-Faculty of Philosophy at Oxford for substantial technical assistance and especially to Jo Cartmell. Without her the task could not have been completed. From earlier times, a variety of philosophical acknowledgements must be carried forward that are no less real for being old: first (from the monograph of 1967) there are special thanks to Professors P. T. Geach, W. A. Hodges and B. A. O. Williams. From 1980, there are acknowledgements to M. K. Davies, E. L. Hussey, D. W. Hamlyn, R. A. Wollheim, C. A. B. Peacocke, M. L. C. Nussbaum, D. F. Cheesman, J. A. W. Kamp, N. Tennant, J. H. McDowell. Debts were incurred on a much larger scale in 1977–8 to Sir Peter Strawson and Jennifer Hornsby. In 1980 I made more general acknowledgements to various papers by Hilary Putnam, Saul Kripke and Richard Cartwright, and to *Leibniz's Philosophy of Logic and Language* by Hidé Ishiguro. In divers and different ways, each of these authors informed or strengthened the various convictions that I needed in order to shape the characteristic, however insufficiently qualified, claims of *Sameness and Substance* concerning the mutual dependence of the ideas of substance, causality, law, and *de re* necessity.

In *Identity and Spatio-Temporal Continuity*, dark claims were entered about the relevance and importance for the theory of individuation of the philosophy of biology. In *Sameness and Substance* it would have been good if there had been more about these matters. After the abandonment of Longer Notes, all that remains here are certain sketchy remarks in Chapters Two and Three. But I shall recall from the 1980 Preface the keen pleasure that I felt at that time on discovering how, in response to all the facts that confront the biological scientist, Professor J. Z. Young had arrived, in chapters Five and Six of his *Introduction to the Study of Man* (Oxford, 1971), at a conception of identity and persistence through time that is strikingly similar, where living things are concerned, to the neo-Aristotelian conception that I defend:

The essence of a living thing is that it consists of atoms of the ordinary chemical elements we have listed, caught up into the living system and made part of it for a while. The living activity takes them up and organizes them in its characteristic way. The life of a man consists essentially in the activity he imposes upon that stuff . . . it is only by virtue of this activity that the shape and organization of the whole is maintained.

Two other good things that have happened since 1967 are the recognition in the philosophical community at large of the persisting conceptual importance, all foolish revivalism apart, of Aristotle's biology and philosophy of life; and the development by Peter Simons (in *Parts: A Study in Ontology*, Oxford, 1987) of a new account of the part–whole relationship that is far less alien to the present inquiry than the works of classical extensional mereology that I criticize so relentlessly in Chapters One, Two and Three.

In 1980 it seemed that there were two important things I had to say about identity and individuation. One came down to this. Identity was an absolute relation, yet, despite this, identity was not bare continuity. *A fortiori*, neither identity nor even the identity relation as restricted to material objects could be the same relation as continuity as such. *Identity and Spatio-Temporal Continuity* (1967) had been a first engagement in the war against this idea, which was no less dispensable, I said, than it was incoherent. Hence came the thesis of Sortal Dependency, labelled **D** in *Sameness and Substance* (1980). This said that behind every true identity claim there stands an identity covered by the concept of some particular kind of thing (in a wide range of empirical cases, a substance-kind). Once **D** was in place, the philosophical work that remained was to show how, in all their strictness, the formal properties of the relation of identity can be sustained by our kind-based individuative practices.

Among the further consequences derived from sortal dependency were a modest but specifically individuative (contrast referential) form of essentialism and the second of the special things I thought I had to say in 1980. This was the doubtfulness of the separation, supposedly obvious or truistic and still widely insisted upon, between ontological and conceptual questions. Here, even if some of the things rehearsed in the previous paragraph have come to be accepted as commonplace, I think I have made scarcely any impression on received ideas about the sharp division of questions of ontology from questions of ideology. (In Quine's sense of "ideology". See *From a Logical Point of View*, Harvard, 1953, p. 131.) As in the 1980 version, the case for this adjustment is expressed in Chapter Five and that which leads up to it. In *Sameness and Substance Renewed*, Chapter Five prepares the way for some fresh reflections, pursued further in Chapter Six, about identity, vagueness, determinacy and the singularity of the identity relation. It is here that I think the conceptualist insight I try to formulate in Chapters Five and Six shines a new light onto certain familiar questions, questions already transformed by Timothy Williamson's sharp critique of received theories of vagueness. See his recent book, *Vagueness* (London, 1995). Before the insight that I call the conceptualist insight falls into the wrong hands, however, let me say immediately that it is all of a piece with the absolute and adamantine hardness of truth. (See Chapter Six, §6.) The same goes for the increasing emphasis placed upon the irreducibly practical aspect of our acts of individuation. This may even amount to a third important thing that I think I have to say.

Chapter Six makes a protest against the idea that, even if identity is strictly irreducible, it must supervene somehow upon other properties and relations of objects, and supervene in such a way that these will constitute locally sufficient grounding for a judgment of identity. By this protest, I position the theory of identity and individuation to see the making of identity judgments in an altogether other way. Let us see it as an extension of our practical capacity to single out things of a given kind and then, in the light of an understanding of the behaviour of things of that kind, to keep track of them. The fully fledged judgment of identity outgrows its primitive origin but, according to my account, it does not lose touch with the original enterprise that it extends.

If I had seen all this clearly in 1980, if I had seen the opportunity it affords for fresh modes of philosophical exposition, I think I might have found a way to treat the questions of identity and individuation otherwise than in the technical-sounding language of principles of individuation, persistence, identity, activity. To dispense altogether with all talk of such principles would have been a noble endeavour. But it would have required a completely new book, one that strained less after generality or that only achieved it by the extended demonstration and discussion of eminent instances. Instead, the thing I shall say here about principles of individuation and so on is simply this: given that any serious or ontologically committal use of language of this kind can only multiply the kind of problems that philosophy has already with entelechies, forms, potentialities, actualities, etc., and given that such use may threaten an explanatory regress (as Penelope Mackie has properly observed, see her *op. cit.* at note 22, Chapter Four), all talk of such things needs to be understood as notional. What would it be to treat it so? Well, here is a start. To see that the principle of individuation for a buzzard is not the same as the principle for a bat, to see that the principle of individuation for a teapot is not the same as that for a housefly – there is no more to this (and no less) than there is to seeing what a difference there is between these things *from the practical point of view of singling them out, of keeping track of them and of chronicling what they do.*

Chapter Seven, the new chapter on personal identity, focuses on human beinghood, and recants anything I have ever said against Bishop Butler's objection to Locke's account of personal identity. The chief aim is to treat personal identity for what it is, namely a special case with a special power to test any emerging answer to the general question of the identity and individuation of substances. The chapter reviews briefly the course of controversy on these matters since the nineteen sixties, when a thought experiment of Sydney Shoemaker's deflected me and many other philosophers towards the neo-Lockean conception of personal identity. My completed recantation, which perseveres in doubts Bernard Williams, Paul Snowdon and I have expressed over a long period, comprises considerations *inter alia* of epistemology and the cognitive activity of human beings. On this basis, I seek to show that there is no non-vacuous sense in which one can say "the ordinary further facts of human personality *supervene* upon the facts of mental and physical continuity and connectedness". (*Pace* the philosophers who say that sort of thing, those mental and physical facts are *already* identity-involving.) I must add, however, that despite the completion of this recantation of all neo-Lockean tendencies, I cling to my admiration of Locke's *Essay* ii·27, not least (now) of his "forensic" conception. This last has usually been taken to support the Lockean over the human being conception of personal identity. In the light of the considerations of physiognomy that I try now to insist upon, I think that the chief contribution of the forensic conception is to make us (the persons that we are) see the difficulty of conceiving of a person (conceiving of one of us) otherwise than as a being with a human form. Rereading the old chapter in *Sameness and Substance* that the new Chapter Seven replaces, I find that this anticipated and spelled out at great length a range of practical and moral apprehensions arising from the prospect of other, quasi-functional or quasi-artefactual, conceptions of personhood gaining ground. The fact that the ensuing twenty years have intensified these apprehensions might be ground for intellectual satisfaction. (For no other.) But the intervening years equally suggest the need to condense the apprehensions themselves into one or two bare paragraphs. At this point of the argument, the thing that matters is the intimate connexion between such apprehensions, familiar as they will now be to almost every reader, and the range of rival conceptions, some of them artefactual, some of them (like mine) anti-artefactual, of what *kind* of thing it is we are concerned to individuate when we ask what a human person is.

Readers who wish to begin by seizing the main essentials of the theory of identity and individuation which leads into all these other things (or so I claim) should not labour too hard over the later sections of the Preamble, which is mainly methodological and terminological. Terminological explanations that are essential – and some of them are indeed essential – are given again or referred back to as and when they are needed in the body of the book. The chief purpose of the Preamble is to place all these explanations where they belong, namely in a single framework within which they will show themselves to be singly and collectively defensible. Those convinced of the wrongness of my substantive conclusions or who object to the method of reaching them ought, in due course, to take the precaution of reading the Preamble through to the end.

Readers who are prepared to skip should read Chapter One, sections 1–5, and then advance immediately to Chapter One, sections 9 and 10, before reading Chapters Two and Three. A summary is given at Chapter Three, section 5, of this material, just as a partial summary is given in §2 and §8 of Chapter Five, to recapitulate Chapters Four and Five.

The chief aim of Chapters One, Two and Three of the book is to place questions of individuation, identity and persistence through time on a firmer and broader basis of theory, but in such a way that the particular point that is at issue in particular problems of identity will be locally determined. Once matters are put onto this basis, there can be securer standards (or so I claim) by which to judge *in situ*, on the basis of the right kinds of consideration, the relevance or irrelevance to the given case of empirical information that is collateral with the case. The resulting conception of individuation is principled, logically founded, yet irreducibly practical. It is *universal*, in so far as it always appeals to ideas that transcend the particular case, but also *dialectical*. It is dialectical not only in respect of how it envisages any particular decision's being reached but in respect of the individuative practices that it justifies. Room is left for these practices and the thing-kind conceptions that incorporate them to proceed in a given case by considerations that are highly specific to it (scarcely general at all). That will not prevent these considerations from being universal in import. For the distinctness of the general/specific and the universal/singular (or universal/particular) distinctions and the compatibility of specificity with universality, I would refer to R. M. Hare, *Freedom and Reason* (Oxford, 1963). (See his p. 39.) Even at this late stage in the specialization of philosophy, light can still be cast on logic and metaphysics from ethics and the philosophy of law.

The explanation of how the conception thus formed of identity and individuation coheres with the invincible strictness of the laws of identity is completed in Chapter Six, which resumes and extends some of the arguments of Chapters Four and Five. Finally, the last part of Chapter Seven (§13 onwards) offers certain general reflections about identity and individuation and follows them through. In these concluding reflections I see some culmination of the efforts of all earlier chapters. I hope that this part can be read on its own without the preceding sections of Chapter Seven.

The price of making the book skippable in this way is paid by the reader who reads it right through. I have tried however to keep to the barest minimum the amount of repetition that is entailed by the policy.

The purpose of the Select bibliography is to include a selection (updated 1999) of certain major and minor classics of the theory of identity and individuation and to make reference to other works that the reader may find useful or on which this book most heavily depends. Only incidentally is it a bibliography of personal identity or of anything else besides the theory of identity and individuation. Numerous other useful or fascinating items not included in this selection are referred to in the footnotes. I know that many books and articles left out of the Select bibliography are just as good as those I have included. Philosophers hate to contemplate such contingency, I know, but the sole aim has been to make this bibliography short enough for it to be useful, useful in its own right or usefully cognizant of the particular intellectual debts it happened the author incurred in writing or rewriting this book. The author/date system is used for references to titles included in the Select bibliography.

The chapter footnotes are part of the final defences of the theory, but they are meant to be theoretically dispensable to the basic understanding of the argument. (One regrettable departure from this policy remains, at footnote 2 of Chapter Three.) But there is no attempt to push into the text everything which points at something important. Most especially I have not attempted this where the matter in the note leads not back to the argument of the text but outwards from it. An example of that is the brief discussion in footnote 14 (formerly 12) of Chapter One of some of the differences between a substance and an event. Another example is the equally old footnote 16 of Chapter Three (now numbered 17), concerning that which I regard as the chief falsehood in the classical or original form of mereology or the calculus of individuals.

The Index is intended to secure the sense of key technical terms, printing in bold the page reference that best indicates what acceptations I have aimed, for the length of a book, to assign stably and definitely to certain technical terms used here.

December 1999   D.W.
New College
Oxford

Preamble, chiefly concerned with matters methodological and terminological

Technical terms are worse to be shunned than dog or snake.
(Leibniz, Gerhardt IV, 140.)

I. AIMS AND PURPOSES

The chief aim of this book is to elaborate a theory of the individuation of continuants, including living substances and other substances. Such a theory ought to comprise at least three things: an elucidation first of the primitive concept of identity or sameness; second, some account of what it is for something to be a substance or continuant that persists through change; third, an account of what it amounts to, practically and cognitively, for a thinker, to single a thing out at a time. Here, with this last task, there is the supplementary question of what it amounts to for the same thinker, having once singled something out, later to single out that same thing *as* the same thing.

From a philosopher's attitude towards the logical and methodological ordering of these tasks one can tell something about his or her attitude towards the idea that the meaning of a word is a function of its use. In this work, it is everywhere accepted that the meanings of such words as 'same', 'substance', 'change', 'persist' and 'recognize' depend upon their use. The life and semantic identity of such terms is only sustained by the activity of singling out or individuating. But the thesis of meaning as use is consistent with two converse or complementary theses (A)(B), which have an equal relevance to what is to be attempted and an equal claim upon rational acceptance.

(A) The relation between the meaning and the use of such words as 'same', 'substance', 'change', 'persist' is in fact reciprocal or two-way. Everything that concerns meaning registers upon use; but, unless we

I

redefine use, that does not imply that meaning can be reduced to use.[1] Among the concerns I began by enumerating, there is no question of collapsing the first two into the third, for instance.

(B) An interpretation of a set of linguistic uses or conceptual practices must speak of the *subject matter* to which they relate. For that reason, it must refer to the various things themselves towards which the uses or practices themselves are directed, together with the properties and relations of these things. The child who is learning to find for himself the persisting substances in the world, to think the thoughts that involve them and recognize the same ones again, grasps a skill and a subject matter at one and the same time. A philosopher who seeks properly to understand those thoughts must proceed accordingly. Let the philosopher elucidate *same*, *identical*, *substance*, *change*, *persist*, etc., directly and from within the same practices as those that an ordinary untheoretical human being is initiated into. At the same time, let the philosopher show by example what good elucidations can be made of such ideas as these. To this end, let him shadow the practical commerce between things singled out and thinkers who find their way around the world by singling out places and objects – and singling out one another. If the meaning of the terms 'same', 'substance', 'change', 'persist', etc., is a function of use and use is a function of the said commerce, then one by-product of this mode of elucidation will be that the task I began by calling the third task is undertaken in concert with the first and the second. The first and second tasks acknowledge the importance of the third; but, by their constant appropriate acknowledgment of this importance, they will in fact absorb the third.

When the reciprocities and mutual interdependencies of concept, practice and thing-singled-out are acknowledged and likened to those of some seamless web, when the primitiveness of all the relevant notions is acknowledged too, how much genuine clarification is it reasonable to expect a philosophical theory of individuation to be able to achieve? Well, we have rudimentary pretheoretical ideas of identity, persistence through change, and the singling out of changeable things. By means of these, we may arrive at a provisional or first explication of what 'same' means and of the actual application of this relation-word. So soon as that is achieved, there is a basis from which to scrutinize afresh and then

[1] Or even to correct and truthful use, which would be a less striking achievement. (I hear someone scoffing at the distinction between use and correct use. Let them note that the correct use of a word or device might only be determinable from within a whole practice, yes, but without its following from this that the correct use was determinable from within practice *in respect of this word or device*. Cognate questions are pursued further in my (1997b).

consolidate our logical and participative understanding of the individuative practices that a thinker's grasp of the concepts of substance, sameness and persistence through change makes possible for him. At the end
of this second phase, nothing will be recognizable as the philosophical
analysis of '='. But no special mystery need remain about how a notion
of the exigency that we ascribe to the identity relation can find application in the changeable world of our experience. Provided we do not
despise the ordinary ideas by which we conduct the untheoretical business of the individuation and reidentification of particulars, we can
remind ourselves well enough of what regulates the principled employ-
ment of '='. We can remind ourselves of what it is for anyone who is
bent on singling out objects to carve off from the world, or isolate from
among the objects of his experience, various continuants or things that
persist through change.

This emphasis on the practical does not mean something that it might
seem to mean if, in the cause of the crudest version of 'meaning as use',
a separate priority were accorded to the third of the three tasks enumerated in the second sentence of the first paragraph. It does not mean that,
for the benefit of his deluded subjects, the theorist is to find a way to see
a world that might as well be one of pure flux in which nothing really
persists through change *as if* that world offered us objects that persist
through change. For persistence through change is not make-believe. No
sensible inquiry could abandon a datum so fundamental or so deeply
entrenched.[2] It means that, arriving at the point programmatically
described, the theorist is to understand as well as he can – discursively,
practically, in the same sort of terms as those who individuate them or
in modest extrapolation from these – what it is for an object to be a
genuine continuant; it means that, when that is done, the theorist is to
describe how the charge that something did not persist is to be considered, namely on its merits, such merits being set out in terms accessible
in principle to those who take themselves to believe in genuine continuants. It is in this way that we shall try to identify the point properly at
issue in some of the most bitterly contested questions of identity.

There are two complaints about the method of elucidations that will
not go happily together: (1) that the method is vacuous, a mere replay of
that which needs to be 'explained'; (2) that the demands which the
method derives from the congruence and other properties of identity
and translates into requirements upon the positive finding of identity are

[2] Nor could flux *as such*, or as coherently conceived, stand in the way of singling out changeable
continuants. See my (1982).

draconian, too exigent, too severe. You cannot make both complaints. But it is better (I hope to show) not to make either.

Where there is reciprocity or mutual presupposition between concepts, analytical philosophy is always tempted into violence or arbitrariness. We find it hard to endure the thought that, in the substantive questions of philosophy, there is no master thread we can pull upon to unravel everything else. Even as I deprecate this idée fixe, however, it may appear that the chapters which follow are victim of the same illusion. For in this book the formal properties of identity, namely the reflexivity of identity and Leibniz's Law (registered in the claim that, if x is the same as y, then whatever is true of x is true of y and whatever is true of y is true of x), will be treated as enjoying a special status. In this way, am I not attempting to insulate from legitimate criticism my opinion that these formal properties determine what can count as someone's singling out or tracing an entity? In the presence of doubt concerning formal properties, is it not simple dogmatism for me to persist in saying (in effect) that the properties of identity regulate, by reference to a claim they make upon reason, the interpretation of thought and action *as* thought and action?

In partial answer to this charge, I can only plead that something is done in the course of Chapter One, §2, to justify the view I take of the formal properties of '='. I do not really think they are given simply *ab extra*. It is true that I liken the status of reflexivity and congruence (along with the symmetry and transitivity that they entail) to that of the Law of Non-Contradiction. But, bracketing Chapter One, §2, my conciliatory view would be that the issue between the opposition and me is holistic and dialectical. If that is right, however, then the question at issue cannot really be resolved until some opposing account of individuation is developed to the same point as the account presented here. These questions will not be resolved until rival descriptions of individuation (and of reference) are compared with one another against the background of all the practices that they purport to describe. (For one small step in that direction, see Harold Noonan's and my exchange in Lovibond and Williams (1996).) The thing I have to hope is that, in the end, the reader will convince himself that the internal difficulties of the ontology and ideology of a position that abandons the Leibnizian conception of identity are overwhelmingly greater than any of the difficulties attaching to the position I recommend. I trust that at that point, if not before, the reader will come to share my conviction that the Leibnizian principle is immanent in any linguistic or reflective practices we can recognize as reference and individuation.

3. NOTIONS

Corresponding to the three tasks mentioned in the first paragraph, we have the notions *identical (same)*, *continuant* and *individuate*.

(i) The notion of sameness or identity that we are to elucidate is not that of qualitative similarity but that of coincidence (as an object, thing or substance), a notion as primitive as predication and correlative with it in the following way: if and only if Socrates is a man, then Socrates is identical with some man, and thus (we shall argue) shares all his properties with him. (This equivalence is offered as a manifest truth, rather than as an analytical definition of 'is a man' or of anything else. It is not offered as a part of a canonical or mandatory definitional sequence. See below, §10.) No reduction of the identity relation has ever succeeded. (See especially Chapter Six, §9.) Nor yet is it called for, once we realize how much can be achieved in philosophy by means of elucidations that put a concept to use without attempting to reduce it but, in using the concept, exhibit its connexions with other concepts that are established, genuinely coeval or collateral, and independently intelligible. (Compare here Wittgenstein, *Tractatus Logico-Philosophicus*, 3.263, 4.026, 4.112.) Not only is identity irreducible. Only in a vacuous sense of 'supervene', or a weak and irrelevant one, does it supervene on the totality of properties and relations other than itself. (See Chapter Six, §9.)

(ii) We have to explicate what it is to be a continuant or a substance. This explication will not amount to a definition. Nor will it be achieved without the ineliminably practical demonstration of the ordinary perceptible individuals of common experience. The explication must go some way beyond mere demonstration. But to set out, as so many philosophers have done in emulation of Book VII of Aristotle's *Metaphysics*, with the high-minded aspiration to achieve an altogether purer kind of definition of substance, and then to abandon the concept of substance just because the result does not satisfy, is to end up doing philosophy that is at once ill-tempered and needlessly bad. It represents the inability to learn from Aristotle's experiment.[3]

---

[3] For my own attempts to learn from it, see my (1995).

Kant writes at §46 of *Prolegomenon to Any Future Metaphysic:* 'People have long since observed that in all substances the proper subject, that which remains after all the accidents (as predicates) are abstracted, remains unknown.' I protest that the substances or subjects we begin with are not unknown but known, that the only abstraction in which we need to be interested is utterly distinct from that which is supposed to result from the notional (mythical) removal of properties from a substance. The interesting and benign form of abstraction is that which results from the ascent from particular kinds of substance to the determinable *substance of some further specifiable kind.* (Ascent to what Wittgenstein in *Tractatus Logico-Philosophicus* called a formal concept.) This form of abstraction cannot part us from our conviction that substances are things which are known to us.

(iii) The *Oxford English Dictionary* defines 'individuate' in terms of 'single out' or 'pick out', and this definition is well suited to the purposes of this book. That which individuates – in the one sense in which the word will be used in this book[4] – is in the first instance a thinker. (Derivatively, but only derivatively, one may find oneself saying that a substantive or predicate individuates.) To single *x* out is to isolate *x* in experience; to determine or fix upon *x* in particular by drawing its spatio-temporal boundaries and distinguishing it in its environment from other things of like and unlike kinds (at this, that and the other times during its life history); hence to articulate or segment reality in such a way as to discover *x* there. To single *x* out though, or even to prolong the singling out of *x* into the effort to keep track of *x*, is not yet (unless 'in thought') to refer to *x* or to designate *x*. And one may well refer to *x*, of course, without in our primary sense singling *x* out at all. This is not to say that, if there were no singling out, there could be reference. Singling out is the sheet-anchor for *information about particulars.*

The verbs 'individuate' and 'single out' are not intensional. If a thinker singles out *x* or individuates *x*, and *x* = *y*, then, whether or not he knows it, he singles out or individuates *y*. Such verbs do, however, permit of a complementation that is intensional. A Greek could have simply singled out Socrates; he could have singled out Socrates as Socrates; he could have singled out Socrates as a certain man or philosopher; or he could have singled out Socrates as the Athenian married to Xanthippe who was represented by Plato to have stressed (*Phaedrus* 265ᵉ) the equal importance, in classification and in carving, of 'dividing where the joints are'. What then is the relation of singling out and singling out *as*? In due

---

[4] Contrast books about logic or metaphysics where the verb is used to stand for the relation between a predicate and some unique thing that satisfies the predicate.

course, we shall discover reason to think that there could be no singling out *tout court* unless there could also be singling out *as*. (This is not a priority claim.) It will be declared that not just any attempt at singling out counts as singling *something* out; that that which is required in a given case derives from what the thing itself is. It will be a consequence of the account of these matters to be given here that, for a thinker to single out or individuate a substance, there needs to be something about what he does, something about his *rapport* with *x* or his relational state towards *x* and his practical sensibility in relation to *x*, which (regardless of whether he articulately knows this or not – for all he needs is clear indistinct knowledge, cf. Chapter Three, note 6 and associated text – and regardless of whether it is a singling out *as*) sufficiently approximates to this: the thinker's singling *x* out as *x and* as a thing of a kind f such that membership in f entails some correct answer to the question 'what is *x*?' For the philosophical cargo carried by this Aristotelian question, see Chapter One and the chapter mottoes prefixed to it from Aristotle's *Categories*. One further and equally Aristotelian part of that cargo makes reference to the way in which *x* behaves, how it acts and reacts. It will be everywhere insisted, moreover, that the singling out at time *t* of the substance *x must look backwards and forwards* to times before and after *t*. And it will be categorically denied in Chapters Five and Six, that, where it is indeterminate what was singled out, we have the singling out of something indeterminate. (Even at this distance the thing denied has the distinctive smell of fallacy.) But at this point in summarizing what is to come, I venture well beyond explanation of terminology and deep into the philosophy of the matter. Chapters Five and Six aim to complete the account of what singling out is. If they succeed, it will become finally clear how and why the singling something out at *t* cannot help but look, as I say, both backwards and forwards to times before and after *t*.

In sum, let the English language fix what will be meant by 'single out' and 'pick out'. Let these verb phrases sustain the practical and epistemological significance of 'individuate', 'individuation' and 'individuative'. Let philosophy then seek to say what individuative acts and thoughts amount to. At this point, a reader who has had enough of preliminaries may want to advance to Chapter One.

4. PHILOSOPHICAL TERMINOLOGY: A MANIFESTO

The explications just given are intended to leave room for me to make the following declaration. Ideally, all technical terms should (i) be defined and

(ii) belong in that part of the metalanguage which does not overlap with the object language. Where there is no alternative but to allow technical terms to penetrate into the object language (e.g. because the object language is poor in schematic devices or devices of generalization), one might hope that technical terms would serve the sole purpose of abbreviation, of summarizing, and of systematizing, in terms not essentially different from the expressions indigenous to the object language, the matters of which the object language already speaks. No doubt the philosophy of any particular science or art will need to use the technical terms of that science or art. But such terms will have needed to pass muster in that art or science itself.[5]

The semi-technical uses in this book of 'concept', 'continuant', 'substance', 'coincidence', 'coincidence under a concept' will stand condemned unless they can conform to these requirements. Maybe they will not always live up to the ideal stated, and will to that extent stand condemned. But my aspiration for them is that they should be devices for the generalization of that which has a straightforward meaning in the object language of English – more specifically, that they will be *determinables* of which ordinary English provides countless *determinations*.[6] This is everywhere important, but it is a particularly important stipulation in connexion with the term 'substance'. If we misunderstand determinable notions such as this, then it is almost inevitable that we shall unintentionally restore the unwanted associations of 'substance' with doctrines of bare particulars and qualitiless substrate.

5. SORTAL PREDICATES AND SORTAL CONCEPTS: AND CONCEPTS VERSUS CONCEPTIONS

A technical term that is associated with 'substance' and the *what is it?* question but belongs in the metalanguage is 'sortal predicate'. I use this

---

[5] In stating that these are the ideals to which I regard myself as answerable, I am not venturing to condemn all philosophy that disregards them or follows some other manifesto. It is enough for me to say that the badness of much philosophy that is bad by almost any standard can be partly explained as the effect, *inter alia*, of disregard for such maxims – or of utter nescience of them.

[6] The *determinable/determinate* distinction was revived by W. E. Johnson (*Logic* I *XI 3*; Cambridge, 1921) out of dissatisfaction with the traditional genus and differentia account of species when it was applied outside its traditional scope. 'To be ultramarine is not to be blue and something else besides, but it is a particular way of being blue', A. N. Prior, *The Doctrine of Propositions and Terms* (London, 1976). *Pace* the traditional doctrine of *genus* and *differentia*, I should say the same of being a cat. It is not a matter of being an animal and something else that is independent of animality. See below on real definitions, §6. Manifestly 'substance' stands for a *fundamentum divisionis* in the traditional scheme. Or, in the language of the *Tractatus*, one may prefer to say it stands for a formal concept. For further discussion, see A. N. Prior, *op. cit.*, pp. 63–4 and 'Determinables, Determinates and Determinants', *Mind*, 58 (1949), pp. 1–20, 178–94.

Lockean term in roughly the manner of the second part of P. F. Strawson's *Individuals* (London: Methuen, 1959). See especially his pp. 168–9. (For a discrepancy not of philosophical purpose but of detail, see Chapter One, section 8 below.) Locke's usage, Strawson's usage and my own are all focused or organized by Aristotle's distinction of predications in the category of substance from predications in the category of quality and the other categories. See the first five chapters of Aristotle's treatise *Categories*, especially the two passages I have prefixed to Chapter One. For Locke's usage, see *Essay* iii, iii, 15:

> it being evident that things are ranked under names into sorts or species only as they agree to certain abstract ideas, to which we have annexed those names, the essence of each *genus* or sort comes to be nothing but that abstract idea which the general, or *sortal* (if I may have leave so to call it so from *sort*, as I do *general* from *genus*), name stands for.[7]

Here, as in other cases, the intuitive semantics we reach for in replacement of the Lockean system of ideas are Frege's or some adaptation of these. (For, however unfinished Frege's original scheme may be and whatever reservations one may have about the further elaborations that he offers of it in *Grundgesetze*, the underlying ideas are as general as they are durable.) Like other predicables, a sortal predicate expresses a sense and, by virtue of expressing this sense, it stands for a concept. Under this concept individual things may fall. See the diagram in Frege's letter to Husserl.[8] To understand a predicate and know what concept it stands for is to grasp a rule that associates things that answer to it with the True and things that don't answer to it with the False. (The extension of the concept is therefore the inverse image of the True under the function

---

[7] At §19 ('Divided reference'), Quine (1960) notes the following variants for 'sortal predicate': (1) individuative predicate; (2) articulative predicate; (3) substance-name; (4) shared, or multiply denotative, name; (5) predicate which divides its reference (extension). Another variant that has had some currency, on which see Woods (1959), is (6) boundary drawing predicate. (Cf. Frege (1950), §54.) All six terms serve to illuminate the difference, partially but only imperfectly reflected in the grammatical division of noun and adjective or verb, between Aristotle's ontologically basic question *What is x?* and less basic questions such as *What is x like? Where is x? What is x doing?* Note that looking at these terms in this Aristotelian way will enforce a *diachronic* interpretation of 'individuate', 'articulate', etc. We shall not be in the business of describing first what it takes for synchronic momentary presentations (things presented) *a* and *b* to be the same dog and *then* describing what it takes for a presentation now and a presentation tomorrow to be 'concanine'. Identity over time is just identity. The same holds of identity at a time. Such truisms should condition any account of the terms of a given identity judgment. Any secure practical grasp of what counts now as a dog regulates present judgments in the light of future and past findings about the same thing. And *vice versa*. See my 'Reply to Noonan' in Lovibond and Williams (1996).

[8] The letter is dated 1894. See Dummett (1973), Chapter Five. The diagram is reproduced in my (1984) and my (1993).

determined by this rule.) To grasp the rule is to grasp how or what a thing must be (or what a thing must do) in order to satisfy the predicate. To grasp this last is *itself* to grasp the Fregean concept. Thus 'horse' stands for that which Victor is and Arkle is, for instance – just as, outside the sortal category, the verb-phrase 'runs swiftly' stands for that which Arkle does. When I declare that to grasp this rule is to come to understand what *horse* is or *run swiftly* is, someone may insist that, in that case, the concept so spoken of, *horse* or *run swiftly* or whatever it may be, is a property. I shall not demur, but simply insist in my turn that the notion of a rule of correlation to which I appeal is pretheoretical. It is not indissolubly wedded to an extensional criterion of concept identity. The extensional criterion is the by-product, not here needed, of the mathematicians' regimentation of an entirely intuitive notion.[9]

The concept *horse* is not then an abstraction such as horse-hood or horse-ness (whatever these are). It is something general or, better, universal; and to that extent it will be philosophically contentious. But *horse* or *mammal* or *carnivore* surely *are* things that we need to speak of or quantify over, in metaphysics and in science.[10] Objects fall under them and so on – and, under this aspect, objects can be seen as belonging to divers assemblages, variously denominated species, sorts, kinds.[11]

Seen in this way, as something with instances, the concept belongs on the level of reference (reference in general being something of which naming is one special case). But there is another use of the word 'concept' which is equally common, if not more common, and this belongs on the level of sense. It is this rival use of the word 'concept' that we find in discussions that are influenced directly or indirectly by Kant. In those discussions, talk of things falling under a concept, or of concepts having extensions, may be less felicitous. Or rather, it will not come to the same thing. Perhaps everything will fall into place, however, and the connexion will be visible between the two uses of the word, if we try to reserve the word 'concept' for the Fregean use and we prefer the word 'conception' to cover the Kantian use (seeing a Fregean sense as a very special case of a conception). The connexion that there is between the two may then be understood as follows:

[9] See B. A. W. Russell, *Introduction to the Mathematical Philosophy* (London, 1917), p. 187, and the further references to Ramsey, Quine and Church given in Aaron Sloman's neglected but valuable article 'Functions and Rogators' (1965). See especially pp. 158, 159, 161.

[10] For more on these, see my (1984), especially the references to Elliot Sober, 'Evolutionary Theory and the Ontological Status of Properties', *Philosophical Studies*, 40 (1981), and my (1993). The quantification in question is over both sortal and non-sortal properties.

[11] In ordinary English and even in ordinary philosophical English, some of these terms lead a double life perhaps, as denoting assemblages *or* as denoting properties.

Thinker T has an adequate conception of the concept *horse* (an adequate conception, as one says in English, of a horse) if and only if T can subsume things under *horse*, knows what it would take for a thing to count as a horse, and has some sufficiency of information about what horses are like, etc.

In a word, the conception of horse is a conception of that which 'horse' stands for, namely the concept of horse, or the concept *horse*. (Similarly, one may speak of an idea of horse and mean by this a conception of the concept *horse*.) On these terms, the right way to understand what a philosopher means when he speaks of grasp of the concept *horse* may be to understand him as speaking in a telescoped way of having an adequate conception of that which the predicate 'horse' stands for, namely horses. Such phraseology as 'grasp of the concept *horse*' was common in *Sameness and Substance*. Given the option of reading it as just indicated, there are places where I have seen no danger in the telescoped terminology's remaining in place.

At this point, with terminological explanations more or less complete (and ready to be repeated later, as and when necessary), the reader who has not yet postponed reading the rest of this Preamble ought probably to advance to Chapter One.

6. REAL AND NOMINAL

Next, in anticipation of something laid out in Chapter Three, a word on the terminology of 'real' and 'nominal'. The use of these terms turns on the distinction between a predicate whose elucidation makes ineliminable allusion (or must *begin* by making ineliminable allusion) to members of its actual extension (real)[12] and a predicate whose elucidation can dispense with such allusion (nominal). In the case of the nominal, the elucidation can often be made fully explicit or articulate. In the pure case of the nominal, it never needs to involve the deictic or demonstrative element that is so typical of the real definition. A typical nominal definition would be Aristotle's formula '*x* is a house if and only if *x* is a shelter against destruction by wind, rain and heat'. By contrast, a typical real definition – I call it a definition only to follow custom, this is not really definition – might run in the following way: '*x* is a water-vole just if *x* is relevantly similar to *that* [demonstrated] *animal* (letting the criterion of 'relevantly' depend at least in part on the nature, whatever it may

---

[12] Pending the completion at some imaginary moment of a science, cf. Chapter Three, section 5, point (v). Compare the way in which the elucidation of the sense of a proper name is *designatum*-involving. Cf. here 'On the Sense and Reference of a Proper Name' (1977), by John McDowell, to whom this Preamble is indebted also in other ways, and cf. my (1993).

prove to be, of the animal actually demonstrated)'.[13] Not only does the real definition depend on real specimens. The question of its application and correctness or incorrectness also depends crucially on the facts about these specimens. All the same, real definitions lie within the province of semantics, as well as of empirical fact. No lifelike elucidation of ordinary discourse could be contrived without them.[14] Let us forget once and for all the very idea of some knowledge of language or meaning that is not knowledge of the world itself. In this way, let us follow through the capital thing which Quine contended for in 'Two Dogmas of Empiricism'.[15]

7. NECESSARY/CONTINGENT AND *A PRIORI* / *A POSTERIORI*

It is to be expected that there should be concepts any passable conception of which requires experience. Such concepts are *a posteriori* or empirical. The semantics of a predicate that stands for such a concept ('elm', 'oak', 'rabbit', 'brazen', 'green', for instance) will be rooted in the actual

---

[13] A definition can be real with respect to *genus* and nominal with respect to *differentia*. The philosophers' favourites like 'sibling', 'oculist' and 'bachelor' have definitions like this.

[14] There may be a measure of injustice to Locke (as well as to certain other philosophers) implicit in this usage. By using terms that are commonly conceived of as Locke's property and stressing constantly the importance of the real, I may seem to be claiming that, in his adherence to what he called the nominal, Locke failed to see things which some say he did see. Locke's doctrine of ektypes and archetypes, and the way he contrasts ideas of mixed modes with ideas of substance, both suggest not only that he had a grasp of the question whether a given predicate has an extension-involving or not extension-involving sense, but also that he may have anticipated the ideas of onus of match and direction of fit which, following Michael Woods (*op. cit.*, in footnote 7) and David Shwayder (1963), p. 9, I have found so suggestive in J. L. Austin ('How to Talk: Some Simple Ways', *P.A.S.* 1952–3) and have allowed to influence the exposition given here of certain thoughts that now have currency in philosophy about substantives and kinds. Such ideas certainly go back to Leibniz. See Leibniz's *Meditations on Truth, Knowledge and Ideas*, Gerhardt IV, especially p. 422. See also *Discourse on Metaphysics* (sections 24–5) and *New Essays* (Akademie, pp. 254–6). Some see the germ of all this in Aristotle's account at *Posterior Analytics* 93^{a21} of how we may effect a preliminary determination of a phenomenon (e.g. a certain noise in the clouds) and then, having picked it out, gradually refine our description of its nature and work back to the rudiments of a real (or as Leibniz would say causal) definition. It may well be that some comparable credit is due to Locke, if he is correctly interpreted. Chapter Three credits Putnam and Kripke with refurbishing such ideas for present purposes.

[15] See *From a Logical Point of View*, pp. 20–46. This view of that which is enduringly important in Quine's argument accrues to me from remarks and commentaries that Hilary Putnam has offered since the nineteen sixties. For the consistency of this thing with the modest essentialism that will be advocated in this book (from Chapter Four onwards), see Quine's later judgment in *Ways of Paradox* (1977 edition): 'There is also in science a different and wholly respectable vestige of essentialism or of real definition . . . It consists in picking out those minimum distinctive traits of a chemical, or of a species, or whatever, that link it most directly to the central laws of science. Such definition . . . is of a piece with the chemical or biological theory itself [and] conforms strikingly to the Aristotelian quest . . . This vestige of essentialism is of course a vestige to prize.'

world. (See the previous paragraph.) Nothing, however, prevents the occurrence of such concepts in judgments that are themselves *a priori*. For instance, 'all rabbits are rabbits' requires (of anyone who understands it at all) a certain quantum of experience; but, once a thinker has got *a posteriori* that which is required to understand it, he needs nothing more to see that it is true. In this sense, the judgment, whose comprehension is in part *a posteriori*, is itself *a priori*. Moreover, it is true no matter what. So it holds necessarily. Notoriously, though, not everything that involves such concepts yet holds necessarily can be *a priori*. Pursuing the deictic demonstration of gold and investigating the relevant similarities of good specimens of the stuff that is denominated 'gold', physical chemists have found ways to light upon the element with atomic number seventy-nine. Since that is the very stuff they were directed to by the deictic demonstration, it seems gold is necessarily the stuff with atomic number seventy-nine. (Use Russell's theory of descriptions and Smullyan (1948) to understand the grammar of this claim.) But the experience that it takes to understand the semantics of 'gold' was insufficient to establish this identity. It holds necessarily but *a posteriori*. The same surely holds good for 'Lucifer is Noctifer'. The *a posteriori* basis on which each of these names is understood does not suffice to establish that Lucifer is Noctifer. Only when that identity is established empirically can modal reasoning convert this discovery into the discovery that there is no circumstance in which Lucifer is not Noctifer. The identity holds necessarily – necessarily but *a posteriori*.

These matters are familiar, even if they still lie on the margin of controversy. But, beyond those treated by Saul Kripke, certain adjacent questions are less familiar. Leibniz writes in *On Nature Itself* (G IV, 512, following §11)

Matter resists being moved by a certain natural inertia (as Kepler well calls it) so that . . . it requires for its motion an active force proportional to its size . . . Just as matter has a natural inertia which is opposed to motion, so in a body itself, and indeed in every substance, there is a natural constancy which is opposed to change.

The point Leibniz draws to one's attention here is a perfectly general condition on the determinable concept *material body or substance*. Relatively few ordinary thinkers are in a position to state this condition articulately or with precision. But a person who had absolutely no conception of this mark of the concept *material body or substance*, or who expected no resistance at all from things that answered to determinations of it (such as *apple, wagon* or *tree*), would be hard to credit with any adequate conception of these concepts (either of the determinable *material substance* or of such determinations of it).[16]

What then is the status of the truth 'a material substance has inertia and requires for its motion an active force proportional to its size'? It is a candidate to hold necessarily. Nevertheless, the truth is scarcely analytic. It does not follow from logic and definitions. (What definitions are available here?) The truth is grounded in the empirical concepts *material substance* and *inertia*. It is grounded there in such a way as to leave no room (apparently) even for the possibility of a material substance without inertia. Moreover, for anyone who thinks through what is involved in a substance's lacking inertia, the very idea of a material substance's lacking inertia may seem to be excluded. Some philosophers may even react to this by calling the truth that material substances have inertia an *a priori* truth. If I do not call it that myself, it is because I strongly suspect that, in thinking through what would be involved in a substance's lacking inertia and finding the way blocked to that state of affairs, one calls upon experience for a further contribution, over and above that which was required to grasp the empirical concepts that are involved.

8. FORMAL NOTATIONS

In the ensuing chapters, there are notations and locutions that may give the impression that, despite protestations to the contrary, I am engaged in the business of constructing a formal system. But the only aim of these notations is to effect abbreviation where abbreviation is needed, or to make fixed and transparent whatever is taken in the context to be the logical and inferential character of certain antecedently familiar forms and locutions. In the case of notations such as $\frac{a = b}{donkey}$, this disclaimer is to be borne particularly in mind. This simply abbreviates '*a* is the same donkey as *b*', where that is to be understood as having whatever meaning the language imparts to these English words. Again, at the outset of the inquiry in Chapter One, the question is put whether *x* can be the same f as *y* without being the same g as *y*. But there is no policy here to diminish dependence on informal English. To make a question in English out of this schema, for instance, replace the letters ' *x* ' and ' *y* ' by names of things and the thing-kind letters 'f' and 'g' by predicates denominating

---

[16] Cf. Christopher Peacocke, 'Intuitive Mechanics, Psychological Reality and the Idea of a Material Object', in *Spatial Representations*, ed. Eilan, McCarty and Brewer (Oxford, 1993).

kinds of thing, e.g. 'donkey', 'horse', 'tree', 'mammal', 'animal', 'beast of burden'. In sum, the codifications proposed should be seen as an invitation to agree in finding a certain meaning in natural language expressions of which the notations are the counterpart, and then to treat these notations as specifying that meaning canonically.

Notation such as this, latching as it does onto one particular understanding of the reusable words that make up some phrase or latching onto one particular reading of the construction in which the words are placed, represents, if you will, a first step in the direction of a systematic account of the logical grammar of English. But it is no more than a first step. Much has been learned from experiments with an approach that is opposite to mine, i.e. with a would-be exact or calculus-building approach. This has advanced some matters by raising questions not previously encountered and identifying all sorts of possible answers to these questions. Yet all too often this top down approach has had the effect of precipitating its proponents rather suddenly into issues for which there had been no discursive or presystematic preparation. In this book, by contrast, the approach is that of the underlabourer – albeit an underlabourer not denied the *distant prospect* of discerning a simple Leibnizian order implicit in the syntax and semantics of English.

9. THE MODE OF COMBINATION INVOLVED IN 'IS THE SAME DONKEY AS'

In the explanation described as a first step, I said how '*a* is the same f as *b*' may be read as a sort of English. This explanation was general. But this particular form is, for purposes of this book, special and specially important. What is the relation between the mode of combination by which 'donkey' occurs in '*a* is the same donkey as *b*' and that by which 'donkey' occurs in '*a* is a donkey'? For the sake of completeness, we need to address this question. Logically speaking, the matter belongs here; even though, as so often with the questions treated in this Preamble, one who does not care yet about the answer may wish to skip or go on now to Chapter One.

According to Quine, '*a* is the same donkey as *b*' is simply a contraction or condensation of the logical form '*a* is a donkey and *a* is *b*'.[17] Thus '– (is) (*a*) donkey' should be read as a predicate distinguishable within the

---

[17] See Quine review of P. T. Geach, *Reference and Generality* (1964); also Perry (1970).

general class of predications only by the non-syntactic marks insisted upon at §5 above. (These marks are further discussed in Chapters One, Two and Three.) A variant that I think Quine might tolerate, and (having scrutinized all extant alternatives) I should myself prefer it, is to see '*a* is the same donkey as *b*' as saying that *a* stands to *b* in the relation of identity *as restricted* to (things that are) donkeys. Hence our notation in this book: $\dfrac{a = b}{\text{donkey}}$. In Russell and Whitehead's official *Principia Mathematica* notation (see Volume I, *35), the approved rendering would have been $(a) = \lceil \text{donkey} (b)$.

The advantage of proposals such as these is that they simultaneously show forth the distinctive contribution of 'donkey' to the linguistic forms that the word 'donkey' helps to make up and show it as made by means of a single mode of combination. Suppose that for one moment we represent this mode of contribution by the invented verb 'to donkey'. Then '*a* is a donkey' becomes '*a* donkeys' and '*a* is the same donkey as *b*' becomes '*a* donkeys and *a* = *b*' or else (essentially similarly, but in a way that brings '=' and 'donkey' better into construction together): *a* has to *b* the relation of identity *as restricted* to things that donkey, or *a* has to *b* the relation same $\lceil$ donkey.

So far so good. Now, helping ourselves to similar verbs for other substantives, we can quickly make sense of 'there is something that *a* is', '*a* is the same what as *b*?', '*a* is the same something as *b*', and so on. For purposes of such contexts, the letters 'f' and 'g', which have served so far as schematic, will need to take on the role of true variables,[18] ranging over the general things which we claimed to discover that thing-kind words stand for. Examples would be person, plant, tree, house, horse, donkey, etc.[19] On these terms, if we continue with our temporary representation of nouns by verbs, we can say that '*a* is something' is true if and only if *a* something-s; that *a* something-s if and only if for some f (one of these general items) *a* f-s, or $(\exists f)(fa)$. Similarly, '*a* is the same something as *b*' is

---

[18] If we were constructing a formal system, it would be a heinous offence to let the same letters f and g do duty sometimes as schematic letters, understood by reference to the role of holding a place for their designated linguistic replacements, and at other times as genuine variables, understood by reference to whatever items 'all' and 'some' range over. But, as I have said, our notation is not introduced for the purpose of constructing a formal system. It is only abbreviatory and disambiguative.

[19] This is second level quantification but of a very limited kind. There is no question yet, of quantifying over everything true of *x*. We quantify over the sorts of thing which this or that given object is, in the Aristotelian sense of this phrase. For this, see again the epigraphs for Chapter One.

true if and only if, for some f, *a* f-s and $a = b$ or, better, *a* has to *b* the relation of identity as restricted to things that f; or, more formally, $(\exists f)$ $\left(\begin{array}{c} a = b \\ f \end{array}\right)$. Note that in the quasi-formalized version, concatenation is taken to do the work of the verb ending. When we revert to the ordinary English form *a is an* f and look back at the quasi-formalized version, this concatenation is seen as having taken over the work of the indefinite article too, bracketing for us the nice question of how much or little significance to attach to the English form '*a* is a(n) . . .'.

In sum, following the variant that I propose on Quine's proposal, we then have the equivalence:

$$a = b \leftrightarrow (\exists f)\left(\begin{array}{c} a = b \\ f \end{array}\right)$$

Let it be as clear as anything can that, in embracing and exploiting this equivalence, one is not agreeing with Geach's claim that always '*x* is identical with *y*' is an abbreviation for '*x* is the same f as *y*' where f 'represents some count noun supplied from the context of utterance' ('or else it is just a half-formed thought').[20] One is disagreeing deliberately and actively with that. If vindication were really needed of the bare '$a = b$', then the right-hand side of our equivalence would vindicate it. It would vindicate it as definite, determinate and well formed. It is determinate in the same way as 'I talked with someone yesterday at noon' is determinate for a truth-value.[21]

In *Sameness and Substance* the question of how $\begin{array}{c} a = b \\ \hline f \end{array}$ and '*a* is an f' are related was left undecided. In so far as it can now be treated as decided, there should be no strict need to argue separately or twice over, as in Chapter One, about the formal properties of '$=$' and '$\begin{array}{c} = \\ f \end{array}$'. There is something to be said, though, for trying to satisfy the reader separately under each head. Again, in Chapter Two, where the doctrine of Sortal

---

[20] See Geach (1972), p. 238. See also Geach (1980), p. 214.

[21] It follows that there are two reasons why there has never been any temptation, either in *Sameness and Substance* (1980) or in Wiggins (1967), in each of which '$a = b$' was treated as guaranteed the same truth-value as '$(\exists f)\left(\begin{array}{c} a = b \\ f \end{array}\right)$', to follow Geach in claiming that '$a = b$' is in any way defective or incomplete. First, no variable is free on the right side. Secondly, being Leibnizian '$(\exists f)\left(\begin{array}{c} a = b \\ f \end{array}\right)$', and '$a = b$' are both determinate in the further sense of excluding the possibility (see Chapter One) that $(\exists g)\left(ga \ \&\ \text{not}\ \begin{array}{c} a = b \\ g \end{array}\right)$.

Dependency is formulated, it may be wondered what strict need there now is for the third clause of Principle **D** to invoke f-coincidence as such. In that third clause, is more required than that there should be no difference at all between the particular f that *a* is and the particular f that *b* is? In the absence, however, of complete reconstructions of the lifespans of *a* and of *b* (and that is the normal case), some idea of f-coincidence does seem integral to the ordinary working or application of the third clause of **D**. In *Sameness and Substance Renewed*, the third clause remains as it was. See Chapter Two, §1.

10. QUESTIONS OF PRIORITY

Do the determinations of the foregoing section mean that there is a danger that we may be forced to concur in a claim that adherents of Quine are apt to repeat sometimes, as if in evidence against positions like **D**? Does it mean that '$x = y$' is prior somehow to the practices, directly and indirectly invoked by **D**, of the individuation of things and the assignment of things to thing-kinds?

> When we do propound identity conditions for bodies, or persons, or classes, we are using the *prior* concept of identity in the special task of clarifying the term 'body' or 'person' or 'class'; for an essential part of the clarification of a term is clarification of the standard by which we individuate its denotata.[22]

Well, no. There is no need at all to concur in the asymmetry Quine has seemed to suggest. For the truth is that there can be no question in this province, where so much is primitive, of *anything's* being absolutely prior – either logically or philosophically or psychogenetically. To be sure, 'Juno donkeys' or 'Juno is a donkey' will seem (so soon as we look at this predication as it appears in English) to mean or imply that Juno is the same as one of the donkeys or is identical with one of the donkeys. But, as we shall see in Chapter Two, there is also an opposite dependence. The practical grasp of identity itself presupposes the capacity to subsume things under kinds, to refer to them and to trace them (or keep track of them). But in order to trace things, one has to trace them in the way that is appropriate to this or that *kind*, and then, by dint of one's understanding of congruence as flowing from identity or coincidence, to assign to an object picked out at one time and again at another time everything that is true of either. But if that is right, then not only does sortal predication presuppose identity. Identity presupposes sortal pred-

---

[22] W. V. Quine (1972). My italics.

ication.[23] These things belong together – or the grasp of each requires the grasp of the other. Identity is a notion coeval with the determinable *entity of some determinate kind*, which brings with it the possibility of the particular determinations that figure in particular sortal predications.

Without thinking very hard about what one is hoping for, one forms too easily the aspiration to discover a starting point from which one could introduce, stage by stage, as if definitionally, the apparatus of naming, substantial predication, identification and differentiation, then other kinds of predication, then quantification over individuals, then quantification over sorts, then abstraction (the prototype of lambda abstraction), then quantification over properties . . . If the process to be reconstructed were intended to be definitional or quasi-definitional, however, then all the hazards of piecemeal definition would have to be guarded against (the hazard of the left hand's undoing or altering what, unknown to the left hand, the right has already done). The difficulties would quickly appear of keeping careful account of what already presupposes what. Given the absolutely foundational nature of that with which we are concerned, however, and the primitiveness of the predicative and other devices that are under consideration, I should claim that it is a false picture that bewitches one who demands such a quasi-definitional sequence. What we have here to confront is a whole skein of connected practices. These practices are intertwined with one another. Their relations can indeed be set out in all sorts of true equivalences. But it does not follow they can be set out in a *developing sequence* of the kind we were meant to be looking for. It is much more likely that the basic

---

[23] Geach seeks to penetrate to a deeper level of analysis of sortal predication, by isolating an underlying mode of combination effected by the attribution of equivalence relations (which are not necessarily, according to Geach, congruence relations) such as *x is the same donkey as y*, *x is the same apple as y*, etc. This relation can then be *derelativized* as in '*x* is the same donkey as *x*', '*x* is the same apple as *x*', etc. Finally, he offers these latter forms as definitions of '*x* is a donkey', '*x* is an apple'.

Geach's proposal can be separated from Geach's case against absolute identity and his denial of congruence.

If the proposal were offered on the level of psychogenetic theory, then it would be implausible. For it is hard to avoid thinking that calling *x* the same horse as *y* presupposes picking *x* out and picking it out as something (as a horse?) simpliciter. If there were nothing more to horse-identity than there was to being a horse, whence could come the relationality that Geach derelativizes?

If Geach's proposal is simply grammatical or definitional in its intent, well, that is more plausible. But it may be less clear than it looks. For as soon as we try to bring Geach's 'same donkey as' forms into the requisite relation with 'the same what?' and 'the same something as', which are indispensable to the whole rhetoric of sortalism, we need to discern structure *within* 'is the same donkey as'. This structure cannot, however, be, for Geach, that which is suggested by the English predicable 'is the same donkey as'. For that apparently reintroduces both absolute identity and simple 'donkey' predication.

forms and devices have to be learned together. Just as the keystone of an arch and the adjoining bricks can be placed together, but only if somehow they are placed there simultaneously or they are put into position with the help of a temporary external support, so each primitive device is learned *simultaneously and in reciprocity* with each of the others.

In the language learning case, there is the possibility of partial and interim grasp of a device. But the full grasp of any one device will require the full grasp of many or most of the others. If semantic devices are well made, then, once they are fully mastered, they will operate smoothly and in concert together. Their mutual relations will indeed allow of their being rehearsed by logical equivalences. If a sceptical question arises, however, about whether in their supposed reciprocity the concepts corresponding to the expressions we are concerned with are well made, the only answer that ought to be promised is that, several chapters into the book, there will be *indirect* assurance that the locutions 'same', 'horse', 'same horse' collaborate securely in the modes of combination of which we avail ourselves in identifying things, placing them in kinds, distinguishing them from other things and attributing other properties to them. For the interim, the most that should be offered in answer to the question broached in paragraph one, §9 above, is a non-definitional and non-psychogenetic account of a single mode of combination linking 'is an f' and 'is the same f'.

CHAPTER ONE

The absoluteness of sameness

Only [species and genera, among predicables,] reveal the primary substances [e.g. Socrates]. For if one is to say of the individual man *what he is* it will be in place to give the species or the genus (though more informative to give man than animal); but to give any other thing would be out of place – for example to say 'white' or 'runs' or anything like that.

(Aristotle, *Categories* 2^{b30-7}, as translated by J. L. Ackrill, Oxford, 1963, but with italics and square bracket additions.)

[*Man* or *animal*] does not signify simply a certain qualification, as *white* does. *White* signifies nothing but a qualification, whereas species and genus mark off the kind of substance – they signify what sort of substance.

(Aristotle, *Categories* 3^{b17-21}, translation and paraphrase based on J. L. Ackrill, *op. cit., vide* p. 88.)

I. A CENTRAL QUESTION ABOUT IDENTITY; AND RIVAL ANSWERS GIVEN BY DEFENDERS OF THE ABSOLUTENESS OF IDENTITY AND THE RELATIVITY OF IDENTITY

If somebody claims of something named or unnamed that it moves, or runs or is white, he is liable to be asked the question by which Aristotle sought to define the category of substance: *What is it* that moves (or runs or is white)? Perhaps one who makes the claim that something moves does not need to know the answer to this question in order to enter his claim. It is not hard to envisage circumstances in which he can know that it moves without knowing what the thing is. Yet it seems certain (for more on this see below, Chapter Two, §2) that, for each thing that satisfies a predicate such as 'moves', 'runs' or 'white', there must exist some known or unknown, named or nameable, kind to which the item belongs and by reference to which the 'what is it' question *could* be answered.

Everything that exists is a *this such*. Where someone *fully* understands what he is judging when he says that this, that or the other things moves, or runs or is white, he will know what the thing in question is.[1]

Secondly, if someone reports further that the thing that runs is the same as the thing that is white, then his judgment cannot be true unless at least two conditions are satisfied. These conditions are that the thing that runs should be the *same something or other* as the thing that is white (the same horse, say, or the same man or whatever) and that the something in question be correlative with or associated with a principle by which entities of a particular kind may be traced or kept track of and re-identified as one and the same.

These two requirements will represent one part of what will be referred to in this book as **D**, or the Thesis of the Sortal Dependency of Individuation. (For **D** as elaborated, see Chapter Two, §1.) But in some readers, neo-Aristotelian formulations of this kind will instantly arouse grave misgivings. Such suspicions will be allayed in the end (if at all) simply by following out the implications of the classical conception of identity. But that is the work of later chapters. At the beginning of a search for a theory of individuation, it will be better to focus on a non-Aristotelian question that requires nothing more of the reader than that he should understand English sentences that employ familiar locutions like 'the same horse', 'the same donkey', 'the same tree'. The universally accessible question to which these locutions naturally give rise is whether *a* can be the same f as *b* without being the same g as *b*. Better and more precisely, the question is whether *a* can be the same f as *b*, and not the same g as *b*, even where *a* or *b* is itself a g.

This is the topic of Chapter One. The answer to the question will be short and negative. But the absoluteness thereby discovered in identity will carry with it certain unexpected consequences, the possibility for instance that a portion of space may be co-occupied at a time by distinct things (provided, at least, that the things in question belong to different basic or individuative kinds). Indeed some of these consequences may be strange enough to prompt someone to reconsider the attractions of the affirmative or relative answer to our question. Let him do so at least once before confronting the larger questions of identity and individuation that will arise later – if only because our answers will need the absoluteness that it is the work of the present chapter to establish.

The thesis of the Relativity of Identity, which I shall denominate **R**

---

[1] Most recently, I have tried to answer the doubts that such claims have provoked in Wiggins (1997b).

and shall steadfastly oppose, may be held in several distinct forms.[2] It will convey the general spirit to enumerate a few of the different and equally correct sortal answers that may be given to the question 'What was the thing that ran?' Suppose the answers are *man, soldier, greybeard, Greek, philosopher, official of the state, the chairman (epistates) for day d, 406 B.C., the subject of a certain portrait bust in the Vatican Museum, stonemason, victim of the wit of Aristophanes, the person whose body was the only human body that was to be discovered at place p at time t in the agora of ancient Athens.* Then an **R**-theorist might suggest that it makes all the difference to the project of keeping track of continuants through space and time *which* of the concepts in such a list one subsumes something under. Might not material particular *a* coincide with material particular *b* when individuated under some of these concepts and not coincide with *b*, but be distinct from it, when individuated under others? From this apparent possibility a defender of **R** may want to conclude that the notion of identity is concept- or sortal-relative, i.e. relative to different possible answers to the question '*a* is the same what as *b* ?'. (For 'concept' and 'sortal', see Preamble, §5.)

 D and **R**, the theses of Sortal Dependency and Relativity of Identity, may seem to be made for one another. For this reason they have sometimes been confused or assimilated; and sometimes, because **R** appears to entail **D**, **R** has been taken to be the one good reason for maintaining **D**.[3] Occasionally, philosophers have even gone so far as to argue from

---

[2] The label is suggested by Quine's review (1964), p. 102 of P. T. Geach, *Reference and Generality* (Ithaca, N.Y., 1962), and Quine's characterization of the doctrine given at p. 157, where Geach says: 'I could not object in principle to different As' being one and the same B . . . as different official personages may be one and the same man.' Cf. also Geach's later articles at *Review of Metaphysics*, 21, 1 (1967), and 22, 3 (1969). See Geach (1972) (1973).
  Among those who have followed Geach in one way or another are Eddy M. Zemach 'In Defence of Relative Identity', *Philosophical Studies* 26 (1974), pp. 207, 218; D. Odegard, 'Identity through Time', *American Philosophical Quarterly* 9 (1972), pp. 29 38; Nicholas Griffin, *Relative Identity* (Oxford, 1977); Harold Noonan, 'Objects and Identity', Cambridge Ph.D. thesis, 1977 (see the extracts in Noonan (1976) and (1978)); Tobias Chapman, 'Identity and Reference', *Mind*, 82 (1973); Richard Kraut, *American Philosophical Quarterly* (1987). See also Noonan (1996).

[3] Some have held that the reverse dependence exists between Relativity of Identity and Sortal Dependency, others that they are equivalent doctrines. The supposition that **D** depends for its rationale on its being possible for *a* to be the same f and not the same g as *b* was made by Professors Geach and Quine in their original controversy about these matters. Professor Geach insisted on the universal legitimacy of pressing the *same what?* demand (see (1962), §§31–4, and Chapter Six); and one of his arguments for it rested on the doctrine that it was logically possible for *a* to be the same f as *b* without being the same g as *b*. Professor Quine in his review rejected out of hand the possibility of *a*'s being the same f as *b* without being the same g as *b*. But it was apparently *on the strength of that rejection* that he strongly questioned the legitimacy of Geach's *same what?* demand and the proposals he took to be Geach's for the treatment of quantified sentences. The one point on which Geach and Quine seem to have been agreed at that time is that the possibility of *a*'s being the same f but not the same g as *b* is what provides the principal rationale of **D**. This is a point on which I am to disagree with them both.

the falsity of **R** to the falsity of **D**. But this is a formally fallacious procedure.

R and **D** are utterly distinct. The falsity of **R** will be argued very
shortly, on the basis of the principle commonly known as Leibniz's Law,
which says that if *a* is *b* then whatever may be true of *a* is true of *b*. It will
be argued that '*a* is *b*' and '*a* is the same f as *b*' are equally and excep-
tionlessly subject to this Leibnizian principle. In Chapter Two, with **R**
put out of the way, the Sortal Dependency of Individuation will be
amplified and refined. **D** will then be applied to the task of finding a
schematic or formal characterization of the notions of substance and
sortal concept. Chapter Three will relate the abstract requirements
upon sortal concepts to the sortal concepts that we actually possess.[4]
Everything else will follow on from that.

In addition to **R** and **D**, there will be occasion to mention a thesis that
I shall call the Counting thesis, or **C**. It says that to specify the something
or other under which *a* and *b* coincide is to specify a concept f which
qualifies as adequate for this purpose *only* if it yields a principle of counting for fs. **C** is no more to be confused with **D** than **R** is. I shall submit
that, however closely it approximates to an important truth, **C** is false.
(See Chapter Two, section 7.)

The realistic discussion of the thesis of the Relativity of Identity
requires formal argument, as in the ensuing section. It also requires the
detailed discussion of examples. That will be the work of the rest of this
chapter.

2. LEIBNIZ'S LAW AND THE DIFFICULTIES OF RELATIVE IDENTITY

The fact that there are many different sortal concepts under which one
may single out some individual *a* does not in itself imply **R**. For all the
alternative procedures of individuation of *a* under alternative covering
concepts might, when they yielded *any* answer, yield the same answer to
that question.[5] My contention is precisely that they must do so. The

---

[4] For other support of **D**, or for related theses, see, e.g., A. Prior, *Analysis*, 17 (June 1957); Hampshire
(1956); D. Wiggins, 'Individuation of Things and Places', *P.A.S. Supp.* 38 (1963), printed in more
correct form in M. Loux, ed., *Universals and Particulars*, 1st edn (only) (New York, 1969).

[5] I shall call an individuative or sortal concept that adequately answers the *same what?* question for
an identity-statement *s*, a covering concept for *s*, and, as prefigured in the Preamble §8, I reserve
the letters f and g to represent such sortal concepts. 'f(*a*)' means that *a* belongs to the sort f – colloquially, that *a* is an f or is one of the fs. In the case of an identity '*a* = *b*' supplemented, as any
fair discussion of **R** will evidently require, with covering concept f, I write $\frac{a=b}{f}$. For the

reflexivity and congruence of identity provide logically compelling reasons why, if *a* is *b*, or if *a* is the same something or other as *b* (same horse, same tree, same planet, or whatever), then all different procedures of individuating *a* (provided they really do individuate *a*) must, if they yield any answer at all, yield the same answer with respect to *a*'s coincidence with *b*. This is to say in the timeless idiom that if, for some f, *a* is the same f as *b*, then for any g such that *a* is a g, *a* is the same g as *b*, or

$$\left((\exists f)\left(\begin{matrix} a = b \\ f \end{matrix} \right) \right) \rightarrow \left((\forall g)(g(a) \rightarrow \left(\begin{matrix} a = b \\ g \end{matrix} \right)) \right);$$

which is to say that **R** is false.

To illustrate this will only require the extension to 'is the same f as' or '$\begin{matrix} = \\ f \end{matrix}$' of the formal properties that logicians associate with '='.[6] The strong reflexivity of *the same* (dyadic identity),

$$(\forall x)(x = x),$$

will have for its *same* f counterpart the reflexivity property

$$(\forall x)(f(x) \rightarrow \left(\begin{matrix} x = x \\ f \end{matrix} \right)).$$

The congruence of sameness that is affirmed by Leibniz's Law or the Indiscernibility of Identicals,

$$(\forall x)(\forall y)((x = y) \rightarrow (\phi x \leftrightarrow \phi y))[7]$$

has as its *same f* counterpart:

$$(\forall x)(\forall y)(\left(\begin{matrix} x = y \\ f \end{matrix} \right) \rightarrow (\phi x \leftrightarrow \phi y)).$$

interpretation of this, see again Preamble §9. Replacements of the ordinary predicate letters phi and psi (ϕ and ψ), as they occur in schemata of first order logic, will embrace both sortal predicates and non-sortal predicates.

[6] On the account of 'is the same f as' that I have proposed in the Preamble §9, this is not a substantial extension at all. We are simply following through the consequences of the claim that this relation is a *restriction* of the relation of identity. But from now until the end of this chapter I shall not simply assume the Preamble account. I hope it will help to confirm that account if I can arrive at the conclusion I shall arrive at without its immediate assistance.

[7] The schematic letter phi holds a place for any predicate that can be true of the things over which the variables of quantification range. Given reflexivity, the schema in the text is derivable from $(x)(y)(x = y \rightarrow (\phi x \rightarrow \phi y))$. See Quine (1963), pp. 12–13. Furthermore, reflexivity and this schema suffice to prove symmetry and transitivity.

Or, treating the letter f not as a schematic letter but as a variable, we have

$$(\forall x)(\forall y)((\exists f)\begin{pmatrix} x = y \\ f \end{pmatrix} \rightarrow (\phi x \leftrightarrow \phi y))$$

$$(\forall x)(\forall y)(\forall f)(\begin{pmatrix} x = y \\ f \end{pmatrix} \rightarrow (\phi x \leftrightarrow \phi y)).$$

So much for being the same f. Now for the thesis **R**. **R** entails that for some a, b, f and g

$$\begin{pmatrix} a = b \\ f \end{pmatrix} \ \& \ not \begin{pmatrix} a = b \\ g \end{pmatrix} \ \& \ g(a).$$

Is that last possible? To answer that question let us suppose that the first conjunct, $\begin{matrix} a = b \\ f \end{matrix}$, holds and let us take the ϕ in the Leibnizian schema

$$\begin{pmatrix} a = b \\ f \end{pmatrix} \rightarrow (\phi a \leftrightarrow \phi b)$$

as including among its replacements any predicable of the form '$\begin{matrix} a = x \\ g \end{matrix}$'.[8] Then we have

$$\begin{pmatrix} a = b \\ f \end{pmatrix} \rightarrow (\begin{pmatrix} a = a \\ g \end{pmatrix} \leftrightarrow \begin{pmatrix} a = b \\ g \end{pmatrix}).$$

But then, by *modus ponens* and the supposition that $\begin{matrix} a = b \\ f \end{matrix}$, we have the consequent

$$\begin{pmatrix} a = a \\ g \end{pmatrix} \leftrightarrow \begin{pmatrix} a = b \\ g \end{pmatrix}.$$

But now, by the reflexivity of '$\begin{matrix} = \\ g \end{matrix}$' and g($a$), as in the third conjunct, we have

$$\begin{pmatrix} a = a \\ g \end{pmatrix}.$$

---

[8] For what follows, see Wiggins (1967), pp. 3–4. For similar derivations see Perry (1970), p. 186; Stevenson (1972), p. 155. Stevenson worked out a formalized framework in which this and other claims could be formally evaluated in Stevenson (1975).

Hence, by *modus ponens*,

$$\left(\begin{array}{c} a = b \\ g \end{array} \right).$$

Hence we arrive at not **R**. So, if we suppose that the first conjunct of **R** holds true, then we obtain the denial of the remainder of **R**. It follows that **R** is not true.

The questions that now arise are whether Leibniz's Law is true (as this derivation presumes) and, if so, whether it is as true for 'is the same f as' as it is for '='. In support of an affirmative answer, I shall urge four considerations:

(i) Leibniz's Law marks off what is peculiar to real identity and it differentiates it in a way in which transitivity, symmetry and reflexivity (all shared by *exact similarity, weighing the same, having exact equality in pay*, etc.) do not.[9]

(ii) How, if *a* is *b*, could there be something true of *the object a* which was untrue of *the object b*? *They are the same object.* People sometimes speak of counter-examples to Leibniz's Law. But these are scarcely more impressive than the counter-examples to the Law of Non-Contradiction.

---

[9] Cf. Frege's remark in his review of Husserl, p. 80 in Geach and Black's *Translations from the Philosophical Writings of Gottlob Frege* (Oxford, 1952): 'I agree . . . that Leibniz's explanation *eadem sunt quorum unum potest substitui alteri salva veritate* does not deserve to be called a definition; my reasons, however, are different from Husserl's. Since any definition is an identity, identity cannot be defined. This explanation of Leibniz's could be called an axiom that brings out the nature of the relation of identity; as such it is fundamentally important.' We may fault Frege's doctrine of definition here, and we ought to note that the *eadem sunt quorum unum alteri substitui potest* principle says more than the principle that I have called Leibniz's Law. But when construed as a contention about Leibniz's Law, Frege's contention seems incontrovertible. (See also *Grundgesetze der Arithmetik*, Jena, 1903, 11 Band, 245.)

The Indiscernibility of Identical was familiar to Aristotle (see *De Sophisticis Elenchis* I 79[a37]). But I follow custom in calling it Leibniz's Law. It is not to be confused with the distinctively Leibnizian (and non-schematic) converse, the Identity of Indiscernibles (to be discussed in §2 of the next chapter). Leibniz's *eadem sunt quorum unum alteri substitui potest* principle presumably entails both Leibniz's Law *and* the Identity of Indiscernibles.

It may be asked what protects the schematic Leibniz's Law from illegitimate replacements for the letter phi (ϕ). I follow Quine in holding that intensional replacements are excluded by 'the incoherence of bound variables in any but referential position'. See *Journal of Philosophy* 61, 5 (1972), p. 490. Quine writes 'This version of the principle of identity is a little broader than the version in terms of properties, since the open sentence represented by 'ϕx' can sometimes exceed the range of properties, for reasons unrelated to substitutivity and related rather to Russell's paradox.' By 'the version in terms of properties', Quine means the non-schematic second level principle that if x is y then every property of x is a property of y, which is discussed and defended by Cartwright (1971), p. 119.

Quine's characterization of the substitutivity schema suffices in my opinion to answer all the questions about paradox that Geach has seen as counting against the congruence conception of identity. See the works by Geach cited at note 2 above, in further reply to which, I would refer to my reply to Harold Noonan in Lovibond and Williams (1996), p. 281, note 17.

Concerning modal and intensional contexts, Frege and his inheritors have shown how ineffective such contexts are to discover to us objects that are at once identical (or numerically the same f) and discernible.[10] At their best, these Fregean arguments are given on the basis of independently plausible accounts of what else is being conveyed in the purported counter examples.

(iii) If Leibniz's Law is dropped, or if classical identity is dropped in favour of some allegedly un-Leibnizian relative identity, then we need some formal principle or other, and one of at least comparable universality, to justify the instances of the intersubstitution of identicals that evidently are valid. The instability, indeterminacy or arbitrariness of all extant emendations and relativizations of Leibniz's Law only corroborate the case for a pure congruence principle such as Leibniz's. (See below, §3, and especially footnote 31.)

(iv) Suppose there were terms t_1 and t_2 both designating z, one and the same donkey, and suppose there were a context $\phi(\ )$ such that the result of supplying t_1 to it was true and the result of supplying t_2 was false. What ought we to say if it were suggested that the open sentence $\phi(x)$ determined a property? Call the putative property Q. We ought to ask: How can the donkey both have and lack the property Q? The question is unanswerable. Let the **R**-theorist note that this argument can be stated, as it is stated here, without showing any special favour between '$=$' and

'$\overset{=}{f}$'. It supports Leibniz's Law for both of these relations. In order to counter it, the **R**-theorists will have to uncover much more complexity than appears to be present in the innocuous locution 't_1 designates z and t_2 designates z'. Nor is that enough. **R**-theorists will need to deny the very possibility of there being such a relation as simple designation. (Chapter Six, §7, footnote 24 bears on these matters.)

3. FIVE WAYS FOR IT TO BE FALSE THAT $\overset{a=b}{\underset{g}{}}$

The previous section showed why we ought not to expect to find any true judgments whose truth requires the relativity of sameness. Nevertheless, given that there is no shortage of apparent examples in the form $\left(\overset{a=b}{\underset{f}{}}\right)$ & *not* $\left(\overset{a=b}{\underset{g}{}}\right)$ & $(g(a) \lor g(b))$, it will be as well to classify them,

---

[10] See 'On Sense and Reference' (Frege, 1952). Frege's defence of Leibniz's Law is fortified in a way independent of his theory of direct and indirect sense and real and apparent reference by Cartwright (1971), p. 119.

however crudely. There are five types of case where a is not the same g as b. Only three of these will provide ways for **R** to appear to be exemplified, but it will do no harm to enumerate all five.

(1) g may simply be the *wrong* covering concept for both a and b where nevertheless $a = b$. The evening star is the *same planet* but not the *same star* as the morning star. For Venus is not a star. This is not a case of

$$\left(\binom{a = b}{f} \& \text{ not} \binom{a = b}{g} \right) \& (g(a) \text{ v } g(b)).$$

(2) Venus is not the *same star* as Mars nor the same anything as Mars. For in this case, for all f, not $\binom{a = b}{f}$. Again this is irrelevant.

(3) We may seem to get nearer to what is required with the case where John Doe, the boy whom they stupidly took for a dunce, is the *same human being* as Sir John Doe, the Lord Mayor of London, yet neither the *same boy* (for the Lord Mayor is not a boy) nor the *same mayor/ex-cabinet minister/father of five marriageable daughters*. (For the boy did not attain office or beget children when a boy.) Yet surely, it may be said, *boy, dunce, mayor, ex-cabinet minister, father of five marriageable daughters* are all sortal words. They furnish perfectly good covering concepts. One can count and identify such things, and so on. So this gives the appearance of a case where we have

$$\binom{a = b}{f} \& \text{ not} \binom{a = b}{g} \& (ga \text{ v } gb) \& \text{ not } (gb),$$

a case that is where a cuts out, as it were, under a sortal-concept g (e.g. *boy*) but persists under another sortal-concept f (e.g. *human being*).

This is not the sort of case the relativist is looking for. The first thing it shows is the necessity for care, care about tenses, care in the interpretation of affirmation and denials of the formula $\binom{a = b}{f}$ or $\binom{a = b}{g}$ and care in the interpretation of Leibniz's Law. Secondly, it shows the possibility of an interesting and highly important distinction within the class of sortal predicates.

If John Doe is still a boy, then John Doe, the boy, *will* one day be a cabinet minister and later the Lord Mayor of London, and he *will* beget five children. If John Doe is no longer a boy, then John Doe the boy (or Sir John Doe, when he was a boy) *was going to be* and *was going to do* these

things. We only thought we had a case of **R** because we confused the
timeless and the tensed way of speaking within one utterance. If 'g(Sir
John Doe)' is to be a tensed statement, it should be read as saying that
Sir John *was* a boy and it is true. If it is a tenseless statement, then it says
of Sir John Doe that he is, was or will be a boy or that at some time or
other he timelessly is a boy. This again is true. If you take tenses seriously,
you may refuse to say 'Sir John Doe *is* the same boy as John Doe', since
it is false that Sir John Doe is now a boy. But it is true and perfectly
unproblematic that Sir John Doe *was* the same boy as John Doe (was). It
is precisely for this reason that Sir John Doe is not now identified or
singled out under the temporally restricted sortal *boy*. From all this it
follows that $not \left(\dfrac{a = b}{\text{g}} \right)$, properly read, is not true. (Similarly, the author
of *Childe Harold* I/II (1812) was the same person as the baby born in 1788
who was christened George Gordon Byron. That author was a poet. But,
if we said the author was the same poet as the baby, that would give the
impression that the baby could write verses when he was a baby and that
is not true. The baby will, however, be the same poet as the author of
Childe Harold I/II.)

   The second matter that type-(3) cases bring to our attention is this.
They underline the need to distinguish between sortal concepts that
present-tensedly apply to an individual x at every moment throughout
x's existence, e.g. *human being*, and those that do not, e.g. *boy*, or *cabinet
minister*. It is the former (let us label them, without prejudice, substance-concepts) that give the privileged and (unless context makes it
otherwise) the most fundamental kind of answer to the question 'what
is x?' It is the latter, one might call them phased-sortals, which, if we
are not careful about tenses, give a false impression that a can be the
same f as b but not the same g as b. But, in fact, they do not conflict at
all with what is to be proved: namely that, for all x and all y, every
concept that adequately individuates x for any stretch of its existence
yields the same answer, either directly or via the principle of individuation for the substantive it restricts, as every other genuinely individuating concept for x or y to the question whether x coincides with y or
not.

   The first appearance of the phased-sortal is probably the best
moment to inveigh against a misunderstanding of identity which has
culminated in attempts to show that the only true identity is the 'identity
at a time' of one and the same phase or thing-moment of a thing, 'identity through time' being held by those in the grip of this conception to
connote some different relation that holds between the different phases

or thing-moments out of which individual continuants are supposed to be combined or concatenated.[11]

Whatever the merits of this idea as a programme for linguistic reform, those drawn to it have never appreciated the true scale of the re-organization that they are envisaging. There is no serious prospect that this view of the identity relation will do justice to any of the actual questions of continuity and persistence that perplex our habitual modes of thought about identity and difference. That which these questions want in the first instance is not replacement by other questions given in terms of phases of things or thing-moments[12] or in an alien four-dimensional mode. The answers these questions require from philosophy ought to be given in language that speaks as simply and directly as natural languages speak of proper three-dimensional continuants – things with spatial parts and no temporal parts, which are conceptualized in our experience as occupying space but not time, and as persisting whole through time.[13] Unlike sets or classes, continuants can gain and lose elements. The terms

[11] Cf. Hume, *Treatise of Human Nature*, Bk. 1, §6: 'We have a distinct idea of an object that remains invariable and uninterrupted through a supposed variation of time; and this idea we call that of identity or sameness. We have also a distinct idea of several different objects existing in succession, and connected together by a close relation; and this to an accurate view affords as perfect a notion of diversity as if there were no manner of relation among the objects.'

[12] Against a related but distinct proposal concerning existence and persistence, see Chapter Two. See also Chapter Six, §8, where some eirenic remarks are offered on the four-dimensional mode of speech. For a discussion of the distinction that Mark Johnston, David Lewis and other writers have made between the endurance and the mere perdurance of things, see §4.10 of my 'Substance' (1995).

[13] It is well worth remarking that, if we respect this way of thinking, then by a transposition we arrive at the everyday conception of event. An event takes time, and will admit the question 'How long did it last?' only in the sense 'How long did it take?'. An event does not persist in the way in which a continuant does – that is *through* time, gaining and losing new parts. A continuant has spatial parts. To find the whole continuant you have only to explore its boundaries at a time. An event has temporal parts. To find the whole event you must trace it through the historical beginning to the historical end. An event does not have spatial parts in any way that is to be compared with (or understood by reference to) the way in which it has *temporal* parts.
    At least in the light of this conception of the differences of events and continuants, there appears to be a terrible absurdity in such claims as 'a material object is just a long event'. For an illuminating specimen of such claims, see C. D. Broad in *Scientific Thought*, p. 54:

> We usually call a flash of lightning or a motor accident an event, and refuse to apply this name to the history of the cliffs of Dover. Now the only relevant difference between the flash and the cliffs is that the former lasts for a short time and the latter for a long time. And the only relevant difference between the accident and the cliffs is that if successive slices, each of one second long, be cut in the histories of both, the contents of a pair of adjacent slices may be very different in the first case and will be very similar in the second case. Such merely quantitative differences as these give no good ground for calling one bit of history an event and refusing to call another bit of history by the same name.

This will not do. *Material object* and *event* are in some sense *duals*. It has recently come to seem more and more important in philosophy to understand the notion of an event (cf. Donald Davidson, 'Causal Relations', *Journal of Philosophy*, 64, 1967). A fair start can be made on these questions if we take note of all the hints of analogy and disanalogy we get from the unreformed language of things and events.

of the identity questions that we are concerned with in this book stand for these continuants themselves, John Doe, say, not for phase-thick laminations of their four-dimensional counterparts, John Doe-when-a-boy, or for infinitesimally thin time-slices of these held fast between perceptual impressions, John Doe-as-caught-sight-of-there-then. And, by the same token, the phased sortals like 'boy' or 'old man' that we encounter in English never denote 'phases' of entities or (if that were different) the entities themselves frozen at an instant. They denote the changeable changing continuants themselves, the things themselves that are in these phases. No faithful elucidation of identity judgments will seek to alter this. People often speak of identity over time and distinguish this from identity at a time. But identity is just identity. (See Chapter Six, §8.)

Experience proves that here there is a choice between tedious repetition and scarcely prevailing against a deep-seated tendency of the human mind towards confusion.[14] In the equivalence *x is a boy at t if and*

---

[14] It is a profound and important question, which one should long keep open, what underlies this nisus towards disorder. That it is not provincial to any particular language or culture is attested by the confusion, misrepresentation and misquotation to which Cratylus and others subjected the gnomically simple insights of Heraclitus, a thinker as innocent of the confusion of 'numerical' and 'qualitative' sameness as he was of any positive desire to equate *opposition* and *contradiction*. Robert Coburn has given an able account of some of the sources of confusion. (See 'The Persistence of Bodies', *American Philosophical Quarterly*, 13, 1976.) For another source, scrutinize the quotation from Hume at footnote 11. The capacity to make inner images is as difficult to control as it is indispensable in most human thinking. Perhaps it will help even to explain the folly Russell describes in 'The Philosophy of Logical Atomism' (*Logic and Knowledge*, ed. R. C. Marsh, London, 1992, p. 247) when he writes:

> Identity is a rather puzzling thing at first sight. When you say 'Scott is the author of *Waverley*', you are half-tempted to think there are two people, one of whom is Scott and the other the author of *Waverley*, and they happen to be the same. That is obviously absurd, but that is the sort of way one is always tempted to deal with identity.

There is another confusion that is a converse of this: its aetiology will deserve equal attention from someone who comes closer than I shall to completing the theory of individuation and identity:

> The question of what we count as survival, as continuing to be the same person, is even more difficult to answer in a precise and definite way. (Joel Kupperman, *Character*, New York, 1991, p. 29.)

Nobody has any choice about going on 'being the same person'. One is bound to do so. In ceasing to be, one does not become somebody or something else. The difficult question is rather this: what it takes, conceptually speaking, to survive or persist. For another case of 'changing my identity', see

> One of Locke's insights was that although under the description 'this lump of matter' I may be changing my identity from moment to moment, under a description 'this person' I am not. (David Sedley, 'The Stoic Criterion of Identity', *Phronesis*, 1982, p. 255. Cf. Hobbes cited below at note 16.)

I am not a lump of matter, even if a lump of matter constitutes me. I cannot then change my identity under the description 'lump of matter'. I cannot change my identity at all in any relevant sense of 'my identity'. (For another sense of 'my identity' that may be needed sometimes, but is not at issue here, see Chapter Seven, §16.)

only if x is a male human being who has not at t reached maturity, we have the substance term 'human being', and two qualifications of it which determine proper subsets of the class of human beings. I have followed Geach in calling these qualifications 'restrictions' of the concept *human being*. It follows that, unlike 'boyhood', 'boy' cannot denote a phase. Still less can 'boy' denote a phase or stage, whatever that would be, of a human being. A boy is a human being. No human being is a stage of a human being, or an 18-year-old cross-section of a year-long space–time worm. Suppose some boy grows up and lives seventy years. If that is how it is, then there is only one answer to the question 'How long did that boy persist in being?' – namely seventy years. He lived seventy years. He did not live seventy years as a boy, but, when he grew up, that growing up was not the passing away of a boy.

So much for confusions that can flow from imperfect recognition of the presence in natural language of phased predicates and the phased sortal concepts that they introduce. Finally, if there were need, further refinements could be introduced at this point, e.g. between predicates like 'infant', 'adult', 'pupa', 'tadpole', which every member of the extension of the substance term that they restrict *must* in due course satisfy if only it lives so long, and predicates like 'conscript', 'alcoholic', 'captive', 'fugitive' or 'fisherman', of which this does not hold. This distinction, like certain others that are there to be made, is not without interest. But we shall not need these refinements to dispose of type-(3) cases represented as cases of **R**.

The point we have now reached is the fourth and fifth types of identity claim where **R** appears to be verified. Here at last we shall find cases with a semblance of plausibility.

(4) is the variant where, in the timeless idiom,

$$\left(\begin{matrix} a = b \\ f \end{matrix}\right) \ \& \ not \left(\begin{matrix} a = b \\ g \end{matrix}\right) \ \& \ (g(a) \text{ v } g(b)) \ \& \ (g(a) \ \& \ not \ g(b)).$$

(5) is the type of case where, allegedly,

$$\left(\begin{matrix} a = b \\ f \end{matrix}\right) \ \& \ not \left(\begin{matrix} a = b \\ g \end{matrix}\right) \ \& \ (g(a) \text{ v } g(b)) \ \& \ (g(a) \ \& \ g(b)).$$

We need some examples which might be said by an **R**-theorist to be of type (4), and then some of type (5). We must understand why these examples give the appearance of being cases of **R** and then understand what reasons there are for interpreting them otherwise.

4. POSSIBLE EXAMPLES OF TYPE-(4) RELATIVITY

(α) I might say to someone 'that heap of fragments there is the jug you saw the last time you came to this house'. They could not be *the same jug* but they might be *the same collection of material bits*.

(β) The visitor might be a person of tiresome ingenuity and cement the pieces of the jug together to make not a jug but, say, a coffee pot of a quite different shape from the original jug's. It might then be said that 'the jug is the coffee pot' is true with covering concept *same collection of material bits* and false with covering concept *same utensil*.

(γ) Perhaps the best and least strained example of type (4) is one of a kind which a champion of the relativization thesis that is given in P. T. Geach's *Reference and Generality* might describe in the following way:

'Leonard Linsky asked in his review of *Reference and Generality*[15] why 'Cleopatra's Needle' could not correspond in use to 'the same landmark' rather than to 'the same (lump of) stone'. And of course it could. For all one knows, 'Cleopatra's Needle' in some people's use does work this way. In that case, if the stone obelisk brought from Alexandria to London in 1877–78 is eroded by the atmosphere, and is continuously repaired with concrete, so that in the end none of the original stone is left, then we shall have to say, 'The same landmark, namely Cleopatra's Needle, was stone and is concrete.' But now, whereas it would be true that Cleopatra's Needle in 1984 is the same *landmark* as Cleopatra's Needle in 1900, it would be false that Cleopatra's Needle in 1984 is the same *stone* as Cleopatra's Needle in 1900 – or, indeed, the same stone as anything. For it wouldn't be a stone in 1984. This gives a case where Cleopatra's Needle is in 1900 both an f and a g, both a landmark and a stone, and goes on being the same f but doesn't go on being the same g.

'To take another case, during the Festival of Britain the stone in Meriden, inscribed to show that it marks the reputed centre of England, was removed from Meriden to London to be put on show. Such a performance is well within the limits of human folly. Well, during transport it will have remained the same stone but not the same landmark as the Meriden stone. Moreover, after its return to Meriden, it is questionable whether it is any longer that same landmark. After its return, old villagers alleged that it was put back some yards away from its old site.'

These cases, (α) (β) (γ) seem to qualify, if they qualify at all, as cases of type (4), though for one or two of them type-(3) analyses might also be suggested.

---

[15] *Mind*, 73 (Oct. 1964).

5. SOME CASES THAT MIGHT BE ALLEGED TO BE OF TYPE (5)

(δ) An argument in Geach's *Reference and Generality*, p. 151, might prompt the following suggestion. Whatever is a river is water. Suppose I moor my vessel at the banks of Scamander when that river is in full torrent. The next day, the river on which my vessel is now moored is the *same river* as the river on which I moored it yesterday. But, even though rivers are water, the river is not the *same water*. The water on which I moored it is now part of the Aegean Sea.

(ε) John Doe the boy is the *same human being* as Sir John Doe the Lord Mayor, but not the *same collection of cells* as Sir John Doe.[16]

(ζ) '[I]t may be said, without breach of the propriety of language, that such a church, which was formerly of brick, fell to ruin, and that the parish rebuilt the same church of freestone, and according to modern architecture. Here neither the form nor the materials are the same, nor is there anything in common to the two [*sic*] objects but their relation to the inhabitants of the parish; and yet this alone is sufficient to make us denominate them the same.'[17] So we may say of Hume's church that the present church is the same *church* as the old parish church but not the same *building* or the same *stonework* as the old parish church.

(η) At Paddington Railway Station I point in 1962 to the Cornish Riviera Express and say: 'That is the same train as the train on which the Directors of the Great Western Railway travelled to Plymouth in 1911.' *Same train*, yes, it may be said, but not *the same collection of coaches and locomotive.*

(θ) A petitioner asks to see the same official as she saw last time. The man she sees is the *same official* but not the *same man*. (Cf. Geach, *op. cit.*, p. 157.)

(ι) The Lord Mayor is *not the same official* as the Managing Director of Gnome Road Engineering Ltd (indeed they often write one another letters) but he is *one and the same man*.

(κ) Dr Jekyll and Mr Hyde were the *same man* but not the *same person or personality*. (Cf. Locke, *Essay*, II, XXVIII, 9 and 23.)

(λ) 'There is but one living and true God . . . and in unity of this Godhead there be three Persons of one substance, power, and eternity; the Father, the Son, and the Holy Ghost.' (Article I of the XXXIX Articles.)

---

[16] Cf. Hobbes, *De Corpore*, Ch. 11, §7: 'It is one thing to ask, concerning Socrates, whether he be the same man and another to ask whether he be the same body; for his body, when he is old, cannot be the same as it was when he was an infant, by reason of the difference of magnitude; yet nevertheless he may be the same man.'   [17] Hume, *Treatise* 1.4 (p. 244 in the Everyman edition).

This is to say that the Father, Son and Holy Ghost are the *same God* but not the *same person*.[18]

Some of these examples are more convincing than others, but none of the examples (α)–(κ) is sufficiently secure to provide an independent argument for the conceptual possibility of (λ), which is the most difficult case. I shall argue that all the perspicuous cases repose on ambiguities of reference or logical form or on special uses of 'be' (e.g. the use I shall call the constitutive use). None of them shows a way for relations like 'is the same horse as', 'is the same river as' (in the usage that ties them to questions of identity and existence) to escape from the congruence requirement. Any reader who is prepared to take this on trust (or can satisfy himself of it) should skip now (or so soon as he is satisfied) to section 9 of this chapter. The suggestion to skip is intended seriously.

6. DISCUSSION OF TYPE-(4) CASES

(α) and (β) hang together. For if the jug is the same collection of bits as the heap of fragments and the heap of fragments is the same collection of bits as the coffee pot, then, by transitivity, the jug must be the same collection of bits as the coffee pot. Either both or neither, then, is a true identity-statement. The difficulty is that if the jug is the same collection of material parts or bits of china clay as the coffee pot, that is if they are one and the same collection of china-bits, then their life histories and durations must be the same. (Call that the life-histories principle.) But the coffee pot *will* be fabricated or assembled at t_3 by my ingenious friend and exist only from then on. The jug won't then exist any more.

(α) will only be what is required as a case of type (4) if the sentence 'that heap is the jug you saw last time' comes to something more than 'the matter you see there is the same matter as the matter of the jug you saw when you came here last time'. Similarly (β) must not be reducible to the unexceptionable claim that the jug and coffee pot are made of the same matter. Otherwise, it is no longer obvious that we have the type-(4) identity-statement the relativist required. To get that, the 'is' in 'is the same collection of china bits' of (α) and (β) must mean '=' and we must take *collection of china-bits* as a straightforward covering concept. The 'is' in question must not be comparable to the 'is' in 'The soufflé you are eating is flour, eggs and milk' or the 'is' of 'The portico is wood and

---

[18] A collection of the writings of the Church fathers on this matter is to be found at pp. 33–7, 45ff., 54ff., 58ff. of *Documents of the Christian Church*, selected and edited by Henry Bettenson (Oxford, 1963). See also *op. cit.* in note 33 below.

stucco'. I shall call the latter the 'is' of *constitution*, contrast it with the 'is' of identity, and shall attempt to prove that it is precisely this constitutive 'is' that we have in (α) and (β). If I am right, then this occurrence of 'is the same collection' means 'is constituted from the same collection'.

Suppose, with (α), that the jug is straightforwardly the same collection of china-bits as the heap of fragments. Then, if this is a type-(4) identity-statement, we are entitled to infer that the jug is a collection of china-bits. (If Hesperus is the same planet as Phosphorus then Hesperus is a planet.) But then there must be some collection of china-bits with which the jug is identical. (If you doubt the principle linking identity and predication of this sort, namely that if x is ϕ then there must be some ϕ-thing with which x is identical,[19] then consider whether you will deny this instance of it: if Hesperus is a planet then there is some planet with which Hesperus is identical.) Suppose there to be some such collection. Then, again, we have trouble from the principle that, if a and b are identical, then they must have the same life history. Suppose I destroy the jug. Do I then destroy the collection? Either I do or I don't. If I do, then both (α) and (β) fail to be true with covering concept *collection of china-bits* and fail as type-(4) examples. If I don't thus destroy the collection, then it cannot be true of the jug that it is a collection of china-bits in the normal predicative sense of 'be a . . .'. Nevertheless it is true, under some other reading of 'be', that the jug is a collection of china-bits. That is to say that it is china-clay. It is true in the sense that the jug is *made of* china-clay or *constituted of* a collection of china-bits.[20] This is what is predicatively true of the jug. So much seems obvious. But the argument requires two supplementary remarks. One remark concerns the behaviour of 'same' in (α) and (β) within the gloss *same collection*, the other remark concerns the sense of 'collection'. Together, these

---

[19] A principle no less true for having prompted false theories of predication, e.g. Antisthenes' identity-theory. Cf. Aristotle, *Metaphysics*, 1024^{b32}; Hobbes, *De Corpore*, ch. 3, §2. It implies no such absurdity. The principle is denied by Noonan in *Mind* (1976), p. 572. Cf. also p. 573, where Noonan claims something can *be* a man by constituting that man *but be not identical with that man*: 'What constitutes a man is not identical with *that* man, but on my account it is identical with something which *is* a man, namely itself.' For further discussion of Noonan's position, see my reply to him in Lovibond and Williams (1996).

[20] I am not saying that the possibility of this paraphrase by itself forces us to postulate this distinct sense of 'is'. I am saying that the independent plausibility of this paraphrase, *plus* the plausibility of Leibniz's Law which would otherwise have to be amended or abandoned, *plus* the difficulties of amending Leibniz's Law or finding any f-restricted version of this principle for *same* f that stands in the right connexion to what it is for an f thing to exist, forces us to postulate this distinct sense of 'is'.

For collateral evidence supporting the hypothesis, as first formulated in Wiggins (1967), that this distinct reading of 'is' needs to be postulated, see the article by Tyler Burge cited at footnote 8 of Chapter Two.

remarks will occupy all seven paragraphs that intervene between here and the transition to example (γ).

The argument for the non-identity of jug and collection does not rely on a special or unfair construal of the term 'collection'. The possible construals seem to be three in number. 'ϕ (A)' where A is in some sense or other a collection can presumably mean either (i) that class A is ϕ or, (ii) that each of the As is ϕ, or (iii) that a *physical aggregate* A is ϕ.

Sense (i) cannot be what we are really looking for, even if skilful and opportunistic reinterpretations of ϕ might hold a set-theoretical interpretation of the 'A' in 'ϕ (A)' onto the rails for an indefinitely long time. In the end, the only way in which one could explain breaking or scattering a set-theoretical entity would have to be parasitic on the way one explained what one had to do to a physical configuration to break or scatter it. At root, the thing we need to be interested in is a notion of collection or manifold for which there can be no empty or null collection,[21] and for which it holds that 'if we take the German Army as our manifold and an infantry regiment as a domain within it, it is all one whether we choose to regard as elements within it the battalions, the companies, or the single soldiers'.[22] Notoriously this is not true of sets.

Sense (ii) of collection is not what we are looking for either. If I repair or destroy an item, I do not repair or destroy each part of it. (Since each part of a part is a part this would be difficult.) Nor in any non-Anaxagorean universe do we wish 'Jug (A)' to mean each of the As is a jug.

Sense (iii) suggests the definition of *sum* or *fusion* in Lesniewski's mereology.[23] An individual X would be a Lesniewskian *sum of* [*all elements* of the class *of parts of the*] *jug* J if all [elements of the class] *parts* of J were parts of X and if no part of X were disjoint from all parts of J.[24] This would certainly seem to be the sort of thing that we are looking for, because, according to this notion, all collections of parts of the jug,

---

[21] 'If we burn down all the trees of a wood we thereby burn down the wood. Thus [in the concrete sense of class] there can be no empty class.' Frege's review of Schroeder's *Algebra der Logik* in Geach and Black's *Translations*, p. 89.   [22] *Ibid*, p. 87.

[23] For a description of mereology (the calculus of individuals) see Tarski (1956), p. 24; or Nelson Goodman's *Structure of Appearance* (Cambridge, Mass., 1951), ch. 2. See also Woodger (1937), ch. III, §1, and appendix E (by Tarski), p. 161.

 For one capital philosophical defect of mereology as thus formulated, see footnote 17 of Chapter Three. I am relieved and encouraged to find my reservations about these mereological systems vindicated in Simons (1987).

[24] The definition of 'Y is disjoint from Z' is 'no individual W is a part both of Y and Z'. The reference to classes in the definition of *sum of elements* is eliminable (as is indicated by the square bracketing). The 'part of' relation is transitive in mereology.

however specified (whether as china-clay bits or as molecules, or as atoms), and all collections of collections of parts of the jug, etc., are intended to define and exhaust one and the same Lesniewskian whole or sum, X, of the jug. If 'collection' is defined in this way, however, and *if* mereology is grafted straight onto that pre-existing scheme of three-dimensional persisting things and their parts that we are operating (and anybody who wanted to obtain our type-(4) or type-(5) contrasts would have to be willing to operate), then perhaps the jug turns out *not* to be the same collection, in this sense of 'collection', as the coffee-pot in (α) and (β). For if $X = J$ then among the parts of X is J itself. For everything is part of itself. So if J is broken at t_2 and there is no such jug as J after t_2, then it looks as if X does not survive t_2 either.[25]

   In fact the problems that would arise in adding mereology to a logical system already possessed of a concept of identity defined for three-dimensional continuants, whose parts are not specified in terms of a pre-determined scheme of logical 'atoms', have been studied insufficiently.[26] The reason for this is that the adherents of mereology have almost always wished to operate a four-dimensional scheme which (as I have already complained) reduces everyday continuants to temporal series of slices, 'thing-moments' or spatio-temporal regions of the space–time continuum, and have usually advocated a most implausible semantic distinction between identity or difference at a time and identity or difference through time. (More is said against this below in Chapter Six, §8.) For the former concept of identity, they say that '$x = y$' can be defined mereologically by the condition that x is a part of y and y is a part of x; whereas for spatio-temporal continuity, or what is sometimes called *gen-identity*, these definitions have to be supplanted or supplemented by special conditions of a quite different character. The thing that chiefly matters here, in a discussion of (α) and (β), is that, no matter how these extra conditions may be stated and whatever alternatives there may be to Lesniewski's general method of defining 'concrete collection' and however three-dimensional wholes may be accommodated, the same fundamental dilemma remains. Either 'concrete collection' is defined in

---

[25] It is pointless to try to counter this by redefining the Lesniewskian whole of J without including J as part of J. One cannot destroy the *non-proper* part of J without affecting the *proper* parts of J and doing something just as drastic to them as to J. For to shatter J, or even break it into two, is to shatter the indefinite number of proper parts of it that lie across the break. This may amount to the destruction of these parts. (That depends on what destruction is deemed to amount to in the mereological framework.) The ordinary continuants of ordinary three-dimensional talk are not built up in any predetermined way from logical 'atoms' and aggregates of these.

[26] This remark dates from before the appearance of Peter Simons's book. For his book, see above, Preface paragraph six.

such a way that concrete collection X has the same principle of individuation as the jug, or it is not so defined. If it is not, then the life-histories principle debars X from identity with the jug and the type-(4) example disappears.[27] But if X does have the same principle of individuation as the jug, then again, for a different reason, we don't have a type-(4) example. For under this option, the jug isn't the same concrete collection as the coffee pot. What is more, the chances are that the whole project of equating thing and matter will then have degenerated into triviality.

If X is to be defined so as to be no more and no less tolerant of damage or of replacement of parts, etc., than is the jug, then sponsors of X will need to help themselves to the everyday continuant concept *jug* so as to secure the right configuration and persistence-conditions for X. But this is to ascend from the level of bits of things to the level of something whole, structured and jug-like, namely a jug. The jug is constituted of certain matter and identical only with a certain whole or continuant at present constituted in a certain way out of that matter. That is to say it is identical with the jug. Unless the project is thus trivialized and concrete collection is so defined, the true statement that the jug or the coffee pot is X must not be allowed by anybody who accepts the life-histories principle to have the standard consequence of the ordinary 'is' that it is identical with the mereological thing X. The 'is' must mean 'is constituted of', and collection of parts will not function standardly as a normal covering concept in the locution 'is the same collection as', as it figures in our examples (α) and (β).

Since 'the jug is the heap of fragments' and 'the jug was the same china-clay as the coffee pot' both boil down to identity of matter, the supplementary remark about 'the same' that was promised seven paragraphs ago is simply this: the words 'the same' can do appropriate duty with constitutive 'is' just as readily as they can do their ordinary duty with 'is' taken in the sense where it yields so-called numerical identity (the sense paraphrasable as 'is the *same substance* or *continuant* as'). So much for (α) and (β).

---

[27] Still a doubt may persist. Isn't the life-histories principle too strong? Might not the jug be identical with a stretch of some Lesniewskian whole X for such time as no part of the jug is broken or replaced? But quite apart from the support we have adduced for the strict life-histories principle, this 'temporary identity' is surely a peculiar sort of identity. See now my reply to Noonan in Lovibond and Williams (1996). We surely cannot give a sense to the supposition that Hesperus might be the same planet as Phosphorus for a bit and then stop being Phosphorus. But then the relation between the jug and the redefined whole X looks as if it cannot be the same sort of relation as that between Hesperus and Phosphorus. The conclusion for which I am arguing is of course just this, that they are related by the one being composed or constituted of the other, not by identity.

Example (γ) also requires considerable unpacking, but I think its power to convince is quite deceptive. We may begin by asking what is meant by 'Cleopatra's Needle'. What it is that someone points to when he points to Cleopatra's Needle. There is here a special difficulty that has to be faced by a consistent defender of the position Geach took up in *Reference and Generality*. To keep (γ) in play at all as a type-(4) example, the defender will have to claim that *landmark* and *stone* give different principles of identity. But by the theory of proper names defended in *Reference and Generality*, the sense of a proper name is given by the principle of identity built into the general term associated with it. It seems to follow that if 'Cleopatra's Needle' had two equally good but different 'nominal essences' then it ought to be ambiguous. In which case (γ) should not surprise or impress us any more than any other startling paradox arrived at by equivocation.

Rather than object in general to this theory of proper names,[28] let us simply examine the different specifications one might give of the received meaning of 'Cleopatra's Needle'. What again *is* Cleopatra's Needle? Is it a stone? If a stone is what it is, if 'it is a stone' properly answers Aristotle's *what is it* question, then, so soon as that stone is rotted away completely, Cleopatra's Needle is rotted away completely. For they are one and the same stone. Cleopatra's Needle, the stone, is not then the same *anything* as anything that exists in 1984. For if the stone, Cleopatra's Needle, no longer exists in 1984 then it is not then the same landmark as anything, even if something different may have come to fulfil the same role as it did.

But perhaps the fact the stone has completely rotted away by 1970 does not imply that there is no longer any such thing as Cleopatra's Needle. *Stone* is not then the sense-giving sortal. It may be that *monument* or *monument suitable for use as a landmark* is what Cleopatra's Needle substantially is. And perhaps monuments can be completely refashioned and still persist. But then 'Cleopatra's Needle in 1984 is not the same stone as Cleopatra's Needle in 1900' need only mean that Cleopatra's Needle is not made of the same material as it was in 1900. The dates surely qualify the verb in any case. Cleopatra's Needle is not constituted in 1984 of the same material as Cleopatra's Needle was constituted of in 1900. Once its matter was a (piece of) stone, now its matter is concrete. In that case the words 'the same' are serving in (γ), with the versatility already remarked upon in connexion with (α) and (β), to indicate that

---

[28] Which could be defended against the criticisms of Linsky all the more effectively if the general thesis of the present chapter were correct.

you can't say about the *material* of Cleopatra's Needle in 1984 what you could have said in 1900. (A type-(3) analysis might also be attempted.)

These are not all the possibilities. One might think *landmark* was what gave 'Cleopatra's Needle' its sense. But there is something rather peculiar about treating 'landmark' as an ordinary substance-concept suitable for giving a proper name a sense. It is really more like a title conferred on an object when it attains a certain position of conspicuousness. Compare 'chairman' or 'official' or 'president' or 'sovereign'. In that case, in one use, *landmark* is a restriction of a sortal concept. It presupposes the availability in principle of some underlying sortal predicate that says what sort of object. This takes us back to the alternatives already mentioned. There does, however, exist the possibility of another use, which one might call a *titular* use, of the phrase 'same landmark'. According to this, for *x* to be the same landmark as *y*, *x* has only to mark the same spot as *y* did.[29] But in this use, something else, something nonidentical with the obelisk and distinct under every genuine covering concept, can succeed it as the same landmark. It must be this view of 'landmark' that (γ)'s defender exploits in suggesting that the Meriden stone ceases to be the same landmark when it is transported to London. 'Cleopatra's Needle' then turns out not to be an ordinary proper name at all. It emerges as an abbreviation for the description 'whatever suitable object of suitable dignity conspicuously marks such and such a spot on the Embankment in London'.

The effectiveness of this critique of example (γ) does not depend on there being a hard and fast or canonically correct answer to the question 'what is Cleopatra's Needle?' The example may owe a specious plausibility precisely to the fact that 'Cleopatra's Needle' can remain ambiguously poised between these and perhaps yet other incompatible interpretations.

With this, the alleged cases of (4) are concluded. It begins to appear why there simply cannot be cases of type (4). Where $(\exists f)\binom{a=b}{f}$ and allegedly $(\exists g)\ not\ \binom{a=b}{g}$ & g(*a*) v g(*b*), either g is a substantial sortal

---

[29] If this use exists and extends to 'sovereign' then all that is required for Queen Elizabeth II to be the same sovereign as Queen Elizabeth I is that she should rule the same country. And perhaps 'The same sovereign was a man, is now a woman' need not signify that anybody has changed sex (unless 'anybody' be thought of as adapted to perform precisely the same trick as 'sovereign'). Queen Elizabeth herself simply succeeded a man.

concept or it is not. If it is not substantial then the champion of (γ) needs to show that we have more than a type-(3) case or a case of constitutive 'is'. If g is a substantial sortal concept, however, then either *a* or *b* has to fall under g without the other falling under g. But that has been excluded.

7. DISCUSSION OF TYPE-(5) CASES AND SOME ATTEMPTED AMENDMENTS OF LEIBNIZ'S LAW

The identity-interpretation of (δ) and Leibniz's Law are incompatible. Unlike the water, the river on which I moored my boat yesterday is not a part of the Aegean. Rivers are indeed water but this means that water goes to make them up. 'Same water' is not therefore a covering concept for an identity statement identifying a river with something.

(ε) is fairly easily unmasked. If 'collection of cells' will do as covering concept, and if 'is a collection of cells' doesn't merely mean 'is made up of cells', then John Doe must be identical with some definite collection of cells, and this will have to share all properties of John Doe. *What* collection of cells? Suppose we make 'collection of cells' mean 'such and such aggregate' (with fixed constituents). But then one aggregate is succeeded by another. John Doe is not similarly succeeded. One aggregate is dissipated. John Doe isn't. But then 'John Doe is such and such collection of cells' has to have the constitutive interpretation. (Compare (α) and (β).) Suppose we make 'collection of cells' mean 'composite with a succession of constituents through time'. Then we no longer have an example of type (5) at all, i.e. change of truth-grounds by change of covering concept. For in this sense man and boy are the same collection of cells.

(ζ) resembles (γ) in a certain specious exploitation of ambiguities. The example has intrinsic interest, but, because the analysis is at once intricate and at least in part predictable, I relegate the discussion to a note.[30]

---

[30] Hume continues in tell-tale manner: 'But we must observe, that in these cases the first object [*sic*] is in a manner annihilated before the second comes into existence; by which means, we are never presented, in any point of time, with the idea of difference and multiplicity; and for that reason are less scrupulous in calling them the same.' Hume has less interest than we ought to have in pressing the point I am about to make because, having distinguished respectable strict 'numerical' identity from what he variously dubs 'imperfect', 'specific', 'fictitious' identity (the lamentable ancestor, I suppose, of 'genidentity', and a notion which on one occasion he even calls a perfect notion of *diversity*), he can then afford to let you say whatever you please about the disreputable second notion. But we must insist – *either* we make up our minds to say the building was annihilated *or* we do not make up our minds so.

If we do say the building was annihilated, then a certain building seems to be found in existence after it lapsed from existence. It is easy to avoid this absurdity. Here are two or three different ways. First take 'church' in its first and third occurrences in 'the present church is the same

In (η) the appearance of a type-(5) case relies entirely on the failure to say what is meant by 'Cornish Riviera Express'. Once this is specified, all semblance of support for **R** disappears. Manifestly, to admit the possibility of an express surviving its present coaches and locomotive is to admit its non-identity with these. But then *collection of coaches and locomotive* is a non-starter for straightforward covering concept, and we have a constitutive 'is'. (Alternatively, perhaps we have a titular use of 'same train' or 'same express'.)

(θ) is equally easily exposed. Suppose official *a* is succeeded by official *b*. The petitioner therefore sees *b* on her second visit. She doesn't see the same office-holder but the holder of the same office, whoever he is. The sentence '*a* is the same official as *b*' doesn't ascribe 'numerical identity' to *a* and *b* at all. It predicates something of them in common, namely holding a certain office. In *the same*'s extensive repertoire this is one of the better-known roles. (Cf. *landmark*, and example (γ).)

(ι) also exploits an ambiguity. Under one interpretation it is simply false that the Lord Mayor is not the same official as the Managing Director of Gnome Road Engineering. John Doe, that tireless official, is both Lord Mayor and Managing Director. So the Lord Mayor is the same tireless official as the Managing Director. The interpretation that makes the first part of (ι) true concerns *what it is to be Lord Mayor* and *what it is to be Managing Director of Gnome Road Engineering*. These Frege might

footnote 30 (*cont.*)

church as the old church' to mean 'building'. Take the second occurrence of 'church' to signify what can persist when a congregation loses its church building. Mark this latter sense by capitals. Thus the sentence signifies something like 'the present church building embodies/ realizes/houses the same Church as the old church building embodied/realized/housed'. If this really is a way of reading the sentence that we are concerned with, then, there must be some 'is' of 'realization' which extends the 'is' of constitution. (Here cf. (μ) later.) To add to the sentence 'the new church building is the same Church as the old church building' the qualification 'but it is not the same *building*' imports a zeugma at 'is', which reverts the second time round to its '=' sense, with consequential change in the grammatical role of the expression following 'same'. A second way is to take 'church' to mean 'Church' throughout in the affirmative sentence 'the present church is the same church as the old church', and to take the addition 'but it is not the same building' as importing a zeugma at the subject place: '… but the new *building* is not the same *building* as the old'. Third, let 'church' mean building at its first and third occurrence and behave in the titular fashion and unlike a proper covering concept at its second occurrence, as it was supposed 'land mark' might behave in (γ) (meaning say 'whatever building houses such and such a congregation'). We lose the type-(5) identity-statement whichever analysis we adopt.

If we do not make up our minds to say that the church was annihilated then either we do not know what to say about the example, or we say that it was not annihilated. It is then false that the new church is not the same building as the old one. It is the same, and has simply been repaired and remodelled. That is what we have decided to say. Again the rebuttal does not depend on its being a hard and fast question how 'church' behaves in the example. As before, the example cannot be permitted to survive by poising itself ambiguously between mutually exclusive alternatives.

have called concepts. And what (ι) then says is that to satisfy the one concept and hold the one office, is not to satisfy the other and hold the other office. To add 'they often write one another letters' is to make a zeugma. For now 'they' must be understood, the second time round, as 'the man who satisfies this concept and the man who satisfies that concept'. And it is in this sense (in which they are the same official) that 'they' are the same man.

(κ) touches on large issues to which we shall return in Chapter Seven. It is certain that neither *human being* nor *homo sapiens* is synonymous with *person*. But this does not prove the point. And the difficulty is this. If, as (κ) says, Mr Hyde and Dr Jekyll are the same man, then, if Mr Hyde visited Tilbury Docks at 9.30 p.m. on 18 December 1887, then Dr Jekyll did so too, and did whatever Mr Hyde did. Now Dr Jekyll the man is a person and he did these things at Tilbury Docks. But then is he not the person who did these things at the docks? How then can he be a different person from Mr Hyde? The only way to make (κ) come out true is to give it a rather odd and implausible interpretation, and interpret it to mean that to satisfy the concept *person who is ϕ* is not necessarily to satisfy the concept *person who is ψ*. To have these personal characteristics is not necessarily to have those personal characteristics. Contingently, though, to satisfy the one concept was (in R. L. Stevenson's story) to satisfy the other. 'Dr Jekyll' and 'Mr Hyde' have then to be read twice over in (κ) to make it come out true, first as standing each for a man (this individual is the same man as that individual), the second time as standing for a certain kind of character or personality. (These personalities, not these men, are different.) But this spoils all prospects of seeing it as a case of **R**; and the example really represents an implausible attempt to postulate philosophically defined schizophrenia without going the whole way and postulating two men sharing one body, each taking his turn to control it.

This brings me to (λ), and that which is becoming overdue, the re-examination of Leibniz's Law. No one could hope to exhaust the theological implications of what is at issue here or examine every possible formulation, but the plain difficulty is that, if the Son who was God was crucified and was the same God as the Father, then, according to Leibniz's Law unamended, the Father was crucified. I understand that this involves one in the heresy of *patripassionism*. What is more, one application of Leibniz's Law is as good as any other. If the Fathers of the Church had allowed the Patripassiani their way, then the three Persons, Father, Son and Holy Ghost, would have been in danger of collapsing into one another. For, in exactly the same way, all the predicates of Christ that applied uniquely to him or applied to him at a time and place will have applied to the Father and Holy Ghost; how then could Christ fail to be the same person as these?

Short of heresy, which offers an indefinite variety of reformulations, the determined defender of (λ) needs to withhold Leibniz's Law. The trouble is that Leibniz's Law underwrites the substitutivity of identity, and this is a principle not long dispensable in any form of reasoning. It follows that the defender must find a way to qualify it or restrict its application. Even as he brackets the full Leibnizian Principle, the defender of (λ) must make positive provision for some however circuitous advance from ϕa and $\left(\dfrac{a=b}{f}\right)$, taken as true of some a, b and f that satisfy any extra condition he requires, to the conclusion ϕb. There must be some condition or other under which the circumstance of b's having a genuine property may be deduced from the circumstance of a's having that property.[31]

A method of dispensing with Leibniz's Law for $\dfrac{x=y}{f}$ that Wilfrid Hodges and I once tried to explore was to make do with this property of $\dfrac{=}{f}$:

$$\text{LL.II:} \left(\frac{a=b}{f}\right) \to (\forall \phi)\left[(\forall x)\left(\frac{x=a}{f} \to \phi x\right) \leftrightarrow (\forall y)\left(\frac{y=b}{f} \to \phi y\right)\right]$$

---

[31] For an attempt to restrict congruence by defining a class Δ_f of predicates such that Leibniz's Law assumes the qualified form:

$$[\tfrac{x=y}{f} \to (\forall \phi)\ [\phi \in \Delta[f(x) \wedge f(y) \wedge [\phi (x) \to \phi (y)]]]],$$

see Nicholas Griffin, *Relative Identity (op. cit.* note 2), pp. 140–1. The conditions Griffin places on Δ_f are as follows:

(i) $f(\xi) \in \Delta_f$
(ii) If $\phi(\xi) \in \Delta_f$ then $\neg \phi \in \Delta_f$
(iii) If $\phi(\xi) \in \Delta_f$ and $\psi(\xi) \in \Delta_f$ then $[\phi(\xi) \wedge \psi(\xi)] \in \Delta_f$; and conversely (provided $[\phi(\xi) \leftrightarrow \psi(\xi)]$)
(iv) If $\phi(\xi) \in \Delta_f$ and $\forall x[\phi(x) \to \psi(x)]$ then $\psi(\xi) \in \Delta_f$
(v)   If $\phi(\xi) \in \Delta_f$ and $\psi(\xi)$ results from $\phi(\xi)$ by the replacement of every occurrence of one or more variables in $\phi(\xi)$ then $\psi(\xi) \in \Delta_f$
(vi) $C_f(\xi,c) \in \Delta_f$, where '$C_f(\xi,\eta)$' is a complex predicate which expresses the identity criteria conveyed by 'f' and 'c' is an arbitrary constant.

S. G. Williams has shown that, on these terms, Leibniz's Law will come back unrestricted. His argument is that, by (i) $f(\xi)$ belongs to Δ_f. So by (ii), $\neg f(\xi)$ belongs to Δ_f, as therefore does $[f(\xi) \wedge \neg f(\xi)]$, by (iii). But $(\forall x)[[f(x) \wedge \neg f(x)] \to \phi(x)] \to \phi(x)]$. So, by (iv), ϕ belongs to Δ_f. But ϕ here can be any extensional predicate. So every such predicate belongs to Δ_f. As Williams remarks, there is something instructive in the way in which Griffin's very natural conditions render back to us the classical Leibnizian principle.

This says that, if a is the same f as b, then whatever properties transfer from a to anything that is the same f as a, these properties will transfer from b to anything that is the same f as b. This is not doubtful. Suppose we know that

(1)
$$\text{Cicero} =_{\text{man}} \text{Tully}$$

and

(2)
$$\text{Denounced Catiline (Cicero)}.$$

Then, by *modus ponens* and universal instantiation, it follows that

(3)
$$(\forall x)(x =_{\text{man}} \text{Cicero} \rightarrow \text{Denounced Catiline } (x))$$

if and only if

$$(\forall y)(y =_{\text{man}} \text{Tully} \rightarrow \text{Denounced Catiline } (y)).$$

But, to get anything more interesting than (3), we need something that cannot be regarded as guaranteed when unrestricted Leibniz's Law is withdrawn, namely the mass of truths such as

(4)
$$(\forall x)(x =_{\text{man}} \text{Cicero} \rightarrow x \text{ denounced Catiline}).$$

In the presence of (4), we could of course deduce

(5)
$$\text{Tully denounced Catiline.}$$

But from whence do we obtain (4)? On what, rather, does the *relativist* take the question of the truth or falsity of claims such as (4) to depend? And what, in the absence of a general principle of congruence for $x =_{\text{f}} y$, does he take to ground the truth of propositions that link particulars and attributes in the way in which (4) links *man*, Tully, Cicero and *denounced*? Why is there no similar true proposition leading to a similar deduction with the subjects The Father and The Son, the sortal predicate *is God*, and the predicate *was crucified at such and such a time and place*? The answer must be that the connexion that holds between *man*, Cicero, Tully and *denounced* and makes (4) true does not hold between *God*, the Father, The Son, and *crucified at such and such a time and place*. It might be said, as Hodges put it, that *crucified* does not 'transfer over' the concept God. But why not? There must be some principle of some sort to be found here from which one could gain an idea of what counts as a consideration for or against claims such as (4).

These questions become more immediately important for present purposes – among which I do not here number attempting to refute (λ) under all interpretations, for all I seek to show is that (λ) is not an identity-statement with any independent leverage in the larger logical dispute – if we ask how the predicate *God who was crucified* can fail to transfer over the concept *God*. Yet, if Christ is God and was crucified, then it seems hard to deny that he is God who was crucified.

One way to block the inference to 'Christ is God who was crucified', and this is a way that has attracted some thinkers, is to deny that it was *qua God* that Christ had a body or was crucified.[32] But if this escape is used, then there is a simpler relativization of Leibniz's Law which promises to provide both the restricted congruence and the adjudication that we have wanted for sentences like (4). It reads

$$\text{LL.III: } \begin{pmatrix} a = b \\ \text{f} \end{pmatrix} \rightarrow (\phi(a) \text{ as an f} \leftrightarrow \phi(b) \text{ as an f}).$$

In assessing LL.III, let us now suppose that LL.II and LL.III are both available. We are to suppose that all identity is reached through relative identity. We are to suppose also that this is our only general account of how a sortal concept f and a property must be related if the property is to transfer from *a* to *b* where $\begin{smallmatrix} a = b \\ f \end{smallmatrix}$. The rest will be given piecemeal, we are to suppose, from the semantics of the various predicates in all their various predicative roles.

Now there are undoubtedly places where *qua* or *as* or similar devices occur essentially and an object has to be characterized (*φa* as an f) and (not-*φa* as a g). But I submit that this is a circumscribed and special phenomenon, ill suited to the larger role for which it is being recruited.

---

[32] This will lead to a division of predicates similar to one which Hodges pointed out to me that Pope Leo made in his *Tome* of 449. 'Deus per id quod omnia per ipsum facta sunt et sine ipso factum est nihil; homo per id quod factus est ex muliere, factus sub lege . . . esurire, sitire, lassescere atque dormire evidenter humanum est.' See also Griffin, *op. cit.*, pp. 140–1.

On any view resting on the non-transferability of *crucified* with respect to *God* new questions arise. For instance, would it then be possible for Christ the God to be the same anything as Christ the person that was crucified? Either yes or no. If no, (λ) disappears. If yes, Christ is the same God as the Father. Furthermore he is a person who was crucified. He is God then *and* he is crucified. But then is he not God who was crucified? Again, what follows, if anything, from the fact that Christ, who was *qua* person crucified, seems to satisfy the complex predicate 'was, *qua* God incarnated, *qua* person crucified'?

(1) It may arise with what have been called *attributive* adjectives such as *big, small, tall, short, real, good, bad*. Thus a ship can be big among destroyers and small among cruisers, a man tall among Japanese but short among Americans, a wooden duck a real decoy duck but not a real duck, a witticism a good joke but not a good thing to say at that particular moment.

(2) There can be reference via *qua* or *as* to a role that some person or thing plays. As a general he was obliged to be present at the Court Martial, as the best marksman in the regiment not. Sir John Doe sent the letter as Managing Director (i.e. in the course of his duties for Gnome Engineering), not as Lord Mayor.

(3) *Oratio obliqua* and straightforward referential opacity can also take cover under *as* or *qua*. *x* sent the letter to Sir John Doe as Lord Mayor not as Managing Director (i.e. *x addressed* or *directed* the letter 'The Lord Mayor'). Philip, who does not know that Cicero is Tully, may believe Cicero, as Cicero but not as Tully, or believe Tully, as Cicero but not as Tully, to have denounced Catiline. Philip may think of him under this name rather than that.

These cases are well demarcated and fairly well understood. What the present proposal seeks to do, however, is to generalize the phenomenon they represent, without doing anything to show us how to determine the relevant '*qua* f ' for each and every property asserted to qualify a given individual, or how to decide the applicability, meaning and satisfaction conditions of the complex predicates thus arrived at. At greater length, a rather more exhaustive and exact typology could have been devised for *qua* and all similar devices. But it is certain that *qua* is not ubiquitous in its operation.[33] Not every adjective has an attributive use. Individuals are many things (satisfy many predicates) otherwise than by virtue of playing some role or other. Referential opacity is not to be found absolutely everywhere. Moreover, *qua* does not always produce a single kind of effect for which a unitary rule of the proposed kind could be laid down. Consider the difference that, with certain precautions, '*qua* f ' is detachable *salva veritate* from affirmative 'ϕ *qua* f ' in types (2) and (3), and not so

---

[33] I owe reference to an example which falls outside these three kinds to Professors Geach and Anscombe. See Aristotle, *Physics*, III.3, 202$^{\rm b}$. Consider the road from Athens to Thebes. It is the same road as the road from Thebes to Athens. But the road Athens–Thebes is uphill and the road Thebes–Athens is downhill. My objection to allowing this example (*qua* Athens–Thebes uphill, *qua* Thebes–Athens downhill) is that either 'road' means an actual feature of the landscape, in which case 'uphill' collects a specification giving the direction of the slope, and there is a simple relational predicate true of that road; or else 'road' means 'journey by road', in which case there is no identity. (The fare for Thebes–Athens may be more than the fare for Athens–Thebes.)

removable in type (1). In kinds (2) and (3), the *qua* is simply explicative and serves to demarcate that which may be detached. Which kind of *qua* is it that is involved in LL.III? Is the intention behind putting forward LL.III to withhold transferability entirely for predicates and verbs that do not need a *qua*? Or is it to require in every case the discovery of some suitable *qua*?

If Jesus Christ could teach the doctors at the age of twelve, then he was by that age good *qua* scholar, that is to say a good scholar. And that was the capacity in which he taught the doctors. This he did *qua* man, not *qua* God . . . So the Father did not teach the doctors at the age of twelve – or so the orthodox will seek to rule. (But was it not *qua* God that Jesus Christ was learned enough aged twelve to teach the doctors?) The intention behind LL.III is clear enough. But nothing else is clear once we insist on making the presence of ϕ *qua* f the general condition of transfer of ϕ from a to some b that is the same f as a – because there is no reason to believe one could say what *qua* would mean and how it would need to be completed when it was adjoined to each of any or every verb or predicate. On the other hand, it is unclear why transfer should be refused to predicates that do not seem to need a *qua*.[34]

8. A MATHEMATICAL EXAMPLE SUPPOSEDLY OF TYPE (5)

This book is not directly concerned with abstract entities but since the arguments that have been used against examples (a)–(λ) have been formal arguments, they ought, if they are good arguments, to work equally well against purported **R**-examples of a mathematical or logical character.

(μ) Suppose we have a relation R that holds only between a and b and between c and d. Then the relation R in extension may be said to be the set $\{\langle a,b\rangle, \langle c,d\rangle \}$, i.e. the set whose members are the ordered pairs $\langle a,b\rangle$ and $\langle c,d\rangle$. Now there are a number of different and equally allowable definitions of an ordered pair. For example, $\langle x,y\rangle$ can be defined either as $\{\{x\}, \{x,y\}\}$ or as $\{\{x\}, \{\wedge,y\}\}$. One might then say (from the *extrasystematic* point of view) that the set S, namely $\{\{\{a\},\{ \wedge, b\}\},\{\{c\},\{ \wedge, d\}\}\}$, was *the same relation* as set S′, namely $\{\{\{a\}, \{a, b\}\}, \{\{c\}, \{c, d\}\}\}$. But it is certainly not *the same set* as S′.

As usual the objection to accepting this apparent type-(5) example at its face-value is Leibniz's Law. If $S = S'$ under the concept of relation

[34] There is now an important essay on the Trinity and such matters by Richard Cartwright, to be found in his *Philosophical Essays* (Cambridge, Mass., 1987).

then whatever is true of S is true of S′ and *vice versa*. But S has $\{\{a\}\ \{\ \wedge,$ $b\}\}$ as a member and S′ does not.

Notice that any project of saving (μ) by some amendment or relativization of Leibniz's Law plus some doctrine or other of categories is manifestly hopeless. Suppose we say that we can only expect what is true of S *qua relation* to be true of S′. Well, either relations are or they are not sets.[35] If they are sets then the plea is absurd, R is a set like S and S′ and we still have the violation of Leibniz's Law. If they are not sets, however, then the true statement 'set S is the same relation as S′' must not be allowed to have the consequence that S or S′ (predicatively) is a relation. We must only allow, when we are looking at this question extra-systematically, that it *represents* a relation. But to block this consequence is to withdraw (μ) as a genuine case of type (5). If we want a reduction of relations of degree n which strictly equates them with something, then we shall have to isolate and utilize whatever it is that all mathematically satisfactory definitions of ordered n-tuples have in common.

If we do block the unwelcome consequences of (μ) (rather than vainly try to settle which is 'the right definition' of ordered pair), then what sort of 'is' do we have in (μ)? Presumably it is analogous to the 'is' of 'Irving is Hamlet' or the 'be' of 'that piece of sugar can be your queen [at chess] while I glue the head of the queen back on'. It may be that the 'identifications' associated with the various proposed reductions of arithmetic to set-theory have to be similarly explained, in terms of realization or representation.[36]

9. CONCLUSION CONCERNING **R**, THE RELATIVITY OF IDENTITY

It may be helpful to conclude with some general remarks about the defects we have discovered in purported type-(4) and type-(5) instances of **R**. Almost all of the readings of these that have given **R** the semblance of support have depended on ignoring one of two things:

  (i) the definite but limited ambiguity of certain uses of 'is' (ambiguity

---

[35] 'Different things cannot be made to coincide by abstraction, and to regard them as the same is simply a mistake. If abstracting from the difference between my house and my neighbour's, I were to regard both houses as mine, the defect of my abstraction would soon be made clear.' (Frege, *Grundgesetze der Arithmetik*, §99.)

[36] For 'theoretical identification', see Putnam's essay in *Dimensions of Mind*, ed. Sidney Hook (New York, 1960), p. 155. For representation of arithmetic in set-theory, see Paul Benacerraf, 'What Numbers Couldn't Be', *Philosophical Review*, 24 (Jan. 1965).

for which we have given some collateral evidence, almost all of it dependent, however, at closer or further remove on Leibniz's Law), most particularly the '*x* is constituted of *y*' reading of '*x* is *y*';

(ii) the deceptive designation of certain referring expressions. ('By 'that Hermes' do you mean 'that statue of Hermes' or "the matter of that statue of Hermes', or what exactly?' Again, it is only in the presence of Leibniz's Law that such questions have any point.)

In the case of some putative examples of **R**, it is hard to say which is the dominant confusion. Different people's appreciation of certain cases may differ. But prolonged experimentation has led me to believe that, even if there is overlap among the **R**-candidates that they disqualify, no one of these diagnoses will account for everything that is going on in the full corpus of apparent examples. Neither diagnosis is dispensable.

The need we have found for the second diagnosis is particularly interesting. At §46 of *The Foundations of Arithmetic*, Frege wrote (in J. L. Austin's translation, my italics):

While looking at *one and the same external phenomenon* [derselben äussern Erscheinung] I can say with equal truth both 'It is a copse' and 'It is five trees', or both 'Here are four companies' and 'Here are 500 men'. Now what changes here from one judgement to the other is neither any individual object, nor the whole, the agglomeration of them, but rather my terminology. But that is itself only a sign that one concept has been substituted for another.

That which is true and unshakeable here is the justly celebrated insight of Frege for which he is preparing to argue in this passage – that numbers attach to the concepts under which objects fall, and not to the objects themselves. But even for a good thesis there will exist both good arguments and bad arguments; and there is at least one bad argument here *if* Frege really meant to suggest that, holding my gaze constant upon one external phenomenon,[37] I can subsume the very same something first under the concept *copse* then under the concept *trees* and, in doing this, assign to the first concept the cardinal number one and to the second concept the number five. Obviously a copse *is* trees. But the copse itself is not identical with any tree *or* with any mereological aggregate of trees. (The copse tolerates replacement of all its trees, for instance, but neither the aggregate nor the class comprising the present trees in the copse can survive such replacement.) There is no real prospect of this 'this' (the 'dies' in 'dies ist eine Baumgruppe' and 'dies sind funf Bäume')

---

[37] Is the *Erscheinung* a sort of internal accusative of *ansehen*, or the whole visual field of the seeing, or the *object seen*? – and, if it is the last, why suppose there is one and only one such object?

having constant reference, even though the stuff (wood) that makes up the this both makes up a copse and makes up five trees.[38] What interests Frege is that, according to which of these choices we make, we either arrive at a concept with the number one or arrive at a concept with the number five. What interests me, however, is that, if we are concerned with the reference of 'this' or of any other designation whatever – concerned that is about what object it designates – then we have to take care to discover whether the 'this' stands for a copse or for a class whose members are certain trees or an aggregate of certain trees. These are not the same thing.

10. ABSOLUTENESS AND SORTAL DEPENDENCE JOINTLY AFFIRMED AND FORMALIZED

Once controversy recedes and the dust settles, the result that we reached by §2 of this chapter may be given again.

Given Leibniz's Law

$$x = y \rightarrow (\phi x \leftrightarrow \phi y)$$

and given, by virtue of **D**,

$$x = y \text{ if and only if } (\exists f) \left(\frac{x = y}{f} \right),$$

we obtain the schema

$$(\exists f) \left(\frac{x = y}{f} \right) \rightarrow (\phi x \leftrightarrow \phi y).$$

So, if we choose any kind at all such that $\frac{x = y}{f}$, x will be ϕ just if y is ϕ:

$$(\forall g) \left(\frac{x = y}{g} \rightarrow \phi x \leftrightarrow \phi y \right).$$

Consider now the arbitrary individuals x and y, each falling under the sort g, the individual x being the same g as the individual y. Then

---

[38] See Wiggins (1968). When Socrates claims in the *Parmenides* that he is one man and many parts, right and left parts, back and front parts, upper and lower parts, all different (enumerated at 129^c, cf. *Philebus* 14^d), Plato seems to say that *Socrates himself* partakes both of one and of many. Of course Frege could not say such a thing. And, if we credit Frege with following through consistently the idea that 'to use the symbol a to signify an object, we must have a criterion for deciding in all cases whether b is the same as a' (§62), then we ought to deny that he is in any way suggesting at §46 that the 'dies' has constant reference to objects. His sole interest is in the shift of concept. ('Neither any individual object' is intended to dismiss the whole question of objects.)

consider an arbitrary individuative sort or kind h. Either x falls under h or it doesn't. If x does not belong to h, then by the principle $T \rightarrow (F \rightarrow p)$, we have

$$\underset{g}{x=y} \rightarrow (h(x) \rightarrow \underset{h}{x=y}).$$

On the other hand, if x does belong to h, then we have

$$\underset{g}{x=y} \ \& \ h(x).$$

But in that case $\underset{h}{x=x}$.[39] So consider x's predicate $(\underset{h}{x=} \cdots)$. By Leibniz's Law and $\underset{g}{x=y}$, the object y has this predicate too. So again we have

$$\underset{g}{x=y} \rightarrow (h(x) \rightarrow \underset{h}{x=y}).$$

Restoring quantifiers, we then have the following conclusion, entailing the denial of **R**:

$$(\forall h)(\forall g)\, (\underset{g}{x=y} \rightarrow (h(x) \rightarrow \underset{h}{x=y})).$$

In sum, let me say that it is on the twin claims of the Leibnizian absoluteness and the sortal dependency of identity that a theory of individuation needs to be founded. It follows that, in order to obtain a theory of individuation, we must try to arrive at a further and better account of the kinds by which we individuate and sort particulars. This will be the work of Chapters Two and Three.

---

[39] If putative type-(3) cases of **R** appear to give trouble, see §3, paragraph one, case (3).

CHAPTER TWO

Outline of a theory of individuation

Upon those who step into the same rivers different and again different waters flow. The waters scatter and gather, come together and
flow away, approach and depart.

(Heraclitus, Diels fragments 12, 91, text and translation after Kirk, *Cosmic
Fragments*, Cambridge, 1954, pp. 367–84.)

In the state of living creatures, their identity depends not on a mass
of the same particles, but on something else. For in them the variation of great parcels of matter alters not the identity: an oak
growing from a plant to a great tree and then lopped, is still the
same oak; and a colt grown up to a horse, sometimes fat, sometimes
lean, is all the while the same horse.

(John Locke, *Essay Concerning Human Understanding* ii, xxvii, 3.)

All constituents of living matter, whether functional or structural,
of simple or complex constitution, are in a steady state of rapid
flux.

(Rudolf Schoenheimer, *The Dynamic State of Body Constituents*, Cambridge,
Mass., 1942.)

1. PROPOSITION **D** AND THE RATIONALE OF THE 'SAME WHAT?' QUESTION

If identity were sortal-relative and sortal-relative just by reason of the
holding of **R** or the Relativity of Identity, then that would help to
support the Sortal Dependency of Individuation or **D**, as that was given
in the Preface and the first pages of Chapter One. For **D** is a thesis that
some champions of **R** have wanted to see as a kind of obverse of **R**. The
obverse they look for says that, on pain of indefiniteness, every identity
statement stands in radical need of an answer to the question *same what?*
But **R** is false, we have decided. It can lend no support to anything, least

of all to the claim that there is some semantical indeterminacy in the plain '*a* is *b*' locution. (See Preamble, §9 *ad fin.*) Let us forget about this obverse.

When **D** is clearly dissociated from **R**, that which remains is this:

D: *a* = *b* if and only if there exists a sortal concept f such that

(1) *a* and *b* fall under f;

(2) to say that *x* falls under f or that *x* is an f is to say what *x* is (in the sense Aristotle isolated);

(3) *a* is the same f as *b*, that is coincides with *b* under f in the manner of coincidence required for members of f, hence congruently . . . [See below §2, paragraph 4.] [For 'concept', see Preamble §5. See also Preamble, §9 *ad fin.*]

Why dwell so particularly upon **D** if the three-place predicable '*x* is the same f as *y*' is going to be Leibnizian? Why is this attenuated version of **D** worth recovering from the wreckage of **R**? It is worth recovering because it registers the way in which, wherever there is a point at issue in matters of identity, this depends in a systematic way upon what *a* and *b* are. **D** unfolds and articulates the collateral and coeval ideas by the possession of which we deploy the ideas of entity, identity and substance upon that which confronts us in experience.

The import and importance of **D** may be brought out by considering the position of a philosopher who proposes to dispense altogether with it. So far as this philosopher is concerned, the point at issue in questions of *a* and *b*'s identity or difference is indeed dependent on what *a* is and *b* is, but only to an unremarkable extent. If *a* and *b* are to count as the same, then *a* and *b* will have to agree in respect of all properties and relations, sortal properties themselves being among these properties.

Suppose I ask: Is *a*, the man sitting on the left at the back of the restaurant, the same person as *b*, the boy who won the drawing prize at the school I was still a pupil at early in the year 1951? To answer this sort of question is surprisingly straightforward in practice, however intricate a business it would be to spell out the full justification of the method we employ. Roughly, though, what organizes our actual method is the idea of a particular kind of continuous path in space and time the man would have had to have followed in order to end up here in the restaurant; and the extraordinary unlikelihood (if the man himself were questioned and these dispositions investigated) of certain sorts of memory-dispositions existing in anyone or anything that had not pursued that path. Once we have dispelled any doubt whether there is a path in space and time along which that schoolboy might have been traced and we have concluded that the human being who was that schoolboy coincides with the person / human being at the back of the restaurant, this identity is settled. And *then* we can say that, no matter what property ϕ is and no matter whether the question of either entity's instantiating ϕ figured in our inquiry into the spatio-temporal paths of *a* and *b*, *a* has ϕ if and only if *b* has ϕ. The continuity or coincidence in question here is that which is brought into consideration by what it is to be a human being.

I am not urging here that our actual method, focused upon the question of this particular path of a human being, gives us a risky but practically indispensable short cut to establishing each of the indefinitely many instances of the schema $\phi a \leftrightarrow \phi b$. Nor am I urging that it happens there is no other way of establishing each instance (though that must be a capital consideration). The contention is rather that to determine correctly the answer to our continuity question, the question about the traceability of things through their life-histories, precisely *is* to settle it that, no matter what property ϕ is, *a* has ϕ if and only if b has ϕ. I am also urging (as the epistemological reflection of a criteriological point) that it is impossible *even in theory* to conceive of some way independent of the prior discovery that $a = b$ by which to establish that *a* and *b* have all and only the same properties. For suppose one were to renounce all elucidations of identity other than one given in terms of *a*'s and *b*'s complete community of properties. Then how would one think about the non-permanent properties enjoyed by an individual *a* identified with respect to the past and the properties enjoyed by an individual *b* identified with respect to the present? One is only justified in pooling the non-permanent properties of *a* and *b* if there is some other basis for the identity of *a* and *b* than their having all their properties in common. Finally, I would urge that, wherever the sortal concept under which *a* and *b* coincide is the sortal concept for a kind of continuant and one can ask 'what is it for an f to persist?', it is the idea of a sequential history of a thing's doings and undergoings that comes into consideration. Without this idea or the willingness to explore analogous points about items that are not continuants, little sense will be made of very much that we actually do with the concept of identity. As Leibniz puts the point that I too have wanted to insist upon, 'By itself continuity no more constitutes substance than does multitude or number . . . *Something* is necessary to be numbered, repeated and continued' (Gerhardt II, 169). Indisputable to our deployment of the ideas of entity, identity and substance is our deployment of our countless ideas of their determinations.

Can some analogous point be made about entities that are not substances or material continuants? Suppose that, in making a tally of the fs, Edward first uses the vocable 'one' then two more vocables. His tally of the fs he gives as 'three'. Suppose Kallias, in making a tally of the gs deploys the vocable 'hen' then uses two more vocables of which the second is 'tria'. Then on this basis alone, we can say that whatever is true of Edward's tally number is true of Kallias's tally number. (Or so anyone will say who subscribes to the idea that natural numbers are objects.) No more is needed. In practice, we don't *start* with $\phi x \leftrightarrow \phi y$. We reach $\phi x \leftrightarrow \phi y$ from identity.

Someone might accept this much and still insist that no philosophical analysis or explanation can ever be achieved along the lines I intend, or without dismantling the question of identity. In the case of continuants, he will seek to dismantle it into a question of relating to some finer-grained continuity relation holding between thing-moments.[1] 'Unless something of this sort is attempted, the only thing that is left for the philosophy of individuation to attempt will be as pointless as it is circular.'

The charge is worth considering, first as directed against the elucidations of particular identities for which **D** provides the recipe, then as directed against **D** itself. In the longer term, though, another answer will appear, namely the peculiar exigency that the method of elucidation will discover in the conditions for significant true application in any particular area of the sentence-form '*a* is the same as *b*'.

2. THE CHARGE OF CIRCULARITY, OR OF EMPTINESS

By the elucidation of identity advocated here, one who knows what he is saying when he says that '$a = b$' ought to be in a position to explain, where *a* and *b* are continuants, that *a* is a continuant which . . . and *b* is a continuant which _ _ _, and then to expand each specification separately in a way sufficient to make it determinate (with the help of the world) which continuant *a* is and which continuant *b* is. In the course of this being achieved, as a necessary condition of the truth of the identity claim, some common sort f will have to be found to which they each belong. That is the point, we are saying, at which the primary question of identity can come into focus. Is the f that *a* is any different from the f that *b* is? Or do these fs coincide? What is there here to invite the charge of vacuity or circularity?

---

[1] For my view of attempts that have been made along these lines, see Chapter One, §3 and Chapter Six, §6. Against the claim that philosophy cannot *dispense* with such efforts, see Preamble, §3.

The first charge might be that, if the author of the statement '*a* is *b*' says in this way what each item is, then his amplification of the judgment already involves the general idea of continuant-identity. Reply: there is no harm at all in this provided two conditions are satisfied. First, the notion of continuity that is invoked must not be the kind of continuity that we have affected to disbelieve in altogether. In so far as continuity is something general, the continuity in question must be the determinable *continuity of such and such sort-specific kind*, of which *man-coincidence, donkey-coincidence, tree-coincidence* can be the determinations. Secondly, when the author of the statement '*a* is *b*' says what the *a* is and what the *b* is, he must be able to do this without prejudging the question of the truth of the identity-claim. But this question *can* be left open. It can be left open even if the answer is, if correct, then necessarily correct.

The second alleged vacuity or circularity relates to the terms of **D** itself. In order to trace *a*, one must find out what *a* is, or so I have said. But what will count as knowing what *a* is in the Aristotelian sense? What counts as a sortal concept for a continuant? Suppose the answer depends in part on the idea of a principle of continuity for *a*. What then of the determinable *continuity* (or *coincidence*) *of such and such sort-specific kind*? Has the nature of this determinable been explained?

Here we are caught in a circle which would be vicious if we thought we were bringing the concept of identity into being by means of other ideas prior and better understood. The circle would be vicious if we could not appeal to some extant *a priori* understanding of the identity relation or we could not invoke a going practice which will effect the sortal articulation of individual continuants as *this* f or *that* g or whatever. Happily, though, we lack none of these things, unless we want to offer up Leibniz's Law to some numen of confusion. So, where the theoretical aim is only to enhance the understanding we already have of sameness, as this is ascribed or not ascribed within the class of continuants, the doubt can be met. For **D** puts us in mind of that which Aristotle's isolation of the *what is it?* question also recalls to us, namely our practical mastery of the business of assigning things to kinds and our capacity to get a grasp upon the nature of a thing. Compare *Metaphysics* $1015^{a\ 10-12}$. It is only by virtue of that capacity of ours that we can keep track of a thing through change and distinguish between doing this correctly and making a mistake in doing it. As for '<u>coincide</u>' (and its correlate 'to be continuous with'), I hope that the meaning of this technical term may be further secured by the following schema:

where f is what x is (in Aristotle's sense), x coincides with y under sortal concept f if and only if the way in which x is f-related to y suffices for whatever is true of x to be true of y and whatever is true of y to be true of x.

Of course, this schema, which is no more than a reminder of matters already rehearsed, requires some collateral understanding of the *what is it* question, of implication and of what it amounts to for the schema ($\phi x \leftrightarrow \phi y$) to hold true no matter what extensional predicate replaces the letter phi. But all this is in fact available to us; and the schema vindicates both the fidelity and the unity of the conception of identity recapitulated by our method of elucidation. We need not exaggerate what has been accomplished, but now let us complete the third clause of **D**, as it is given at the start of this chapter, by supplying the words 'congruently, that is in such a way as to entail the Leibnizian community of what is true of a and true of b'.

This approach to identity will rightly remind the reader of divers doctrines of 'criteria of identity'. Some philosophers have used 'criterion' to mean 'way of telling' or 'conceptually determined way of telling'. Where they have meant that, however, there is a contrast with the proposal advanced here. An answer to the *what is it* question does both less and more than provide that which counts as evidence for or against an identity. It does less because it may not suggest any immediate tests at all. It does more because it provides that which *organizes* the tests or findings. It organizes that which has been wanted by those who have asked for a criterion of identity in the constitutive sense of 'criterion' in which Frege asked for such a criterion.

My approach here is only a variant on Frege's. If it differs in any important way, that is only in virtue of a pessimism (corresponding to a difference of subject matter) that I feel about the prospects for strict philosophical analysis. It is true that some who have followed Frege (*Foundations of Arithmetic*, §62) in asking for the criterion of identity have required from such a criterion some breakdown of identity into materials that are singly independent of identity. But this was not necessary. Nor is the Fregean demand inextricably linked with the puritanism of those who have insistently required criteria of identity in fanatical pursuit of ontological parsimony. Such philosophers have wanted to refute claims that this, that, or the other kind of entity exists. That is not my present concern, however. Nor was it Frege's.

The real and abiding interest of the demand for the criterion of identity is surely this. Wherever we suppose that entities of kind f exist, we are committed to ascribe some point to typical identity questions about particular fs; and, in so far as identity is a puzzling or problematic relation, the first concern of the philosophy of any subject matter must be to enhance our powers of finding the elucidation (whether or not we use here the language of criteria) for its disputed identity questions. We need to reinforce and enrich our powers of determining what it is we must look to in order to answer these questions. ('What does the matter turn on?', we must ask.) Such explications or glossings may be as discursive and heterogeneous as we will from case to case, and as irreducibly practical (which implies that they will not be fully expressible in mere words), provided that they all originate from something we can recognize as a unitary understanding of *identical* and *the same*. Once it is understood what organizes the tests or methods that we actually use to answer questions of identity, it will be possible to see the way backwards from any tests we do use to the underlying point of these tests or methods; and that is the trail back to what the tests are tests of, and why they are tests of it. The special effectiveness of the 'what is it' question is that, in the case of continuants, it refers us back to our constantly exercised idea of the persistence and life-span of an entity; and it makes manifest the connexion, which it was always evident that there must be, between the entity's identity through time and its persistence, between its persistence and its existence, and between its existence and its being the kind of thing it is.

3. THE IDENTITY OF INDISCERNIBLES

It is no confusion of epistemology with philosophical elucidation or analysis to require, as we have, that 'for all ϕ, a has ϕ if and only if b has ϕ' should be the consequence and not the criterion of an identity judgment's being true, or so I conclude. Furthermore, as will emerge in the course of the elaboration of the consequences of **D**, there really can exist for a kind k some effective, albeit not verbally explicit, condition for '$=$' whose satisfaction by any a and b belonging to k will have the amiable property of securing that, no matter what property ϕ is, a has ϕ if and only if b has ϕ. But, in the meanwhile, it will be useful to enlarge for the length of one short section upon a principle that has been in the background for some time now. That is the Identity of Indiscernibles. This is the principle which results from taking the converse of the first level schema that I called Leibniz's Law, and transposing it to the second level – the need for this transposition can scarcely be sufficiently emphasized

– by prefixing to the antecedent a second-level quantifier with scope confined to that antecedent.[2] Thus the Identity of Indiscernibles is

$$[(\forall \phi)\, (\phi x \leftrightarrow \phi y)] \leftrightarrow (x = y).$$

The shortcomings of this principle are intimately connected with the failings of community of attributes and relations as an elucidation of identity, and also with the failure of all reductive accounts of '='.

Leibniz's own view of the principle may be made plain by quotation:

There is no such thing as two individuals indiscernible from each other. An ingenious gentleman of my acquaintance, discoursing with me, in the presence of her Electoral Highness the Princess Sophia, in the garden of Herrenhausen; thought he could find two leaves perfectly alike. The Princess defied him to do it, and he ran all over the garden a long time to look for some; but it was to no purpose. Two drops of water, or milk, viewed with a microscope, will appear distinguishable from each other. (*Correspondence with Clarke*, p. 36 in the H. G. Alexander edn, Manchester, 1956.)

I have said that it is not possible for there to be two particulars that are similar in all respects – for example two eggs – for it is necessary that some things can be said about one of them that cannot be said about the other, else they could be substituted for one another and there would be no reason why they were not called one and the same. Moreover, if they have diverse predicates the concepts too, in which these predicates are contained, will differ. (Pp. 476–7 in F. Schmidt, *Leibniz: Fragmente zur Logik*, Berlin, 1960; cf. p. 9, L. Couturat, *Opuscules et fragments*, Paris, 1903.)

If we ask about the strength of the antecedent 'for all ϕ, $\phi x \leftrightarrow \phi y$' in this rendering of Leibniz's reading of his principle, then it is clear that it is as if he considers the principle to be protected from triviality by his excluding from the range of this variable 'ϕ' not only predicates compounded from '=' itself but also such predicates or relations as 'five miles S.W. of Big Ben'. Indeed, he must think all predicates presupposing place-, time- or thing-individuation are excluded.

It is always necessary that beside the difference of time and place there be internal principles of distinction . . . thus, although time and place [external relations, that is] serve in distinguishing things, we do not easily distinguish them by themselves . . . The essence of identity and diversity consists . . . not in time and space. (*Nouveaux Essais* II, 27.1 and 3; cf. II, 1.2, and letter to De Volder, Gerhardt II, 250.)

---

[2] At the same time providing for the concatenation of property variable and individual variables to be understood as effecting predications. So, officially speaking, the Identity of Indiscernibles, given in the maximally perspicuous form, says that x is identical with y if and only if, for all pure properties ϕ, x has ϕ if and only if y has ϕ. For the question of which properties are pure, see the ensuing paragraph.

Not everyone who has wanted to defend the Identity of Indiscernibles has been prepared to follow Leibniz into his theories of relations, space and time. But, unless one is prepared to follow argument where argument leads and delimit the range of the property variable in something approximating to Leibniz's manner, the formulation 'for all ϕ, $\phi x \leftrightarrow \phi y$' becomes a relatively trivial condition. Once predicables involving '=' or its congeners and its derivatives are included within the range of the variable, the formula is neither an analytical explication nor even a serviceable elucidation of identity. For the formula manifestly presupposes identity. It presupposes it in such a way that any particular issue of identity will move round and round in a small circle.

On the other hand, if one gives the principle of the Identity of Indiscernibles the Leibnizian and more interesting interpretation, or if (as I note that Leibniz probably did not) one envisages the principle being used, not merely for the refutation of identity claims, but for their positive or effective determination, then strange results follow. Wittgenstein noted at *Tractatus Logico-Philosophicus* 5.5302 that the Identity of Indiscernibles rules out a possibility that involves no evident incoherence at all, namely that of two objects' having absolutely all their properties in common. Max Black and others have explored the difficulties one will have in trying to deny the logical possibility of a universe consisting only of two qualitatively indistinguishable spheres. (See Black (1952).) This matter will be resumed in Chapter Six, §8.

4. PROPOSITION **D** FURTHER EXPLICATED AND AMPLIFIED: AND **D**(ii) AS THE PROPER DEVELOPMENT OF **D**

At this point we must revisit a claim already entered, namely that, no matter how disparate in respect of temporal and other identifications the two designations are that flank the identity symbol in a true identity of the form '*a* is the same f as *b*', a phased or restricted sortal predicate can always be supplanted *salva veritate* by a comprehensive unrestricted sortal predicate, or (as I shall say) a substance predicate, to produce an equally true affirmative identity-statement.[3]

---

[3] There are many sortal predicates whose status as restricted sortal predicates is not syntactically or even etymologically manifest, e.g. boy, foal, cub, gaffer, *graus* (Greek for an old woman); and many whose precise status is not only structurally unmarked but has also to be discovered empirically, e.g. tadpole, caterpillar. In the end, though, all phased sortal concepts are either latently or manifestly restrictions of underlying more general sortal concepts. *Boy* is definable as *human being that is male and biologically immature*, and so on. [footnote continues]

This is the point at which it becomes necessary to distinguish between two claims. I shall call them **D**(i) and **D**(ii). **D**(i) says that for all times t at which a continuant a exists there is a g under which a falls at t; or more perspicuously

$$\mathbf{D}\text{(i): } (x)(t)[(x \text{ exists at } t) \rightarrow (\exists g) (g(x) \text{ at } t)].$$

As will be apparent, all that this guarantees for each continuant is a *succession* of phased sortal concepts. It does not guarantee the availability of one concept with application for all times. It does not guarantee the thing the substance assumption envisages, namely that there will be some preferred concept in a hierarchy of sortal concepts that a thing will fall under throughout its existence. If the idea of continuity is to elucidate the truth-conditions of identity statements in the special way envisaged by **D**, then we need a stronger principle. It is this

$$\mathbf{D}\text{(ii): } (x)(\exists g)(t)[(x \text{ exists at } t) \rightarrow (g(x) \text{ at } t)].$$

Here, as before, 'x' ranges over three-dimensional continuants, 't' ranges over times and the letters 'f' or 'g' range over individuative or articulative concepts which 'divide their reference' and answer the question *what is x?*

I hold that **D**(ii) is true. But let us begin with a putative counterexample to it. Consider the story of Lot and his wife, as given in Genesis, chapter 19:

17. . . . And it came to pass, when they had brought them forth abroad that [t]he [Lord] said [unto Lot]: Escape for thy life; look not behind thee, neither stay thou in all the plain . . .

18. Then the Lord rained upon Sodom and upon Gomorrah brimstone and fire from the Lord out of heaven . . .

20. But his wife looked back from behind him [Lot] and she became a pillar of salt.

footnote 3 (*cont.*)

Nothing in the argument to follow here is meant to depend upon a certain conceptual conservatism from which philosophical inquiry into substance and identity should be free, viz. the supposition that simply by being a language-user one can tell for any given sortal, e.g. the sortal *tadpole* or *pupa*, whether or not it is a substance-sortal or merely a phased sortal. Room must be found for the empirical and surprising discovery that there is something which is first a tadpole and then a frog – let us designate what goes through the whole cycle, what becomes this and then turns into that, *batrachos* – or is first a pupa or chrysalis and then becomes a perfect insect. The ensuing argument will leave room for that.

'Another type of linguistic shortcoming [in biology] is illustrated by the persistence of our tendency to identify *organisms* with *adults* . . . it is not just adults we classify when we classify organisms . . . We can speak of the egg as the primordium of the future adult, but not of the future organism because it already is the organism': J. H. Woodger 'On Biological Transformation', in *Growth and Form: Essays for D'Arcy Thompson*, ed. Le Gros Clark and Medawar (Oxford, 1945).

Encouraged by this narrative, one who doubts **D**(ii) will say that we can understand the story through and through. He will urge that it corresponds to a possible world, declaring that the champion of **D**(ii) must make a difficult choice. Either that champion trivializes **D**(ii) altogether by inventing arbitrarily a concept *woman-pillar*, which a thing satisfies by being first a woman and then a pillar of salt; or else the champion must postulate a real and substantial discontinuity (as judged by standards of the answer given there to the 'what is it?' question) between Lot's wife and the pillar of salt.[4]

At the outset let it be agreed between me and the objector to **D**(ii) that, if we avoid the trivializing alternative, then there is no substantial sortal concept suitable to cover the identity between Lot's wife at the beginning of the story, before she looks back, and the forty-foot pillar of salt that is still there to be encountered on the Jebel Usdum near the Dead Sea. Indeed if we could invent sortal concepts simply at will, then the real content of the assertion that something lasted till *t* and then ceased to exist would be trivialized completely. For if one were unconstrained in the invention of a substantial concept by which to represent that a thing persisted, one would be equally unconstrained in the invention of a substantial concept by which to represent that it failed to persist. We could have it either way, so to speak. We do not think of things like this, however. As Aristotle perceived, there is an important difference that we mark between a thing's changing and its being replaced.[5] If we took the

---

[4] The counterexample to **D**(ii) might be fortified by suggesting that, in the story, the change in question was continuous. The opponent of **D**(ii) may suggest that one may imagine that at one stage in the process narrated there was something that was a candidate to count both as a human body and as something crystallizing into salt. In defence of the claim that the story determines a possible world, he will point out that, as told, the story does not even require violation of a plausible principle that adds to **D**(i) but is weaker than **D**(ii). This might be called the *principle of sortal continuity*:

> If an entity x survives from *t* to *t′*, then there is some articulation of the time between *t* and *t′* into periods $P_1, P_2, \ldots P_n$ such that, for every period P_i, $(\exists f)$ $(f(x)$ throughout $P_i)$ & $(f(x)$ throughout the adjacent period $P_{i\pm1})$.

This principle marks adequately the necessity (he will say) to distinguish between the persistence of a thing through change and its replacement by some quite other thing. The story of Lot's wife respects this principle, the critic will insist.

For further discussion of the example of Lot's wife, see Wiggins (1997a).

[5] Cf. Aristotle: 'Unqualified coming to be and passing away takes place when something as a whole changes from *this* to *that*. Some philosophers hold that all such change [coming to be and passing away] is mere alteration. But there is a difference. For in that which underlies change there are two factors, one relating to the *logos* of the subject [i.e. what it is], the other relating to the matter that is involved. When the change affects both of these, coming-to-be or passing-away will occur. But when the change is not in the *logos* but only in the qualities [i.e. in respect of categories other than substance], i.e. when the change is a change in accidents, there will be alteration' (*De Generatione et Corruptione*, 317^{a21} ff.). Aristotle's is a stronger claim (given Leibniz's Law and the

Lot story seriously, if we treated it as if it were a historical narrative, then, enamoured as we are of the change/replacement and true/false distinctions, we should need to interrogate the narrative very closely, and press all sorts of questions about what sort of a being Lot's wife really was. We should need to think of that question as one to which an answer could be discovered 'in spite of ourselves'. But we do not do so. It is simply a story. It is perfectly notorious that not every story corresponds to a possible world. (Chapter Three, §1, bears on this, as does Chapter four.)

If we do not want **D**(ii) to be trivially true, then we need to begin by taking seriously the sortal predications we actually use. (That is how I arrive so swiftly at the denial of identity between Lot's wife and the pillar of salt.) But even if we follow this counsel, some may ask: what forces us to think that the mass of as yet uninvented sortal predicates which might be truly applied to a woman such as Lot's wife have to cohere together in the kind of structure that is needed to verify **D**(ii)?

Well, remembering that all the sortal predicates that apply to a thing at all can be used to cover identity claims concerning it, let us now deploy our previous finding that **R** is false. If **R** is false, then all the sortal concepts that apply to a thing at all must be *concordant* with respect to such answers as they furnish for identity questions relating to the thing. If, as I suppose, the best explanation and characterization of this concordance is that all true sortal attributions to a given thing are restrictions of one substance-concept (or are restrictions of a *set* of substance concepts that are individuatively concordant), then that will make sense of other facts such as this: in practice, something or other almost always lends a high (even indefinitely high) degree of determinacy to questions we ask about whether, at a given time, an object *a* still exists. Our capacity for massive agreement about this is much more remarkable than our occasional disagreement.[6] The question I urge upon anyone reluctant to accept **D**(ii)

---

footnote 5 (*cont.*)

arguments that are shortly to be presented for **D**(ii)) than the principle of Sortal Continuity. But the power of both is attested by the lengths to which poets and story tellers will go, when concerned to pass off unqualified passing away as persistence-through-alteration, to create the however mendacious impression that the conditions for alteration are scrupulously respected. The trick is to describe the change as happening very gradually. See particularly Ovid, *Metamorphoses*. One must add that the metamorphoses of Proteus — see, e.g., Homer, *Odyssey* IV, 453–63 – represent a special artistic problem, corresponding to a conceptual impossibility of really imposing dimensions. See Chapter Three, §1.

[6] If there are any disagreements, that will suggest that sortal predications can be *contestable*. For the idea that it can be seriously contestable, in a way that can stir moral disquiet, what this or that provisionally identified thing is, see Chapter Seven, especially §16 following. The concordance requirement, so far from being inconsistent with any of this, helps to bring out what may be at stake.

is this: what could better or more plausibly ensure that, if an individual appears to fall under several sortal concepts, then these concepts agree in the identity and persistence conditions that they ascribe to it?[7]

How could an entity escape this argument (such as it is) for **D**(ii)? It could escape only by lacking a principle of identity and persistence made fully determinate in the manner we have envisaged by a substance-concept. But it would be no great defect of the argument for **D**(ii) if, at this point, we rested it perfectly explicitly upon such an assumption. The assumption says that in the ordinary business of individuation, questions about the identity and persistence of the substances that we have knowledge of possess definite answers, answers that are not normally undiscoverable in principle. The same assumption says that, within the ontology of changeable Aristotelian continuants to which so many of these familiar things belong, we find ourselves committed to think that many things have definitely ceased to exist.[8]

---

[7] Nicholas Griffin (see *Relative Identity, op. cit.*, p. xi and p. 84 note) has complained about this argument that it assumes that no two ultimate sortals can overlap (overlap, that is, without one's being a proper part of the other). But the argument does not assume that. It implies it. The picture the argument in the text motivates is this. If we have a structure comprising only sortal concepts (concepts that answer the *what is it?* question and autonomously assign principles of individuation to objects that instantiate them) and these concepts stand in relations to one another such as that of having members in common, one concept's restricting the other, identity etc., and if the structure is not closed to further or 'missing' concepts or individuals, then, where concepts C(1) and C(2) have any members in common, there will be three cases:

The first case is where neither C(1) nor C(2) is a restriction of any other concept and each is an ultimate sortal. Here, if the concepts have common members, then, because they will cover identities relating to these common members and **R** is false, C(1) must be identical with C(2) or extensionally equivalent to it.

The second case is the case where one of the two sortal concepts C(1) and C(2) is ultimate and the other is not. In this case, if there are common members, then the non-ultimate one restricts the ultimate one.

The third case is the one where neither C(1) nor C(2) is ultimate. Here, if C(1) and C(2) have common members, there may be overlap without either concept subsuming the other. This is the case of cross-classification. But then some sortal concept that is ultimate will subsume both C(1) and C(2).

It is my conjecture and hope that this picture of things, founded in the nature of sortal concepts and the absoluteness of identity, concedes everything that deserves to be conceded to the over-stringent demand that sortal concepts should form a hierarchy. (On which see Woodger (1937), p. 42; Richmond Thomason, 'Species, Determinates and Natural Kinds', *Nous*, 3 (1969), pp. 95–101, who was criticized by Howard Kahane, 'Thomason on Natural Kinds', *Nous*, 4 (1970), especially p. 410. Thomason's proposal deserves to be dissociated from the idea that the hierarchy must be arrived at by a process of dichotomous division. Cf. Aristotle, *De Partibus Animalium*, 642[aff] and Plato, *Politicus*, 262[d].) At the same time, the picture I am suggesting does not, I think, rule out the sorts of cross-classifications that seem indispensable to ethology, linguistics, etc. On cross-classification, see Chomsky, *Aspects of the Theory of Syntax* (Cambridge, Mass., 1965), pp. 79–80.

[8] This implies that there are no principles of conservation that apply to continuants as such. But to deny that there are such principles is not of course to deny that the *matter* of such continuants

If we defend **D**(ii) in these terms, then a question remains whether an entity could escape from the space where these assumptions hold good. In Chapters Five and Six an argument will emerge for the claim that none can escape. But that argument (and a limitation upon it that will emerge in Chapter Seven, §16 following) must wait for its moment.

Rather than pursue undecidable fantasies about what it would be like if the presuppositions of our practice were groundless and unjustifiable or search for every conceivable pretext not to take them seriously, I urge the reader first to observe and marvel at the near unanimity that has been reached (and is almost effortlessly extended to a whole range of new cases) about what constitutes the ceasing to exist of an everyday continuant of this or that kind.

5. EXISTENCE AND SORTAL PREDICATIONS

The story of Lot's wife has the effect of facing us with another question to which sortal concepts are no less relevant than they are to identity. What is it to cease to exist? An orthodox account says: to cease to have any properties. But this is not necessary. Of Aristotle, the author of *Nicomachean Ethics*, I believe that he was bald. So this Greek, though long since dead and non-existent, now has the property of being believed by someone to have been bald. Similarly Heraclitus is still misunderstood and Frege has become famous since his death. Are these not properties? Suppose we devised a stricter notion of property to exclude these and we said that ceasing to exist was a matter of ceasing to have any strict properties. Would that count as a full answer to the original question? I do not think so. The question about tensed existence arose from the desire to know what it was for an individual to be *no longer available* to have such and such properties. Maybe it will cast light on that question, however, if we respect the distinction between predications in the cate-

footnote 8 (*cont.*)

is subject to such principles as physics and chemistry can demonstrate. Nor is it to deny that continuants may share this matter with the other entities, if any, for which there do exist principles of conservation.

We pass close here to the problems of the continuance of stuff. There are profound and difficult questions to be asked about this. I do not deny that these questions interact with some of the most difficult questions in the philosophy of chemistry and physics. It would be a wonderful thing, if life, will, and the mixed economy lasted so long, to embark upon them. But those questions are not these questions. And these ones are easier.

For a careful and searching exploration of the attempt, by what he calls the Relational Theory, to circumvent the claim in the text to which the present note is affixed, see Burge (1975), see especially p. 74) – a gratifying vindication also of the constitutive 'is' and of the constitutive approach to things and their matter that was advocated in Chapter One.

gory of substance and predications in the category of quality or relation, and we follow in an older tradition to say that an individual *a*'s having ceased to exist at *t* is a matter of there being nothing identical with *a* that belongs to the extension at *t* of the ultimate or substance kind that is *a*'s kind.[9]

A little more still needs to be said about the meaning of **D**(ii). There are countless predicates in English that have the appearance of sortal predicates but are purely generic (*animal, machine, artefact*) or are pure determinables for sortal determination (*space-occupier, entity, substance*). Like a substance-concept for *x*, these apply to *x* at every moment of *x*'s life-span. But to adduce any of these as verifying the existential claim that we find in **D**(ii), 'there is a g ... (etc),' would sell the principle short. The reason why **D**(ii) is true has to do with the special role of the substance-concept *man, horse, willow tree* ... in marking simultaneously what a thing is, what matters turn on with regard to its persistence and what matters turn on with regard to identity claims relating to it. It will be the work of subsequent **D** principles (and of later chapters) to suggest the further conditions that will need to be placed on the sort-variable f if **D** is to possess itself of the whole strength that it is intended to enjoy.

6. FURTHER **D** PRINCIPLES

It will be inquired in the next Chapter how any predicate at all could measure up to the responsibilities that go with the title of standing for a substance-concept. But, in advance of Chapter Three, let us assess the magnitude of the office that it now appears such a concept must discharge and try to reckon up in some further principles, without any regard to economy or completeness or independence of statements, the duties that have already been laid upon it.

---

[9] Note that '*a* exists at *t*' is not on the theory we have advanced here an incomplete assertion. It says ($\exists$f) (f is a substantial concept for *a* and *a* is in the extension at *t* of f). This is a complete assertion, and it well reflects the apparent completeness of actual denials and assertions of temporal existence. Someone bent on rejecting **D**(ii) might advance a theory to be sharply distinguished from mine. He might claim that '*a* exists' is an incomplete assertion and propose a doctrine of *relative existence*. By this theory of existence, the distinction we have drawn between phased and substantial sortal concepts is simply misconceived. For by this new theory, *whatever* concept f is, a thing may always cease to exist as an f but continue to exist as a g. About this proposal I should remark that it may well be the only consistent option for someone bent on rejecting **D**(ii); but it would constitute a daring reconstruction of the principles of the continuant ontology and of the whole way we at present think and speak. As I have said already, **D**(ii) was intended to reflect the ontology implicit in our *present* way of thinking and of puzzling ourselves about everyday identity questions. According to that, many things do definitely stop existing.

nb

First, in summation of what has been said already, we have

D(iii): *a* is identical with *b* if and only if there is some concept f such that (1) f is a substance-concept under which an object that belongs to f can be singled out, traced and distinguished from other f entities and distinguished from other entities; (2) *a* coincides under f with *b*; (3) ⌜coincides under f⌝ stands for a congruence relation: i.e. all pairs ⟨*x*,*y*⟩ that are members of the relation satisfy the Leibnizian schema ϕx if and only if ϕy.

D(iv): f is a substance-concept only if the grasp of f determines (with or without the help of further empirical information about the class of fs) what can and cannot befall any *x* in the extension of f, and what changes *x* tolerates without there ceasing to exist such a thing as *x*; moreover f is only a substance-concept if the grasp of f determines (with or without the help of further empirical information about the class of fs) the relative importance or unimportance to the survival of *x* of various classes of changes befalling specimens of f (e.g. how close they may bring *x* to actual extinction).

Clause (3) of **D**(iii) answers to the requirement that community of properties should be not the basis but the consequence of the satisfaction of an acceptable criterion of identity. It may seem either emptily unattainable – in the case where it is not allowed that anything at all could guarantee the satisfaction of the Leibnizian schema – or magic of some sort. But it is not magic. **D**(iii) simply recapitulates the principle on which in our actual practice, sustained as that is by the idea of the nature of an object and (where applicable) its life-span, predicates are applied to *a* and *b* or (as the case may be) withheld from *a* or *b* in respect of any instant or period belonging to the life history of this (these) persisting continuant(s). This is not to say, however, that it will always be possible to *write down* an explicit f-involving condition that suffices for the identity of *a* with *b*. The thing we can write down will only be some verbal expression of the larger practical understanding enjoyed by one who can convert his grasp of the concept of an f into some capacity to determine what is at issue in any particular case where it is asked, with respect to an *a* or a *b* which is an f, whether *a* is the same as *b*.

No doubt a sceptic may say that our practice has no business to be sustained by such ideas as that of an object's life-span or nature, etc., however filled out in particular cases. He will say that any practices founded in them must be precarious in the extreme. But here, as usual, our chief concern must be to describe from within and to sustain from within the ideas that the sceptic attacks, and then to enumerate such sources of support as they do have. It is not the purpose to render them immune to all doubt or difficulty – still less to minimize the considerable commitment that someone incurs when he says what something is. Such commitment is indeed precarious, but no more precarious than anything else that is worth the candle. It should be added that it will be rare for any sortal concept that qualifies by **D**(iii) as a substance predicate (or as determining a principle of tracing) to come up to the standards a positivist would propose for *observationality* or direct *experiential confirmability*.[10] I do not think this prevents a predicate that qualifies by the standard set by **D**, **D**(i), **D**(ii) and **D**(iii) from furnishing a principle of individuation for members of its extension. Nor does it prevent **D**(iii) from determining and organizing any recognizably empirical tests that may be elaborated for whether *a* or *b* is an f thing, for whether *a* is the same f as *b*, and for *a* or *b*'s continued existence.[11]

Connoisseurs of the literature of identity and individuation will have noticed that little room has been left in these formulations of **D** principles to accommodate the distinction of which so much has sometimes been made between synchronic principles of boundary drawing (sometimes called criteria of distinctness) and diachronic principles of reidentification (criteria of 'transtemporal' identity). This is not an oversight.[12] It is my contention that, as principles that purport to be of one or the

---

[10] Across the full range of their received applications, not even 'white' or 'flexible' or 'soluble' do.
[11] The same point, or almost the same point, can be seen from a completely different angle. Consider the biologically informed description of the Protozoon Paramecium (Class Ciliata):

> Paramecium reproduces by both asexual and sexual means . . . Sexual reproduction is by means of a process called conjugation. In Paramecium not all individuals are alike: there are two different classes which are known as mating types . . . Conjugation begins with a pairing and then partial fusion of the anterior ends of two individuals of opposite types. The micronucleus in each undergoes meiosis and then there is an interchange of nuclei between the two individuals. In each individual a new micronucleus is formed by the fusion of one of its own micronuclei with one from the other individual. This is essentially fertilization. The macronuclei degenerate. (J. A. Moore, *Principles of Zoology* (New York, 1957), p. 106.)

Contrast with the above the description that might be given by an observer who was attentive but not biologically informed. Such a description would leave room for the possibility that the individual paramecia *a*, *b survive* the process described. It is principles **D**(iii) and **D**(iv) that articulate the rationale for insisting, on the basis of Moore's description, that they cannot survive it.

With **D**(iv), it should become finally clear why, in the sense of 'coincide' that I employ in order to elucidate identity, a thing does not coincide with its matter. Coinciding is not simply being in the same place at the same time. Just as there is no such thing as mere continuity so there is no such thing as coinciding otherwise than under a concept. A house, for instance, does not coincide with its bricks and mortar. For in 'the house is bricks and mortar' the *is* is constitutive. Here we do not have identity. Cf. Chapter One, §6.
[12] See my symposium paper 'The Individuation of Things and Places', section v, *Proceedings of the Aristotelian Society, Supplementary Volume* 37 (1963); see M. J. Woods's reply, *ibid.*; see Woods (1965). See also my reply to Harold Noonan in Lovibond and Williams (1996).

other sort are filled out in the direction of adequacy, the distinction disappears. It is of course a severer test of someone's grasp of the concept of cat to ask him to determine whether this cat is the same cat as the cat that licked the saucer clean on Monday of last week than it is to ask him to count the cats in the parlour now at 3.06 pm, making sure that none is counted twice. It does not follow, though, that the thing tested by the first assignment can be seen as built up from the cat-lore needed to meet the second assignment plus some altogether different kind of lore or some different sort of grasp of what cats are.

In so far as the sense and semantics of substance words come into question here, or our grasp of this sense, these things must wait for Chapter Three, §§1–2, as must the justification and full explication of the **D**-principle I shall place next:

> **D**(v): f is a substance-concept only if f determines either a principle of *activity*, a principle of *functioning* or a principle of *operation* for members of its extension.

The Leibnizian echo of 'activity' is deliberate – as will emerge when the *activity* of natural things is distinguished from the *fulfilment of function* that is characteristic of organs and artefacts.[13] In Chapter Three, where this distinction will be made, a key role will be played by a principle that is a direct consequence of **D**(iii):

> **D**(vi): If f is a substance-concept for *a*, then *coincidence under f* is fully determinate enough to exclude this situation: *a* is traced under f and counts as coinciding under f with *b*, *a* is traced under f and counts as coinciding under f with *c*, yet *b* does not coincide under f with *c*.

Consider what happens when an amoeba divides exactly in half and becomes two amoebas. We are committed by **D**(vi) and the other doctrines of this chapter to find that neither of the resultant amoebas qualifies as coinciding under the concept *amoeba* with the original amoeba. Chapter Three will show how the peculiar facts about a natural kind, discovered *a posteriori*, could in any given case be enlisted to support this ruling. But two things are immediately obvious. The first is that, since not both amoebas can be identical with the original, and since neither has a better claim than the other, no sensible theory

---

[13] In advance of Chapter Three, however, let me commend Hacking (1972). The Leibnizian echo made by 'activity' is deliberate but, outside the monadological framework, it does not have to import anything very different from 'way of being, acting and reacting' – something a stone might have.

will want to count either amoeba as identical with the original one.[14] The second obvious point is that judgments of coincidence and identity must not be withheld *ad hoc* simply because transitivity is threatened. There must be something that one who grasped the *a posteriori* concept *amoeba* could see (not necessarily independently of general knowledge of the kind) was lacking in any idea of amoeba-coincidence that was ready or poised to count amoeba division as a way of persisting for amoebas.

Let us not make the wrong denial here. The process of division is of course the process by which Amoeba proteus, for example, is perpetuated. Particular amoebas perpetuate it. But Amoeba proteus is not a substance or a particular. It is something universal (a kind or a clone of organisms or cells all produced asexually from one ancestor or stock from which they are genetically indistinguishable). The thought we were concerned with in relation to **D**(vi) concerned not Amoeba proteus but the particulars that instantiate and perpetuate it. So the second point that we were concerned with in the paragraph preceding this may be beneficially expanded to run like this: if amoebas (amoebas plural, the particulars) are to be objects of reference, then there must be something or other that one who understood amoebas *and* grasped the *a priori* constraints upon the determinable *continuant-identity* (is the same something or other as) could in practice find to be independently wrong with the suppositions that generate the contradiction that **D**(vi) proscribes. Moreover, there *is* something wrong, as would be apparent to anyone who contrived to observe and understand this general process of division.

One other thing deserves remark. Principles such as **D**(vi) not only enforce our formal understanding of the identity relation. As we see from the work that they do here, they bear witness to our grasp of the distinction between particular and universal.

---

[14] Contrast Prior, 'Time, Existence and Identity', *P.A.S.*, 66 (1965–6). The view I have put in the text conforms with the only thorough attempt that is known to me to work out a logic of division and fusion, namely that of Woodger (1937), p. 61. One amoeba becomes two amoebas. But here, in a manner that will remind the reader of a thesis frequently defended in Chapter One, the verb 'becomes' receives an analysis making it correspond to the ordinary 'becomes' in the same way in which constitutive 'is' corresponds to the ordinary 'is' of predication and identity. The matter of the original amoeba – the 'it' – is the fusion, or the matter, of the two new ones taken together. There is matter such that first *a* was constituted of it, and then *b* and *c* were constituted of it.

Further light is shed on the amoeba question by the 'Only *a* and *b*' rule of Chapter Three, §4. We shall call this **D**(x), a principle that will come into its own in Chapter Seven.

7. MISCELLANEOUS FURTHER PRINCIPLES; AND A DOUBT ABOUT COUNTING

From the falsity of **R** we have

D(vii): there are no essentially disjunctive substance-concepts (f *or* g) coincidence under which might allow *a* to be the same (f *or* g) as *b* and allow *a* to be the same (f *or* g) as some *c* that was distinct under every covering concept from *b*.

Some disjunctive sortal predicates are innocuous in this regard, e.g. when one disjunct f is subordinate to a higher sortal. (For example, *animal or mouse* is innocuous. *a* cannot be the same mouse as *b* and a different animal from *b*. The sortal predicate reduces here to *animal*.) Disjunctive sortal predicates will be innocuous when the corresponding conjunctive sortal is a satisfiable concept (e.g. *animal and mouse*, which reduces in the opposite direction to *mouse*). But for that case disjunctive sortals seem to be as superfluous as they are innocuous.[15] The argument for **D**(vii) is not, of course, an argument against the essentially disjunctive (f *or* g) being *a concept*. It is an argument against its being a *sortal* concept.

D(viii): If f is a substance-concept for *a* then, however indefinitely and unforeseeably the chain of *a*'s f coincidents *a*, *a'*, *a'*, *a'''* . . . extends, whatever is truly or falsely applicable to one member of the chain must be truly or falsely *applicable* to every member of the chain whatever. But then all fs must belong to one *category*.

This follows *a fortiori* from Leibniz's Law, and is trivial. But it is worth deducing for the sake of the things it brings out against certain allegedly possible metamorphoses, for instance that of Proteus into fire at Homer, *Odyssey* IV, 453–3. These difficulties will present themselves again in Chapter Three.

I now come to the doubt. It would be all of a piece with the speculative tradition to which these speculations belong to add

D(ix?): f is a sortal concept only if it furnishes the materials for the question, and for the determination of a definite and finite answer to the question: 'How many fs are there in region *r* at time *t*?'

This is more or less the claim **C** of the first section of Chapter One. Many or most of the concepts that it is the aim of this and the next

---

[15] It is sometimes objected that we must have disjunctive sortals for certain kinds of counting operation. But 'There are 7 women or shadows here' means 'The number of women *plus* the number of shadows = 7'. We do not need disjunctive sortal concepts to find our way here.

chapter to characterize do satisfy this principle. For all I know, everything traditionally accounted a concept of material substances satisfies it. But it is one thing to be able to say how many fs there are in some particular context and another thing to provide the conceptual prerequisite for the thing that **D**(ix) seems to require: namely a general method of enumerating fs. Subject to any doubts that Hobbes's puzzle of Theseus' ship may arouse concerning artefact kinds (see Chapter Three, §3), the concept *crown* gives a satisfactory way of answering identity-questions for crowns. But there is no universally applicable definite way of counting crowns.[16] The Pope's crown is made of crowns. There is no definite answer, when the Pope is wearing his crown, to the question 'how many crowns does he have on his head?' Something similar will apply in the other cases of homeomery.

Given that someone knows how to count and can also be relied upon to count correctly in some particular situation, then to see if they give the right answer there to the question 'how many fs?' shows whether they can pick out fs and isolate them correctly from their background and from one another. That is what carries **C** of Chapter One, §1 and the putative principle **D**(ix) so close to the truth. But the objection to taking these general principles as necessary for a concept's being individuative is that someone might be able to tell reliably whether this arbitrary f-thing was the same or not the same as some independently identified f-thing, even though there were far too many different ways of articulating f-things for there to be any definite answer to the question how many fs there were to be found in this or that given place. To ask for the latter as well is to ask for more than is needed to ensure that f is a sortal concept.

Frege wrote in *Foundations of Arithmetic*, §54, 'only a concept which (a) delimits what falls under it in a definite way [der das unter ihn Fallende bestimmt abgrenzt], and (b) *which does not permit any arbitrary division of it into parts* [und kein beliebige Zertheilung gestattet] can be a unit relative to a finite number'. His condition (a) could be naturally developed to

---

[16] Cf. *wave, volume of fluid, worm, garden, crystal, piece of string, word-token, machine.* This is a rag-bag. These are all kinds of individual decomposable into matter, though there is a good sense of 'substance' in which not all are kinds of substance. So far as concerns any general doubt or the general logic of identity and individuation, it must be worth taking note of homeomerous items in other categories, such as colours and their shades, quantities, wanderings, wonderings, readings, insults.

With the exception of this minor disagreement about countability taken as a necessary condition of a concept's being a sortal concept, there is here no disagreement with Strawson's account of these matters in *Individuals*, or with the written and oral tradition concerning these predicates. The intention has not been to cut loose of that tradition, but to correct and enlarge it.

cover precisely that which we have intended by our conditions upon being a sortal concept. But there is no reason to think that the second condition, italicized here, is for Frege's special purpose otiose. His particular interest in this passage concerns counting, and the second condition, condition (b), seems to represent a precise further requirement that has to be satisfied for there to be a universally applicable distinction between right and wrong answers to the special question 'how many?' Like **D**(ix), this requirement goes appreciably beyond any requirements it would be sensible to place upon the generality of sortal concepts that are enjoined upon us by our concerns with the *what is it?* question.

D(ix) fails. But **D**(ix) is not the last candidate to consider. Chapter Three, §4, will introduce another, namely **D**(x), the *Only a and b* rule. In due course, anyone who follows through the rationale for articulating such principles will surely want to frame others.

Sortal concepts: and the characteristic activity or function or purpose of things falling under them

The barley drink disintegrates and loses its nature unless it is constantly stirred.

(Heraclitus, Diels fragment 125.)

Nothing is permanent in a substance except the law itself which determines the continuous succession of its states and accords within the individual substance with the laws of nature that govern the whole world.

(Leibniz, Gerhardt II, 263.)

That which is a whole and has a certain shape and form is *one* in a still higher degree; and especially if a thing is of this sort by nature, and not by force like things which are unified by glue or nails or by being tied together, i.e. if it has in itself the cause of its continuity.

(Aristotle, *Metaphysics* 1052^{a22-5}, as translated by W. D. Ross.)

I. THE SORTAL PREDICATES OF NATURAL KINDS

Among the best candidates to play the roles of sortal and substantial predicates, as these roles were described in Chapter Two, are natural kind words. We now reach the question whether even these will fill the bill. Given a kind k associated with the sortal concept c introduced by some sortal predicate or substantive, how can c determine what is at issue, what the matter turns on, when it is asserted or denied that x and y, which instantiate k, are one and the same? **D**(iii) as glossed by **D**(v) requires something to be latent or implicit within the sense of a natural kind identification that will determine, for x, for y, for typical other members of the kind, some further specifiable principle of activity. It seems that here the natural kind concept c must make some constitutive link between the relevant questions of identity and the empirically ascertainable causal and dispositional properties of members of the kind, as we find them in the actual world. But how is this link secured?

It is certain that, if we are looking to the sortal concept to play this role in matters of identity and individuation, then there is no help to be got with the problem from the explications of kind words offered in the tradition of nominal essence as traditionally conceived, or from accounts that seek to specify the sense of 'sun' or 'horse' or 'tree' by a description of such things in terms of manifest properties and relations or in terms of appearances. It is now a very familiar point that these are unsatisfactory, even when taken on their own terms. If we read proposals of this sort literally or in the way in which they invite us to understand them, they always fail either of necessity or of sufficiency for membership in the intended kind. Nor is this their only failure. By the very form in which nominal essence accounts are given, it is impossible that they should reconstruct our actual understanding of natural kind substantives. They leave unexplained not only the way in which our conceptions of a given kind of thing can evolve while still being conceptions of the very same natural kind, but also the non-arbitrariness of that evolution. A more satisfying account will emphasize the contribution that the world itself makes to those conceptions and paint into the picture the instinctual, cultural and technological preconditions of our catching hold of one another's public meaning when we make reference to kinds. These last are an indispensable part of the background for our collective interest in natural kinds and the advancement of our shared understanding of them.[1]

---

[1] 'To be sure – there has to be a great deal of stage-setting before one can read a [dictionary] definition and guess how a word is used. But in debunking . . . the fact that something so simple . . . *can* convey the use of a word [certain philosophers] forget to be impressed by it . . . there is a great deal of stage-setting, but it is rarely stage-setting specifically designed to enable one to learn the use of *this* word.' See Putnam (1970), p. 198.

In subsequent writings Putnam has stressed how any good account of these matters must incorporate not only stage-setting but also the division of labour and the dependence of non-experts on experts in the identification of natural and other kinds:

The ['probability theory of meaning'] cannot as it stands incorporate either the linguistic division of labour (the fact that confirmation procedures for *being gold*, or *being aluminium*, or *being an elm tree*, or *being N.N.* are not the property of every speaker . . . speakers defer to experts for the fixing of reference in a huge number of cases), or the contribution of the environment (the fact that the extension of a term sometimes fixes its meaning and not *vice versa*). In my view, the criteria used by experts to tell whether or not something is gold are not 'part of the meaning' of *gold* (e.g. the word doesn't change its meaning in the language if the experts shift to a different set of tests for the same metal), yet they are part of a mechanism for fixing the extension of gold. ('Reference and Understanding', the *Collected Papers*, Vol. II (Cambridge 1975).)

Compare Leibniz, *Nouveaux Essais*, 3.10.18, 3.11.24. See also 4.6.4, which suggestively anticipates and answers some of the difficulties that have been found in the deictic–nomological account,

Hilary Putnam's counter-proposal is now well known.[2] This proposal (or reconstruction, if you prefer to call it that) holds that, for the explication of the sense of a substantive or a sortal predicate, the thing that needs to be laid down is that *x* is an f (horse, cypress tree, orange, caddisfly . . .) if and only if, given good *exemplars* of the kind that is in question, the best theoretical description that emerged from collective inquiries into the kind would group *x* alongside these exemplars. (See also Preamble §6, and my (1993).) An object *x* is an f just if *x* is similar in the

e.g. by D. H. Mellor in 'Natural Kinds', *British Journal of the Philosophy of Science*, 28 (1977). Take an element and one of its isotopes. Which one is the natural kind? Leibniz would surely say that it was a mistake to insist on any general decision. It may be implicit in our however provisional classificatory practice that the stuff we are aiming for is the most specific kind possible. But Leibniz also leaves room to say that it is implicit in our use that what we are aiming at is a kind of stuff that plays a certain role in a particular kind of explanation. In the case of isotopes (one may insist), that which is fundamental is the part played by the element in chemical reactions. Electron shell usually matters more in this connexion than atomic number. Normally then the relevant similitude should embrace both isotopes under one element. (But there may be grounds for another decision in special cases, e.g. those that were marked by the name 'deuterium'). This does not reduce real classification to our decision. The decision relates to the identification and refinement of the interest that is in question, *not* to the inclusion or exclusion as such of a given thing or stuff.

[2] See also Kripke, Lecture III, 'Naming and Necessity' (1972). Compare Leibniz, N.E. 3.6.14. Related conclusions have been reached by Vernon Pratt (1972), pp. 305–27. See also W. V. Quine (1969); and Hidé Ishiguro (1972).

  The terminology in which I shall expound all this will coincide with Frege's usage wherever Frege had a serviceable term, and will sometimes diverge from Putnam's. A sortal predicate has a *sense*, a *reference* or *designation*, and an *extension*; and there pertain to it both a *concept* (which may have *marks*) and a *conception*. On these matters see my (1984) and (1995) and see Preamble §5 and following. Summarizing these, here is the terminology I try to adhere to:

[1] The *reference* of a sortal predicate such as 'horse', i.e. what 'horse' stands for, is the concept *horse*, the general thing horse.

[2] The *extension* of a sortal predicate such as 'horse' consists of the entities falling under the concept it designates, i.e. horses.

[3] The *sense*, or *contribution to truth-conditions*, of a sortal predicate may be elucidated by specifying what concept the predicate stands for, and seeking to impart a certain *conception* of that.

[4] A *conception* of horse is a set of beliefs concerning what horses are, or what it is to be a horse. The conception is in no way the same as the concept. The conception is *of* the concept.

[5] Finally, a *mark φ of a concept* f is any φ such that $(\forall x)(x \text{ is an } f \rightarrow \phi x)$.

I remark that almost any appreciable change in people's beliefs about horses might constitute a shift in their conception of horses. Such a shift, taken far enough, might in the end deserve to be accounted as a change in sense. But only in a rare or extreme case could a change in conception result in anything so extreme as a shift in the reference of 'horse'. This is not to deny that it may result in a correction of previous conceptions of that extension.

  I have tried to present Putnam's theory in a manner that (a) is compatible with a supplementary doctrine of his about the stereotypes which support human understanding of substantives (stereotypes being standardized sets of beliefs or idealized beliefs associated with terms, and belonging with conception); (b) leaves sense itself *relatively* insensitive to minor shifts in conception, and to minor changes in the criteria used by experts; but (c) involves no unnecessary or dubious claims to the effect that the sense (contrast reference) of a natural kind word is invariant through change in theories, beliefs or conceptions. On these matters see, *mutatis mutandis*, J. H. McDowell (1977), and above, Preamble, §4 and following.

relevant way to genuine exemplars (where the proper standard of relevance is not abstract or general but internal to the nature that would be revealed by study of f-exemplars). It should be noted that Putnam's account, like that of Kripke, not only bears upon the semantics of words for natural kinds whose instances are particulars or substances. It also bears upon the semantics of words for natural stuffs. That matter is equally important, and the parallelism is important and illuminating. In this book, however, the chief or central concern is with particulars/substances and their kinds.

It is fully compatible with Putnam's suggestion (which should not be read as a recipe for the production of formal definitions of the substantives to which it applies, only for real definitions in the sense of Preamble §6) that the theoretical description that comes into question in a given case should make reference to both the microphysical and the macrophysical. (Some of the useful theoretical notions in this area, *gene-pool* for instance, really make reference to both.) As this figures in Putnam's account, the act of deixis will not prescribe at what level the relevant facts should lie. Nor is it implied by Putnam's proposal that the people who use a natural kind word will know what the true theory of the kind is – only that, if they take the word seriously as the name of a natural kind, then their linguistic practices will finally depend upon the supposition (however inexplicit, and not always borne out)[3] that such a theory is there to be found. All the doctrine implies is that the determination of a natural kind stands or falls with the existence of lawlike principles, known or unknown, that will collect together the extension of the kind around two or three good representatives of the kind. In order for the name to stand for a natural kind, everything depends on whether there is some nomological grounding for the application of the name. If there is, and if the predicate is worthy to survive as a natural kind term, then the holding of the relevant principles is constitutive of its exemplification by its instances. To be something of that kind *is* to exemplify the distinctive mode of activity that they determine.

In this conception we are driven back to an unmysterious but pre-empiricist notion of substance (a notion that is here to be progressively enriched) which it would have been both possible and advantageous for Aristotle to distance from his concern with final causes:

---

[3] Witness what befell 'caloric', 'phlogiston', and Leuwenhoek's 'hominids'. On such terms see Kripke, *op. cit.* (footnote 2), and Lecture One, *ibid.*, paragraph one, and his addendum at pp. 763–4. See also G. Frege, *Nachgelassene Schriften*, ed. H. Hermes, F. Kambartel, F. Kaulbach (Hamburg, 1969), p. 133.

Things which exist by nature . . . such as animals and the organs of these or plants and the elementary stuffs . . . have in them a principle of change or rest (in respect of place or growth and decline or alteration generally) . . . the nature of a thing being the source or cause of non-accidental change or rest in anything to which it [the nature] belongs . . . (*Physics Book II*, Ch. 1);

and which Leibniz did divorce from all final causality except that of God's decree:

Aristotle has well called [nature] the *principle of motion and of rest*, though that philosopher seems to me to take the term more broadly than its accepted meaning and to understand by it not only local motion and rest in a place, but change and stasis or permanence in general (p. 499) . . . [The] divine law once established . . . has truly conferred upon [things] some created impression which endures within them, or . . . an *internal law* from which their actions and passions follow (p. 500) . . . if the law of God does in fact leave some vestige of him expressed in things . . . then it must be granted that there is a certain efficacy residing in things, a form or force such as we usually designate by the name of nature, from which the series of phenomena follows. (*On Nature Itself, or on the Inherent Force and Actions of Created Things*, Gerhardt IV, 504 ff., as translated at pp. 499 ff. by Leroy E. Loemker in Leibniz, *Philosophical Papers and Letters*, 2nd edn, Dordrecht, 1969.)

Putnam's account of natural kind words, as combined with the importance we ascribed to the *what is it?* question, provides a fresh understanding of one part of the point of these doctrines. However rough and unfinished such a suggestion may seem when compared with the variety and complexity of all the classifications that are implicit or explicit in our linguistic practices (consider our divers substantives for genera, species, subspecies, crossbreeds, variants, etc), it has the signal virtue of revealing or recalling to us a possibility scarcely even imagined by those who have preferred to theorize in abstraction from particular kinds of substantive, or preferred to erect transcendental arguments upon the foundation of such supposed truisms as 'because all our concepts are tools for the intellectual handling of our sensory intake, we cannot make sense of any statements about the world except ones admitting of a broadly phenomenalistic analysis'.[4]

---

[4] Jonathan Bennett in 'The Age and Size of the World', *Synthèse*, 23 (1972). Of the numerous philosophers who have been party to this conception I know only one who dared to draw the proper conclusion, viz. Nietzsche.

We speak of a 'serpent'; the designation fits nothing but the sinuosity (the *serpere*), and could therefore appertain also equally to the worm. What arbitrary demarcations! What one-sided preferences given sometimes to this, sometimes to that, quality of a thing . . . What therefore is truth? A mobile army of metaphors, metonymies, anthropomorphisms; in short a sum of human relations which become rhetorically intensified, metamorphosed, adorned, and after

Not very many things are entirely new in philosophy. The insight we have borrowed here has been anticipated several times. But that which earlier attempts have lacked, with the exception perhaps of Leibniz's, is the explicit combination of two distinctive features: (1) the component of *deixis*, which requires of any candidate for kind f that it be relevantly like something that is directly or indirectly identifiable and is actually an f, and (2) the explicit acknowledgment of the indispensable part played in the determination of standards of relevant likeness by the laws or lawlike propensities of the real world. With or without this feature, however, all views of this kind have the distinctive consequence, which is attested by experience, that it is possible for what appear astonishingly like fs to be not fs, whereas the most improbable seeming specimens may turn out to be fs after all. (Hidden structure dominates apparent, as Heraclitus puts this at fr. 54 Diels.) It can also be a matter of prolonged and difficult inquiry gradually to improve currently accepted standards or conceptions of what it is to be an f.

According to the account suggested by Putnam, the semantics of a kind word will accommodate all this. There is room for one and the same concept of *what it is to be an* f, anchored as it is to examples that are grouped together in virtue of resemblances that are nomologically grounded, to be unfolded gradually in a succession of different and improving conceptions. As the primitive mentality gives way to the protoscientific, it can be predicted that human beings will entertain the thought that it is extraordinarily mysterious what the most ordinary objects are. They may come to believe they are gradually awakening from a pre-conscious state in which they never grasped properly what

footnote 4 (*cont.*)

> long usage seem to a nation fixed, canonic and binding; truths are illusions of which one has forgotten that they *are* illusions. (*On Truth and Falsity in the Ultramoral Sense.*)

Ingenuity and elaboration of the phenomenal conception can postpone this outlandish conclusion. The conclusion Nietzsche draws about truth can be *blurred* by the deliverance of common sense that worms do not in fact belong to the extension of 'serpent'. But might they just as well have? If the semantical conception that sustains Nietzsche's inference to his conclusion is in violation of common sense – and, in the presence of an alternative conception of the working of substantives, it becomes all the easier to suspect that the phenomenal conception enjoys no special obviousness of its own – then the common-sense finding that worms are not serpents is irrelevant and the ingenuity is misplaced. It is a mere postponement of the startling conclusion that Nietzsche draws.

Semantical fact is almost always more interesting than transcendental philosophical fiction; and for the imagination a hundred times more potent. We do not really have to choose between (1) the phenomenal cum reductive way of Berkeley and Mach, which assimilates the criterion for being an f to some set of tests for f-hood, and (2) the opposite way, which assimilates what would be required by way of a real test for f to the constitutive criterion for f-hood.

they encountered, nor comprehended it even when they learned to recognize it.[5] Moreover, the doctrine illustrates in a schematic way how a word can enter the language on the slenderest and most provisional basis of theory – just enough to yield what is required for the recognition of an extension (which can itself be subsequently purified) – and draw credit on a draft that Nature may *or may not* finally honour.

Once one has seen the possibility of a natural kind word's having such a debut, one will be tempted, in the case of natural things, to replace all doctrines that distinguish in the customary way between the real and nominal essences of a given kind of thing (contrast our use of these notions at Preamble, §5) by an account of the different *stages* in the unfolding of what it is to be an f. Let us try to understand and describe a process by which clear but indistinct knowledge – knowledge sufficient for recognition but without the enumeration of distinguishing marks – is replaced by clear, more distinct (better itemized) or more adequate knowledge.[6] In the light of an adequate account of this, it should pose no difficulty to suggest that one could pick out (say) a tadpole and identify its kind by saying 'the members of the kind are anything relevantly like this', while leaving the actual standards of relevance to be scientifically determined at macrolevel and microlevel; then that one can be surprised to find a principle of individuation for members of the kind committing one to count into the kind a frog – not of course as a present tadpole, but as a member of the very same kind as the Batrachian specimen recently demonstrated. Here the discovery may or may not result in some modification of the received sense. But all that it needs to be is a realization of the possibility, which was always there, of fuller or more detailed specification both of what it is to be an f and of *which* things are f.[7]

---

[5] Cf. Heraclitus fragments 17, 26 Diels; and Leibniz '[les hommes] sont empiriques et ne se gouvernent pas que par les sens et les exemples, sans examiner si la meme raison a encor lieu' (*Nouveaux Essais*, Gerhardt v, p. 252). See also §4 of the Preamble, with footnote 15.

[6] Leibniz describes this process in several places and connexions. See especially his account of clear but indistinct knowledge at 'Meditationes de Cognitione, Veritate et Ideis', Gerhardt iv, *op. cit.*, especially p. 422. The Leibnizian distinction between clarity and distinctness is one I have availed myself of constantly, here and in subsequent chapters, in developing the account given here of sortal concepts and our conceptions of their determinables and determinations. See also my 'Reply to Fei Xu' (1997a).

[7] Again someone might pick out an amoeba under a microscope, say '*that* cell [or *that* creature], and anything [relevantly] like it, I call an amoeba', and commit himself in that way to the existence of some (as yet unknown to him) standard of scientific similarity. What he commits himself to is to live with that standard and the associated principle of activity when he finds it out, and to arbitrate persistence questions, when he graduates to these, in empirical and logical accord with these. We have seen in Chapter Two (see **D**(vi)) how this minimal commitment leads into a

Frege said that the sense of an expression determined its reference, and not the reference the sense. If Putnam's theory is correct, this order of determination ought not to be expected to hold in the case of natural kind words. Just as the sense of a proper name (contrast definite description) is best explained by saying what its reference is, so, in the process of the teaching and elucidation of the sense of a natural kind-predicate, everything depends upon providing specimen satisfiers of the predicate. These are held as hostages for that which Frege would have called its reference – or as hostages, one might say, for the *what it is to be* an f. (For the real coherence, despite verbal differences, of Putnam's and Frege's views see my (1993).) Putnam's suggestion does not, however, imply that reference is *prior* to sense. The principal effect of this supposedly salutary exaggeration would be to raise difficult and perfectly irrelevant questions about the possibility of prelinguistic *deixis* and the preverbal categorization of experience. Putnam's suggestion only implies that at this point sense and reference are mutually dependent and correlative notions.

Suppose that all this is even roughly right. Then it contains most of the answer to the problems that we have posed about the demands of **D**(iii), **D**(iv), **D**(v) and all the other **D** principles. If there have to exist true lawlike principles in nature to underwrite the existence of the multiply instantiable thing that is the reference of a natural kind-predicate, if lawlike principles of this kind have to exist in order for that general thing's extension to be assembled around the focus of actual specimens or for a reality-invoking kind of sense to be conferred on the term standing for the concept f, then they must also determine directly or indirectly the characteristic development, the typical history, the limits of any possible development or history, and the characteristic mode of activity of anything that instantiates the kind.

The conclusion is not a novel one:

I also maintain that substances cannot be conceived in their essence as bare or without activity, that activity is of the essence of substance as such . . . above all it is necessary to consider that the modifications that can befall a subject naturally or without miracle derive from limitation and variation in a real kind, or from a constant and absolute original nature . . . and wherever one finds some quality in a subject, one must believe that if one understood the nature of the subject and of the quality then one would understand how the quality could

footnote 7 (*cont.*)

> further commitment in this case – the commitment to count every splitting of an amoeba as the demise of that amoeba. The commitment, though its working is logically constrained, is empirically grounded. It is grounded in the actual activity of these unicellular creatures. (For the interaction of logical and empirical, see further Chapter Six, §§5–6.)

result from them. So in the order of nature it is in no way arbitrary whether substances have these qualities or those, and God will only give them those qualities which naturally befit them, that is the qualities which could be derived from the nature of the substances themselves as intelligible modifications of them. . . . Everything that is must be such as to be intelligible distinctly, if only one were admitted to the secret of things . . .[8]

The deep interest of this conception of the activity of a substance and of Leibniz's idea that the nomological foundation of activity is something supervenient upon fundamental laws of nature (see Gerhardt II, 263, quoted at the head of this chapter) utterly transcends all the particularities of Leibniz's finished view of substance (which in the end dethroned Aristotelian continuants, seen as imperfect from this point of view, in favour of monads). Its implication for the theory of individuation outlined in Chapter Two may be summed up in an idiom that is officially alien to this book but, for the purposes of this particular thought, very concise. Where fs make up a natural kind, the only possible worlds we need consider, for these are the only possible worlds having within them any entity that is an f, are worlds sufficiently similar in nomological respects to the actual world to exhibit specimens relevantly similar to actual specimens. This means that, for the special case of natural kinds, we find that ordinary necessity virtually coincides with physical necessity, and ordinary possibility with physical possibility. (Cf. Ishiguro *loc. cit.*) It was difficult, until we thought about the sense of natural kind words in Leibniz's or Putnam's fashion, to imagine how the requirements of the last chapter could possibly be satisfied. But the principal difficulty that now remains is epistemological, and is shifted to another point, which is at once right and familiar: how to assure oneself, once one realizes what a considerable commitment such an identification will involve, that any particular entity really is an f, or a g, or whatever.

It may be instructive at this point to try to illustrate how the theory of individuation, the semantics of natural kind words and general findings of theoretical biology are in a certain way made for one another. (The

---

[8] Leibniz, *Nouveaux Essais*, preface. Compare, in connexion with the contentions of the preceding paragraphs, Leibniz in Couturat, *Opuscules et Fragments Inédits de Leibniz* (Paris, 1903), pp. 16–24.

> I think that in this series of things there are certain propositions that are most universally true, and which not even a miracle could violate. This is not to say that they have any necessity for God; but rather that when he chose the particular series of things he did choose, he decided by that very act to observe these principles as [giving] the specific properties of just this particular series of things. (Cf. Gerhardt II, 263, quoted at the head of this Chapter Three.)

I have followed here the interpretation of Leibniz's view that is defended in chapter IV, especially §3–4, of Hidé Ishiguro (1972 and 1990) .

significance of this exceeds the simple pleasure one might have in finding such Leibnizian anticipations as Gerhardt II, 264: 'For there to be a certain persisting law which involves the future states of that which we conceive as one and the same continuant, this is what I say constitutes a substance's identity.') Starting off with the almost pre-theoretical idea of a sortal predicate whose sense is such as to depend on the sort of thing that lies in its extension – the kind of predicate that cries out for real definition – we are led to speculate what holds together the extension. So soon as we find that, we find lawlike norms of starting to exist, existing, and ceasing to exist by reference to which questions of the identity and persistence of individual specimens falling under a definition can be arbitrated. Such norms will supervene on basic laws of nature, we have supposed; they may be understood as certain *exploitations*, so to say, of these laws. But now we are led by simple conceptual considerations to precisely the account of living substances that biologists can fill out *a posteriori* by treating them as systems open to their surroundings, not in equilibrium with those surroundings, but so constituted that a delicate self-regulating balance of serially linked enzymatic degradative and synthesizing chemical reactions enables them to renew themselves on the molecular level at the expense of those surroundings, such renewal taking place under a law-determined variety of conditions in a determinate pattern of growth and development towards, and/or persistence in, some particular form.[9] (In certain cases there may be definite alternative forms keyed to different environments, e.g. locust/grasshopper, axolotl/salamander, but again this is something that is founded in the solid basis of lawlike propensities.)

2. THE OTHER SORTAL PREDICATES

Almost everything that has been said so far has been mainly directed at words standing for the various species of natural substances. The account could be extended and adapted without overwhelming difficulty to predicates of *genera*, wherever these were still determinate enough to be autonomously individuative. (See especially requirements **D**(iv) and **D**(v).) And *mutatis mutandis* certain of the claims so far made would also apply to words for the natural organs, *heart*, *liver*, *foot*, *brain*, and even to

---

[9] Cf. Aristotle, *Physics*, 199[b15]: 'For these things are natural which, by a continuous process originated from an internal principle, arrive at some end. The same end is not reached from every principle, nor any chance end, but always the tendency in each is towards the same end, if there is no impediment.'

geographical or geological terms such as *river, lake, spring, sea, glacier* or *volcano*. In the latter case, it will not be wildly inappropriate to speak of principles of activity. In the former, we can honour **D**(viii) in terms both of principles of *activity* and of *modes of functioning* or *operation*. It would be interesting to enter into detailed questions about just how well these predicates measure up to the **D** requirements of the previous chapter; then to enter all the appropriate and considerable reservations.[10] But, apart from the intrinsic interest of these kinds of entity, it would be distractive, and it would be seen as mere postponement by those who hold that it is on artefact kinds especially that the individuative theory proposed in Chapter Two must stumble.

Consider ordinary artefact-words such as *clock, chisel, drinking vessel, drill, stove, pen, spade, table*. Putnam's account is not happily extended to these. Of course the easiest way to explain, in a given case and context, what a tool or artefact of some sort is might be to proceed by the use of examples. But the deictic nomological method is scarcely indispensable. Moreover, in the absence of the right sort of commentary, it could be positively confusing or lead to an implausible narrowing of the reach of the artefact kind. There are virtually no lawlike sentences to be had about particular utensil, implement or tool kinds *as such*. There scarcely could be. Clocks, for instance, may be made of a variety of different kinds of material and may function by radically different kinds of mechanism (cf. Locke, *Essay*, 3.6.39). Artefacts are things to be encountered in nature, and subject to its laws. But they need not be collected and classified together as this or that artefact by virtue of internal resemblances or scientific resemblances. Artefacts are collected up not by reference to a theoretically hypothesized common constitution but under functional descriptions that are precisely indifferent to specific constitution and particular mode of interaction with environment. A clock is any time-keeping device, a pen is any rigid ink-applying writing implement, and so on. The description gives what it is usually impossible to specify in the other cases, an explicit nominal essence; whereas a finite and determinate set of marks fully suitable for definitional purposes is precisely not what the members of natural kinds

---

[10] There need be no one physiological theory to cover all animal hearts of all kinds. There is no one specific structure which a heart must have, nor any one fully specific mode of biological functioning that a heart must as such exemplify. To be a heart (simply contrast a human heart, a sheep's heart) an organ need only be an organ of *some* definite physiological kind or other playing a particular role in the circulation of the blood.

Such terms may seem then to be hybrid between functionally defined terms shortly to be characterized and natural kind terms.

endowed with a scientifically palpable real essence may be expected to have in common.[11]

For the theory of individuation generally, and for the theory here advanced especially, there is then a crucially important difference between natural things and artefacts, both in respect of conditions of persistence through time and in respect of the satisfaction of the require- ments upon sortal predicates sketched in Chapter Two. Where there is dispute concerning an object identified as a member of a natural kind, one can readily conceive of getting more scientific facts. Consider the nineteenth-century discovery that the elvers *Leptocephali* were in fact the young of the species Conger Eel, or the humbler but in some sense proto-scientific discovery that tadpoles become frogs and maggots houseflies. These discoveries changed conceptions (not concepts). In the light of the deictic/nomological theory, it will be apparent how such dis- coveries can engage with the semantics of 'eel' or 'frog' even as they advance the collective grasp of concepts. (For the thing they reveal is allowed for in advance in the fixing of the designation of the kind word).[12] We can see why identity questions about members of natural kinds may be expected to find the notion of identity at its best. Empirical discovery playing the part it does play here, it is plain too why they are the most unsuitable of all candidates for any conventionalist treatment.[13] By reference to the natural propensities that constitute the foundation of the natural kind concept, we can make a clear distinction between normal activity and what happens under conditions where there is inter- ference. (Cf. Chapter Seven, §17.) It is in no way up to us what to count as persistence through change or through replacement of matter. There

---

[11] Concepts of artefact kinds, being verbally analysable in a way that is excluded for concepts of natural kinds, offer more prospect of generating truths that are analytic (in the strict sense of 'analytic', viz. truths reducible by explicit definitions to truths of logic). Even here though, and in the place where such truths would be less interesting, the matter is not unproblematic – if only because of the high degree of actual vagueness inhering in the definitions of artefact kinds and the scope there is here for innovation. In any case, neither here nor in other chapters does any- thing whatever hang on analyticity. It would do no damage whatever to the doctrines of nature, substance and necessity put forward in this book if the only analytic truths were the logical truths of first order logic, as afforded by means of formally correct, purely stipulative definitions.

I have claimed that Putnam's account of natural kind words is not happily extended to arte- fact words. But I ought to mention Putnam does seek to apply his account to such words, e.g. to 'pencil'. See 'The Meaning of "Meaning"', at pp. 242–4 of *Mind, Language and Reality*, Philosophical Papers, Volume 2 (Cambridge, 1975).

[12] Here, as throughout, I hope to maintain the terminology proposed in footnote 2 of this chapter and the disposition set out in Preamble §5 and §6.

[13] For the original impulse to conventionalism, see Plato, *Symposium* 207[d3] and following, and Thomas Reid (1785), II, 4. For the association between conventionalism and parts, see Peter Simons (1987), Chapter 5.

is some sort of contrast here with the identity problem of artefacts. To some limited extent, there may be shadowy counterparts even for artefacts of that which a natural kind concept furnishes straightforwardly. But in the case of damage to a watch, say, or extensive replacement of its parts, there is nothing theoretical or extra to discover, once the ordinary narrative of events is complete. For there is no such thing as the natural development of a watch or a lawlike norm concerning the behaviour of watches as such.

It will be useful then, before we grapple with the problems of artefact identity, to return to the first chapter of Book Two of Aristotle's *Physics*:

animals and their organs and the elementary stuffs . . . differ from what is not naturally constituted in that each of these things has within it a principle of change and of staying unchanged, whether in respect of place or in respect of quantitative change, as in growth and decay, or in respect of qualitative change. But a bedstead or a cloak or whatever, *qua* receiving the designation 'bed' or 'cloak' . . ., i.e. in so far as it is the product of craft, has within itself no inherent tendency to any particular sort of change. Though in so far as an artefact happens to be composed . . . of whatever mixture of natural elements, it does incidentally, as so considered, have within itself the principle of change which inheres in its matter. So nature is a *source or principle of change and staying unchanged* in that to which it belongs *primarily* i.e. in virtue of the thing itself and not in virtue of an incidental attribute of the thing. I say 'not in virtue of an incidental attribute' because, for instance, a man who is a doctor might cure himself. Nevertheless it is not in so far as he is a patient that he possessed the art of medicine. It was incidental that he satisfied both descriptions. And something similar holds of everything that is an artificial product (192^b8–28).

There is an insight here that is so important that it deserves a formulation free of the locutions 'qua', 'in so far as', 'considered as' at which Aristotle clutches to give voice to his thought. (These are the locutions by which some Aristotelians still persist in obfuscating this and many other good thoughts: compare the discussion in Chapter One, §7 under (λ).) Let us say instead that a particular continuant *x* belongs to a natural kind, or is a natural thing, if and only if *x* has a principle of activity founded in lawlike dispositions and propensities that form the basis for extension-involving sortal identification(s) which will answer truly the question 'what is *x*?' For purposes of this chapter, and for purposes of the theory of individuation, it is not the question of whether a thing was fabricated but rather the difference between satisfying and not satisfying this condition that makes the fundamental distinction. Loosely, and because there is no other handy term, I shall continue to call objects that fail this crucial condition 'artefacts'. But this is without prejudice to the question, which is scientific not philosophical, of the possibility (which I have no wish to prejudge) of the artificial synthesis of natural things.

It should go almost without saying that the distinction of natural thing from artefact is presented here in a fashion conformable at every point and in every particular with the plausible scientific belief that, however we have arrived at the individuation of a given thing, the thing will be subject to the fundamental laws of physics and chemistry. For the purposes of that belief, there is no more difficulty in our distinction between natural things and other things than there is in making a further distinction, *within* the class of natural things, between (a) those things which, being alive, are not in chemical and energy equilibrium with their surroundings but suck from their environment the energy that they need for their typical activity or their molecular self-renewal and replacement, and (b) those natural things that maintain a typical mode of activity without being alive and cannot help but be in equilibrium with their surroundings. (Take the Chesil Bank, for instance, or the River Nile or the Caspian Sea.) It is true that live things exemplify most perfectly and completely a category of substance that is extension-involving, imports the idea of characteristic activity, and is unproblematic for individuation. But not all extension-involving concepts are concepts of live things and I should stress that non-equilibrium with surroundings is an additional and special distinguishing mark. In fact, terrible confusion will result from mindless assimilation of the *live /not live* distinction to the other two distinctions. In other words, (1) *extension involving* or *not extension involving, with respect to the specification of their concept*; (2) *not synthetically produced* or *synthetically produced*; (3) *live* or *not live* (as elucidated in terms of non-equilibrium and of self-renewal at the molecular level) – these are *three* distinctions, for all that living animals fall on the same side of each of them. Moreover, once we move in this way towards a more fundamental basis of distinction, we need not flinch from trying to understand some harder cases: an india rubber ball for instance (individuated by a stuff sort that is extension-involving and that simultaneously lends nomological import to a thing-kind, the ball itself being something artificially produced, not live) – or even a wasps' nest (something individuated by reference to other things which are themselves individuated in the extension-involving fashion, an animal artefact not a human artefact, an artefact constrained in respect of its material constitution, not live).

3. PROBLEMS OF ARTEFACT IDENTITY

Our concern passes now to the problems associated with singling out artefacts and the similar difficulties we shall have with other things that cannot furnish the theorist of identity with a principle of activity. Summing up the argument so far in the general (if qualified) claim that natural things are individuated by reference to a principle of activity naturally embodied, but ordinary artefacts are individuated by reference to a parcel of matter so organized as to subserve a certain function;[14] and advancing next to the consequences of the finding that there is nothing nomological to make up for the logical indeterminacy that seems to inhere in the individuation of artefacts, one feels the temptation looming to exaggerate the degree to which questions of artefact identity are matters of arbitrary decision. Even here, though, and even for the most typical cases of our own artefacts, conventionalism is not immediately plausible. For human purposes and decisions might enter into the invention and modification of human artefact-kinds without its following that any particular questions of identity and difference (between this artefact and that artefact) should qualify for decision by stipulation.

Artefact identity does, however, present some difficult problems. **D**(iii) requires that the contribution that is made by an artefact-word such as 'clock' to the sense of 'x coincides with y under the concept *clock*' should suffice to render this relation both an equivalence relation and a congruence relation. But how is this to be secured? And how are we to get for artefacts the effect that was got for natural things by the notion of activity? (The conceptual effect, I mean.) It would be unrealistic and absurd to suppose that coincidence under the concept *clock* required a clock's continuous functioning or expect the functioning spoken of in **D**(v) to be more than remotely analogous to the activity of natural things. A clock may stop because it needs winding up. Such a pause does not prejudice its persistence. A clock can stop because it needs to be repaired; and again it persists, however long the lapse before the repair. (The nominal essence of *clock* does not make 'broken clock' problematic for existence or peculiar in the manner of 'dead person'.) The nominal essence of *clock* must involve a stipulation of some sort concerning the capacity to tell the time. But surely the uninterrupted continuance for all t of the capacity at t to tell the time at t will not be stipulated. This is too strong. The

---

[14] Contrast works of art, which do not normally, *qua* works of art, have any *function*. See below, Chapter Four, §10.

Concerning the expression 'principle of activity', see Preface.

only loss that could count to any appreciable degree against the persistence of a clock is a *radical and irretrievable* loss of the time-keeping function.
(Sometimes, even under this circumstance, the clock itself may be held to
have survived, however irreclaimably damaged.) Another reason why a
clock-persistence condition has to be undemanding is that the repair of a
clock apparently permits both disassembly and replacement of parts. We
do not look back to the time when a clock was being repaired and say that
the clock's existence was interrupted while it was in a dismantled condition. For a thing starts existing only once; and in the case of a clock its
proper beginning was at about the time when its maker finished it. In the
case of dismantling, there is not even a time limit upon reassembly.

When these several points of discontinuous functioning, disassembly,
and part replacement have been accommodated, the condition of coincidence and persistence for clocks that emerges is not merely weak. It is
so undemanding that there seems to be nothing to prevent one clock,
identified a description applying at the time when it was functioning
normally, from *clock*-coinciding (i.e. coinciding in a manner supposedly
sufficient for identity) with two distinct clocks, each identified under a
description applying to it after some radical repair or muddled reassembly in a moderately disorderly clock maker's workshop. But the coincidence of one thing with two things breaches requirement **D**(iii), **D**(vi),
and almost every other interesting declaration made in Chapter Two.[15]
Nor is there one piece of clock – the spring, the regulator, the escape-
ment, the face, the case . . . which the concept *clock* could suggest that we
should revere as the 'focus' or 'nucleus' of a clock, and which can help
us past this difficulty. Here, and in the extremes of ingenuity and opportunism to which such problems pushed the Roman laws of *accessio* and
specificatio (cf., for instance, Justinian, *Institutes* Bk II, 1.34 *et passim*), we see
that, however questionable it may be, Leibniz's transition in the decade
of his writing the *Discourse of Metaphysics* from Aristotelian substances to
Leibnizian monads, and his demotion of things with parts to the status
of mere aggregates (for a characteristic statement see Gerhardt II, 261),
did not arise from a simple misconception of the logical level of the
number word 'one'.

A good place to embark on the difficulties of artefact identity is with
a case that Thomas Hobbes put forward expressly against those who
regarded 'unity of form' as a *principium individuationis*: on this view, he
suggests,

---

[15] It is worth noticing that it fails even the weaker requirements that relative identity theorists would
have to place upon the relation *is the same clock as*.

Two bodies existing both at once would be one and the same numerical body. For if, for example, that ship of Theseus, concerning the difference whereof made by continued reparation in taking out the old planks and putting in new, the sophisters of Athens were wont to dispute, were, after all the planks were changed, the same numerical ship it was at the beginning; and if some man had kept the old planks as they were taken out, and by putting them afterwards together in the same order, had again made a ship of them, this, without doubt, had also been the same numerical ship with that which was at the beginning; and so there would have been two ships numerically the same, which is absurd.[16]

The unity of form theory that Hobbes means to attack here is not dissimilar from ours. In our version of the theory, the finding of *a*'s coincidence with *b* under the concept *ship* needs to be the makings of a sufficient condition of *a*'s being the same ship (unless the concept *ship* is to be not a sortal concept). It might seem that in our theory the difficulty Hobbes mentions is escaped because our theory favours the repaired ship. For the constant availability of this ship, and its uninterrupted service as the sacred ship by which the annual voyage was made from Piraeus to Delos, may seem to mark this ship out as the one that is continuous in the manner of a ship with Theseus' ship. But is such a fact really enough to trump *all* the claims of a reconstituted ship, which may well be much closer not only in matter but in its design, its manoeuvrability and its handling qualities to the ship that Theseus sailed? Can one who favours the working ship ignore all of this? Cf. **D**(v).

Few of us will hurry to make a choice between the two options as so far specified. Some will even say we do not have to choose. They will ask us to imagine its being decided, in an age that no longer believed in Apollo but still believed in Theseus, to erect a monument to Theseus and to put his ship upon the monument. Then antiquarians might say that the ship put together from discarded planks was the right one to raise up there. But dispute might break out about this matter between them and

---

[16] *De Corpore*, II, H (Molesworth, p. 136). Hobbes's source for the puzzle is Plutarch's life of Theseus:

> The vessel in which Theseus sailed and returned safe with these young men went with thirty oars. It was preserved by the Athenians up to the times of Demetrius Phalerus [floruit 280 B.C.]; being so refitted and newly fashioned with strong plank, that it afforded an example to the philosophers in their disputations concerning the identity of things that are changed by addition, some contending that it was the same, and others that it was not. (§§22–3; cf. Plato, *Phaedo* 58ᴬ; Xenophon, *Memorabilia* 4.8.2.)

I do not know who proposed the final twist in the story that made it into Hobbe's objection. An addition to our modern store of problems in this area is furnished by Jonathan Barnes in 'Bits and Pieces' in *Matter and Metaphysics*, ed. J. Barnes and M. Mignucci (Bibliopolis, 1986); another by T. W. Rhys David's *The Questions of King Milinda* (New York, 1963).

the superannuated priests who favoured the working ship.[17] The difficulty (it will then be said) is a certain incomparability between the positions. It might be eirenically suggested that, if one party is looking for an
archaeological relic and the other for a functionally persistent continuant, then the whole dispute ought really to be traced to a disagreement
about what it is for something to be such a sacred ship. The antiquarian
who favours the reconstituted ship has a different interest, it might be
said, from the priest who favours the continuously repaired ship. Both
are stuck with the identification *ship* but, having different interests, they
do not mean quite the same thing by 'ship'. The priests and the antiquarians find different entities with different principles of individuation in
one and the same place.[18] Neither party can vindicate its view by reference to the 'laws of development' of a ship.[19] There are no such laws.

[17] A mereologist making reference to the mereological definition of identity

$$(a = b) =_{df} [(a \text{ is a part of } b) \ \& \ (b \text{ is a part of } a)]$$

might well side with the antiquarian and against the priests. Evidently, though, it is a precondition of the acceptability of the mereological definition of identity, supposing that this is what is
invoked on the antiquarians' behalf, that, for any non-empty class of individuals α, there should
be one and only one sum of all elements of α. That is to say that the sum axiom of mereology
must be unrestrictedly true, true whatever entities we admit into the class α, including continuants that persist through loss or gain of parts. (The sum axiom is the second postulate in the
tenseless presentation of mereology given by Tarski, *op. cit.* in footnote 23 of Chapter One. See
the text of Chapter One for the definition of 'sum'.) Under the conditions stated, however, it no
longer looks obvious that this axiom is true, unless 'part' is given a sense specially designed to
save the plausibility of Tarski's postulate II. In that case, any mereological definition of identity
that depends upon the axiom loses any direct usefulness it might have had for the antiquarian
cause. For my own conversion to the view that Tarski's second postulate is false, see Wiggins
(1968). For a general account of the doubtful status of the second postulate see now Simons
(1987). Note also that, on a strictly mereological view, it is neither here nor there for the sum or
fusion whether the elements are together in one place.

Relative identity theorists are apt to claim for their view of such puzzles as Theseus' ship a
particular naturalness. Griffin in *Relative Identity*, p. 178, provides what he calls the 'simple and
appealing' solution that the original ship of Theseus is not the same ship as the reconstruction,
though it is the same plank collection. There is then nothing peculiar at all about the case. The
reader will have to decide for himself whether it is a virtue or a vice in the relative theory that it
so easily distances the disputants from the issue which they suppose they disagree about – and
from the ontology of absolute identity.

[18] For careful discussion of some of these issues, see Brian Smart, 'How to Reidentify the Ship of
Theseus', *Analysis*, 32. 5 (April 1972), pp. 145–8, and 'The Ship of Theseus, the Parthenon, and
Disassembled Objects', *Analysis*, 34.1 (Oct. 1973), pp. 24–7. But see also the response by Francis
W. Dauer, 'How not to reidentify the Parthenon', *Analysis*, 33 (1972–3), p. 63.

[19] There may then be a temptation to dismiss the question as merely psychological. But we must
not confuse the fact that it is in some sense a psychological matter whether we ourselves come to
adopt the priests' or the archaeologists' view with its being a merely psychological matter which
one is Theseus' ship – or an arbitrary matter. Compare Frege (1950), §26:

The objectivity of the North Sea is not affected by the fact that it is a matter of our arbitrary
choice which part of all the water on the earth's surface we mark off and elect to call the 'North
Sea'. This is no reason for deciding to investigate the North Sea by psychological methods . . .

This third view seems as unsatisfactory as the uncritical ship-continuity view and the antiquarian-cum-mereological view. Let us call it the naïve conceptualist view. Admittedly it divorces the antiquarian view, sensibly enough, from crude mereologism. But in the process it makes the antiquarian view seem unstable. By its nature antiquarianism looks back to Theseus. But Theseus looked forward to the priests who would continue the cult he took himself to be establishing. The competing conceptions of Theseus' ship really are rival views. Philosophical quietism is a sensible outlook upon some questions, but in the present case it does not convince. We need at least one more idea.

4. TWO APPROACHES TO THE PROBLEM OF ARTEFACT IDENTITY

Two further methods suggest themselves for the resolution of such difficulties. These will define a fourth and a fifth view of the example. The fifth will emerge in the form of an improved application of the unity/continuity of form view advocated in this book. The fourth is an alternative approach widely adopted in the present-day literature of identity and individuation.[20] This runs contrary to the spirit of Chapter Two and involves our seeing a certain further complexity in the notion of f-coincidence.

The fourth view proposes that we start with the relation in which x and y stand just in case y is a coincidence-*candidate* (of type f) for identity with x. We then say that y *veritably coincides under* f *with* x if and only if y *is an* f-*coincidence candidate for identity with* x *and nothing distinct from* y *is as good an* f-*coincidence candidate for identity with* x *as* y *is.* If one wanted to proceed like this, one could then elaborate an account of the degrees of strength in a candidature, and arrange to distinguish best from second best, third best . . . claimants. In application to the present case, the best candidate theorist might say (i) that, where Theseus' ship is constantly repaired without any retrieval of the parts that are shed, the working ship persists into an open future; (ii) that, where a ship is reconstituted and the

---

If we say 'The North Sea is 10,000 square miles in extent' . . . we assert something quite objective, which is independent of our ideas and everything of the sort. If we should happen to wish, on another occasion, to draw the boundaries of the North Sea differently . . . that would not make false the same content that was previously true. (Cf. Dummett (1973), p. 576.)

[20] I am indebted to my colleague Naci Mehmet for persuading me to take this approach more seriously than once I did and helping me to understand it better. He will wish me to enter the normal disclaimers on his behalf.

working ship is no more, the reconstituted ship is Theseus' ship; (iii) that, where a ship is reconstituted from discarded planks but the working ship is not destroyed and continues working, the working ship is Theseus' ship and persists into an open future. (These decisions reflect the perceived strengths of considerations that are meant to count, however defeasibly, in favour of an identity.)

In the application to our case, the best candidate proposal, so given, perpetuates some questionable preferences, especially concerning the working ship. (Does it really not matter, as in (i), provided that the working ship continues and is the sole candidate, what changes the candidate undergoes? Could Theseus' ship continue in the shape of a Dutch barge or a Chinese junk?) But the proposal might easily be hedged or qualified. Nor is it necessary to take exception to the fact that the best candidate theorist's method is dialectical or (in the correct and non-condemnatory sense) casuistic. The chief objection is rather that this approach proves inappropriate, as so far characterized, to questions of identity. The most general form of the objection is this. *In notionally pursuing object a in order to ascertain its coincidence or non-coincidence with b, or in retracing the past history of b to ascertain its identity link with a, I ought not to need to concern myself with things that are other than a or other than b.* This is not to deny that singling *a* out or singling *b* out may involve contrasting *a* or *b* with a background of other things. But the identity of *a* with *a*, of *b* with *b*, and of *a* with *b*, once we are clear which things *a* and *b* are, ought to be a matter strictly between *a* and *b* themselves. Let us call this **D**(x) or the *Only a and b* rule and adjoin it to the other **D** principles of Chapter Two.[21] In its official form – see the sentence italicized above, as glossed by the two succeeding sentences – this is not a principle that is stated in the object language. Contrast **D**, **D**(i), **D**(ii), **D**(iii). It is akin to **D**(iv) or **D**(v). It is a dialectical rule for the adjudication of persistence and coincidence claims founded in the nature of the identity relation.

Consider the cases (ii) and (iii) mentioned in the last paragraph but one. Here it is supposed that the reconstituted ship claims identity with Theseus' ship; and whether this title is accorded to it or not depends at least in part on the presence or absence of the working ship. Does that contravene the *Only a and b* rule proposed in the previous paragraph? It

---

[21] Compare Bernard Williams (1960), a discussion antedating in the philosophical literature of identity the rediscovery of Miss Barcan's proof (1947), of the necessity of identity. See also his (1970), pp. 161–80. At *Philosophical Explanations* (Oxford, 1981), pp. 32–5, Robert Nozick animadverts sceptically upon this insight of Williams's. But I do not think he measures up to its full logico-metaphysical rationale.

appears that it does. In the present version, the best candidate theory sees the reconstituted ship as a *weaker* claimant than the working ship.[22] If so, then the working ship candidate and the reconstruction candidate must be distinct. But then (as remarked) the reconstruction's identity with Theseus' ship, wherever it is identical, seems to depend on a third thing.

I should expect that, at this point, someone will ask why one should not simply reword the fourth view. Why not say that, where the claim of the reconstituted ship is good, namely in case (ii), this ship, precisely by reassembling Theseus' ship, *ipso facto* reconstructs a ship that was at one point a working ship, was constantly repaired, then broke up (though some of its parts were recovered)? That suggestion, it will be said, has the effect of preserving the *Only a and b* rule. And I agree that it does. But to preserve the rule in this way effectively dispenses altogether with the best candidate formulation. (See below, the fifth view.) The reconstructed ship is Theseus' ship, if that can be made out, not because it is the best candidate for the role but because it is in this reconstruction from the original materials that the effort to track Theseus' ship from its beginning onwards finds Theseus' very ship. One finds the ship that is Theseus' ship *and* thereby one finds a ship that was reconstituted by restoring to Theseus' ship, after accidents that befell it at some intermediate moment, original planks and materials.

The only candidate

Someone who was as sure as Hobbes was that working ship and reconstituted ship could coexist might try to salvage the *rivality* that the best candidate view assumes by asking us to consider the reassembled ship 'on its own' – or as it might have been if it had been put together before the breaking up of the working ship. But that only starts more trouble. Do we want to say of this reconstruction that it is premature but, if only it had appeared later, it would have been identical with Theseus' ship? Or do we want to say that at the break-up of the working ship, the prematurely reassembled ship *becomes* identical with Theseus' ship? (Can literal sense be made of being not identical at one moment and then

---

[22] For that which is surprising in the very idea of weaker and stronger claimants, compare Arnauld, letter of 13 May 1686 to Leibniz:

> I can as little conceive of different varieties of myself and a circle whose diameters are not all of equal length. The reason is that these different varieties of myself would all be distinct from one another, otherwise there would not be many of them. Thus one of these varieties of myself would necessarily not be me: which is manifestly a contradiction. (Gerhardt II, 30, translated by H. T. Mason.)

becoming identical?[23]) Neither of these suggestions is at all promising. Let us remember that the title in question is not the title to the sobriquet 'Theseus' ship'. It is the title to identity with Theseus' ship, a particular ship originating from the eighth century BC.

Similar troubles arise for the best candidate view where the finding is that we have case (iii), namely the working ship's defeating the candidate by reconstitution. The best candidate theorist says that the working ship is Theseus' ship by virtue of its being a stronger candidate than the reconstructed ship. That infringes the *Only a and b* rule. Of course, we can respect the rule better if we can find some other basis on which to say that the working ship is indeed Theseus' ship. But here we must remember that this other basis might have nothing to do with the relative 'strength' or 'weakness' of the claims of reconstituted ships against working ships. One might say instead that, in tracking Theseus' ship through its journeys and various repairs, one comes upon the working ship, not a reconstruction from original materials. The idea of candidacy and strength of candidacy could, of course, be restored to the scene by someone's pointing insistently to the reconstructed ship, and describing its claims as not quite good enough, etc. But once that line is preferred, there is further trouble. We are laid open to the thought that this reconstructed ship, now lying in Piraeus, this very ship – if only the working ship, which is the so-called 'better candidate', were not still extant and plying once yearly to Delos – *would have been* Theseus' ship. Someone might perhaps say that. But the idea that on these terms, namely the simple absence of the stronger contender, the ship now deemed the worse candidate would have been Theseus' ship itself seems

Right

[23] I will give an argument that literal sense ought not to be made. Suppose that we can make sense of *a* and *b*'s being identical *at time t*, or

$$a = b$$
$$f, t$$

Suppose then that it is true that

$$a = b$$
$$f, t$$

and suppose that, in addition to existing at *t*, *a* will also exist at t′. Then so will *b* exist at t′. For *a* is at *t* the same f as *b* is. So

$$a = b$$
$$f, t'$$

Indeed, anything that can be truly said at t about *a* can be truly said about *b* too, whether the thing said be past, present or future. Either that or we don't know what it is for *a* and *b* to be identical at t. How then can temporal identity require anything less than full Leibnizian congruence. Generalizing then, we have for any f,

$$\exists t \left(\frac{a = b}{f, t} \right) \rightarrow \forall t' \left(\frac{a = a}{f, t'} \rightarrow \frac{a = b}{f, t'} \right).$$

to be absurd. There is a temptation to add as a separate modal step: nothing might have been a different entity from the entity it actually is. (Compare Chapter Four, §3.) But it is the utter oddity of such a claim about the weaker candidate that discovers to us the real intuitive grounds for doubting that anything might have been a numerically different entity from the one it actually is. The absurdity of the idea confounds the understanding of '=' that is implicit in everything we think and say about identity. If the issue is one of what founds what, then the impossibility of conceiving of an entity's not being identical with that with which it is in fact identical seems to be the real foundation for the modal claim, rather than the other way about.

A simple conclusion suggests itself – that the best candidate theory, lacking obvious means to talk sensibly or intelligibly about plural candidates for identity, must cede place to a theory that identifies, for a given circumstance and a given question of identity, the best way to think of a thing and the best way to track the thing. Preferably this will be a theory that excludes, by its operation and application, the very possibility of distinct *rivals* for identity with Theseus' ship. Such a theory will surely regulate the dialectic of same and different by the *Only a and b* rule. An adherent of this fifth view will say that $\mathbf{D}(x)$ could only be abandoned on pain of forswearing any claim to the effect that the dialectic just spoken is a dialectic of real sameness and difference.[24]

The search for the fifth view already promised and hinted at may usefully take off from a simple reflection: the problem with which Theseus' ship confronts us is that of conjoining the ordinary commonsensically strict notion of identity with the commonsensically loose requirements that we place upon artefact persistence. Even if we are to relax cautiously the demands we have been placing on artefact identity or we are to recognize the tolerance that so many of our conceptual practices require and in real life rarely abuse, we can scarcely grant ordinary artefact concepts or the things that satisfy them an indefinite tolerance of disassembly, repair, discontinuance of function, *and* part replacement. Unless we grasp this nettle, and are prepared for some degree of reform, either of concepts or of the philosophical account we give ourselves of our concepts, we shall not disarm Hobbes's ship paradox. Will this mean that we are faced here with a stark choice between abandoning the laws

---

[24] This is not of course to deny that a third thing may be *evidentially* relevant (as in detective reasoning) to the question whether $a = b$. For further discussion of $\mathbf{D}(x)$ see Harold Noonan, 'Wiggins, Artefact Identity and Best Candidate Theories' and 'The only X and Y Principle', both in *Analysis*, 45 (1985). But see also Nathan Salmon (1981), pp. 219–29.

of identity and abandoning – in the spirit of the maxim *no entity without identity* – the received ontology and ideology of artefacts? That fearful outcome is to some extent anticipated in the high metaphysical tradition of substance that seeks, for related reasons, to demote artefacts from the status of genuine entities.[25] But in truth, the data before us suggest a much less exciting conclusion.

Suppose that we forget analogies with living substances and, running to the opposite extreme, we remake our conception of artefact persistence on the model of the identity-condition for quantities that has been proposed by Helen Morris Cartwright.[26] The condition she proposes does not exclude change, but it excludes all addition or subtraction of matter whatever. As remodelled and adapted to the formulation of a persistence condition for artefacts, this condition would need to be made more demanding in one way, in order for it to require some however vestigial continuance of the thing's capacity to subserve the roles or ends the artefact was designed (as that very artefact) to subserve. (Cf. **D**(v).) On the other hand, the 'no subtraction' condition could be relaxed somewhat without our confronting the risk that condition **D**(vi) will be breached. Even on these revised terms, the possibility can still be excluded of competition à la Hobbes between different candidates for identity with Theseus' ship. Some of an artefact's matter may perhaps be exchanged with matter from its surroundings, provided that all replacement of material parts is referred back to the first state of the finished artefact, and provided only, if the reader will forgive the comical precision of this first attempt, the artefact retains more than half of that original matter (or provided that it retains, where such is definable, the material of some individuatively paramount *nucleus*). Under this condition there will never be more than one claimant to the title of ship of Theseus. Under this condition, it can remain determinate whether the ship of Theseus itself has been traced effectively through time. (For the requirement of determinacy, see Chapter Six, §4, thesis (iv).) Finally, by reference to some strict condition like the one we began with or some

---

[25] Aristotle maintained that natural things are the real beings par excellence to which everything else is secondary. Leibniz maintained that the title of real unity must be reserved to 'animate bodies endowed with primitive entelechies'. Cf. Leibniz, *Nouveau Essais*, 3.6.24: 'It is true that there appear to be species which are not really *unum per se* (i.e. bodies endowed with a genuine unity or with an indivisible being which makes up their whole active principle), any more than a mill or a watch could be . . .': 3.6.42. 'In a word, perfect unity should be reserved for animate bodies, or bodies endowed with primary entelechies; for such entelechies bear some analogy to souls and are as indivisible and imperishable as souls are.' Cf. also 2.24.1, on which see R. Coburn (1976). For further discussion, see my (1995), p. 242.

[26] See Helen Morris Cartwright (1970), pp. 25–42.

modification of that, it becomes possible to see our linguistic practices as underhung by a sort of safety net that justifies the confidence we feel in our capacity for controlled opportunism. The lesson we find ourselves learning from Hobbes is one that we can see to be reasonable in itself, namely that the 'unity of form' conception of individuation needs to be carefully constrained in its application to things that evolve in a way that is not nomologically controlled and that submit to repair by replacement of parts. The question of their persistence needs to be stringently regulated by considerations relating to change of matter. (This is not, however, an essentialist claim. It relates only to the limitations upon change. See below Chapter Four, §11. Nor yet is it surprising.[27] See Chapter Six, §6.)

I do not want to claim too much for the fifth approach. It is doubtful whether any admissible relaxation of the strict condition we began from can be guaranteed to account for each and every judgment of artefact identity by which we are rationally tempted. But in respect of the more audacious judgments of artefact identity, where the concept will exceed its strength and take us too far from the original function or material constitution of the artefact, the time has come to point out that it is not at all obvious that the judgments in question always do demand to be read literally as statements of identity. When someone gives his watch to the watchmaker to clean and repair, the thing he wants back may, on a very sober and literal minded construal, be either that very watch (by the unproblematic criterion) or else a watch with a certain obvious relation to his (a watch of the same kind, in better working order, enjoying considerable community of parts, etc.). If he wants more than that, if he thinks of his watch as an antiquarian or historical relic from a better age or as a work from the hand of a great artist, then he should take more precautions than we normally do take. He should care about its original constitution. The truth is though that, for some practical purposes, we simply do not mind very much about the difference between artefact survival and artefact replacement. (A negligence that in no way undermines the real distinction between these.)

So much for how matters seem to stand with the normal artefacts which, in everyday life and outside the museum, we freely permit to

---

[27] It is not surprising in itself. But one or two of its consequences may surprise (in advance at least of legitimate qualification). Where the repairs to a working ship are reaching their constitutive limit, you will not always be able to tell by one careful look whether the ship in front of you is the same as the ship you saw yesterday. There is moreover one conceivable circumstance where carrying a plank from one place to another and joining it to a reconstruction that is in progress from discarded original planks will count as shifting Theseus' ship itself from one place to the other.

be repaired, altered and (without our realizing it very well) replaced. But could there not be artefact concepts that were less permissive in their definition (as required by **D**(iv) and **D**(v)), were more like natural kind terms in the specificity of what they required of their instances, and did not raise the problems that are raised by artefacts that are subject to disassembly, part-replacement and discontinuance of function? The answer to this question is that there surely could be. True, I have not been able to find any normal artefact concepts which require of their exemplifications anything remotely analogous to unremitting obedience to some specialized principle of activity that conditions the sense of the artefactual substantive itself. There is, however, one very special kind of artefact whose survival-requirement is extremely detailed and specific. This is the work of art. We shall postpone the special features of this and cognate concepts until the last section of Chapter Four, where we shall maintain that the conceptual need which a natural law will supply for the identity of a natural thing but not for an ordinary artefact kind, the artist's conception of his activity and its eventual product can supply for the work of art. But works of art and their like are in a special class of their own among artefacts, and most especially perhaps for purposes of the theory of individuation.

Rather than explore this or other analogies with the principle of activity of a natural substance (e.g. the analogy furnished by such social arte-facts as an *administration*, or a *governing body* recruited and replenished by a formal procedure) or seek to extend further the discussions begun in this chapter, [28] it is time to provide an outline of what is supposed to have been achieved in the first three chapters.

5. SUMMARY OF CONCLUSIONS TO DATE: AND A METHODOLOGICAL REMARK

(i) The formal properties of identity, both '$=$' and '$\underset{f}{=}$' and 'the same something as', are transitivity, reflexivity, symmetry, and the congruence defined by Leibniz's Law, although the dyadic relational predicates 'is the same as' and 'is, for some f, the same f as' have a content that amounts to more than could be explained, to one who lacked the

---

[28] Since the time when this chapter was first laid out, the most important new contribution to these questions of criteria of identity is that of Timothy Williamson, *Identity and Discrimination* (Oxford, 1990).

concept of identity altogether, by a bare rehearsal of these principles.[29] A fortiori, the principles themselves are not dispensable.

(ii) If (i) above is true, then **R** is false.

(iii) There are two distinct standpoints from which **D** as stated at the beginning of Chapter Two can be maintained. It may be held that *a* could be the same f as *b* without being the same g. That is the philosophical contention **R**. Or it may be held that to say what *a* is is to subsume *a* under a predicate which either gives *a*'s principle of continuity and individuation – its principle of activity or its mode of functioning – or else restricts some other predicate that gives this principle. This principle furnishes the wherewith to vindicate the absoluteness of identity.

---

[29] See Chapter Two, §1, and Chapter Six, §10. Neither there nor in the sentence to which this footnote is affixed do I seek to controvert Quine's claim that, for a given language, 'we can settle objectively and absolutely what predicate to count as the identity predicate, *if any*, once we have settled what notations to count as quantifiers, variables and the truth functions . . . The requirements [on treating] an open sentence '$\phi\, x\, y$' as '$x = y$' are strong reflexivity and substitutivity . . . If 'ϕ' and 'ψ' both meet [these] requirements . . ., then they are coextensive'. See 'A Reply to Professor Marcus' in *Ways of Paradox* (New York, 1966), p. 178.

Quine's claim itself is not to be gainsaid. But the two words I have italicized, namely 'if any', are not unimportant. They need to be there, as Quine points out, because it may be that in a given language *no* open sentence in 'x' and 'y' is strongly reflexive and substitutive. There is also another reason why they have to be there. This too can be put in Quine's words: 'If the universe is taken as that of persons, and the predicates are interpreted in ways depending on nothing but people's incomes then the proposed manner of defining '$x = y$' will equate any persons who have equal incomes; so here indeed is an unfavourable case where '$x = y$' [defined in the manner indicated here and in 'Reply to Professor Marcus'] does not come out with the sense of genuine identity.' (W. V. Quine (1963), §1, p. 15.)

The first conclusion that I draw from the difficulty that Quine acknowledges is that one cannot say perfectly generally that the sense of '=' in a given language L is exhausted by the fact that it is a reflexive relation and a congruence relation with respect to L-predicates. (Compare Chapter Six, §9.) The second thing I think I see here is support for something I have already contended: namely that questions about identity and questions about kinds of thing are not clearly extricable from one another. The indefinable primitive forms '$x = y$' and 'x is an f' need one another. Each must be present for the other to operate. See Preamble (*ad fin.*).

Whatever Quine might say about these conclusions, they are oblique to Quine's interests in the passage I have cited. He goes on to consider there the suggestion that matters might be straightened out by reconstruing the members of the universe as whole income groups. (Cf. (1953), p. 70.) He says that, whether or not we do that, 'no discrepancies between [the surrogate for identity] and genuine identity can be registered in terms of the theory itself'. I don't think this last would furnish everything he needed to one who wanted to dismantle the identity relation into reflexiveness and congruence. But in the background is something else that is well worth questioning: namely whether absolutely everything that grounds interpretation for a given language must be such as to register in the explicit predicative repertoire of the language itself. It would not suffice for these purposes to say (plausibly enough and in line with everything we have said in Chapters Two and Three) that there is a process by which an interpreter's implicit or practical understanding of the role of language in the life and conduct of its speakers can be made *more and more* explicit. For, first, the process may not terminate. Secondly, in so far as the process does not terminate and the predicative resources and repertoire of the language are constantly extended towards semantic saturation, the intended definition of surrogate identity given by means of exhaustion of predicates will never *quite* be available. See further Chapter Six, §10.

(iv) The absoluteness just spoken of is vindicated as follows. A substance-predicate's standing by virtue of its sense for a kind f as in (iii) ensures this: that a's coincidence with b under the concept f will imply the community of all of a's and b's predicates. In so far as this requirement on the sense of substance predicates is satisfied, it will follow that f-coincidence is not only an equivalence relation, but also a congruence relation. Indeed, nothing less will suffice for a theory of individuation of the continuants of our accepted ontology.

(v) The absoluteness requirement stated in (iv) is satisfied by concepts introduced by sortal predicates whose definition is extension-involving and deictic-nomological in the manner described by Leibniz, Putnam, Kripke and others. These are natural kind terms. The requirement is not so straightforwardly satisfied by ordinary artefact concepts, which are not extension-involving or nomologically founded. Artefact kinds confront us with serious problems. Here some revision of what might appear to be our current individuative practices or intuitions may seem to be required. But one suspects that tacitly these practices respect already some corresponding restriction. It may be that the most that is required is some revision of distorted or ill-considered conceptions that accord too little significance to the original matter of an artefact.

(vi) All this has been explained by talk of the coinciding of entities under a concept. The locution 'coincides', rare though it is by comparison with the other words and forms we are using it to elucidate, and technical though my use of it may be, is not an invented one. Whenever we have written 'x coincides with y under the concept f', our sentence could be rewritten (without loss of anything but the strictest synonymy and occasional convenience) in the form 'x coincides with y as an f – in the manner, that is, of an f'. The most this new version can do perhaps is to prompt a reader who thinks he needs something more to *remind himself* of what is there already, latent in his own irreducibly practical understanding of 'the same f'. For all I know, 'coincides' could drop out of the object language altogether if a better observed and more complete account were achieved of what it is to say what a thing is. But, pending that's being achieved, it is by talk of coinciding that one may hold substance, identity and individuation far enough apart to give a view of the many strands by which they are connected. Note especially here the relative perspicuity of the right-hand side of the schema by which 'coincides' is explicated in §1 of Chapter Two. (See especially there paragraph four.)

(vii) Neither in **D** as further elaborated nor in any other place has it been supposed that, in the normal business of making identity judgments, we deduce the judgment in question from other claims about other properties and relations. Judgments of identity are *sui generis* judgments. (They are refutable, no doubt, by reference to other properties and relations but they are not deductively based on them.) In their own way, they represent the prolongation and diversification of our powers of carrying out the practical business of singling out and keeping track of a thing. With this prolongation and diversification there comes into being a dialectic of same and other. It is the regulation of this dialectic of same and other by **D** principles, which *themselves* arise from the formal properties of identity, that qualifies the dialectic as centrally concerned at the levels of action and thought with the strict relations of identity and difference. **D** principles give partial expression to practical and logical norms for judging matters of persistence and non-persistence, identity and difference. These norms articulate the Leibnizian conception of identity that is stated in (i) (ii) (iii) (iv) and developed further in Chapter Six. Not least among the **D** principles (and central to that which marks identity off from other notions) is **D**(x), the *Only a and b* rule.

6. TRANSITION TO CHAPTERS FOUR AND FIVE

It will be instructive to try to apply all this to persons, to works of art and to other special cases of natural and artificial things. But, in advance of all that, the view of individuation that has begun to emerge must be brought into some relation with the larger questions of Realism, Idealism and Conceptualism to which a theory of individuation is finally answerable.

Call the philosopher who denies **R** and denies **D** the Bare Absolutist. Call the philosopher who accepts **R** the Relativist or **R**-theorist. Call an upholder of my position a **D**-Absolutist. Chapter Four draws out certain of the individuative and essentialist consequences of **D**-Absolutism. Chapter Five seeks to communicate my conviction that it is typical of the **R**-theorist to exaggerate the autonomy of thought in the singling out of objects of reference. In Chapter Five and then in Chapter Six, I try to create the conviction that, by contrast with the **R**-theorists, the Bare Absolutists, if they genuinely believe in continuants at all, are disposed by their denial of **D** to take too lightly the conceptual preconditions of singling out. I think of it as the role of the **D**-Absolutist to see the articulation of reality in a way that corrects both faults at once. The mind (you may feel moved to say) *conceptualizes* objects. Yet objects *impinge* upon the mind.[30] On the basis of this double claim, a new response will be mustered to the problems of identity and vagueness. When that has been done, the ground will have been cleared for an application of all these thoughts to the case of persons and their identity.

[30] One who defends such a thesis can scarcely fend off too soon certain misreadings of what he means to be committed to. Perhaps 'the mind conceptualizes objects' will appear to carry the suggestion that *the very same objects* could have been conceptualized in different ways, had the mind been differently constituted. But, if so, then the suggestion that appears to be carried is hereby cancelled. That is not what the sentence in the text means or implies. On these matters see further Chapters Five and Six.

If the sentence to which this footnote is annexed still seems to conflict with the sentence preceding, then it is worth reflecting that for the mind to 'conceptualize an object *x*' is not for it to construct *x*, or even for it to construe *x* (whatever that would mean). Rather (the person with) the mind, making sense (so far as possible) of divers lookings and explorings and perceivings, being ready to deploy clear indistinct ideas of sorts or kinds of thing (see note 6), *finds x* – which is not yet to say that *x* was the *only* thing there to be found. Almost always there will be other things there to be found.

CHAPTER FOUR

Individuative essentialism

Nature loves to hide.

> (Heraclitus, Diels fragment 123.)

We despise obvious things, but unobvious things often follow from obvious things.

> (Leibniz to de Volder, Gerhardt II, 183.)

I. INDEPENDENCE FROM THE EXPLICITLY MODAL OF THE FOREGOING THEORY OF INDIVIDUATION

Little or no use has been made up to this point of the notion of necessity. We have resisted the idea that a theory of individuation must be a set of judgments about all possible worlds, or occupy itself with problems that are special to the making of statements of explicit necessity *de dicto* or *de re*. In the case of the things that belong to natural kinds, we went to some lengths to show that, for all the purposes of identity and individuation that have concerned us so far, it is enough to have regard for the lawlike propensities of members of the kind. It is enough to look for true generalizations, open and counterfactual-sustaining, about the past, present and future entities of this world. (Enough and more than enough. Our practical understanding of identity and individuation makes do with less.) It is true that, in connexion with artefacts and at the point when the argument for the *Only a and b* Rule was introduced, something modal appeared to be involved. But in so far as modality obtruded itself there, it was consequential upon the pretheoretical perception of an absurdity that would be marked as such by almost anyone who reflected on the implications of the business of individuation.

Marking the end of modal abstinence, I now follow matters through to the 'essentialist' consequences of the theory of individuation

expounded in the preceding chapters. Someone who finds these consequences incredible will have the choice between criticizing the theory for
entailing them and criticizing the derivations now to be attempted. But
the final product will be an essentialism that is at once modest and (in
case that is thought to matter) austerely extensional. In the argument to
be offered here, which will not depend on the idea of reference to this
or that particular thing but on the necessary condition of that very
thing's being singled out from the rest of reality or individuated (not,
however, on the suspect idea that these necessary conditions will
combine to form a distinguishing or particularizing essence of the thing),
any gaps that the reader finds should be criticized under the head of
argumentative insufficiency. Deficiencies should not be supplied from
principles or premises offered by philosophies that aim for something
stronger. To the adherents of *possibilia*, substantive possible world theories or individual (particularized) essences, as to champions of essential-
isms that deliver easily or immediately the conceptual indispensability to
anything of its actual origin, the essentialism of particular substances
offered here may seem laughably modest or timid. But I am uncertain
of the rationale for maintaining anything stronger.

2. PRINCIPLES AND MAXIMS GOVERNING THE DERIVATION OF A MODEST ESSENTIALISM

First an enumeration of the principles and assumptions ((A) – (H)) that
will govern the derivation of essentialism to be attempted in later sections. By a derivation nothing very formal will be intended. (A) – (H)
simply prepare the way for a dialectical exploration of that to which we
are committed by our simplest thoughts about continuants and our simplest individuative practices:

(A) The first maxim is to dispense, in everything relating to the derivation, with *possibilia*. Compare Arnauld

I have no conception of these purely possible [individual] substances, that is to
say the ones that God will never create . . . One can conceive of possibilities in
the natures which he has created . . . but I am much mistaken if there is anyone
who dares to say that he can conceive of a purely possible substance, for I am
convinced in my own mind that, although one talks so much of these purely
possible substances, nonetheless one never conceives of any of them except
according to the notion of those which God has created.[1]

---

[1] Arnauld to Leibniz, 13 May 1686, Gerhardt II, 31–2, as translated by H. T. Mason. Cf. W. V.
Quine, 'On What There Is' in his (1953).

(B) The second principle is the requirement that the argument should be independent of (and go deeper than) the model theory of possible worlds.[2] In so far as possible worlds are mentioned, they are intended only as an expository device.

(Γ) The third principle or assumption I shall need is given succinctly by A. J. Ayer:

> We can significantly ask what properties it is necessary for something to possess in order to be of such and such kind . . . the answer may be to some extent arbitrary, but at least some answer can be looked for. On the other hand, there is no such definition of an individual.[3]

It is the consequence of this that, to make clear which thing thing *x* is, it is not enough, *pace* the friends of individual or particularized essences (by which I mean essences that it is supposed can be specified without the use of identity yet determine an identity) to say however lengthily that *x* is *such and such* or *so and so*. We have to say that *x* is *this* such and such, or *that* so and so. This is perfectly obvious when we think of trying to specify one particular entity by mentioning short or simple predicates (other than *identical with x* or the like). Is there any reason to believe that by making ordinary predicates ever longer and more complicated one will overcome the obvious non-sufficiency or non-necessity for identity with just *x* that infects all the relatively simple predicates true of *x*? Let us be realistic then and forget about individual or particularized essences.

(Δ) The fourth assumption or principle can again be given in alien words, again those of Arnauld[4] and Ayer (*ibid.*):

> I can think that I shall or shall not take a particular journey, while remaining very much assured that neither one nor the other will prevent my being myself. So I remain very much assured that neither one nor the other is included in the individual concept of myself.

> [But] we have to maintain some anchorage in reality if our references are to be successful . . . There appear to be no *general* rules for deciding what this anchorage may be . . . One could imagine that the Pyramids were built at a different time, or perhaps even in a different country. If one anchors Dickens to

---

[2] See Williamson in Lovibond and Williams (1996), p. 3 and following.
[3] *The Central Questions of Philosophy* (London, 1973), p. 197.
[4] The source of the quotation is the same letter from Arnauld to Leibniz, Gerhardt II, 33, translated by H. T. Mason. My citation of Arnauld should not be taken as tantamount to agreement with him about the interpretation of Leibniz. Leibniz was not an essentialist. See my (1987a). It would have clarified his purposes to distinguish always, as he sometimes did, between the Leibnizian concept of an individual and the essence of that individual. Always, though, Leibniz insists on the contingency of my going or not going on a journey (say).

other items in his biography, one can conceive of his not having been a writer: if one identifies him by his writings one can perhaps conceive of his having lived in a different century. But could we consistently place him in the distant future, or in prehistoric times? . . . It is a rather arbitrary question in this sort of case.

Appearances perhaps to the contrary, one positive thing Ayer is claiming here does not depend upon the theory of reference as such. Nor does it depend (even if Ayer expresses the point in a way that invites this charge of confusion) upon a denial that one can counterfactually conceive at *t* of some individual *x* not having the properties by which, for the purpose of conceiving at *t* of *x*'s being otherwise, one identifies this *x* in the actual world. Rather the point is that, if serious conceiving is to have to do with real metaphysical possibility and it is excluded that a given thing can be just anything, then we shall need to arrive at an understanding of conceiving that yields the following conclusion–: For any entity, there are properties or complexes of properties such that nothing could count as conceiving of that entity as possessing them; likewise properties or complexes of properties such that nothing could count as conceiving of the entity as lacking them.[5] It is among the things brought to light by the Chapter Three discussion of **D**(x), the *Only a and b* Rule, that one of the excluded conceivings is the conceiving of a thing as not the very individual that it is. That point will now be argued further, as will the exclusion of the conceiving of an individual's having a different principle of individuation from its actual principle.

The positive point of agreement between Ayer and me may be set out as follows then. Where a thinker A conceives of an individual *x* as ϕ (and by moving from 'refer' to 'conceive of' we can only make Ayer's claim more foundational), ϕ cannot assume just any value. There are restrictions on ϕ and they depend on which entity in particular the entity *x* is. What we have in (Δ) is not a reduction or elimination of necessity and possibility (that is not our purpose), but the following elucidation of possibility and necessity *de re*:

---

[5] The idea of metaphysical or conceptual possibility invoked here is the dual of metaphysical or conceptual necessity. (Which is not to say that the latter is our sole route of access to it.) The conceptual necessity of things being thus or so must not be confused with or assimilated to the analyticity of the sentence that says that things are thus or so. Nor must concepts be assimilated to meanings understood *a priori*. The concept of a *horse* or *tree* is an *a posteriori* concept. The truths involving horses or trees that are truths one has to be aware of in order to grasp fully the concept *horse* or *tree* (i.e. in order to get an in any way adequate conception of the concept *horse* or *tree*) are *a posteriori* truths. Those truths are semantically enabling for that kind of discourse. Here, in saying this, it may be that we exceed any claim Ayer could even have contemplated approving. (For more on these questions, see Preamble, §7.)

(i) x could be ϕ if and only if it is possible to conceive of x's being ϕ, where the intended acceptation of the verb 'conceive' ($\approx$ 'think right through and in such a way as to count oneself as impeded by any incoherences or contradictions') is to be worked out in tandem with the sober essentialism that is here and now to be excogitated (see below, footnote 20);

(ii) x must be ϕ if and only if it is not possible to conceive of x being not ϕ;

(iii) The position of the boundary between what one can conceive of x and what one cannot conceive of x depends on x, i.e. depends on which thing or what thing the thing x *actually* is; the position of this boundary may depend on a matter of degree, or appear to be somewhat arbitrary; in which case, it must be unsurprising that at least some of the properties that it is definitely impossible (i.e. well beyond the last point of possibility) to conceive of x's not having are rather *unspecific*.

(E) The next guiding principle for the construction to be attempted is that the relational claim *A conceives of x's being ϕ* or *A conceives of (λz) (z is ϕ) of the entity x* may be cleared of all extensionalist and nominalist suspicions by viewing its connexion with *A conceives that* on the model of Quine's theory of the relation holding between *believing of* and *believing that*.[6] The relation we are concerned with is between the thinker A, the entity x (however described), and an attribute $\hat{z}$ (fz) or $(\lambda z)(fz)$. The relation is triadic. (Quine has shown how, at a certain price, the attribute which is its third term can be nominalistically reconstrued, but nominalism is not the issue here.) Similarly, 'x is such that it is possible to conceive (λz) (z is ϕ) of x' represents a complex dyadic relation between x and this attribute.

(Z) Ordinary intuitive grammar suggests that 'necessarily' and 'possibly' can either govern a complete sentence (as in sentences that submit naturally to treatment within what Quine calls the second grade of modal involvement, namely complete sentences lying wholly within the scope of 'necessarily') or govern a simple or complex predicate. (Or might they somehow govern the predicative tie by which one who makes an essentialist attribution seeks to link the subject of his attribution and some property? I shall not enter into the question here of whether, strictly speaking, the 'necessarily' qualifies copula or predicate.) If it is asked what is meant by the latter usage, which lies outside all grades of

---

[6] See 'Quantifiers and Propositional Attitudes', *Journal of Philosophy*, 53 (1955), reprinted in *Ways of Paradox* (New York, 1966), at pp. 183–94. For an important amplification of the theory, see Brian Loar, 'Reference and Propositional Attitudes', *Philosophical Review* (1972), p. 57.

modal involvement approved by Quine,[7] then I reply first that this is something the reader is already familiar with, under the verbal forms '*x* can be ϕ', '*x* could be ϕ' and 'it is possible for *x* to be ϕ'; secondly, that (Δ) above was already a partial elucidation of some such usage; thirdly, that anyone who speaks English is already deeply committed to a whole range of locutions that resemble this one in lying outside Quine's canon.[8] For, if we supplant *de re* 'possibly ϕ' and 'necessarily ϕ' by 'can/could (be) ϕ' and 'must (be) ϕ' ('cannot / could not help but (be) ϕ') we shall notice that, so far as logical form goes, they seem to have formal affinities with the *de re* predicates of ability, obligation, capacity or disposition, which people who have heard nothing of possible worlds apply effortlessly to the actual things of the actual world when they say that A can do otherwise than he is doing, that D could not help but strike C, or that X, Y and Z are soluble or fragile or fusible.[9] None of these claims has a natural *de dicto* translation.

(H) I represent with the sign NEC the undifferentiated *de re* 'must' or 'necessarily' that I presume to underlie as a genus the various species of *de re* concept. For the corresponding *de re* 'can' and 'possibly' I use the sign POSS. NEC and POSS are interpreted here as working with predicates abstracted in a manner now to be described.[10] To form the expressions

---

[7] See W. V. Quine, 'Three Grades of Modal Involvement', *Proceedings of the XIth International Congress of Philosophy. Brussels 1953*, Vol. XIV (Amsterdam: North Holland Publishing Co., 1953) reprinted in *Ways of Paradox* (see footnote 6), p. 157. See also 'Reference and Modality' in Quine (1953), 1st edn (this essay was rewritten for the 1961 edition).

[8] Compare Ian Hacking (1975) for an analysis which is amenable to the same semantical treatment and delivers the same results as the present chapter seeks to establish.

    The truth predicate is defined for a language containing this 'necessarily' in my 'The *De Re* "Must": A Note on the Logical Form of Essentialist Claims', and for a richer language containing it by C. A. B. Peacocke in 'Appendix to David Wiggins' "The De Re 'Must'"', both in *Truth and Meaning: Essays in Semantics*, ed. Gareth Evans and John McDowell (Oxford, 1976). See also my (1979).

    For the idea of treating 'necessarily' as a modifier of predicates, or (which is not quite the same) of the copula, see 'The Identity of Propositions', in Geach (1972), p. 174; R. Cartwright, 'Some Remarks on Essentialism', *Journal of Philosophy*, 65 (1968); Wiggins (1967), p. 42; R. Stalnaker and R. Thomason, 'Abstraction in First Order Modal Logic', *Theoria*, 3 (1968); G. E. Hughes and M. J. Cresswell, *An Introduction to Modal Logic* (London, 1968), note 131; John Woods 'Essentialism, Self-Identity and Quantifying In', in *Identity and Individuation*, ed. Milton K. Munitz (New York, 1971); Wiggins (1974). See also Christopher Kirwan, 'How Strong are the Objections to Essence?', *Proceedings of the Aristotelian Society*, 71 (1970–1); Tyler Burge, 'Belief *De Re*', *Journal of Philosophy* (1977). For the historic sources of this view of the matter, see for instance Aristotle, *Prior Analytics* 30^{a15-23}, *De Interpretatione* 21^{b26ff}; *De Sophisticis Elenchis* 166^{a23-3a}.

[9] See also pp. 349–50 of Wiggins (1974).

[10] The decision to signal these occurrences specially by this particular notation begins without prejudice either for or against the appropriateness of $\square$ and $\lozenge$ to this role. The decision leaves it open whether the pairs NEC and $\square$ and POSS and $\lozenge$ will prove to be related as an ordinary truth-definition for open and closed sentences involving the logical constants relates (say) predicate-negation and sentence-negation.

to which NEC and POSS are to apply we take any open sentence, say 'x is a man' or 'if x is a man then x has the property G' or 'x is identical with y', and bind the free variable or free variables in the open sentence with an abstraction operator λ. Thus: $(\lambda x)[\text{Man } x]$ or $(\lambda x)[\text{Man } x \rightarrow Gx]$ or $(\lambda x)(\lambda y)\,[x=y]$. These abstracts may be read 'the property that any x has just if x is a man', 'the property that any x has just if, if x is a man, then x has property G', 'the relation in which any x and y stand just if x is y' respectively.

We may now express the judgment that an entity or a sequence of entities $\langle \ldots \rangle$ falls in the extension of some property or relation so designated as follows:

Caesar has $(\lambda x)\,[\text{Man } x]$
Everything has the property $(\lambda x)\,[M(x) \rightarrow G(x)]$
$\langle$the evening star, the morning star$\rangle$ have $(\lambda x)\,(\lambda y)\,[x=y]$,

or, more handily and conventionally, we may exercise the option to employ a simple juxtaposition of the λ-term and a subject term, to be marked by angle brackets, thus:

$(\lambda x)\,[\text{Man } x],\,\langle\text{Caesar}\rangle$
$(\forall z)\,((\lambda x)\,[M(x) \rightarrow G(x)],\,\langle z \rangle)$
$(\lambda x)\,(\lambda y)\,[x=y],\,\langle$the evening star, the morning star$\rangle$.

So far these are mere λ-equivalents of simpler sentences. But putting NEC or POSS to work on these abstracts, and leaving the subject term incontrovertibly outside the scope of the modality, we have

$[\text{NEC } (\lambda x)\,[Mx]],\,\langle\text{Caesar}\rangle$
$(\forall z)\,([\text{NEC } (\lambda x)\,[M(x) \rightarrow G(x)]],\,\langle z \rangle)$
$[\text{NEC } (\lambda x)\,(\lambda y)\,[x=y]],\,\langle$the evening star, the morning star$\rangle$.

The last says that the evening star and the morning star necessarily have the relation that any x and y have if and only if they are identical. It is a second level sentence introduced by means of λ-abstraction. More colloquially and idiomatically, it says that it is necessary for the evening star and morning star to be identical. Informally, there is much use of such versions in this book. Indeed I would emphasize that the modal enrichment of the first order logical framework by modality and second level notions is explained in the English vernacular. Once the second level framework is in place, however, the official explication runs in the language of properties and the having of properties – and predicate letters take on the official role of variables. In this way things are managed in such a way that the *de re* 'necessarily' starts life with credentials no worse than those of Quine's relational senses of saying and believing (already referred to in (E) above). Just as Ralph believes of the man in the brown hat (or of the man seen at the beach; it makes no difference, for they are identical) that he has the property or attribute λx (x is a spy), or just as the man in the brown hat (*alias* the man at the beach) is universally believed to have the attribute spyhood – so, in this *prima facie* innocuous sense of 'necessarily', Caesar (or the conqueror of Gaul, or the consul of 69 BC, it makes no difference how you refer to him and it makes no difference what philosophical account is given of definite descriptions) is necessarily such that he has the attribute *man*. Following the parallel, we can say that the relational '[NEC (λx) [Mx]], ⟨Caesar⟩' stands to notional '□ (Man (Caesar))' as the relational 'Of Caesar is universally believed (λx) [Man x]' (≈ 'It is universally believed of Caesar that he is a man') stands to the notional 'It is universally believed that (Man (Caesar))'. Compare (E) above.

At the point where the λ-abstraction operator first appears, let one example and five equivalents illustrate the two-way rule under which it operates:

(a)   Caesar is a man
(b)   Caesar has the property of being a man
(a′)   Man (Caesar)
(b′)   (λx) (Man x), <Caesar>
(c)   the value for the argument Caesar of the function from objects to truth-values (λx) (Man x) is the truth-value *true*.

English permits the two-way transition between (a) and (b). The λ-abstraction rule permits a similar two-way transition between (a′) and (b′).

3. THE NECESSITY OF IDENTITY AND THE NECESSITY OF DIFFERENCE

Taking Leibniz's Law in a second-level form

For all F such that F is a genuine property of x or y,
$(x = y) \rightarrow (x$ has $F \equiv y$ has $F)$

and making the assumption (against which no argument from opacity or unintelligibility now presses) that NEC properties are genuine derived properties, let us begin by obtaining a proof of the complete coincidence of the necessary satisfaction and the actual satisfaction of the predicate of identity. In other words, let us try to construct the NEC counterpart of the quantified modal theorem, sometimes controverted:

$$(\forall x)\,(\forall y)\,((x=y)\to\Box\,(x=y)).$$

Consider any individuals H and P (Hesperus and Phosphorus say) such that

$$H = P.$$

Now H is necessarily H, so the following is a truth about H:

$$[\text{NEC } \lambda x\,\lambda y\,(x=y)],\,\langle H,H\rangle;$$

and, the scope of this NEC being confined to the abstract, there then exists the abstractable property of being necessarily identical with H or

$$(\lambda z)\,[[\text{NEC } \lambda x\,\lambda y\,(x=y)],\,\langle z,H\rangle].$$

But H itself has this property, and whatever property H has P has. So

$$(\lambda z)\,[\text{NEC }[\lambda x\,\lambda y\,(x=y)],\,\langle H,z\rangle],\,\langle P\rangle.$$

Then by the two-way rule of λ-abstraction, we have

$$[\text{NEC }[\lambda x\,\lambda y\,(x=y)]],\,\langle H,P\rangle.$$

But now, since nothing depended on the particular choice of the H and P which were such that $H = P$, we have the necessity of identity:

$$(\forall x)\,(\forall y)\,((x=y)\to[\text{NEC }[\lambda x\,\lambda y\,(x=y)]],\,\langle x,y\rangle)).$$

This proof adapts a famous proof of the necessity of identity which was given by Ruth Barcan Marcus in 1947.[11] Its merit when given in this form is that it makes evident that all substitutions within the Barcan proof can be made on manifestly extensional positions, lying outside the scope of 'necessarily'.[12] (To show this is the chief point of deploying λ-abstraction here.)

Miss Barcan's proof was long received with incredulity by those committed to the mutual assimilation (much criticized in more recent times by Kripke and others) of the categories of *necessity* and *a priority*, and rejected on the grounds that the identity of evening and morning star was an *a posteriori* discovery. But even if *statement ascertainable a priori*

---

[11] See Barcan (1947), Wiggins (1974). For an exemplary restatement of the Barcan proof, with a reasoned review of all the formal and philosophical issues, see Williamson (1996).

[12] This holds of both the deduction and the truth definition required for that minimal fragment of first order logic which adjoins NEC to abstracts of the form $[\lambda x\,\lambda y\,(x=y)]$ in the object language. In the metalanguage the additional requirement is to adjoin NEC to abstracts of the form

$$[\lambda x\,\lambda y\,(x \text{ satisfies } y)]$$

to be true and *necessarily true statement* coincided perfectly in their extensions, Miss Barcan's theorem could still stand in our version. For the conclusion is not put forward here as a necessarily true statement. (On this we remain mute.) It is put forward as a true statement of *de re* necessity. The thing that the proof comes down to is simply this: Hesperus is necessarily Hesperus, so, if Phosphorus is Hesperus, Phosphorus is necessarily Hesperus. The only conceivable point left to argue is whether there is a *de re* use of 'must' in English. But the onus is on the contingency theorist and the anti-essentialist at last. The latter has to dispel as illusion what seems to be fact – that in English there exist many such *de re* uses.

That is not all. By showing that all identicals are in fact NEC identicals, the proof will furnish one other thing to anyone who is party to a natural intuition: the intuition that designations of things that are necessarily identical ought to be intersubstitutable within the scope of 'necessarily'. One who is party to that intuition no longer needs any act of faith to believe that the ordinary modal logic of $\Box$ and $\Diamond$, permitting quantification into the 'necessarily' and 'possibly' contexts represented as $\Box$ and $\Diamond$ contexts, can give blameless expression to *de re* necessities. The NEC identity of all actual identicals revindicates this as an entirely reasonable belief. And, on this basis, we need not demur at the necessity of identicals given in the familiar form

$$H = P \rightarrow \Box\, (H = P).$$

Advancing from this point, one may argue for something more controversial, namely the necessary distinctness of things that are actually distinct. Improving on earlier derivations that invoked stronger principles, Kripke gave a proof of this on the sole basis of the necessity of identity and the so-called Brouwersche principle

$$\text{not } A \rightarrow \Box\, (\text{not } \Box\, A),$$

which is equivalent to

$$A \rightarrow \Box\, \Diamond\, A.[13]$$

Once one is given the Brouwersche principle and its NEC/POSS counterpart in the lambda notation, the NEC difference of actually different

---

[13] A model theoretic vindication of this formula would depend on the claim that accessibility between worlds is symmetrical. For discussion of this see my p. 280, note 8, in Lovibond and Williams (1996) and the paper by Williamson in the same volume. Williamson offers a more general discussion, of the Brouwersche axiom and of whether it is indispensable to the proof of the necessity of difference.

things is readily available. But, in the light of the revindication of the □ and ◇ notation now afforded by the NEG version of the proof of the necessity of identity, the reader may be spared the vexation of following Kripke's proof in the NEG notation.

When stated in the □ ◇ notation, Kripke's proof may be given as follows (see Williamson, *op. cit.*). Begin with the necessity of identity as in Barcan and Kripke,

$$(H = P) \rightarrow \square (H = P).$$

Contraposing this, we have

$$\text{Not } \square (H = P) \rightarrow \text{Not } (H = P).$$

Being proven from a theorem, this is a theorem. So we have the necessity of it:

$$\square (\text{Not } \square (H = P) \rightarrow \text{Not } (H = P)).$$

And then, by the modal principle $\square (A \rightarrow B) \rightarrow (\square A \rightarrow \square B)$, we have

$$\square (\text{Not } \square (H = P)) \rightarrow \square (\text{Not } (H = P)).$$

But by the Brouwersche principle, we have

$$\text{Not } (H = P) \rightarrow \square (\text{Not } \square (H = P)).$$

In which case, by virtue of the last two formulae and the transitivity of $\rightarrow$, we have

$$\text{Not } (H = P) \rightarrow \square (\text{Not } (H = P)).$$

In other words, if Hesperus is different from Phosphorus, then it is necessary that Hesperus be different from Phosphorus. And the same for all other cases. If Venus is distinct from Mars (and it is), then Venus is necessarily distinct from Mars.

Such formal results as this help to confirm and consolidate a metaphysical conception which the necessity of identity alone might almost have sufficed to vindicate. According to this conception, facts about the identity and difference of individuals are part of the necessary structure of reality and are completely invariant across possible worlds. (See Williamson (1996).) It is simply not an option for us even to describe or envisage possible worlds in a way that would conflict with the identities and distinctnesses that actually hold. Rather, actual identities and differences have to condition the specification of any world whatever that counts as a candidate to contain actual things – things of the real world.

Moreover (again as Kripke has emphasized), the identities of the things within a possible world are specified along with their other properties or relations.

4. CONCEIVABILITY, THEORY AND ESSENCE

So much for the first step towards the modest essentialism that was promised. It remains to be seen whether, within the apparently immobile framework that these theorems discover to us, there is anything interestingly essential to establish about this or that given individual. In this search let us begin gently, however, mindful of all the doubts that are still provoked by the very idea of essence. And let us consider first a thought that is drawn from an area where extensionality reigns absolutely, namely set theory. This thought is most aptly expressed in our NEC notation, because that is better suited than is the $\square \diamond$ notation to mark a certain asymmetry that appears immediately here between sets and the objects that are members of them:

$$(\forall x)\,(\forall \alpha)\,(x \in \alpha \rightarrow \text{NEC}\,[(\lambda z)\,[x \in z]],\,\langle \alpha \rangle).$$

This claims that, even if an object might have belonged to different sets, any set that contains an object contains it necessarily.[14] In this way, expression is given to an idea (not in practice completely incontrovertible, but our chief interest in it is *exempli gratia*) which lurks unacknowledged in the explanations that certain friends of extensionality who are also set theorists give of the identification and individuation of classes, as these are conceived in mathematics.

'What sets attributes apart from classes is merely that, whereas classes are identical when they have the same members, attributes may be distinct even though present in all and only the same things.'[15]

---

[14] On asymmetrical formulae such as these, see my (1976) and (1974) cited at note 8; also Kit Fine, 'Essence and Modality', *Philosophical Perspectives*, Vol. VIII, ed. J. Tomberlin (Atascadero, Calif., Ridgeview Publishing Co., 1994); also (a work in which my grasp slipped of the point stressed in footnote 16 of Chapter Three) 'Mereological Essentialism, Asymmetrical Essential Dependence, and the Nature of Continuants', *Grazer Philosophische Studien* 7/8: *Festschrift for Roderick Chisholm* (1979), 297–315.

[15] Quine (1953), p. 107. (Cf. Quine (1960), p. 209: 'Classes are like attributes except for their identity conditions.') The reader is urged to focus for a moment on the 'may' in the sentence I have cited in the main text. For another use of the same 'may', see p. 151 of Goodman's 'A World of Individuals' (*Problems and Projects* (1972)), 'While a class of individuals is uniquely a class of just those members, a whole made up of individuals may also be made up of quite other parts.' Neither of these is an epistemological 'may'. Nor yet is either of them *de dicto*. Do they exemplify any grade of modal involvement officially approved by Quine?

'We use the word 'set' in such a way that a set is completely determined when its members are given.'[16]

Suppose that we try to apply these criteria, and we are invited to think of a thing α simply identified as the entity (whether class or attribute we do not yet know) to which there belong the items x and y and only these. Then it seems that, if we are to envisage α for what it is, the question we have to ask is whether α, the very thing α, could have dispensed with the particular entities x and y. If it could – if α could lack x or could lack y – then α is not a set or a class.[17] That is the thought that is suggested by Quine's distinction of classes and attributes, and suggested equally by received justifications of the axiom of extensionality given in terms of membership determining set-identity.

The idea that motivates this way of talking is that, whereas there is no constitutive connexion between being this or that property and any actual extension, or between being this or that man and some actual particular position in space–time, there *is* such a connexion between the membership and the identity of a set. The thought that is needed – and I should hope by now to have cleared it of the suspicions expressed by Quine in 'Reference and Modality'[18] – is the *de re* modal thought that, if α is a class containing x and y, then α could not have lacked x.[19] Set

[16] Patrick Suppes, *Introduction to Logic* (Princeton, N.J., 1957), p. 178.

[17] Compare Kit Fine, 'First Order Modal Theories I – Sets' *Nous*, 15 (1981), pp. 177–205.

[18] In pursuit of a different purpose, one critical in effect of the 'may' we seem to have found (note 15) even in texts of Goodman and Quine, Cartwright has expressed a reservation that is cognate with Quine's:

> $(x)\,(y)\,(z)\,((z \in x \leftrightarrow z \in y) \rightarrow x = y)$ . . . will be a theorem of any pure theory of classes but presumably of no pure theory of attributes . . . but it is a difference between theories, and I know of no coherent way in which it can be supposed to carry over to the objects dealt with in the theories. It does, of course, reflect a difference between the *concepts* class and attribute.

Richard Cartwright: 'Class and Attribute', *Nous*, 1 (1967). (See also R. Sharvey, 'Why a Class Can't Change Its Members', *Nous*, 2 (1968).) My claim is that the formal proposals that have been sketched in §2 save from Quine's doubts *and* Cartwright's doubts not only the essentialist 'must', 'may', 'can', 'could', 'able/unable' and not only the usage into which Quine and Goodman themselves seem sometimes to lapse, but also the kind of language cited in note 27.

[19] Suppose someone doubted the necessity of the membership relation. Then the question would be whether he could combine his doubt with any argued or principled affirmation of extensionality, or advance on behalf of extensionality such claims as 'a set is nothing more than a unity constituted by its members' (Richmond Thomason, *Symbolic Logic* (London, 1970), p. 284). If there is no other way of identifying such a unity than via its constituents, and such a unity can be given *simply* by giving all its members, then is not its identity derivative from these, and derivative in a way in which the identity of a perceptibly demonstrable horse or tree is not derivative from that of any particular cells or derivative from the identity of any particular sequence of spatio-temporal positions or particular sequence of paired space–time positions and material components? Against those not convinced, here is a final or Parthian shot: try conceiving the unit set of x, namely $\{x\}$, as the unit set of y where $y \neq x$. Now try conceiving the pair set $\{x,y\}$ as lacking either x or y. . . .

theorists who say that it is a peculiarity of sets to be determined by their members, or who distinguish sets from attributes in Quine's way, are surely saying at least this. And it need occasion no surprise that, in order to delimit an area within which extensionality will reign, in order to justify intuitively the axioms of extensionality for the mathematicians' world of sets and exclude attributes from the intended interpretation of Greek letter variables, one has to trespass for a moment outside the delimited area and talk in a language of richer expressive resources.

Suppose so much can be accepted. Then, given (Δ) of section 2, one might say that the pair set {Eiffel Tower, Crystal Palace} is essentially a set, and essentially a set with just these members, because nothing could count as envisaging that very set in a way that implied that it was not a set, or that it lacked these members.

At risk of recycling the obvious but warned by experience that there is often no alternative, I stress that the claim under discussion is not that it is impossible to envisage such sets as {Eiffel Tower, Crystal Palace} under any other *description* than 'pair set whose sole members are Eiffel Tower and Crystal Palace'. One might conceive of this set under the description 'the pair set whose members are in Z's opinion the most remarkable works of nineteenth-century engineering in the capital cities London and Paris', or in indefinitely many other ways. To show that the set itself, the very one we are concerned with, could lack Eiffel Tower, one must envisage *that set* as lacking Eiffel Tower. Once we tried to do this, the question would be *what* it was we could succeed in envisaging as lacking the Eiffel Tower.

It may seem for a moment that one can envisage anything of anything, even 'lacking Eiffel Tower' of {Eiffel Tower, Crystal Palace}, provided that the identification the envisager *starts off with* is as vague as, say, 'entity mentioned or had in mind at *t* by F. Hausdorff'. But that is the same mistake in another guise. Starting off with so vague a description of the thing mentioned by Hausdorff should not make it easier but harder for the would-be envisager to be sure that he has, in the serious sense, conceived of *that* entity under the description 'lacking the Eiffel Tower'. The sort of possibility we are interested in should not be such as to be *augmented by ignorance*.[20] The same goes for the necessity and possibility that Ayer was discussing in his own enunciation of principle (Δ). The conceiving must be with regard to some determinate thing that answers to some specification that identifies it, however contingently, as

---

[20] Cf. Arnauld's Objection 'De Natura Mentis Humanae', against Descartes, at p. 201, vol. VII of *Oeuvres de Descartes*, ed. Adam and Tannery (Paris, 1897–1913).

that particular thing. Then the question must be how this thing can be counterfactually envisaged; and what it is possible to envisage of it must depend on what the particular entity is, whether Dickens, the Pyramids, or whatever. The more you know about the thing, the more authoritative your findings of possibility and impossibility ought to be.

5. CONCEIVABILITY CONTINUED

A handy way of summing up (Δ) (E) and (Z) as they combine with the conception of individuation just illustrated is this: x could have the property ϕ, or it is possible for x to have ϕ,[21] if and only if it is genuinely possible to conceive of x's having ϕ; and a thinker genuinely conceives of x as having ϕ only if there is *some* sortal concept f such that: (i) f adequately answers the Aristotelian question what x is, and commits anyone who singles a thing out as an instantiation of f to an identity-cum-persistence condition for x; (ii) f and ϕ are cosatisfiable by x, and if x had the property ϕ that would not preclude x's being singled out as this very instantiation of f.[22] Let us call this the anchor constraint. It may be protested that it does not render it an entirely clear or non-disputable matter whether x could or could not have had the property ϕ. But this is no ground for complaint. For often it really isn't an open or shut question. (The contestability in question echoes that of questions to be explored in Chapter Seven.) The role of philosophy here is not to render hard questions easier, but to cast light upon what is at issue. This anchor constraint will be further elaborated just once, at the beginning of §10. But it will not be amended or modified.

[21] See Hacking (1975), for this variant. For the distinction of *could* and *can*, which could be made explicit here by the identification of a place for a *relative to what supposition* parameter ('could' representing here the bare supposition that x exists), see e.g. S. A. Handford, *The Latin Subjunctive*, pp. 130f. (cited by J. L. Austin at *Collected Papers* (Oxford, 1961), p. 164) and Alan R. White, *Modal Thinking* (Oxford, 1975), Ch. Two. See also my *op. cit.* in Lovibond and Williams (1996), p. 233. In the language of that piece let me say that I am focusing here on the *flat* sense of 'could' and the correspondingly exigent dual sense of 'must'.

[22] What would refute this contention and its expansion at §10 below? A weaker requirement that arose equally naturally from a theory of particular identification, respected the absoluteness of identity, and represented the substantial requirement that (Δ) puts upon the *de re* relation of conceiver, object and attribute. The case for this requirement is that it makes sense of our more reflective practice when we make suppositions. (Our practice, I mean, where it does not idle or substitute fantasy for the careful conceiving, the careful thinking right through, of the alternatives to the actual.)

It follows that the proper response to the proposal is dialectical: to propose a weaker or different principle that promises the same sort of friction or impedance upon claims of possibility that are idle or baseless. This is one part of the reply to Penelope Mackie (1994). For another part, see Preface, paragraph 10. See also note 26.

The interest of this elucidation lies not in a claim to be an analysis or reduction of *de re* possibility – it is multiply disqualified from those tasks by its re-use of the modal concepts and the importing of a notional thinker to do the conceiving – but in the stringency of the necessary condition that it proposes for *de re* possibility. It illustrates how there might be such a thing as a *de re* necessity to which a concrete particular was subject. And it sees the issue of *de re* necessity as all of a piece with the practical business of individuation.

According to this elucidation, it is possible, for all that has been shown so far, to conceive of Caesar's having a different career; it is possible to conceive of this very man's not being consul in 69 BC, or his not conquering Gaul, or his not crossing the Rubicon, or even of his not in fact being male or not living through adolescence. Maybe it is even possible to conceive of Caesar's not having his actual parents. If there is a difficulty about that, then we shall come to it in due course.[23] What then do the constraints so far framed suggest that it is properly impossible to envisage of Caesar? The *this such* conception of individuation and the paradigm of the previous section, combining in the elucidation now proposed, suggest that among the things it is hardest to conceive of Caesar's not being is human being. For if anything plays here the part that we found the concept *set* or *class* to play in our specimen argument, then the concept *human being* plays it. Or so it would appear.

I allow that there is one doubt even about this restriction. Someone might concede to me that there must be *some* sortal concept f such that, whatever else Caesar is envisaged as being, no genuine envisaging of Caesar excludes his being this instantiator of f. But, despite conceding that, the questioner might wonder whether there was a less specific sortal concept than *human being* that was capable of fixing the persistence conditions of this entity and answering the question 'what is Caesar?' Could not the generic property *animal* serve in the role of f? (See §9; and see Chapter Seven for the other candidate, namely *person*.) It may be said that all that Caesar needs is to be such and such an instantiator of *animal*.

This is by no means the only obscurity or perplexity to be encountered in adapting the {Eiffel Tower, Crystal Palace} argument to the

---

[23] For Kripke's argument for the opposite conclusion see below, §10. A word is needed here on the status in my treatment of claims that something is *de re* possible. They are by their nature provisional, and they are defeasible by further arguments why the property in question cannot after all be conceived of some object. Chapter Six, §7, bears on the reasons for this.

things to be encountered in nature. But before we prune back the doctrine it must be allowed to put on more leaf.[24]

6. INDIVIDUATIVE ESSENTIALISM AND ITS CONSEQUENCES

Suppose that every natural thing x satisfies throughout its actual existence some sortal concept that any thinker who singles out x has to treat as invariant (cf. **D**(ii)), and has to treat as invariant even when engaged in conditional and counterfactual envisagings of states and histories alternative to x's actual states and history; and suppose that this concept is a natural kind concept which not only says what x is but also leads *a posteriori* to a passable criterion of identity and persistence for members of its extension.[25] Then not only will such sortal concepts be owed the kind of honour once upon a time accorded by Aristotle and by Leibniz to the *infima species* (cf. Aristotle, *Metaphysics* Z; Leibniz, *Nouveaux Essais* III, 6.36; III, 3.6), provided only that they really do represent the least specific account of their bearers that will suffice to articulate these very bearers from the rest of reality. It will also be possible to derive some potentially surprising *a posteriori* consequences.

Suppose that 'human being' (and every other natural kind term, whether species or genus) has its sense fixed by reference to some hypothesized generic constitution, a constitution which users of the term are committed, despite their ignorance concerning it, to think of as exemplified (under the physical laws of the actual world) by the actual instances that they encounter and group together as men. (Suppose the simple fact of their use of the term commits them, as claimed in Chapter Three.) And suppose G is some predicate standing for an abstract property, e.g. one pertaining to the gene pool perhaps (albeit not only to that, see Chapter Three, §1), and scientifically partially definitive of that constitution and/or determined by that constitution. Now consider anything that is a human being. Surely he or she is necessarily if-a-human-then-G. It may be objected that the conditional governed by this 'necessarily' is no genuine necessity, because it is

---

[24] There are anti-essentialists of a moderate persuasion who might let pass the set-theoretic argument of Chapter Four, section 4, on the grounds that sets are abstract things and not identifiable independently of a mathematical theory, but resist strenuously the extension I have attempted to material substances. It seems dubious, however, that conceptual-cum-individuative dependence on a mathematical theory is the real principle of the distinction between abstract and concrete. Witness the entities of modern physics.

[25] I find my arguments about this anticipated in part by A. MacIntyre's article 'Essence and Existence' (1967).

contingent upon the laws of nature and lawlike propensities that actually obtain and other laws and propensities might have obtained. But already Chapter Three has confronted that. If the concepts of *man* and *human being* behave in a manner consonant with the deictic explications of 'man' and 'human being' envisaged in that chapter, then the very existence of such things as human beings is contingent on that same thing. For it is on the same actual laws that the delimitation and significance of the human being-definitive constitution depends.[26] Since the G-property and *human being* depend for their instantiation on the very same circumstance, and nothing counts as human entirely independently (as it has now appeared) of possessing the G-property, it follows that a human being is necessarily if human then G. Moreover, once that is established, we can advance beyond this merely conditional property. We already have the beginnings of an argument to show that whatever is a human being is necessarily a human being. If that is right (cf. Preamble, §2, on 'individuate'; Chapter One, mottoes and §1; Chapter Four, §2 and in due course §9), then we can necessitate the consequent of the conditional. It will be true *a posteriori* that anything that is a human being is necessarily G.[27]

---

[26] See again Chapter IV of Ishiguro (1972). Our concern is with the general form of this kind of argument. Once that was accepted, the time would come to enter into the differences between (a) Aristotelian *infimae species*; (b) the kinds furnished by zoology or other sciences, which need not perhaps be depended upon to do from their own resources the right sort of justice in the right sort of terms to the sort of differences we might want there to be between a St Bernard dog and a Pekingese; and (c) the individuative kinds (not necessarily articulated in a zoological way or another scientific way) that are promoted by our construction in this chapter. On these matters see P. F. Strawson's Critical Notice of *Sameness & Substance* (1980), *Mind*, 90 (1981), pp. 603–7.

[27] The argument relies of course on the NEC counterpart of $\Box\,(p{\rightarrow}q){\rightarrow}(\Box\,p{\rightarrow}\Box\,q)$. See p. 348 of Wiggins (1974).

It is my hope that in the account here employed of the *de re* 'must' and 'can' there resides some justification for modes of expression that are very natural to some scientists, and possibly indispensable to the attempt to describe how scientific theory explains *what* certain things are. For a passage susceptible of this interpretation and best explained, not by an implausible transposition into *de dicto* terminology, but by *de re* necessity backed with a notion of conceiving not open to the charge that the less you know the more you can conceive, consider Erwin Schrödinger's explanation, at p. 49 of *What is Life? The Physical Aspect of the Living Cell* (Cambridge, 1944), of the Heitler–London quantum theory of the chemical bond:

> a number of atomic nuclei, including their bodyguards of electrons, when they find themselves close to each other, forming 'a system', are unable by their very nature to adopt any arbitrary configuration we might think of. Their very nature leaves them only a very numerous but discrete series of 'states' to choose from . . . The transition from one of these configurations to another is a quantum jump. If the second has the greater energy ('is a higher level'), the system must be supplied from outside with at least the difference of the two energies to make the transition possible . . . the molecule will of necessity have a certain stability, the configuration cannot change unless at least the energy difference, necessary to 'lift' it to the next higher level, is supplied from outside.

It is sometimes complained that essences 'explain nothing'. But if the foregoing argument is correct then, apart from the least interesting and least controversial necessary properties (e.g. *identity with Caesar*, which is too special, and *self-identity*, which is too general), they do have a philosophical function. For, first, there are predicates that stand for essential properties of a thing and register the condition whose satisfaction is a direct or indirect prerequisite of the very thing's being articulated *at all* from the rest of reality. These predicates are not in the business of explaining anything much, because they are presupposed to there being anything to explain. But then, in the second place, there are more interesting predicates, like G above. These correspond to *a posteriori* or scientific accounts given by some (at the appropriate level) relatively fundamental theory of the natural kind or articulative sort to which a thing belongs, a theory whose *non-availability even in principle* would subvert the possibility of a sound deictic demonstration of the particular kind or articulative sort presupposed to the thing's being what it substantially is. It is to the satisfaction of this complex requirement that such properties as the G-property owe both their place in the theory of individuation and their necessary application to human beings.

We may add to the maxims of §4 a principle long since acknowledged in every interesting or thoughtful essentialism of natural substances.

(Θ) The practical scientist does the business; but the philosopher keeps the books. (Nelson Goodman, *Problems and Projects* (Indianapolis, 1972), p. 168.)

I agree with those who deny that forms are to be used in seeking to explain specific and special causes. (Leibniz, *Specimen Dynamicum*.)[28]

7. THAT THE IDEA OF 'HAECCEITAS' IS AS MISBEGOTTEN AS THE WORD ITSELF IS UNLOVELY

Particular individuals have essences without which they would not 'be what they are' – would not exist. But apart from logically particularized

---

[28] *Leibnizens Mathematische Schriften*, ed. C. I. Gerhardt (Berlin and Halle, 1849–55), Vol. VI, p. 235. Cf. *Discourse of Metaphysics*, Ch. x (Gerhardt, *Philosophischen Schriften*, Vol. IV). 'I agree that consideration of these forms is of no service in the detail of natural philosophy, and must not be used for explaining phenomena in particular. And it was in this that our scholastics failed, and the Physicians of past times following their example, believing that they could account for the properties of bodies by mentioning forms and qualities without going to the pains of examining the manner of operation; as if one were willing to content oneself with saying that a clock has the horodictic quality resulting from its form, without considering in what all this consists . . . But this failure and misuse of forms must not make us reject something knowledge of which is so necessary in Metaphysics.' (Translation by Lucas and Grint.) Cf. also Chapter XI *ibid*.

essential properties such as *necessarily identical with Caesar*, which are specified through a designation of the thing in which they inhere, we must
expect the *de re* essences of individuals to be shared or shareable in principle. The requirement that essences determined otherwise than
through identity itself should be unique to particulars (like almost any
other attempt either to say anything or to deny anything by means of the
idea of *haecceity* or this-ness) is the product of confusion. We get from the
'this' of 'this f' (where f represents some sortal specification) all the par-
ticularity that is required for anchorage to the actual entity of which we
are to conceive in various counterfactual ways. Whether or not Strawson
has demonstrated the necessity for thought as we know it of individuals,
he would appear to have shown at least this: that, wherever thought *does*
recognize individuals, the functions of 'this' and 'such' are in the end
(regardless of any limited interchangeability of role) mutually irreducible. (Cf. Chapter Six, §10.) It is true that Russell's Theory of
Descriptions may be seen as a proposal for redrawing one apparent frontier between predicating and designating. But whatever we make of that
theory, naming or designating (which is a linguistic function that is *entity-
involving* in a way in which predicating need not be) and predicating are
two functions. So far, we lack any reason to believe in the existence of
any *haecceitas* that is defined or manufactured otherwise than via designation of the owner of the property in question. It is hard to think of
anything true and significant that could be said using the idea of this-
ness (which-ness?) not better said while respecting the distinctions *desig-
nation/predication* and *particular/universal*. It is harder still to imagine an
approach to the identity of a thing that makes its explanatory beginning
with *haecceitas*.

Conspicuous among the non-particularized properties of Caesar that
pass the test of being invariant under all counterfactual speculations that
can count as successful *de re* conceivings of Gaius Julius Caesar, we must
expect to find properties with negations not coconceivable with his sortal
identification *human being* (or, more weakly, not coconceivable with
animal, see below, §11). Our provisional expectation is that each of the
properties (save those defined through identity itself) that Caesar must
have will in principle be multiply satisfiable.

8. THE ESSENTIALIST 'MUST' AND 'CAN'

Of course the locutions 'can' and 'must' are normally put to other, more
specific, work. The range of available meanings of these modalities is

highly various. *De re* modal claims are usually based upon people's abilities or inabilities, their capacities or incapacities as of some time and in relation to the circumstances of that time, or upon their obligations or debts or compulsions of that time.[29] If someone must repay £5 then the source of the necessity is perhaps a borrowing transaction and a consequential state of indebtedness from which they have not been released. Or if someone cannot help but slide down a slope then that which necessitates their falling may be a trip, the gradient of the slope, and their lack of the strength that would be needed to regain control. This is more unalterable than a state of being obliged to pay money (except perhaps in Sicily). But the proposal that is put forward in this chapter is that we should see the *de re* necessity of essence as the limiting case of the other *de re* necessities with which their form appears to group them. The essential necessity of a trait arises at that point of unalterability where the *very existence of the bearer is conditional* upon the trait in question. Here, at this point, a property is fixed to its bearer by virtue of being inherent in the individuation of it – inherent in the very possibility of the drawing of a spatio-temporal boundary around the object in the light of some principle of activity of the thing. The closer the source of the attribute to the singling out of the thing itself – the more it is bound up with the whole mode of articulating reality to discover such an object there – the more exigent, obviously, is the necessity that, *if there is to be any such thing as the bearer*, it should have the feature in question. The *de re* 'must' of causal inflexibility here passes over at a certain threshold into the inflexibility of the metaphysically necessary or the (in one defensible sense) conceptual (the concept being the *a posteriori* concept of being identical with that very thing). This metaphysical necessity is not of course analytical or (in any but the loosest sense) logical (see Preamble §8). There is no reason, I believe, why this should make the essentialistic *de re* attribute any less of a real attribute of the thing itself.[30]

---

[29] There are constant temptations to confuse differences in the grounds for modal attributions with differences in their meaning. It is not necessary to settle here the question whether we have here an array of distinct senses disposed around a focal idea, or a univocal idea which can conjoin with different parameters to yield a variety of different kinds of semantic output. See also my *op. cit.* in Lovibond and Williams (1996), pp. 232–5.

[30] *Pace* Wittgenstein who, for the same sort of reasons as I am rehearsing in this chapter, isolated such attributions but dubbed them non-descriptive.

There is a sense in which an object may not be described. This is that a description may ascribe to it no property whose absence would reduce the existence of the object itself to nothing. Description may not express what would be essential for the existence of the object. (*Philosophische Bemerkungen* §§93–4. Cf. also *Tractatus Logico-Philosophicus* 4.123.)

9. AVOIDING OVERSPECIFICITY, ALLOWING VAGUENESS

Individuative essentialism has put on more leaf. Ought it now to be pruned back? We need to consider the charge of overspecificity in the choice of *human being* as the highest individuative sortal for Caesar. Thereafter, we can explore yet other directions in which this essentialism might grow.

The objection we postponed was this: why could not the necessary anchor between the actual Caesar and some thinker's envisaging something putatively of Caesar be secured by virtue of the subject's being individuated under the description *this mammal* or even *this animal?*

Suppose first that this objection were correct, and that one of these unspecific sortal specifications were a good enough sticking point. Even then there would be *de re* necessities to be discovered. *Animal* excludes *stone, insect, paddle steamer, number* (and even *mereological fusion of animal parts*). The objector might say that the resulting essentialism lacked much of the interest of the position first stated. But our doctrine of natural kinds would still have a real point even at the level *mammal* or *animal*; and, even at such a distance from the specific, there might still be something to be made of scientific discoveries, however much more abstract the choice for the G property of §6 would then have to be. The damage the objection can inflict is limited then. But the real reply to the objection ought to be that 'this animal' is not a good enough identification of Caesar to sustain the envisaging of him as not a man. Or (better) so soon as we supplement 'this animal' in the way in which it needs to be supplemented in any context in order to be properly individuative there, or in order for it to furnish any answer to the question 'which thing is being referred to?', that which results is more specific than 'this animal'.

It is not to be denied that the words 'this animal' suffice to express a rough and ready identification in ordinary contexts of what things are. But this is because 'animal' so easily takes on an individuative force from a context and/or some other sortal predicate that is ready to hand.[31] But

---

[31] Or because it does not matter very much to know more than roughly what the thing in question is. 'What's under that blanket?' 'It's an animal – I should sit on the other blanket if I were you.' In the context, it is probably perfectly obvious that it is not a leopard or a gila-monster under the blanket. This is ordinary indoor life. (One can sit next to the blanket, for instance.) It doesn't matter whether it's a cat or a dog or a nanny goat under the blanket. It doesn't matter *exactly* what is under the blanket.

At *New Essays* 3.3.6 Leibniz represents Locke as saying, 'les mots deviennent généraux lorsqu'ils sont signes d'idées générales, et les idées deviennent générales lorsque par abstraction on en sépare le temps, le lieu, ou telle autre circonstance, qui peut les déterminer à telle ou telle existence particulière'. In his objection to this doctrine, Leibniz exploits the distinction that I am

the designation 'this animal' is complemented in all sorts of *different* ways. In itself it determines no single principle of individuation. (Cf. **D**(iv), **D**(v).) How then would it be complemented in the context of the claim 'N.N. conceived of this particular animal's not being a man', where *ex hypothesi* there was nothing like 'man' to supplement 'animal' in the anchorage of the object conceived to the conceiving? The chief deficiency of *animal* construed as an *autonomously* individuative concept is that in taking something for an animal simpliciter we are not committed to conceiving of it as a thing with any particular way of coming into being, of behaving, of interacting with other things, of developing or of ceasing to be. But if anything at all is to be singled out determinately as 'this particular animal', then there is no alternative but for the answer to the *what is it?* question to rest on some sufficiently specific causal generalization to provide conditions of identity and persistence for members of its extension. (These are generalizations to which, whether or not he knows or wishes it, anyone who subsumes a thing under the concept will be committed.) This requirement will be breached in the attempted envisaging of Caesar as not a man, unless there is a sortal term that is lower than 'animal' and either coextensive with or higher than 'man' or 'human being', *and* this term is individuative *and* it suffices to fix Caesar with Caesar's very principle of individuation. These conditions are not empty. Their purport is brought out in conditions such as **D**(ii), **D**(iii), **D**(iv) and **D**(v) of Chapter Two. If someone can find such an ultimate sortal concept for Caesar, if it is higher than *man* or *human being* and it is sustained by generalizations sufficiently specific to fix the identity and persistence conditions that are presupposed to individuation, then they are at liberty to substitute it for *man* or *human being* throughout the argument of previous sections, and weaken all my claims accordingly. They will not have been reduced to nothing.

At this point, however, it may seem that an element of the vagueness that Ayer predicted (and we anticipated at (**Δ**) of §2 above) has crept in.

pressing here. The principles we have to use in keeping individuals under continuous observation can be made to yield genus terms. There is abstraction from species to genus. (Cf. Ishiguro (1972)). But there is no abstraction from individuals to species. The principle we use in observing and tracing a particular does not come with a species concept which we get by *abstraction* from individuals. That would be impossible, for in so far as we have a species concept for an individual, the possession of this concept and the ability to pick out the thing under it cannot be *separated*. For genera terms, however, which *presuppose* individuation, there is no such difficulty. 'Je ne disconviens point de cet usage des abstractions, mais c'est plutôt en montant des espèces aux genres que des individus aux espèces. Car (quelque paradoxe que cela paraisse) il est impossible à nous d'avoir la connaissance des individus et de trouver le moyen de déterminer exactement l'individualité d'aucune chose, à moins que de la garder elle même.'

But it is no part of the essentialist's purpose to deny that in exploring the grounds of *de re* modal attributions we encounter matters of degree. Vagueness in the delimitation of kinds is not a new admission.[32] Nor does the need to decide whether or not a certain threshold has been reached entail that the choice to make or not make a given modal assertion is unprincipled or arbitrary, or a matter of no moment. For the admission does not undermine any of the point or interest or determinacy we have shown how to attach piecemeal to these questions, or degrade the complexity of what is involved in seeking to establish, well below the level of how things superficially appear to be, whether one can or cannot envisage some property ϕ of Caesar. In the end, it may or may not prove, in given cases, that there is *indeterminacy*. If (over and above vagueness) there is indeterminacy, then it may be expected that this will be an echo of the *contestability* that can attach to the practicalities of individuation itself – a matter resumed at some length in Chapters Six and Seven.

10. OTHER *DE RE* NECESSITIES, REAL OR PUTATIVE: A FRAMEWORK FOR FURTHER INQUIRY

The derivations of §3 and the consequential reflections of §4 and §5 placed us in the following position. The identities and distinctnesses of individuals make up a metaphysical framework for counterfactual speculation. That framework constrains us in how we can envisage any given individual's being or acting. Translating this into the language of possible worlds, one might say (with Kripke) that, when we construct worlds that are alternatives to the actual world, the specification of a world needs to specify, in so far as anything hangs on this, *which* individuals they are that figure in that world.[33] Moreover, to place a particular individual

---

[32] Leibniz made it willingly in *Nouveaux Essais*: 'Les passages d'espèce en espèce peuvent etre insensibles, et pour les discerner ce seroit quelquefois a peu pres comme si on ne sçauroit decider combien il faut laisser de poils à un homme pour qu'il ne soit point chauve. Cette indetermination seroit vraye quand meme nous connoistrions parfaitement l'intérieur des creatures dont il s'agit. Mais je ne vois point qu'elle puisse empêcher les choses d'avoir des essences réelles independamment de l'entendement, et nous de les connoistre: il est vrai que les noms et les bornes des espèces seroient quelque fois comme les noms des mesures et des poids, où il faut choisir pour avoir des bornes fixes' (3.6.27). Compare also 3.3.14, 3.5.9 and 3.6.38.

[33] Just as we have to be ready, if it matters, to write into the construction of alternative worlds the colours or weights of objects, unless this information be deductively entailed by other specifications already given. If you find it incredible that this specifying should be needed, you are not taking into account what identity and difference amount to or the proper content of these notions. It is likely that you are holding onto the illusion that pure properties and relations can fix identities. For a further attempt to show that this really is an illusion, see Chapter Six, §9.

within a construction/supposition/world limits that construction/sup-
position/world. For *x* cannot be represented there in a manner that is at
variance with what *x* itself substantially is – or in a manner at variance
with anything that flows from that. Here, as so often in this book, the
sense of 'what *x* is' is the one that Aristotle marked out for philosophy.
Apart from being human and having the property G, are there any other
limits on how Caesar can be suppositionally represented? What else
flows from the requirement that, in our envisaging any φ at all of Caesar,
φ should be cosatisfiable with some individuating sortal concept f for
Caesar (*human being*, say)?

The anchor constraint given in §5 suggests at least one further
essentialist thought. Wherever φ is genuinely conceivable of *x* and *x*
could have or could have had the property φ, the property and some
sortal identification f of *x* co-satisfy the following requirement: that if
x had φ then that would not stand in the way of *x*'s being singled out
as *this* particular instantiation of f; *x*'s having φ would not be in conflict with this f-identification of *x*. It is only possible for *x* to have φ if
x's having φ would not obstruct *x*'s being identified somehow, for the
purposes of conceiving of *x*'s having φ, as the particular f it actually
is.[34]

Let the property of being not-ψ be the negation of a long, long disjunction of interesting properties of *x*, properties that would normally
be invoked in the support of a demonstrative identification or (as for us
now) an indirect identification of Gaius Julius Caesar. Suppose it is asked
whether Caesar could have the property not-ψ. Consistently with the
supposition of Caesar's having not-ψ, could he be singled out or individuated as this or that identical-with-Caesar-instantiation of the concept
human being? Or would the putatively total disruption of Caesar's actual
properties that is postulated by the putative envisaging of Caesar as
having not-ψ subvert the very possibility of finding a collateral description in the form 'this or that instantiation of *human being*' that both
homed upon Caesar and was co-conceivable with not-ψ?

Let it be clear that we do not ask this question because we expect the
satisfaction of the predicate ψ to establish the *title* of suppositions that

---

[34] At p. 234 of 'Replies' in Lovibond and Williams (1996), I promised that on some other occasion
I would attempt to expand the Aristotelian account of what an individual is, in order to enrich
the Aristotelian constraint on the construction of suppositions. That is what I am attempting
here. The outcome will be methodologically consistent with that earlier effort, though in detail
different. The aim is to look for more limitations and necessities than were discernible from anywhere on the route chosen on that other occasion. I have not tried to incorporate here all the
points about essentialism argued in that earlier discussion.

project it onto Caesar to be suppositions relating to Caesar. The suppo-
sitional exercise itself confers that title. (It confers it as of right, which is
not to say that that title cannot be put into jeopardy.) The point at issue
is only that, if the answer to the question posed is that the supposition of
Caesar's having not-ψ does indeed rule out the kind of identifiability just
spoken of (for provided that ψ is carefully enough and laboriously
enough constructed, that does seem to be the right answer), then ψ
stands for a property that Caesar must have. Moreover the necessity of
Caesar's having ψ is something over and above the necessity of his being
a human being. The thing shown is the strong *de re* necessity of a
complex property, the one ψ stands for, that is neither in the category of
substance nor yet imported by something in that category.

What if anything does all this suggest about certain familiar *de re*
necessities philosophers claim to be able to discover about individuals?
Saul Kripke once asked 'by what right' one would call a person sprung
from different sperm and egg from the actual ones 'this very man'.[35]
Kripke's question is surely not intended to imply, in a manner at variance with Kripke's own insights in this area, that every counterfactual
speculation about Julius Caesar involves the thinker who undertakes it
in establishing his title to identify the individual concerned as Julius
Caesar. Perhaps Kripke's argument in the passage cited for the necessity to a thing of its actual origin is that the speculator has to be able
to *rebut* the charge that he has lost his grasp of his subject of discourse
if he conceives of this subject with changed parents or origin. But now
one must ask: can one not rebut the charge of losing the subject of the
supposition by claiming to speculate about how the man whom Brutus
murdered in 44 B.C. would have fared if (secretly, say) Marius had
been his father? To rebut the charge of losing the individual, there
must always be available to the speculator, *consistently with his speculation*
and in a way not destructive of the framework in which the question
is posed, some way of specifying the man the speculator means by
Julius Caesar. That seems right. Could a convincing argument be
made along these lines for the thesis of the necessity of origin? It may
well be that a determined attempt to follow through the implications
of the anchor restraint will reveal an important asymmetry between
earlier and later identifying attributes of an individual.[36] That will not

---

[35] See p. 314 of Kripke (1972).
[36] In her admirable new paper 'Identity, Time and Necessity', *Proceedings of the Aristotelian Society*, 98,
    1 (1998), pp. 59–78, Penelope Mackie explains the plausibility that so many have found in the
    thesis of the necessity of origin by showing how it can be based in a branching model of pos-

carry one all the way to Kripke's own arresting contention however – or so I hazard.

11. THE ESSENCES OF ARTEFACTS AND THE MATTER OF ARTEFACTS

Suppose someone responds to the hardness of problems of artefact persistence rehearsed in Chapter Three not with proposals about how to dispense altogether with claims of identity in the more extreme cases of subtraction, addition and repair, but with a more demanding condition for a's counting as the same artefact as b – a condition arrived at by the incorporation for each artefact kind of its nominal essence and then by some further requirement about addition and subtraction of matter. Might this sort of enrichment of the survival conditions of a given artefact kind (already touched upon in Chapter Three, §4) be the basis of certain *de re* necessities that are frequently mooted for artefacts?

Before we try to reach any conclusion about artefacts and their matter, we have to be on our guard. We have tried everywhere to distinguish the question of survival through change – how the object must be at stage $n + 1$ *given that it was thus and so at stage n* – from the question of what can be envisaged of an entity only conditionally upon the existence of the entity. Let us be sure to maintain that distinction in what follows and let us focus on the second question. Conditionally upon its existence, and only upon that, one surely can envisage a given table's not being so polished, not being quite so tall, not being chamfered at the corners. That is not very hard. But can one envisage in this way its being not a table, or its not even being a piece of furniture fabricated for a cognate

---

sibilities concerning actual individuals. According to this model, the ways in which an individual might have been different are restricted to divergences from actual history: 'It follows that any *complete* alternative possible history for Julius Caesar must have some segment that is the same as some portion of his actual history' (p. 70). Mackie calls this the 'overlap requirement'. She calls it this without enthusiasm – for she deliberately confines her efforts to explaining why the thesis of the necessity of origin is found attractive and refrains from advocating the thesis herself – and she bases the need for some such requirement as that of overlap on a version of the 'anchoring requirement' that has motivated the present chapter. See Ayer's wording of our (Δ) in §2 above. I note, however, that, for obvious reasons, she moderates the literal force of the overlap requirement to avoid the 'absurdly strong principle [as it applies to x within an alternative world] that requires *complete* coincidence of properties at some time. Nor . . . need it be taken to require that the overlap include sameness of temporal or spatial location' (footnote 31). But then the question arises why overlap must be interpreted to require either sameness of material constitution or coming from the same sperm and egg. Perhaps this doubt about whether there is here any argument for the necessity of origin as such converges upon the unspoken reservation that discourages Mackie from coming out in any positive advocacy of the necessity of origin.

purpose, or conceive of its enjoying the negation of the disjunction of all predicates that relate to its having been fashioned for cognate purposes? That is too much. One cannot envisage any of these things. These suppositions fail requirements analogous to those already argued for. Let us search then for *de re* necessities lying between these extremes of ease and difficulty in envisaging the table as otherwise than it is.

Let us ask first: can one genuinely envisage my table's being made of different wood?[37] Here there is little or nothing we can postpone to the day of an empirical discovery. For all the physical facts upon which the problem is based may be available already. My provisional answer is this: that difference of material is something one can envisage without jeopardizing the title of the supposition to relate to this very table.[38] The essence of this or that table does not demand any particular matter, only the right kind of matter for that artefact.

Here, in front of me, is a table, one much used and leant upon in writing, a table damaged ten years ago by an inundation of water through the roof, but carefully repaired, revarnished and repolished. Its whole simple history is known and available back to the occasion of its being bought in Chalk Farm, London, NW3, in 1969. Let us suppose that its previous owner and user was also its maker. Let us suppose the table came into being in 1942, after the intending artificer came upon several pieces of some Indian hardwood. Could the artificer not, when he made the table, have taken other pieces? Surely he could. The table came into being when he did whatever he did to the pieces that he managed to find. That which constitutes the table he then constructed and distinguishes it from anything else at all, is something that resulted from the acts he visited upon the pieces he took at the moment of making it and the kind of wood those pieces were to which he did whatever he did in order to make the table. Why look for more? The table can in principle be traced back to the time when it was made. But, consistently with everything that we can show in *this* way, surely this table

---

[37] I venture to think that the argument given at footnote 56 of Kripke (1980) for the necessity of constitution depends on treating constitution as if it were identity. For the distinction, see Chapter One, §6.

[38] Let us contrast a table, taken together with its wood, and an *objet trouvé* (on which the artist might stamp his initials, suppose, and the date and place of the find), taken together with the object itself *before* the artist confers upon it that status. In the second case, <objet trouvé, the object itself>, simply by virtue of the genre, the object found is not *transformed* into the work of art. Or rather it is not transformed in the way in which the hardwood is transformed into a table. The *objet trouvé* is not transformed thus, even if the artist crops, trims or polishes the thing found. For in the case of *objet trouvé*, the stuff of the work of art is the object itself. Contrast the situation (as I claim it appears) with <table, hardwood pieces>.

could (metaphysically could) have been made from other pieces of wood. This is not to say that it easily or non-disruptively could. If we knew more about the table's actual history, then we might find that the pieces actually employed were the only suitable pieces of wood that were in any way available to its maker for a table anything like this. We might find that amazingly many things would have had to be different for the table to have been made in 1942 from different pieces of hardwood – especially when we realize that, as a matter of fact, placed as he was, the previous owner was the only craftsman who was in a position to make such a table and we remember that, at that time, suitable wood for making furniture was very scarce. In that case, not only is there no categorical 'could have been differently constituted' to be affirmed here (in the sense of *potuit* or *poterat*). There rarely is in such cases. Maybe all the hypothetical 'coulds' that are true (all the 'coulds' that have the sense of *potuisset*) are surprisingly remote from reality. That would be interesting, in its way. But not even this would show there is no world where the table has different matter. If there is just one such world, then that suffices for the flat metaphysical 'could have'. And what on earth could make the supposition of its having other matter incoherent?

Would I go so far then as to say that we are free to distinguish between two worlds as qualitatively similar as you like, each containing one table very like my table, and free to do so by identifying the table in the one world but not the table in the other world as my table? I am committed to reply that we can do this.

Suppose though that the only relevant difference between the two worlds is this: that in world one the table has the matter of my table in the actual world, and in world two it doesn't. Even here, in the face of this description of the two worlds, I should say that I can complete the supposition corresponding to world two. I think I can do this by stipulating that in world two, and not in world one, it is my table that the supposition relates to. What could prevent that? Where such a supposition is entertained, all that has happened is that our supposition about where the table is has been separated from our supposition about where such and such a parcel of matter is, taking advantage of their independent specifiability and of the non-identity between table and wood.

'But how *can* you, where two worlds are qualitatively indistinguishable, make a ruling of identity in defiance of the one thing that remains to distinguish the one table from the other, namely the identity of the matter?' Answer: How can *you*, who ask me this question regarding two worlds that are qualitatively indistinguishable, insist that the table in one but not in the other world is made of such and such matter? Only surely by allowing *supposition* to settle which pieces of wood in which world are the actual pieces making up my actual table. So 'supposition' is my answer too, subject of course to the Aristotelian constraint. Worlds are the shadows of our suppositions and they take on their identity from these. Suppositions themselves take on their identity from (*inter alia*) the objects they relate to. If they sever themselves from these objects, then they collapse (or cease to relate to that to which they purport to relate). But the supposition that involves the table's being constituted from different matter does not sever itself from the table that stands in front of me.

12. ONE SPECIAL KIND OF ARTEFACT: WORKS OF ART AND THE ESSENCES OF THESE

Where does this leave us? It seems wrong, or so I conclude, to expect that concepts of particular sorts of artefacts will be more prolific than concepts of particular sorts of natural things in the *de re* necessities that they confer upon their instantiators. And, apart from properties such as that imported by the predicate constructed in paragraph 3 of §10, which will be as readily available for artefacts as for natural things, the necessary properties of particular artefacts will come nowhere near to being logically peculiar to them.

Nevertheless it is natural to ask: could there not be some special sort of artefact-kind for which, as a very special case, something closer to a Scotist theory of individual natures held? And could not such an individual nature also constrain the identity of the matter making up a given member of this artefact-kind?

To obtain even an approximation to a case where a Scotist theory of individual nature was applicable we should need a thing-kind which was special in one particular way. The instantiators of the thing-kind would have to be like this: to understand what this one or that one is, to understand what it is and which one it is, would be to understand countless particular details as so central to the instantiator's identity that its *integrity* depended on the presence of all of them, and its *existence* depended on virtually all of them. Particular objects of this thing-kind, being essentially conceived so particularly, could scarcely be envisaged at all as lacking very many of the particular properties thus designated as theirs. It follows that any variation in the central set of properties which were specific to one such special object's being the particular that it is would then – for this is the consequence of the requirement – have to count as a definite step towards the destruction of the thing or the replacement of it. At the same time, though, if we are to find here any approximation to particularized natures, then anything belonging to this special kind of artefact kinds would have to be an individual, a *material particular*. It must not be a mere type, or a recipe instantiable by different material particulars.

Are there any sorts of sorts like this? I have argued in another place that easel pictures, carved sculptures and frescoes come as close as anything can come to meeting such requirements.[39] In the culture of the West, as in certain other cultures, we think of the artist as making something which is calculated by him to have an effect which cannot be characterized in instrumental or non-aesthetic terms, and cannot be identified independently of some totality of relevant features that are the individuating features of this or that individual work. It follows that, once the work is finished, to visit any interference upon the features comprising this set is to threaten the work with obliteration, or with destruction by replacement, however gradual.[40] At the same time, works of art seem to satisfy the other condition we specified. For we do not conceive of an easel picture, fresco or carved sculpture as a template for the reproduction or multiplication of some particular image. Finally, we attach no less importance to the artist's effect being brought about by the same material means as the artist envisaged and contrived than we attach to the effect's itself remaining agelessly utterly indiscernible from one age to the next.[41] What a principle of activity does very completely for a natural thing, and the function of an ordinary artefact does imperfectly for the artefact (see above, Chapter Three, §4), the artist's conception of his own making of the work, his conception of its outcome and his calculation of the effect of the work on an ideal spectator must do for a painting. We do not look for law-like principles of activity for paintings or particular paintings; and it is equally true that, being no ordinary artefacts, paintings and carved sculptures do not have a function. But any particular work has an aim, a highly particular aim, that is internal to its

---

[39] See Wiggins (1978), pp. 52–68.

[40] Note that there is vagueness here, because partial destruction, hostile to integrity but insufficient to bring the work to the point of destruction or replacement *tout court*, is an idea that makes sense in this sort of case. That, after all, is the sad condition, all too easily aggravated by mindlessly scientistic restoration, of many fine works.

[41] We may not require the second of these things at all – if only because the artist himself cannot have expected it. He may have expected change, patina, fading or whatever. He may even have counted upon these alterations.

being that very work. The hypothesis I advance for consideration is that this at least can generate very particular *de re* necessities.

The work of art has necessarily – is such as to be *de re* inconceivable or unenvisageable as definitely lacking – any sufficiently rich complex of features that has essential occurrence in the artist's own implicit or explicit practically realized account (placed where it is in whatever context of artistic understanding) of this very piece of his work. This is the claim. It entails that there was an important residue of truth in certain idealist accounts of works of art. At the same time, I submit that this way of conceiving these special things is precisely not the way in which to conceive of an ordinary substance or of an ordinary artefact. The contrast that this brings to light serves well to mark something note-worthy in the understanding we have so far accumulated of ordinary substances.

Conceptualism and realism

Quand nous ferons naître la pensée, elle naîtra ainsi dans un univers déjà rangé.

When we come to exhibit the birth of thought we shall find that it is born into a universe that is already ordered.
> Simone Weil, *Leçons de Philosophie*, ed. A. Reynaud (Paris 1959), p. 24, translated by Hugh Price, *Lectures on Philosophy* (Cambridge, 1978).

The relation between my consciousness and a *world* is not a mere matter of contingency imposed on me by a God who happened to decide the matter this way rather than that, or imposed on me by a world accidentally preexisting and a mere causal regularity belonging to it. It is the *a priori* of the judging subject which has precedence over the being of God and the world and each and everything in the world. Even God is for me what he is in consequence of my own productivity of consciousness. Fear of blasphemy must not distract us here from the problem. [But] here too, as we found in the case of other minds, the productivity of consciousness does not itself signify that I *invent* or *fabricate* this transcendency, let alone this highest of transcendencies.
> Edmund Husserl, *Formale und Transzendentale Logik* (Halle (Saale), 1929), pp. 221–2.

I. ANTI-REALIST CONCEPTUALISM AND ANTI-CONCEPTUALIST REALISM

Chapter Four was an exploration of the conceptual limits of our thinking about the things that belong to this or that particular ultimate individuative kind. It pointed to the riches that will lie hidden within any individuative kind which is a natural or real kind. In the examination of how we are constrained in our thought about individuals belonging to kinds that need to be deictically-cum-nomologically specified, we were discovering that which plays in the determination of the essences of such particulars the part that verbally explicit definitions can play in determination of the nominal essences of particulars such as artefacts. In both sorts of case, the constraints on thought derive directly or indirectly from that which is meant by what we think or say. But in the deictically specified case, where the sortal predicate is like 'frog' and unlike 'house' and has its sense fixed in a manner that is reality-involving, meaning is conferred (or so we claimed) in a distinctive way. And this in its turn generates conclusions that appear to go well beyond those conventionally accounted as semantical. To anyone who thinks he knows how to make such distinctions, it will seem to be a metaphysical thesis, not a semantical thesis, that being a human being or having the G property (see Chapter Four, §6) is an absolute individuative prerequisite for anything's being Caesar. For this reason, the arguments of Chapter Four will attract the hostility of at least two schools of thought. Designating my own position (simply for brevity and convenience) *conceptualist realism*, I suggest that one of its likeliest critics may be called the *anti-realist conceptualist*, and another the *anti-conceptualist realist*.

The anti-realist conceptualist may or may not be an **R** theorist, and may or may not have found intelligible the defence of principle **D** attempted in Chapter Two. What he is certain to find questionable in the extreme is the purported absoluteness (non-relativity to topic, context, or level), of the necessity that I have alleged (*exempli gratia*) to attach to the particular entity Caesar's being a human being.[1] The anti-conceptualist realist, on the other hand, whose position is addressed at §5 following, will scarcely object to the categorical conceptions of necessity, substance, truth or whatever that lurk in earlier chapters; but he will doubt (as Michael Ayers does, for instance)[2] that anyone ought to count as a realist who is prepared to embrace the sort of conceptualism that informed the argument that I gave for **D** and that motivated the derivation of *de re* necessity. There is a third form of opposition that might come from latter-day Humeans who are convinced of the theoretical impossibility of a *de re* necessity that is not reducible to the analyticity of some sentence. But I have said my piece against this school, and shall now direct attention upon the other two.

'It is all very well', my new opponents are likely to object, 'talking as you did in the previous chapter of the constraints on envisaging a thing.

---

[1] See Bas C. van Fraassen (1977–8).
[2] See Michael R. Ayers (1974). See also Parts One and Three, Vol. II of Ayers (1992).

Suppose that the place marked by the z-variable in "it is possible to envisage z's being ϕ" *is*, as you claim, an extensional position and somehow confers extensionality upon "z" in "z can be ϕ". We shall not object. We are also ready to suppose that, when Quine claimed that to be necessarily greater than seven was not a trait of a number but depended only on the manner of referring to the number,[3] he overlooked the kind of necessity that you have found outside the range of Quine's three grades of modal involvement and claimed to find traces of in Quine's and Goodman's own writings. We shall not even demur when you claim that, if a thinker genuinely conceives of z as ϕ, there must, for purposes of the kind of possibility you were concerned with, be some sortal concept f such that z can be identified as this or that instance of f, f and ϕ being coconceivable of z. This last requirement may perhaps justify you in adopting, for purposes of your brand of possibility, what Quine called an "invidious attitude towards certain ways of specifying a thing and favouring [some over] other ways [of specifying x] as somehow revealing the essence of the object". But these concessions, in the particular form in which you are trying to extract them, are perfectly unimportant. For the most you can ever obtain by these means is a conceptualism that is shaped and conditioned by human powers of envisaging. These powers are the product, both time-bound and culture-bound, of a conceptual scheme which is determined by interests that are very special. However deep seated they may seem to us, such interests in the world that surround us are scarcely implanted in us by nature in order that our beliefs or theories should mirror nature itself. You are deceiving yourself if you think you have found some philosophical engine by which to invest with real essences the concrete entities of the world. For us, there is no doubt a certain apparent indispensability in the everyday conceptual scheme that *we*, from our limited and cosmically insignificant point of view, bring to bear upon the world. But the real entities of the real world are whatever they are, independently of whether human beings exist or not. They are perfectly indifferent, so to speak, in this matter of how human beings conceive of them. That is not our only complaint. A further charge that we should urge against you is that the conceptual scheme for which you are working to get this privilege is scarcely very different, even now, from the scheme that systematically delayed the progress of natural science beyond the jejune approximations of Aristotle.'

---

[3] See Quine (1953), pp. 148 and 155.

The moral that the anti-realist conceptualist seeks to draw from all this is that the aspiration to contemplate, however distantly, the real essences of concrete things is best forgotten about. For in nature itself, he will say, there are no modalities.

The moral drawn by the anti-conceptualist realist, on the other hand, is not that essentialism as such is mistaken. The conclusion he will come to is that the realist aspiration is inimical to any position like the conceptualism that I have been arguing for. He will persist in the idea that the realist ideal is to be valued above any supposed conceptualist insight. But he will hold fast to his conviction that, in the long run, there must be some better approach than that which is supposed to lead through (A) – (H) of Chapter Four to the real essences of concrete things.

In answer to these critics, I shall be content for the most part to clarify the claims of the particular conceptualism defended here to be one form of realism. For the objection I have just rehearsed comprehends in each of its two forms a number of misapprehensions whose removal will be far more instructive and far more liberating of thought than exhaustive responses to the divers accusations and counter-suggestions that each critic could muster on his side. Once conceptualist realism is recognized for what it is, its metaphysical plainness will be manifest.

2. FOUR CLARIFICATIONS

(a) The objection given in the previous section depends partly on a misunderstanding of one point that Chapter Four will have made familiar. The conditions that have been characterized as peculiarly central to the articulation of this or that particular thing and its division from the rest of reality concerned, not the world's need to contain Caesar, but only the kind of thing *Caesar* had to be *if* there was to be any such thing as Caesar, namely (say) a human being. The necessity in question is at once crucial with respect to the question of the individual's being there to articulate, and peculiarly innocuous. The necessity is categorical with respect to Caesar, but from another point of view it is a conditioned necessity. The singular thing about this necessity resides in the character of its condition. The condition comprehends all states of affairs in which there exists . . . well, the very entity in question.[4]

---

[4] For the reasons for putting the matter in this way, see §13 of my article 'The Kant – Frege – Russell View of Existence: a rehabilitation of the second level view', in *Modality, Morality & Belief*, ed. Sinnott, Armstrong, Raffman and Asher (Cambridge, 1994).

(b) To put a sentence forward as a true statement of *de re* necessity (or as a *de dicto* necessity for that matter, if the *de dicto* were in question) is not to put the sentence forward as in some special way proof from revision, correction, or the boredom of our descendants. Those who object in such terms to essentialism as an expression of the stick-in-the-mud mentality or of ill-advised reaction have insufficiently distinguished these several statuses.

(c) It is necessary to reiterate the sincerity of the essentialist adherence to principle Θ of §6 of Chapter Four. Essences of natural things, as we have them here, are not fancified vacuities parading themselves in the shadow of familiar things as the ultimate explanation of everything that happens in the world.[5] They are natures whose possession by their owners is the precondition of their owners being divided from the rest of the reality as anything at all. These natures are delimited by reference to causal or explanatory principles and purposes that are low level perhaps; but they are fully demanding enough for something to count as their being disappointed or frustrated. (Witness the longish list of would-be sortal concepts that have definitely failed.) It is true that, whatever these principles may once have seemed to be, the principles we have called the laws of development of individual natural substances (that is the laws associated with individuative kinds of natural things) are not themselves the *scientifically basic* laws of the physical world. (Or rather, they need not be.) Nor in general are they reducible (in the strict and proper sense) to such basic laws. Nevertheless, the kind-bound laws of coming to be, of distinctive activity, and of passing away are nomologically grounded. They are *supervenient upon*, or better (as Leibniz might put it) *consentient with*, the more basic laws that are immanent in all things.[6]

---

[5] We do not look for scientifically ultimate explanations at this level of conceptualization. By the standards of 2,300 years ago it was not necessarily unscientific to look for them there, as Aristotle justifiably and non-vacuously did. (See the interpretation offered by Alan Gotthelf in 'Aristotle's Conception of Final Causality', *Review of Metaphysics*, 30 (1976).) Of course, it has been discovered since Aristotle that the search for fundamental explanations and principles, and for mechanisms underlying the phenomena, requires not only a new vocabulary but also a new ontology. On this see below, §7. But let us take a sane view of all this. The failure of Aristotelian science is final. Its failure does not entail, however, that science has shown that every explanation in any way worth having of anything worth knowing must eventually find expression at the level of the science that has displaced the human world view.

[6] Cf. Leibniz, Gerhardt II, 263, *op. cit.* at head of Chapter Three. Not only are these ideas separable from the teleological view of nature (see Chapter Three, Section 1). They are separable also from the teleological conceptions of certain theorists of Natural Law about the levels of excellence that natural things may realize or attain to. For an amusing and summary account of these ideas see H. L. A. Hart, *The Concept of Law* (Oxford, 1961), p. 185.

(d) The realist conceptualist may cheerfully admit that the sortal concepts of which we are possessed, and which he argues to be presupposed to our articulation of reality, are (in a certain fashion and sense – see §7 below) the creatures of our interests (provided that these interests are generously enough conceived to include our curiosity). He may also allow that (often at least) there may be no one way in which we *must* articulate reality, nor any one level at which we must. The thing that does not follow from any of this, he will say, is that, *relative* to some determinate epistemological-cum-practical interest, there is arbitrariness in the discriminations we make, or in the existence conditions that we ascribe to the members of the natural and artefact kinds under which our interests (as properly and generously conceived) oblige us to make sense of experience. For the supposed arbitrariness of whether or not this or that concept is brought or not brought to bear upon reality – better (see Preamble §5) the supposed arbitrariness of whether we deploy the conception corresponding to *this* concept and look for fs in reality, or deploy the conception corresponding to *that* concept and look for gs in reality – cannot be translated into any corresponding arbitrariness in the articulation of the things themselves that fall under the concept.[7] Arbitrariness or vagueness that attaches to the determination of the extension of the sortal concept has a different source (see Chapter Four, §9).

Nobody will find any of these confusions or misapprehensions very inviting – at least when they are anatomized in this way. But that does not mean that they are dead or inert or have no indirect influence. Moreover, confusion apart, it must also be allowed that the thinking the anti-essentialist opposes to the essentialist conception is sustained by the enchantment of an image that is vivid in the extreme.

3. A CONVENTIONALIST RECONSTRUCTION OF OUR MODAL CONVICTIONS: A CONCEPTUALIST ANTI-REALIST VIEW OF ESSENCE

'At bottom, everything that can be said about the world, can be said in purely general statements, without modalities. There is no thisness beyond suchness, but every actual individual is individuated already by the properties it has in this world; hence can be denoted in principle by a definite description in which the quantifier ranges over actual existents alone. At this bottom level the only necessity we can countenance is purely logical or verbal necessity which, like God, is

---

[7] Cf. p. 288 and other remarks I make in §1 of 'The *De Re* 'Must': a Note on the Logical Form of Essentialist Claims', in *Truth and Meaning: Essays in Semantics*, ed. Evans and McDowell (Oxford, 1976).

no respecter of persons. In this modality whatever Peter can do Paul can do also. A semantic representation of this will use a conventional identification of individuals in different worlds, but since every individual plays each possible role in some possible world, *every* choice of conventional identifications which does not violate the identity principle that no two existents in world α have all the same properties in α yields the same result.

'To make sense of our world in a *convenient* fashion, however, we raise certain regularities to the status of laws and (not independently) certain attributes to the status of natures. In the formal mode, this means that some statements assume the office of assumptions which may be tacitly used in all reasoning, and certain predicates are chosen to form a classificatory scheme. Once this is done, we produce relative or tacitly conditional modal qualifiers . . . A proposition P is *peculiarly about* individual *e* if we can change the truth value of P by permuting *e* with another individual *e'* (while leaving all other individuals fixed), but cannot change that truth value by any permutation which leaves *e* fixed . . . In a full model, no proposition peculiarly about a particular entity can be necessary; for [in a full model] the necessary proposition is closed under all permutations.'[8]

What Van Fraassen describes here is a sort of reconstruction in two stages of how it is possible for us to have our present ideas of substance and *de re* modality. The reconstruction is meant to tell us what we should make of these ideas and of the fact that we have them. Not too much, he suggests. The reconstruction is not put forward by Van Fraassen as an ordinary historical hypothesis or even as a piece of psychogenetic theory. Taking it rather as it is intended, we shall find that one thing is crucial to the reconstruction, as to the attitude that it recommends towards substance and modality: the two stages of which it speaks must be intelligible to us and describable by us, the theorists, in just the relationship that the account postulates. How otherwise can we credit Van Fraassen's own words with even the semblance of intelligibility?

The difficulty in this respect attaches to the first stage. Here, whatever Peter can do Paul can do also (Van Fraassen says) – indeed any individual whatever can do. For anything, it seems, can do or be anything at this level, the only constraints being those imposed by logical necessity in the

---

[8] Van Fraassen, part IV of 'Essence and Existence' (1977–8). Cf. part I:

> The nominalist's first and basic move in this game is to say that all natural necessities are elliptic for conditional verbal necessities. This sheet on which I write must burn if heated, because it is paper – yes. But the only necessity that is really there is that all paper must burn when heated. This is so, but means only that we would not call something paper if it behaved differently . . . When sufficiently refined, the position that all non-verbal necessities are ellipses for conditional necessities *ex vi terminorum* can be held.

Cf. also the same author's 'The Only Necessity is Verbal Necessity', *Journal of Philosophy* (Feb. 1977).

narrowest sense which, whatever dues it pays to 'indiscernibility at a world', is 'no respecter' of identity in the proper sense. The question then is: can we really understand this first stage of the reconstruction? Only, I submit, if we can make sense of an entity that is nothing in particular. (Cf. the justification and refinement of Δ of Chapter Four, section 2, undertaken in §5 and §9.)

Van Fraassen's adherence to the Identity of Indiscernibles is important here. Contrast with his explicit reliance upon the principle everything that we have claimed in Chapter Two against the Identity of Indiscernibles and have elsewhere implied (in agreement with P. F. Strawson, *Individuals*, the chapter on monads and *passim*) about the indispensability and irreducibility of the demonstrative function. To turn *this* into *this-ness* and, having found no way to understand *this-ness* as a sort of *such-ness*, to seek then to patch matters up by espousing the Identity of Indiscernibles – this is a counsel of confusion, confusion that is needless. But there is scarcely anything unconfused that can be said or denied by the use of the words *haecceitas* and *this-ness*. What these words purport to help one to say *or* deny is no less mixed up than the noises that they make are unlovely. (Cf. Chapter Four, §7.)

Finally, I would claim that the whole charm of Van Fraassen's picture depends on one's allowing that one can first have an ontology of particulars conceived as bare, and then at a second stage introduce, as an instrument of understanding, explanation and discovery, what Quine and Geach have called an *ideology*. But is it not a mysterious suggestion that a whole range of attributions, including sortal attributions which say what various everyday things are, could be determined at this second stage (in radical dependence, Van Fraassen suggests, on some human viewpoint), by being superimposed upon a completed first stage ontology which is at once bare yet existentially determinate? For anyone versed in the notion that an ontology is by no means an empty or uncommittal thing, this is as strange as being asked to believe that one could distinguish between (first) a neutral or concern-uncontaminated ontology of jokes (what it is for x to be a joke, or for x and y to be the same joke, or for there to be such a joke as z), and (second), a quite separate and interest-contaminated range of predicative attributions to jokes ('funny', 'comic', 'witty', 'off-colour', 'whimsical') or things in jokes ('incongruous', 'ludicrous', 'absurd'). Is it compatible with a good theory of existence to suppose that the first stage (ontology) could have been provided for while leaving absolutely everything else to be determined at the second (ideology)? Let anyone still charmed by Van Fraassen's picture rehearse these questions again, *mutatis mutandis*, for natural numbers, quantities, shades, . . .

Obviously, if ontology were completely insensitive to all changes in theory, in ideology or in how things are conceived, and if one and the same fixed set of entities could be descried by conceptions of the world that were different to just any degree that you like, then that would subvert not only Chapter Four but also the account offered in Chapter Two, §5, of the relationship between existence and belonging to a sort. I should hope that the positive account of existence offered there had the attraction of simplicity. There is a range of basic sortal attributions that we apply to various everyday things – 'this is a horse', 'this is a tree', 'that is a man'. These belong to the level of ontology and, at least to this extent, ontology and ideology must contaminate one another immediately. What is strange is that the anti-essentialists whom I am attacking[9] accept all these attributions in their unmodalized form, and then (one stage too late, in my opinion, for they have already consented to pick out the thing and to involve themselves, however minimally, in some proto-theoretical conception of entities of the relevant kind) adduce as a reason to deprecate the suggestion that any of these things *had to* be a horse, or a tree or a man, the anthropocentricity of the view-point that underlies and conditions the attributions. But here as everywhere the question is: of *what* could one ever be speaking if one allowed that it might equally well have been a prime number or a fire shovel, though it was in fact neither?

4. A HYPOTHESIS CONCERNING THE SOURCES OF ANTI-ESSENTIALISM

I advance for the reader's consideration a hypothesis: the anti-realist case against essential properties has rested on a sequence of three ideas.

(1) It is conceivable that, in the absence of creatures capable of thought as we know it, the particular kinds of individual substance that we ourselves recognize in this world would never have been discovered. (Indeed nothing forces anyone to discover in a place even that which is there to be discerned in terms of his own conceptions.) In that place, in the room of what we ourselves find there, or (so to say) out of its matter, another race of creatures might have articulated and

---

[9] Russell was an opponent of essentialism. But these paragraphs are not directed at his position. For he pursued the logic of his position (and the logic of my paragraphs here) to the point of rejecting the ontology which is presupposed to saying 'this is a man'. See *op. cit.* note 7.

individuated quite other kinds of things with very different principles of individuation.

From this questionable if not altogether implausible premiss the conceptualist anti-essentialist goes on to conclude:

(2) It is perfectly possible for what is there to be discovered in a given place, e.g. for a substance which is there, to be conceptualized in at least two quite different ways. The progress of science would precisely consist in conceptualizing it in better, and radically different, ways. So, he argues:

(3) The constraints arising from the conceptualization and individuation of the particulars that we recognize in the world, and can draw spatio-temporal boundaries around, must not be represented as necessities on what is actually there independently of mind or thought. The most objectionable feature of all the objectionable features of essential attributions is that they purport to record such necessities.

It is at stage (2) that everything goes wrong here. What is this substance out there that can be conceptualized in radically different ways, which can be seized upon in thought by the anti-essentialist, but can have radically different principles of existence and persistence ascribed to it? This is surely an entity with inconsistent properties. If the charge of having a ridiculous conception of substance sticks anywhere, it sticks on anyone who argues via (2) from (1) to (3). But it is only by means of some such conception that an anti-realist philosopher could crowd out altogether the possibility, which is important but always neglected, that, even if a conceptual scheme capable of exploring and understanding the physical world might dispense altogether with the articulation and isolation of x from its environment (because it could afford to ignore x altogether), still the essential attributions upon x record or reflect conditions at once fundamental and invariant upon x in particular's existing and being singled out in reality.

5. AN EXAGGERATION OF CONCEPTUALISM, DEPRECATED AND CORRECTED IN THE LIGHT OF CERTAIN TRUISMS; AND THE REPLY TO THE ANTI-CONCEPTUALIST REALIST BEGUN

If the preceding section succeeded to any significant extent, it will have gained favour for some sort of conceptualist view of individuation. But conceptualism may seem to have strange consequences.

Leszek Kolakowski writes:

'The picture of reality sketched by everyday perception and by scientific thinking is a kind of human creation (not imitation) since both the linguistic and the
scientific division of the world into particular objects arise from man's practical
needs. In this sense the world's products must be considered artificial. In this
world the sun and stars exist because man is able to make them *his* objects, differ-
entiated in material and conceived as 'corporeal individuals'. In abstract,
nothing prevents us from dissecting surrounding material into fragments constructed in a manner completely different from what we are used to. Thus,
speaking more simply, we could build a world where there would be no such
objects as 'horse', 'leaf', 'star', and others allegedly devised by nature. Instead,
there might be, for example, such objects as 'half a horse and a piece of river',
'my ear and the moon', and other similar products of a surrealist imagination.'[10]

I am bound to agree with any anti-conceptualist realist who asserts that
what Kolakowski says here is impossible to believe. I should hold that any
conceptualism which is bent on picking its way past the confusions that
have sustained for so long the conflict between realism and idealism must
indeed strive to do justice to the insight for which Kolakowski is seeking
expression. But it will see the whole interest of these problems as residing in the problem of finding the elusive, correct and unexciting formulation of that insight. A conceptualism that aspires to the title of a modest
and sober realism must keep at arm's length any such 'sense' as the sense
in which horses, leaves, sun and stars could be supposed to be artefacts.
It must hold on to the distinctions so laboriously worked out in Chapter
Three, §2. It must leave itself room to express all the proper reservations
(concerning the lack of appropriate causal or explanatory principles,
etc.) about the prospects of finding a genuinely sortal notion with the
same extension as *half a horse plus a piece of river*. And it must hold a nice
balance, adjusted to what is in fact a subtly reciprocal relation, between
(1) the extent to which the conceptions that we bring to bear in order to
distinguish, articulate and individuate things in nature are our inventions
and (2) the extent to which these conceptions make reference to concepts
that we find or permit nature itself to discover to us, *thereby* informing and
regulating our conceptions of them. (For the distinction of conceptions
and concepts, see Preamble §5.) Conceptualism properly conceived must
not entail that, before we grasped these concepts, their extensions did not
exist autonomously. It must insist that natural things and their concepts
existed independently of whether our conceptions of them were destined to be fashioned or the things themselves were destined to be dis-

[10] Leszek Kolakowski, *Towards a Marxist Humanism* (New York, 1968), pp. 47–8. My attention was
first drawn to this passage by Michael Ayers, who has expressed doubts whether my own sort of
conceptualism leaves me in a position to disagree with it.

covered falling under these concepts.[11] Its most distinctive contention is that, even though horses, leaves, sun and stars are not inventions or arte-facts, still, if such things as horses, leaves, sun and stars were to be singled out in experience at all so as to become the objects of thought, then some scheme had to be fashioned or formed, in the back and forth process between recurrent traits in nature and would-be cognitive conceptions of these traits, that made it possible for them to be picked out.

For someone to single out a leaf or a horse or a sun or a star, or what-ever it is, that which he singles out must have the right principle of indi-viduation for a leaf or a horse or a sun or a star . . . For to single out one of these things he must single *it* out. Such truisms would scarcely be worth writing down if philosophy were not driven from side to side here of the almost unnegotiable strait that divides the realist myth of the *self-differentiating object* (the object which announces itself as the very object it is to any mind, however passive or of whatever orientation) from the *substratum* myth that is the recurrent temptation of bad conceptualism.[12] It is easy to scoff at *substratum*. It is less easy to escape the insidious idea that there can be the singling out in a place of a merely determinable space-occupier awaiting incongruent or discordant substantial determinations (individuatively inconsistent answers to the question of *what it is*).[13] But no substance has been singled out at all until something makes it deter-

---

[11] Cf. Hobbes's definition: 'a body is that, which having no dependence upon our thought, is coin-cident or coextended with some part of space'. *De Corpore* II, 11 (Molesworth, p. 136).

[12] Rebounding from all this, there is a temptation to add nonsense to confusion and say that a thing is nothing but a sum (in some inexplicable sense of 'sum') of properties and/or appearances, or a set of universals each sitting in the next one's lap. This is in fact the notion of thing favoured by some anti-essentialists and sometimes also attributed to Leibniz (entirely wrongly, see my (1995)). How it is to be combined with the idea that objects so conceived have no essences finally passes comprehension. Consider, for a start, the negation of the conjunction of these properties. And if the reply to that is that these collocations of properties have shifting membership, then inquire after the principle determining membership. The answer to this will smuggle back the notion of a substance or a continuant.

[13] There will exist too indefinitely many items with too many distinct principles of identity and per-sistence which you might find in that place – the thing, the parcel of stuff that makes up the thing, and the mereological sum of all the components of that parcel, to name but three. See also here A. M. Quinton, *The Nature of Things*, p. 67. For the claim that the same portion of space can be co-occupied by different things, see my (1968).

Against all such arguments, Michael Ayers has written (1974, p. 132; and compare M. C. Bradley's critique at *Australasian Journal of Philosophy*, 47 (1969) concerning the principles of tracing that have been defended in Chapter Two):

> it might be thought that in unravelling the sweater we remove or destroy one principle of unity, and [that] by cutting the [woollen] thread [of the ball of wool from which the sweater was knitted] we remove a second. Each operation is possible without the other, and so each principle of unity seems independent of the other [giving in one and the same place two different things of different kinds]. The latter and more realistic view, however, is that, if a sweater consists of a single thread, then this means only that the different parts of the wool

minate *which* entity has been singled out; and for this to be determinate, there must be something in the singling out that makes it determinate which principle is the principle of individuation for the entity and under what family of individuatively concordant sortal concepts it is to be subsumed (see Chapter Two, §7).[14]

6. THE PERFECT CONSONANCE OF SOBER REALISM AND SOBER CONCEPTUALISM

An anti-conceptualist realist who takes exception to the essentialism arrived at by means of principle Δ of Chapter Four will view with suspicion any suggestion that truisms are available from which, in the presence of a strict notion of identity, anything like this will follow: that the individuative scheme we bring to bear upon experience or the fashion in which (as a race, or as a culture, or as a culture at a time) we articulate reality can determine the kinds of thing we shall single out (fs, gs or whatever).[15] Such claims may seem to the realist to be tantamount to saying that the active inquiring mind does not merely construe reality but constructs it – as if under certain conditions the mind could fashion not only concepts or conceptions but truth itself. Is this not a particularly unappealing form of idealism, he will ask?

The literal purport of the conceptualist claim which the realist has put under discussion is not that mind constructs reality. If it comes close to seeming to say that, this is only because the truth has here to rub shoulders with two opposing doctrines that are so similar in their pretensions

hang together in more than one way, and so have a unity that is more difficult to destroy than would otherwise be the case. Roughly, the unity or structure of a sweater knitted from a hundred separate threads is destroyed by unravelling, and the unity of a single thread by cutting; while the unity of a sweater knitted from a single thread survives either operation but not both. Thus no serious doubt is cast on that apparently essential ingredient of a realist theory of the identity of physical objects, the principle that the same matter cannot be subjected to more than one principle of unity at the same time: i.e. cannot compose more than one individual simultaneously.

If this says that in some cases (composition from one thread) unravelling a sweater is not a way of destroying it, but that in other cases (composition from several threads of wool) things are so different that unravelling is enough for destruction, then I am happy to let the reader assess the price of Ayers's 'realist principle'. I hope it will be clear why I believe that the principle is dispensable to realism, to objectivity, and to the nomologically grounded conception of substance. (Compare here certain difficulties that I claim to see in a similar principle of Eli Hirsch's: see footnote 4 of my (1974).) Singling out that sweater is not singling out that wool.

[14] A fallacy for the unwary: *It is indeterminate what thing A singled out; therefore A singled out something indeterminate.*

[15] Michael Ayers (1974), Eli Hirsch ('Physical Identity', *Philosophical Review* (1976), especially pp. 36of.) and Fei Xu, among others, have taken exception to these claims. See now Wiggins (1997a).

and underlying absurdity as to leave only a small space between for truth to stand. Our claim was only that what sortal concepts we bring to bear upon experience determines what we can find there – just as the size and mesh of a net determine, not what fish are in the sea, but which ones we shall catch. It is true that the individuative conceptions that are brought to bear at any point will come with notions about the ways in which things of a given kind behave. These notions will bear on persistence conditions. But this does not imply that, once things of a given kind, fs or gs, are lighted upon, the individuative scheme we bring to bear will *itself* determine something further – a principle of activity or a persistence condition. What that principle is for fs or gs depends only on fs or gs. We discover it in tandem with grasping the concept of an f or a g and applying our conception of it to the fs and gs we light upon. Moreover, our conception of the things that answer to the concept is given to us in a reciprocal process of the kind that Chapter Three was meant to illustrate, a process comprising not only deixis, not only allusion to the nature whatever it may be of that which is demonstrated, but practical and probative interaction with the things themselves that are in question.

Much hangs here on identifying correctly the point, if any, where there is choice or freedom in the articulation of reality. The near certainty of incomprehension of the tenets of conceptualist realism by a different kind of realist is so great that even the reader who has seized what I would say here may forgive me for attempting one more statement of the point at issue (and for returning to the matter once again in the course of Chapter Six). As soon as a set of individuative concerns is determinate, and an interest and a set of sortal concepts is fixed upon, nothing that can be done by one who grasps the concept will determine whether or not there is anything at a given place and time that actually satisfies the given concept. Any freedom we enjoy must come at an earlier point. Whatever may be the truth to be found in the idea that what concepts (better, what conceptions of what concepts) a thinker applies to the world depends on his inventiveness in the fashioning of conceptions and the devising of hypotheses, whatever the truth of the idea that the accident or caprice of his interests and/or the thinker's conceptual daring and enterprise will carry him at his pleasure to places that nothing else would have carried him to – this *exhausts* his freedom. For, once arrived at a place, what he finds there is not at his pleasure. Whether or not there exist things that answer to the concept f, and what they are like, cannot depend on his invention or his concerns.

7. THE REALIST REQUIREMENT RESTATED, REFURBISHED AND SATISFIED

It is not enough to remove confusions. The anti-conceptualist realist is not necessarily someone confused by anything at all, except the difference between good and bad conceptualism. And he is most unlikely to think it relevant to what he has to say that one can count as objectively as you like, and answer the question *what is it?* as accurately as you like under sortal concepts of utterly provincial or frivolous provenance. His real preoccupation is surely not with objectivity, for it presupposes that. He will probably allow that we have well-tried canons for recognizing the correctness or incorrectness of subsuming this or that object under such and such a concept. Nor is he bent on denying that the truth with which such predications are concerned can transcend our means of recognizing truth. Evidently, the thing that chiefly concerns the anti-conceptualist realist is to preserve our thought's prospects of passing beyond the narrowly anthropocentric.[16] But here it seems to me that an essentialist of my persuasion can make common cause with him. For, as we have conceived it, an individuative scheme for the articulation of reality and the singling out of natural things can be wide open to reality. There is nothing to prevent the scheme from being regulated and corrected constantly by the things in reality themselves and/or our evolving conceptions of things in reality. Here I would hark back, of course, to the distinction proposed in Chapter Three and Preamble §6 between nominal or stipulative definitions, e.g. those founded in the function of artefacts (whose nature depends on us, or has depended on us, collectively), and the real or causal definitions (strictly not 'definitions') that we hunt after in nature, identifying their targets by 'tacit reference to the real essence of this or that species of body' (Locke, *Essay* III.10.19), first annexing these essences by marks that can *stand proxy* for them (marks that 'tiennent lieu', Leibniz, *Nouveaux Essais*, 3.6.14). With the second kind of definition, deictically directed and provisional in content, we cannot of course avoid the risk in which our explanatory aspirations inevitably involve us, namely that, where we are unlucky, we may have been searching for something that was not there to be found. But here

---

[16] For the distinctness of these concerns, and for the Peircean conception of the advance of science beyond and away from the anthropocentric, see 'Truth, Invention, and the Meaning of Life', in my *Needs, Values, Truth* (1987, 1991; 1997), pp. 120–1.

 I find that my conception of realism here is in some respect anticipated, albeit in terms more optimistic than I should think necessary or desirable, by Milton Fisk in 'The World Regained', *Journal of Philosophy* (1972), see especially pp. 667–8.

too, when all goes well, things themselves can shape our conception of things.

'You assert that the notion of substance is formed from concepts, and not from things. But are not concepts themselves formed from things? (Nonne ipsi conceptus formantur ex rebus?) You say that the notion of substance is a concept of the mind, or an entity of reason as they say. But the same can be said of any concept.' (Leibniz to de Volder.)[17]

In so far as Leibniz is making a completely general claim in this passage, it is no doubt falsified in part by the case that he always ignores (or, where he does not ignore it, underestimates), *viz.* artefact kinds and cultural objects where things are fashioned to answer to a conception and there is no question of shaping the conception of the concept to the things that prove to fall under the concept. But in the other case, there need be nothing to prevent human understanding from coming ever closer to finding features of the world whose articulation is not sensitive to the more narrowly practical or provincial explanatory interests that first moved us to inquire into the nature of things. It may be true that the normal thing-kind concept (even where the understanding sees that not as the creature of our understanding but as something in nature that the understanding has prepared itself to be able to discover or light upon) is rarely an absolutely basic concept conceived as basic by physical science – still less a concept so fundamental that *no* real understanding of nature could ever look past the extension of this concept. It may also be true that, however deep we go, an intelligence of a superior kind might latch on to a more fundamental and explanatorily more basic class of things whose identifying attributes pulled their weight in a far better and more universal theory than do any of the kinds that we, in our lowly condition, shall ever discriminate. Let us not argue here about that. To whatever extent this is true, the causal-cum-explanatory interests that give us the most sophisticated and scientific sortal conceptions we possess may indeed be somewhat provincial. But if that is so, then a proper answer to the realist critic ought not to insist that the concepts these conceptions are conceptions of are never provincial to *any* degree. One part of the better answer is that the critic has not shown that all genuinely explanatory insights must be framed at the deepest level of fundamental theory. Moreover, even for purposes of the purest theory of science, the critic may be in error. His doctrine would certainly be unmanageable in the daily practice of giving expositions of the relatively fundamental theo-

---

[17] Gerhardt II, p. 182. Cf. *Nouveaux Essais*, 3.6, §13.

ries we do possess. The less exigent condition of acceptance that is imposed on the sortal notions that we continue in practice to employ is not in any case an empty one. And equipped as it is with such notions, our present scheme of ideas surely does represent a respectable, however unimpressive, stage in some however gradual process of the revelation of reality. Only sneering discontent with all would-be factual thought or speech as such, or a gloating dissatisfaction with it as any sort of a record of reality (and these are not the vices of the anti-conceptualist realist), could prompt someone to deny this.

8. CONCLUDING SUGGESTIONS

By way of partial summary of this and the previous chapter, I shall close with some suggestions or speculations concerning the relation of the scientific world view and the less theoretical view of reality which lags behind the scientific world view but is practically indispensable to the sustaining of any meaning that might be attributed to our thoughts.

(i) Many of the scientifically significant shifts in our conceptions of the world represent not shifts in our conceptions of a settled ontology, or shifts in the individuative conceptions proper to one and the same set of entities, but the abandonment for certain explanatory purposes of the old set of entities and the old ontology. The 'ingredients' that composed the things of the old ontology may then be inventoried, if that needs to be the question at issue, in other counts of the stuff of the world. In so far as questions about the old set of entities are answered rather than simply abandoned, the answer may be given under the new order by bridge principles (whose *ad hoc* character it will do no harm to acknowledge) or even by recourse to considerations (again *ad hoc*) of a mereological kind.

(ii) Where a shift in conception is a genuine revision of the old conception of the old entities and the same entities are recognizable, i.e. where the shift is an improvement or development of the individuative conceptions which were constitutive of the old ontology, the old ontology can happily take over the improvement. (Cf. the G property of §6 of Chapter Four.) If the deictic-cum-Leibnizian account of concept-formation is correct, then conceptual schemes are designed from the outset to allow for this kind of improvement.

(iii) Scientific progress towards an explanatorily more fruitful conception of the world that abandons an old ontology for certain explanatory purposes may or may not need to discredit the ontology of the older, less theoretical conception of the world. (Cf. Chapter Six, §8.) There will be cases where that older ontology still counts as adequate in its own terms. The older ontology may yet be cotenable with the more theoretical conception. Contrasting the actual discrediting of entities of some kind, palpable or impalpable, with the discovering of new entities at the atomic or subatomic level, let us not conceive the latter as determining the level to which everything else must be reduced (in the serious sense of 'reduce'[18]), even if this is the level at which macroscopic events are promised certain sorts of explanation. Let us note too that these promised explanations may or may not be forthcoming and may or may not be completely formulable at that level; and may, even if forthcoming, leave high and dry but perfectly unharmed the familiar macroscopic entities in which we cannot abandon our interest. Indeed there are some practical interests we *cannot* become blind to, and some entities in which it is impossible for us to lose our interest (most notably perhaps the entities to be treated in Chapter Seven).

(iv) A new conception of the world and its accompanying ontology will not come bare of individuative concepts or of *de re* necessities of its own. As always, the thing that generates these *de re* necessities will be the requirement that everything conceivable of the new entities be coconceivable in the new ontology with that which is their most fundamental sortal identification. Principle Δ of Chapter Four concerned a necessity that is not in the narrow sense logical necessity. But its *strength* (contrast certainty) is equal to that of logical necessity. For once the theoretically fundamental sortal property f is fixed upon and its extension comes to light, it is not for thought to renege, even hypothetically (lest thought lose its grasp of its object), upon the determination of how a thing falling within that extension has to be in order to be an f (belong to f).

---

[18] For the serious sense of 'reduce' deployed in philosophy, let me commend the following:

> Most people are natural metaphysicians, and it is an easy passage for them from the unassailable methodological doctrine that physics and chemistry are applicable to biological objects, to the metaphysical doctrine, that living organisms are 'nothing but' physical systems. This . . . retards the search for explanatory hypotheses on the biological level, just as a purely behaviouristic approach to psychology retards and discourages the search for other hypotheses in that science . . .
> There is one more point to be mentioned in connexion with the doctrine of the reducibility of biology to physics and chemistry: people who hold the doctrine do not in fact believe it. If you want to reduce biology to physics and chemistry, you must construct bi-conditionals which are in effect definitions of biological functors with the help of those belonging only to physics and chemistry; you must then add these to the postulates of physics and chemistry and work out their consequences. Then and only then will it be time to go into your laboratories to discover whether these consequences are upheld there. From the fact that people do *not* do this, I venture the guess that they confuse *reducibility* of biology to physics and chemistry, with *applicability* of physics and chemistry to biological objects. (J. H. Woodger, *Biology and Language*, Cambridge, 1952, pp. 336–8. Compare also Alfred Tarski's Appendix E for Woodger's earlier work, *The Axiomatic Method in Biology*, Cambridge, 1937.)

Identity: absolute, determinate, and all or nothing, like no other relation but itself[1]

> *Wherever identity is real, it admits of no degrees.*   Thomas Reid (1785)

> *Identity is the vanishing point of resemblance.*   Wallace Stevens

I. THREE CONTRASTED VIEWS OF SINGLING OUT AN OBJECT

When something is singled out, an object of some sort impinges on a conscious subject, and the subject, in having the *de re* thought that he has when he is so impinged upon (a thought that may issue in a claim such as 'That bald man has been standing out there in the snow for four hours'), takes the object for something that it is (a bald man). The subject apprehends the object in at least one way correctly (even if, in all sorts of ways that are neither cognitively nor practically crucial, he misapprehends it). Let us label this claim (I). (I) is not drafted in order to exclude animals from the role of subject.

We can also say (II) that, when the subject singles out an object, his thought is answerable for its success to the nature and condition of the object singled out and his thought counts as the kind of thought that it

---

[1] For those sensible enough to have reached this point by skipping the many pages that stretch back from here to the summary of the first three chapters (see Chapter Three, §6), or for those who simply prefer to begin the book here, I resume at this point one key theme, repeating certain essentialist and conceptualist claims in order to push them further. (For some of these, see the partial résumé furnished at Chapter Five, §8.) Bearing in mind the interests of those stalwart enough to have arrived hither by the longer route, the résumé is made in a fresh, albeit highly partisan fashion. At some points the text derives from my contribution to T. Pettit and J. McDowell (eds.), *Subject, Thought and Context* (Oxford, 1986). See also my (1968).

A signpost for the reader: first, this chapter seeks to support Reid's claim and kindred claims about identity. The chosen route is through a further development of the thesis of conceptualist realism. Then the chapter seeks to confute a general conception of identity apparently visible in Wallace Stevens's dictum (torn disobligingly from its context) and in related formulations. (I cite Stevens from Anne Righter in *Shakespeare and the Idea of the Play* (London, 1962), p. 192.) Identity will emerge in this chapter as determinate, irreducible, autonomous and not interestingly supervenient on anything else whatever – like unto no other relation.

is by virtue of being answerable in that particular way to that particular object.

At this point, the contentions of Chapter Five will suggest a further claim (III): that, when an object is singled out by a subject in the manner described in (I) and (II), it will not be determinable without reference to the content of that sort of thought on the subject's part what object it was that impinged upon his mind. For the question of what impinged on his mind is not a simple question of what material something bumped into his sensory-cum-neural apparatus. At any given time all sorts of things will have done that. (Was his thought of a substance, of a stuff, of an event . . ., and, if of a substance then a substance of what kind, size, or typical life-span?)

Among philosophers favourably disposed to the conjunction of (I) and (II), there is one who will deprecate any suggestions which the verb 'impinge' may seem to carry of a material-or-causal transaction yet take keen pleasure in the important (however inadequate) concession to his viewpoint that he sees in (II) as strengthened by (III). For the sake of having a name, let us call this philosopher, among the various inheritors of **R**, an idealist. (Why an idealist? Compare the however reluctant use Kant makes of the appellation in the *Critique of Practical Reason*, Preface, *ad fin.*: 'Names that designate the followers of a sect have always been accompanied with much injustice: just as if one said that N is an idealist. For although N not only admits but even insists that our ideas of external objects have actual objects or external things corresponding to them, yet N holds that the form of the intuition does not depend on them, but on the human mind' (trans. Abbott).)

Another kind of philosopher may be content enough with (I) but reject (III) and be markedly unwilling to allow that it is *only* by reference to a *de re* thought *conceived as irreducibly de re* that it can be determined what object impinged on the consciousness of the subject. Let us call this philosopher, who is among the inheritors of not-**R**, a materialist.[2]

There is a third stand someone may take. Let us give the name of conceptualist or a conceptualist-realist to anyone who is eager to deny **R** and accept (I) and (II) together (as literally understood); happy to say that any full or proper development of (I) and (II) taken together would issue in (III); and happy to deny that there is any reductive level (of retinal

---

[2] He is to be numbered among the bare absolutists of Chapter Three, §6. In practice, not all bare absolutists will want to call themselves materialists. Nor will all dissociate themselves vehemently from every distinctive claim that is comprised under (II) or (III). Here, as in Chapter Three, §6, philosophical stereotypes are useful in exposition, but will not carry any weight in argument.

stimulation or whatever) at which some theory could keep track together of objects singled out and of thoughts of such objects. (He is likely to say that, if such objects and thoughts are to be conceived together in the kind of reciprocity already adumbrated in the conjunction (I) (II) (III), then a theory of this kind is impossible.) Such a philosopher is to be numbered among the **D**-absolutists of Chapter Three, §6. That is my crowd. His position grows out of the claim developed in Chapter Five that our cognitive access to objects in reality is made by *this such* conceptions, where *this such* conceptions were said to be present in advance of the recognition of any particular object as this or that kind of a thing, but were seen as wide open to correction in the light of empirical discoveries relating to entities of the general kind to which some particular thing belongs.

2. BACK AND FORTH BETWEEN THE OBJECT AND THE THOUGHT OF THE OBJECT

So much for the three contrasted views we have conventionally labelled idealism, materialism and conceptualism. My hopes rest, of course, with conceptualism, as developed and defended in the preceding chapters yet still held open to further refinement. My belief is that, as we explore further among the logical properties of the sameness relation, this third doctrine will make it intelligible, in a way that no other doctrine can, how a relation of such logical exigency as identity can have actual application to the world of experience.

The thought of the object is the kind of thought it is (we said) by virtue of being answerable to that object and the condition of that object. That is one dependence. But, according to (II), as poised to assimilate (III), there is an opposite (though unequal) dependence. The object is what it is, whether or not it is singled out. But the object does not single itself out.[3] Nor need the simple commitment to engage with nature and that which is there independently of us require *us* to single it out. What thing-kind conceptions we have or deploy is not determined under this kind of

[3] Here (I am aware) I yield to the temptation to try to convey something by issuing the denial of something that is really nonsense. What would it be for an object to single itself out? The claim may best perhaps be read as a grammatical remark (made in the material mode) following from the explanation of 'single out' given at Preamble §3. One more remark about this misgiving. Even when (on other occasions) I have yielded to allied temptations and tried to convey the point by denying that there are 'lines in Nature', I have never taken this to be a denial that there are *edges* in nature, or that edges can be causally efficacious. Indeed they can inflict wounds or abrasions. Rather, I have wanted to insist that edges of that kind mark out imperfectly or scarcely at all the boundaries that are drawn by the singling out of continuants or substances.

compulsion. Nature does not reach down and lodge them in a pigeon hole or letter box for us. But nor yet is the matter determined quite arbitrarily. Rather, our store of thing-kind conceptions comes into being under the influence of our experience, our constitution, our ways of dwelling in the world and in reciprocity with our active concerns, practical and intellectual alike. The thing-kind conceptions that we arrive at in this way play an indispensable role, the conceptualist says, in the business of individuation. As always, however, the claim this imports, namely that 'which sortal concepts we apply to experience determines what we shall find there', needs to be understood in the unexciting way in which one understands 'the size and shape of the net determines the catch'. The size and mesh of a net determine not what fish are in the sea but which ones we shall catch . . . (for the rest, see Chapter Five, §6) – even as our expectations of what was there to be caught conditioned our choice of that net and affected at an earlier point some netmaker's design for that net.

Conceptualism thus stated will be drawn inexorably to the idea, already apparent in Chapter Five, that x is only a genuine continuant if, in a sense of 'single out' to be gradually refined, x could in principle be singled out as this such-and-such or that so-and-so, where the singling out of x is answerable to multiple constraints that are at once empirical *and* logical. It is to that idea that I should have recourse if I were called upon to justify the assumption I have made throughout this book that, in a case where it is indeterminate what has been singled out, we should not say that the thing singled out is something indeterminate. (Would that not be the merest fallacy?) Rather (I have said) *no substance at all* is singled out until something makes it determinate which entity has been singled out; for *this* to be determinate, there needs to be something in the singling out, something from the sides of the object *and* the thinker, which would yield a principle of individuation for the entity; so the singling out of a substance s at time t must reach backward and forward to any or all of the times, before and after t, at which s exists. What after all is an indeterminate object? What other idea can we have of such a thing than that of an entity that is individuatively indeterminate? And what other idea can that be than the idea of an entity with regard to which it is indeterminate which thing it is – the idea of a thing that is the creature of time t, is 'synchronically' perfectly identical with itself, but is 'diachronically' possibly less than perfectly identical with all sorts of more or less 'other' things? These notions are so strange in themselves, so apparently ludicrous, that I think one's first duty must be to show how readily and easily they can be dispensed with and how unnecessary it ever was to suppose that the relation of identity could suffer from indeterminacy. On the other hand, I know that in philosophy the strangeness of notions such as indeterminate identity may even lend them some positive allure. So there is no alternative but to seek to draw out their logical implications. For the purpose of showing that these are unfavourable to indeterminate identity, I shall follow a line of argument first pursued in another form by Gareth Evans.[4] (See below §4.) Evans's derivation points, I believe, in the direction in which the conceptualist is headed already. Meanwhile though, in advance of the attempt that I shall make to show that the conceptualist notion of an object is inescapable, it is time to lower the level of abstraction and have in front of us two or three would-be examples of an indeterminate object.

3. SOME PUTATIVE EXAMPLES OF INDETERMINATE OBJECTS

(*a*) Imagine a monstrous birth apparently possessed of two heads but having only one trunk, heart, liver . . . 'It is indeterminate', it may be suggested, 'whether this is one animal or two animals. So, by suitable pointings supported by suitable explanations, it will be possible to have a case where it is indeterminate whether *this* ostended thing (that which was born, let us say) is the same as *that* ostended thing (the animal whose head this is, for instance).'[5]

(*b*) 'Circumstances can arise that make it unclear whether or not a club started at some date is the same as a club that exists at some later date . . . The question of identity has no answer; the facts do not determine one.'[6]

(*c*) As we saw in Chapter Three, Hobbes adapts Plutarch and offers us a story in which Theseus' ship is gradually repaired with new spars, while the old planks and spars are simultaneously collected and reassembled in a reconstruction of the ship in its original condition. Suppose someone wishes to maintain, as I myself have in partial response to such puzzles,[7] that in such cases an entity can persist through some measure

---

[4] There have been disputes about the interpretation of Evans's article, 'Can there be Vague Objects?' (1978), p. 208. And there is no firm consensus about the best way of resolving the inconsistency between the two stipulations that Evans enters about the relationship between his Δ and his ∇. Leaving these disputes behind, I follow Williamson (1996) and the line of argument given in my (1986).

[5] Michael Ayers suggested that I must consider such examples and furnished this one.

[6] Cf. John Broome, 'Indefiniteness in Identity', *Analysis*, 44 (1984), referring to Derek Parfit.

[7] For the rest of the response and further discussion, see Chapter Three, §3.

of disassemblage, loss of parts, reassemblage of these parts elsewhere and replacement of present parts, but that there are further extremes of simultaneous disassemblage of the thing, loss of parts to other structures, or reparation with new parts, that are simply *too extreme* relative to the proper reference point, which is the original condition and matter of the entity – too extreme, that is, for the repaired entity to count as having persisted. If that is right, it may be claimed (though I am not sure that I myself should claim this), then there are bound to be relatively late stages in the story of something's enduring changes of this sort at which it is not yet fully determinate whether the original entity has survived or ceased to be.

4. IF OBJECT *a* IS THE SAME AS OBJECT *b*, THEN *a* IS DETERMINATELY THE SAME AS *b*

When we are faced with such examples, it may be asked what there is to be said in favour of a theory of individuation that does not hasten to make room for objects that are indeterminate in respect of identity (objects such that it is indefinite which things they are).

Suppose that *a* is *b*. Then, given Leibniz's Law, whatever is true of *a* is true of *b*. Now *a* is determinately *a*. But if so, then *b* is determinately *a*. So, by conditional proof and the symmetry of identity, if *a* is *b*, *a* is determinately *b*. In which case there is no future in the supposition that one could say that *a* was *b* but refuse to affirm that it was determinately *b*.

Putting the matter more formally, and letting 'Δ' mean 'determinately',[8] we have

(i)	$a = b$	(Hypothesis)
(ii)	$\Delta\,(a = a)$	(Truism)
(iii)	$\Delta\,(a = b)$	((i), (ii), Leibniz's Law)
(iv)	$(a = b) \rightarrow \Delta\,(a = b)$	(conditional proof)[9]

---

[8] Note that this is not Evans's use of Δ. The resemblances between Evans's argument and the one now to be presented would need to be taken point by point, and on their merits. Note also that, if the sign ∇ were introduced here, it would mean 'not determinately not' and, being duals, Δ and ∇ would be consistent. The relation of the two signs would be similar to that of $\square$ and $\diamond$. Never mind that there is no one-word translation of ∇ into English.

[9] There may also be doubt about the use of the rule of conditional proof in the derivations of $a = b \rightarrow \Delta a = b$ and $a \neq b \rightarrow \Delta a \neq b$. For recent discussion, see Richard G. Heck, Jr, 'That There Might Be Vague Objects (So Far as Concerns Logic)', *Monist*, 81 (1998), pp. 274–96. See especially p. 288 following. Heck offers a scrupulous commentary on Evans's argument with Δ understood not as here (see note 8). But Heck's general conclusions, not less his constructivist inclination, transcend that framework and they will cohere in substance with those defended in this chapter.

The reader will perceive instantly the parallelism between this derivation and the Barcan Marcus proof of the necessity of identity given in Chapter Four, §§2–3. The parallelism will be equally apparent between the interpretive issues that arise in each case. If there is doubt about the kind of context that is created by 'determinately', for instance, then it may be that the doubt is to be circumvented by recognizing a predicate adverb and forming complex predicables by λ-abstraction. (See Evans, and see again Chapter Three, §3.)

When he has explored these parallels, the reader will be able to come to his own view of the prospects of following the paradigm of Chapter Four and extending the proof of $a = b \rightarrow \Delta \, (a = b)$ into a proof that $a \neq b \rightarrow \Delta \, (a \neq b)$. Just how hard it would be to deny even the second and stronger of these claims has been shown by Timothy Williamson.[10] (Compare the proof in Chapter Four of the necessary distinctness of non-identicals.)

Again, it will be equally obvious that the derivation (i) (ii) (iii) ⊢ (iv), is available for any interpretation at all of Δ that verifies premiss (ii) and preserves the referential transparency of the context it creates. For instance, if we read (ii) as 'a is absolutely identical with a (i.e. not as a matter of degree)', then we can deduce Reid's conclusion that if a is b then a is absolutely b (not as a matter of degree).

5. WHAT, IF ANYTHING, FOLLOWS FROM SUCH FORMAL DERIVATIONS?

Let it be clear that (iv) should not be understood as entailing that every true identity sentence will remain true when prefixed with 'determinately'. That runs counter to the intention of those who advance (iv) as a truth. For identity sentences may contain descriptions, and indeterminacy of an irrelevant kind may result from vagueness in these descriptions. Consider the not altogether implausible claim 'The greatest ruler was the wisest ruler'. There is indeterminacy in this claim. At the outset, it may be insufficiently clear what wisdom or greatness are, as they figure here. And, even when that is made clearer, it may not be open or shut who is the greatest or who is the wisest. The one thing to be insisted upon and read as following from (iv) is only this: once we prevail sufficiently over indeterminacy by elaboration of the signification and point of the

---

[10] See Williamson (1996) in Lovibond and Williams (1996). In 'Replies' (in Lovibond and Williams (1996)), where Williamson seeks to persuade me of the necessity of difference, I abandon previous reservations and accept the proof that he offers. See also Chapter Four, footnote 13.

original judgment, and once we identify the candidates to satisfy this description and that description, we shall find that, if *a* is *b* at all, then *a* is determinately *b*. *That* matter is open or shut.[11]

At this point, and allowing (they will say) for the explanation just given, opponents of (iv) may yet argue that, if *a* is a vague or indeterminate object, then we cannot claim that *a* is determinately *a*. It is here they will say (that is, at (ii)) that all derivations of principles like (iv) are bound to fail. But to this I should reply that, even if identity were a matter of degree and *a* were an indeterminate object, we still ought to be able to obtain a (so to speak) perfect case of identity, provided we were careful to mate *a* with exactly the right object. And surely *a* is exactly the right object to mate with *a*. Their indeterminacy or vagueness matches exactly.[12] (Here I aim to speak in terms these opponents will find it more difficult to reject as unintelligible than I need to find it.)

A more sophisticated philosopher will intervene here with a different reservation: 'I believe that the world leaves many things vague or indeterminate, even about substances. But that does not mean that I shall be found rejecting the principle (iv) that you claim to have proved. The thing I say is that the world can leave it vague or indeterminate whether *a* is the same as *b*. I do not say that *a* can be the same as *b* but indeterminately so. Who on earth would want to say that? Rather I say the world may *leave it indeterminate* whether *a* is the same as *b* at all. This is just one of the many consequences of the claim to which I really do sub-

---

[11] We may say, if we wish, that the 'determinately' in 'If *a* is *b* then *a* is determinately *b*' has a smaller scope than any description that stands in the places marked by '*a*' or '*b*'. Thus the central question about the determinacy of the *relation of identity* will evade the approach of, for example, Richmond Thomason, 'Identity and Vagueness', *Philosophical Studies*, 37 (1981), pp. 329 ff. In making this proposal about scope, I follow Arthur F. Smullyan (1948).

[12] I am going along with the thought (which is the sceptic's and not mine) that a vague object needs to be an indeterminate object. As will appear, I am not an enthusiast for that, either as a thought about 'vague object' or as a thought about 'indeterminate object'. See text below and note 13.

A related idea, which may exert some adverse influence in this dispute and may make (ii) seem more dubious than it ought to seem, is that 'determinately' cannot be prefixed at all, without destroying full truth, to a sentence in which vague expressions occur. But consider familiar cases innocent of all suggestion of indeterminate objects and well outside the disputed area, where indeterminacies manifestly trade off:

Determinately, it is raining if and only if it is raining.
Determinately, the evening star is as famous as the morning star is.

And a similar response may be directed against the complaint that Leibniz's Law is suspect within this controversy, because (as someone has said to me) it was never formulated to manage vague predicates. Any vagueness in the open sentence for which 'ϕ' holds a place in the equivalence '$(\phi a \leftrightarrow \phi b)$' within the Leibnizian scheme $a = b \rightarrow (\phi a \leftrightarrow \phi b)$ will surely trade off against a similar vagueness in the same open sentence on the other side of the equivalence.

scribe, namely that we live in a world of real and considerable vagueness and indeterminacy.'

Such a protest may seem to invite cross-examination under the triple auspices of the principle (iv), of the principle of contraposition transforming (iv) into the thesis that, if a isn't determinately b, then a isn't b at all, and the principle (as secured by Williamson) of the determinate difference of things that are not identical, $a \neq b \rightarrow \Delta\,(a \neq b)$. Even without the benefit of the principle of classical logic $(a = b) \lor (a \neq b)$, the issue is not in doubt. Indeed, if the contestants simply limited themselves to (iv) and the weak form of contraposition that is permitted in intuitionist logic, the issue still would not be in doubt. Surely then the space that the sophisticated philosopher tries to point to does not exist. Or so says one in my theoretical position. But the thing that has become apparent in the years since the publication of Evans's article is that, given the endless possibilities for variant logics of indeterminacy, the cross-examination just described may not be the right way for a conceptualist to create conviction. In order to undo the present deadlock, it may be better to focus upon three other questions.

The first question relates to the status of the presumption that the vagueness whose existence nobody doubts entails indeterminacy. There should be no such presumption.[13]

Second comes the question of what account the sophisticated philosopher is assuming of what 'the world' is. Of itself, in the absence of a

---

[13] For the dissociation, see Williamson (1996 and 1995). For Williamson, the question of vagueness and identity is one battle in a larger and longer campaign against a host of semantical proposals that engage with vagueness and borderline cases by modifying the scheme of valuations that classical logic furnishes for reference, predication and judgment. Questioning the coherence of these alternatives, Williamson has defended the determinacies of the classical scheme and interpreted vagueness as a phenomenon not calling for new kinds of valuation but as a product of the predictable unknowability within certain subject matters of cut-off-points. An expression will be vague, according to Williamson, if it generates borderline cases where such ignorance is to be expected.

On this kind of basis, one might want to say that being such as to generate borderline cases of this or that kind was one feature among others of the *sense* of certain sorts of predicate; that from this feature of sense nothing automatically follows about these predicates' reference or semantic value, or about the valuation of sentences involving them. One might also be tempted to think that, once this sense/reference distinction is enforced, there is nothing in the phenomenon of vagueness to support a presumption to the effect that reference or truth themselves might have graduated or non-classical valuations.

Since the question chiefly at issue in this book is not the sustainability in general of Williamson's position but the specific question of identity and the interaction between identity and vagueness, there is no evident need to enter into Williamson's general thesis. The thing I shall aim to supply for this special case, however, is that which others may ask Williamson to supply much more generally, namely an account of what will ensure determinacy or supply determinacy positively to a subject matter that trades actively in considerations importing vagueness.

significant question with a point and a clarifiable sense, the world determines nothing. In the presence of such a question, however, and such a sense – and that is a part of the point of introducing the contribution of the individuating subject – there is no predeterminable limit to what might be objectively determined.

Third there is a more specific question, which is the chief question here. If one of the main points of the objector's intervention is to defend the picture of a world of indeterminate objects, what sort of things will such a world contain?

It may be said that one candidate is some mountain the ordinary individuation of which leaves over numerous questions of the form 'Is this foothill a part of x? Is that foothill a part of x?' But this is a strikingly poor illustration of what would be needed. For it can be *perfectly determinate* which mountain x is without x's extent's being determinate. A mountain is not, after all, something essentially demarcated by its extent or boundary.[14] It is not as if there were just as many mountains to be found with x's peak as there were rival determinations of x's boundary. An idea like that could not even occur to one with the good fortune to be innocent of classical extensional mereology.[15]

If a mountain of indeterminate extent is a bad model for an indeterminate object, then how *is* the idea of an indeterminate object to be lent significance? We are thrown back on the bare and abstract specification which says that an indeterminate object is an object that is such that it is indeterminate which object it is. But if the opponent's plea is that, in *this* sense, there are indeterminate objects, then my response is as follows: let x be such an object. Surely it is not indeterminate that x is the same object as x. Whatever else may be indeterminate about x, x is determinately x. Suppose then the question arises whether a certain object y is identical with x. The candidate y can only be x if y has every property x has. One of the object x's properties is that of being determinately the same as x.[16] Unless y has that property, y isn't x. So it seems that, what-

[14] Contrast perhaps a sea, and all the special difficulties that flow from the plausible idea that a sea is simply some roughly designated area of water. How serious though (one is moved to ask) is our existential commitment to seas as such? Contrast our undoubted commitment to quantities or expanses (e.g. of sea water). These do admit of arbitrarily exact determination. Nb. also the falsity of **D**(ix), explained in Chapter Two, §7. On these matters, see also R. M. Sainsbury, *Concepts without Boundaries* (Kings College London, Dept. of Philosophy, ISBN 0 951 729 9 0X, 1991).

[15] See Chapter Three, note 17. 'Classical extensional mereology' is Peter Simons's term. See Simons (1987).

[16] Among other points, surely this was Evans's point, or one of them. See also the discussion by Nathan Salmon in *Reference and Essence* (Princeton University Press, 1981) at pp. 219–29.

ever candidate is presented for identity with x, it can in principle be resolved whether the candidate is identical with x. But now – what can remain of the idea of an object such that it is indeterminate (rather than merely unknown) which object it is? And what remains of the idea of a world of indeterminate objects? In the end, I think we must set more store by questions such as these than on the question whether, in strict canonical logic as such, the principles of the determinacy of identity and determinacy of difference can or cannot be vindicated as theorems in a manner that no party to these disputes will have any right at all to regard as question-begging. (By this time, there are too many such parties.) How then are these inquiries to be pushed forward?

I could scarcely prove that there is only one way forward. But now is surely the moment for the conceptualist to offer an alternative conception. The world is not an object that is determinate or indeterminate. Nor is it an assemblage of indeterminate objects. If something simply *has* to be said in the form 'the world is . . .' (and how could it be shown that that is a legitimate demand?), it may be better to say 'the world is simply the possibility of singling out and referring to actual things which have properties and relations'. Furthermore, if that will do for the present, then this is the moment for the conceptualist to deploy the plausible idea that every judgment can be filled out *ad libitum* from the context of its cognitive formation; then to explain positively and constructively (quasi-constructivistically perhaps) *how it can be* that every well-made singular term with a reference has a determinate reference; then to explain how it can be that every question that is genuinely an identity question[17] is determinate for an answer known or unknown; and how it can be that (understood in the manner described in the first part of this section) every identity that holds at all holds fully determinately and indeed absolutely.

6. TREATMENT OF EXAMPLES (*a*) (*b*) (*c*) OF §3

Before any such explanation is attempted, there is illumination to be had from the consideration of the three examples (*a*), (*b*), (*c*) already provided. I hope that examination of each example will lend plausibility to the claim that the contextual supplementation spoken of in §5, paragraph one, is already one part of our standard practice. That practice

---

[17] A question may be none the worse for not being in my exigent sense an identity question. The continuum question has the appearance of an identity question. But the appearance is inessential. Ask instead whether a totality with a larger cardinality than the totality of natural numbers can have a cardinality smaller than the totality of the real numbers.

deserves an emphasis independent of the theorem status I would claim for our determinacy principles.

Example (*a*) is the birth comprising two heads, one trunk, one heart, one liver. . . . In a case such as this, further inquiry may suggest that the right thing to say is that we have here one non-viable animal and it has two heads. Or it may suggest that there are here two animals, each as capable as unseparated Siamese twins can be of separate life and independent conation. In that case the totality of that which was born comprises two animals.[18] So far, there is no relevant sense in which we have an indeterminate object. All we have is an event of giving birth that either issued in one animal or else issued in two animals. To say that much is not yet to say that we have a thing singled out and it is indefinite which thing it is. But now someone may ask this: what if there is simply no point in insisting that one of these options is the better one? And what will one in my theoretical position say if someone exploits the supposed equal acceptability of those options to declare that it is indefinite whether that which was born is or is not the same as *that object* (that two-headed animal) and indefinite again whether that which was born is the same as *the animal to whom that* [indicated] *head belongs?* My reply is that, if my opponent says this sort of thing, then the time has come to protest that, even if (*ex hypothesi*) you can take each of two options, that does not entail you can take both at once. If *there is* a two-headed animal in the offing, then what was born *is* or *was* a two-headed animal. Relative to that decision the identity is definite. Or if that seems wrong because the associated identity is *not* definite (e.g., because a mere decision is not enough to make it definite), then there is no identity. But that entails that, so far from the options being equally good, the other specified option is better. If so, we have established that that which was born comprised two animals. (Compare again the case of inseparable Siamese twins that survive into maturity.) More generally, it is just an illusion that there is a *this* we can avail ourselves of here which will make as good a reference as you like, as well-backed as you like, and make this reference regardless of whether the identity question *still* remains indeterminate.

Example (*b*) was the club. Suppose it is alleged that the association of persons meeting in 1985 is indeed the same as a club that appeared to its

---

[18] Perhaps then we have an *animal* that comprises two animals. This is simply a case of homeomery, not of indeterminate objecthood. For individuation and number concepts, see Chapter Two, *ad fin.*

For more general issues that arise here about ostension, see Chapter One, especially §6 and §9.

members to be lapsing (or to have lapsed) in 1963. The first question is whether there is any good reason to allege this identity. It cannot be made to hold by a simple decision on the part of those meeting in 1985 (even if decisions on the part of the founders are relevant to the question). On what terms, if any, was the club dissolved in 1963? What had been the articles of association? The thing that really needs to be made out is the point of the claim of identity, and the case *for* the identity. If the case is not good enough, then the thing that we are prompted by (iv) to say is that the clubs are not the same. Why object to that?

Example (*c*), Theseus' ship, is a more complex matter (as we have seen already in Chapter Three, §3). But what does the question of identity turn on here? Without using the idea of identity, one cannot say. But using it freely and imagining a set-up where we are not unduly hampered by problems of unknowability, perhaps one can contrive to say something at least. First, we have a reference to Theseus' ship; and then (let us suppose) we have a reference to the ship whose late return in 399 BC delayed Socrates' drinking of the hemlock. Behind each reference stands the singling out of the object of that reference. What exactly did each of these singlings out catch hold of? To determine that, we have to find some common way of further amplifying, developing and specifying *each* singling out,[19] reaching backwards and forwards along the life span of each object, working towards a more and more complete answer to this question. (Advice: it will save work and serve clarity to do what we normally do without thinking, namely begin work on the object that is specified by reference to the earlier time.) In the end, either we shall find that we have rendered it completely manifest that, as fully spelt out, these are the singlings out of one and the same ship, or else we shall find that we have collected an *x* and *y* such that, for some genuine predicable ϕ that is true of one or other of *x* and *y*, it holds that ϕx and it does not hold that ϕy.

On what principle, then, must we determine the temporal extent of the life span of Theseus' working ship? Well, it depends in the first instance on what ships are and what *that* ship was. We have said that one can allow for the occasional disassembly of the ship; that one can allow for a measure of replacement of parts; that one can allow for modifications of the ritual or religious functions of the ship, with or without structural alteration. The thing one cannot allow (or so it was

---

[19] This stipulation, which ensures the compatibility and commensurability of the singlings out as further amplified, corresponds to the 'there exists a sortal concept *f* such that . . .' clause in the statement of principle **D** given in Chapter Two above.

declared in Chapter Three), if *Theseus' ship* is to be that which is being singled out, is arbitrarily much of all three kinds of change. (If we do allow arbitrarily much of all three, we may find we have let in Hobbes's competitor ship.) Perhaps each such change is *pro tanto* insignificant. But that which matters at each point is the *overall distance* of the new condition at that point from the original condition of the ship that Theseus dedicated to Apollo. (If we are careful about this, if we recognize that any real candidate to be the ship whose late arrival delayed Socrates' death in 399 BC must inherit the answerability of that 399 BC ship to the condition of Theseus' own ship, if we insist also that not arbitrarily much of the matter of Theseus' ship can be discarded, then nothing can colourably emerge as a rival ship during the lifespan of the ship.) And in the end we must say *no* (or refuse to say *yes*) when too many such changes are too variously combined with one another or too much of the original matter is lost from the ship. The better our understanding of what is at issue, the more exact our sense will be of when to say *no*.

Needless to say, this way of regulating Sorites reasonings respects the vagueness of predicates that are vague. Identity is not one of them. It respects also the graduability of predicates that can qualify a thing to some degree. Identity is not one of these either. Note also that that which the determinacy of identity enforces is that each and every positive decision of identity must be judged by the same strict standard as we ought to require for determinate (and absolute) identity.

That ruling is tailored to identity. But what is so unfair or so unmanageable about it? Suppose that, in reaching forward from the origin to later times, we get to a point *t after which*, using that backward-looking standard, we cease to be satisfied that the very same thing is being singled out. Then we shall say that what we have *at t* is indeed Theseus' ship. But, when confronted with something picked out by reference to times later than *t*, we shall refuse to affirm that Theseus' ship is this ship. Contraposing (iv), it will then be open to us to find that Theseus' ship is *not* identical with any item we are presented with that is found after *t*. Before we thought, we might have been in doubt. But having thought about what identity involves, it will be apparent to us that there is no alternative but to permit the logic of identity to regulate our individuative thinking. By this logic, a ship found after *t* has to be a new and different ship that emerged from the process of successive remodellings of a ship that was older and different. Provided we see this decision as itself arising from the exigencies of singling out a continuant that has a history and an original condition that cannot be read off it at a glance, the decision will appear reasonable and inevitable.

7. SENSE AND POINT; AND SENSE AS THE WORK OF THE MIND

Evidently, as one engages with putative examples of objects that are indeterminate and one presses certain questions about them, the position one finds oneself moving toward is this. If that which presents itself as a simple identity question has a real point and this point is the point attaching to a veritable identity question that is open and in good standing,[20] then the question must relate to objects each of which could be identified in its own way. In that case, the sense of each of the terms that figure in the question will allow of some sufficient completion for the term to engage with some conception of an object that is singled out and marked off from all other things. My caricatural idealist is wrong if he supposes that a conception of this sort is in any sense the free creation of the thinker. It is empirically conditioned and *a posteriori* at every point. But the idealist is not wrong to call the conception of each object – as opposed to the object that answers to the conception – the work of the mind. Moreover, that mind-work is not only empirically constrained. It is constrained by the determinable idea of an object, by Leibniz's Law, and by anything else at all that Leibniz's Law can deliver to us.

According to this picture, the sophisticated philosopher who said he was prepared to accept (iv) but went on to declare that it was still open to him to maintain that the world might leave it indeterminate whether object *a* was object *b*, invokes an idea of object-hood which is as difficult as it is dispensable. If it does not make sense to speak of such objects, if every putative example disappears on examination, then one ought not to allude, even indirectly, to the possibility of such objects. Not only that. According to the conceptualist, the kinds of entity invoked by the sophisticated philosopher are entirely superfluous. In describing how a thinker who singles out objects finds these things in the world, we do not need to say that he conceives or fashions them out of preconceptual objects. As theorists, we do not need to speak of indeterminate things at all in order to do justice to the thinker's conceptual activity. Nor yet do we need to abandon realism. For even if, *pace* the materialist, individuation

---

[20] Contrast the question about the wisest and best ruler when it is reconstrued as a question about the relation (of subsumption or whatever) between certain virtues and excellences. See also note 17.

is (as the idealist says) mind's work, this work, in so far as it is constructive, lies entirely at the level of sense. It is work of construal, of making sense of our experience, of seeking things and finding them or of making oneself ready to happen upon objects and recognize them for what they are.

No doubt, as we have said already, different practical or cognitive purposes will make different sorts of construal necessary, and these may be expected to issue in different 'versions of reality'. But (*pace* the Nelson Goodman of *Ways of Worldmaking*, to whom, however, not everything in the present chapter ought to be alien or unwelcome), these cannot be allowed to be *conflicting* versions. Emancipation from the correspondence model of truth is one thing. Emancipation from truth or logic is another. If two versions conflict, not both are right. But in order to conflict, they must have the same subject matter. In so far as I am allowing for different versions with different *a posteriori* conceptions applied for different practical or cognitive purposes, it is sensible for me to expect that different things will be singled out and different subject matters will be proposed. Finally, I point out that, if there are different versions of reality, that does not mean that anything and everything is a correct version (or a version correct by its own lights).[21]

Every significant sentence, by being the sentence it is and having the contextually completable sense it has, sets itself a goal that it either attains or fails to attain. But, in doing this, it does not itself make the verdict on whether that goal has been attained. In the same way, every singling out of a thing, being the singling out of this *f* or that *g*, construes reality in a certain way. But it does not construct the *f* or the *g* from its own *a priori* materials, as if to validate itself. It no more validates itself than the focusing of a camera fixed deliberately at a certain spot creates that which the camera records when set there at that focus. A *de re* thought that is a singling out thought uses tested *a posteriori* materials to set a standard for itself that the world can disappoint or gratify, in accordance with whether there is or is not to be discovered the very object the thought purports to be a thought of. Even if it takes a particular sort of empirically and logically constrained search to light up the object, the object is not posited into being. The mind *recognizes* by the exercise of conceptions the object that is there to be recognized, even as the object

---

[21] None of this would be worth saying at such length if so many would-be modern persons had not got excited at the prospect of coming to conclusions I am warning against or they did not take the conclusions they threaten us with for a liberation or a triumph. As things are, I shall go on remorselessly, for two more whole paragraphs.

impinges upon the mind that has the right sort of thought to single out that object.[22] (See Chapter Three, at the end.) Finally, then, the world can disappoint or gratify the claim that object *a*, singled out under one mind-originated conception, is the same as object *b*, an object singled out under another mind-originated conception.

In sum, once we differentiate that which a judgment contrives by mind's work to say from reality's verdict on what is said, once we distinguish sense from reference or truth-value, sober conceptualism is indistinguishable from a sensible version of realism. (Compare the conclusions of Chapter Five.) Indeed, once we distinguish sense from reference, individuative constructivism emerges as the one form of realism that explains how reference can be determinate, explains how veritable identity questions can be determinate for an answer, *and* explains how whatever identities actually hold can hold both absolutely and determinately.

8. ON THE LEVEL OF REFERENCE, THINGS CANNOT BE SIMPLY CONCEIVED INTO BEING OR POSTULATED INTO EXISTENCE – NOT EVEN MATERIAL THINGS WITH MATTER PUTATIVELY READY AT HAND

So much for the role of conceptualism as it conditions the concept of an object seen as the correlate of an act of singling something out. And so much for the way in which the relation of identity between objects admits neither degrees nor approximations. (For more on the latter, see below, §11.) If it is a pre-condition of such a relation as this coming to seem exemplifiable and possible that there be some freedom that one enjoys at the level of conception, then now is the moment to fill out the account (already begun) of that which *limits* that supposed freedom and effortlessly contains it.

In the third and last edition of *Reference and Generality* (Cornell University Press, Ithaca and London, 1980, see p. 215), P. T. Geach refined a puzzle he had first proposed for discussion many years earlier.[23]

---

[22] Even in the case where the thing singled out simply confronts the thinker, rather than being the object of his search, there has to be some however inchoate conception of things of the kind that is instantiated by the object. There needs to be some sort of readiness. In the absence of that, think how easily one can look directly at something without seeing it. Of course, one can also see a thing without knowing what it is. For the sort of account I should offer of that, see 'Reply to Fei Xu' (1997a).

[23] Professor Geach communicated the puzzle to me in 1966 or 1967 and no doubt to other philosophers. For my then response, see 'On Being in the Same Place' (1968), p. 94. Geach traced the idea for the puzzle to something he had found in William of Sherwood. For earlier versions of

The fat cat sat on the mat. There was just one cat on the mat. The cat's name was 'Tibbles': 'Tibbles' is moreover a name *for* a cat.[24] – This simple story leads us into difficulties if we assume that Tibbles is a normal cat. For a normal cat has at least 1,000 hairs. Like many empirical concepts, the concept (*single*) *hair* is fuzzy at the edges; but it is reasonable to assume that we can identify in Tibbles at least 1,000 of his parts each of which definitely is a single hair. I shall refer to these hairs as $h_1, h_2, h_3, \ldots$ up to $h_{1,000}$.

Now let c be the largest continuous mass of feline tissue on the mat. Then for any of our 1,000 cat-hairs, say h_n, there is a proper part c_n of c which contains precisely all of c except the hair h_n; and every such part c_n differs in a describable way both from any other such part, say c_m, and from c as a whole. Moreover fuzzy as the concept *cat* may be, it is clear that not only is c a cat, but also any part c_n is a cat: c_n would clearly be a cat were the hair h_n plucked out, and we cannot reasonably suppose that plucking out a hair *generates* a cat, so c_n must already have been a cat. So, contrary to our story, there was not just one cat called 'Tibbles' sitting on the mat; there were at least 1,001 sitting there! Of course this would involve a great deal of overlap and sharing of organs among these 1,001 cats, but logic has nothing to say against that; after all, it happens on a small scale between Siamese twins.

All the same, this result *is* absurd. We simply do not speak of cats, or use names of cats, in this way; nor is our ordinary practice open to logical censure.

The verdict of absurdity is if anything understated. By this account of matters, Tibbles, who is an ordinary cat, must have among his proper parts at least 1,000 cats. By similar arguments, will not just any Tib that Tibbles contains prove to contain cats among its proper parts?

Geach's response to the questions raised by Tibbles is as follows-:

Everything falls into place if we realize that the number of cats on the mat is the number of *different* cats on the mat; and c_{13}, c_{279}, and c are not three different cats, they are one and the same cat. Though none of these 1,001 lumps of feline tissue is the same lump of feline tissue as another, each *is* the same cat as any other: each of them, then, is a cat, but there is only one cat on the mat, and our original story stands.

footnote 23 (*cont.*)
  the puzzle that have become visible as a result of Geach's discussions, see *Stoicorum Veterum Fragmenta*, 2.397, and the commentary thereon given by David Sedley at pp. 269–70 of 'The Stoic Criterion of Identity', *Phronesis* (1982).
[24] Geach's explanation of this usage may be reproduced as follows: a name *for* an A can be explained as a name associated with the criterion of identity: *Same A*. Whereas a name *of* an A names something which is an A, but need not be associated with the criterion of identity.
  Chapter One (see also my reply to Noonan in 'Replies' (Lovibond and Williams, 1996)) will have made it clear that, on my view, one who uses a name *n* for an A object *x* is committed to the possibility of making it determinate which of the As he has picked out by the name *n* and is equally committed to the possibility of making it determinate that it is to *x* rather than the matter or the parts of *x* that he is referring. (Cf. Chapter One §6 on the 'is' of constitution.) But to make that determinate is to commit oneself to the principle of individuation for *x*. In practice there is simply no need for a name of an A that is not a name for an A.

Thus each one of the names '$c_1, c_2, \ldots c_{1,001}$', or again the name '$c$', is a name of a cat; but none of these 1,001 names is a name *for* a cat, as 'Tibbles' is. By virtue of its sense 'Tibbles' is a name, not for one and the same *thing* (in fact, to say that would really be to say nothing at all), but for one and the same *cat*. This name for a cat has reference, and it names the one and only cat on the mat; but just on that account 'Tibbles' names, as a shared name, both c itself and any of the smaller masses of feline tissue like c_{12}, and c_{279}. For all of these are one and the same cat, though not one and the same mass of feline tissue. 'Tibbles' is not a name *for* a mass of feline tissue.

So we recover the truth of the simple story we began with. The price to pay is that we must regard ' —— is the same cat as —— ' as expressing only a certain equivalence relation, not an absolute identity restricted to cats; but this price, I have elsewhere argued, must be paid anyhow, for there is no such absolute identity as logicians have assumed.

That, no doubt, is one way to answer. But for those who reject **R** and affirm Leibniz's Law,[25] there must be another response. I think the best response would be one that adds nothing to the description of the puzzle situation, but shows instead how something needs to be taken away. My suggestion is that one should scrutinize carefully the purported definition of c_n. Our freedom to single out *this* rather than *that* was not the freedom either to remake the concept *cat* or to reconfigure its instantiations. Suppose you take the concept *cat* as you find it, you look for its instantiation in object c_{901} and you count c_{901} *as a cat*. Then you are committed to track down all of c_{901}.[26] But that (if it is anything at all) is nothing lesser than Tibbles. If Tibbles has such a hair as h_{901} (or has a tail), then you cannot define c_{901} into existence as the cat that *lacks* the hair (or lacks that tail). For there is no such cat.

At this point, the reader will remember the analogous claim that was advanced in Chapter One, §3, namely that, if John Doe was a boy and later a man, there is no possibility of picking out or fixing upon an object, a boy, John-Doe-as-a-boy, that is distinct from the substance John Doe, who grew old and was by 1958 an old man. (This is not to say that one could not in 1910 have picked out John Doe as a boy. But here the

---

[25] My response to Geach's charges against the coherence of Leibniz's Law and absolute identity is given at 'Replies' (Lovibond and Williams, 1996), p. 242.

[26] There is here a faint but interesting analogy with something that Robert Nozick has urged. See *Philosophical Explanations* (Oxford, 1981), p. 57. The point that I think I see there in Nozick is in no way proprietary to the Closest Continuer theory, defended by Nozick. The point I think I see in Nozick's discussion (see especially his citation from Tversky) relates to the level of conceptions or senses. It is a *misunderstanding* of the concept *cat* (and a failure to grasp the point of the concept) not, in applying it to the set-up Geach describes (namely, Tibbles on a mat), to deploy *the whole reach* of the concept. It is worse still, having denied the concept its full application, to institutionalize this misdemeanour in the manner of Geach's definition of c_n.

'as a boy' is to be read in construction with the verb 'pick out', not with 'John Doe'.)

The technical sophistication of those who tinker with the proposals I am opposing here is completely out of scale, I suggest, with the small heed they are prepared to pay to the most invaluable commonplaces of the logical theory of definition, not least its admonitions concerning creative definitions.[27]

9. ONCE AGAIN (ONE LAST TIME) THE THINGS TO WHICH SIMPLE IDENTITY SENTENCES MAKE A REFERENCE

At this point, at least one sceptical response is to be expected against the claims entered in the course of the preceding sections: 'In this chapter you purport to be showing, against the current of much present day opinion, that identity is determinate, all or nothing, and much else besides. You also purport, by constrained redeployment of an idealist insight, to explain how identity and difference *can* be all these things. But your whole effort depends upon something you will scarcely permit to be scrutinized – the assumption that the items to be singled out in association with the terms of an identity sentence must themselves be continuants to whose earliest and latest moments all true reference must reach out. You pay no attention to the conflicting opinion that the real purport of an ordinary judgment of identity over time is to say that the references of the two terms (thing-moments, phases or whatever one chooses to call them) stand in a "unity" relation, the relation of making up some given whole. This option has been described many times in the literature of identity in a manner that you will say is alien to your concerns.[28] But it can also be described in terms congenial to your sortal approach:

'The sortal [predicate] helps identify the referents of a statement by giving the relation that holds between occurrences – parts, instances, stages, phases, etc. – of the appropriate sort when they are occurrences of a single object of the indicated kind: specifying this relation and designating an occurrence identifies the referent. When an occurrence is identified but no sortal provided, indefiniteness occurs because an occurrence can be an occurrence of different kinds.'[29]

---

[27] Here, as elsewhere, I would refer to Chapter 8 of Patrick Suppes, *Introduction to Logic* (Princeton N.J., 1957).

[28] See, for instance, Rudolf Carnap, *Introduction to Symbolic Logic and its Applications* (New York, 1958), pp. 157ff., 198, 213ff.).

[29] John Perry, review, *Journal of Symbolic Logic*, 25 (1970), p. 448. Compare his article 'The Importance of Being Identical', in *The Identities of Persons*, ed. A. O. Rorty (Los Angeles, 1976).

In the light of this thought (the objector continues) why should it not be suggested that a statement of diachronic identity such as "*a* is the same horse as *b*" qualifies as true if and only if the stage or occurrence *a* and the stage or occurrence *b* make up not just any old concatenation but a suitable concatenation of horse-stages? Understanding the substantive "horse" involves understanding what sort of a concatenation this has to be. Can you not recognize here a point that you yourself want to urge – albeit in different words? (Indeed I would refer you here to your own (1968).)'

Anyone who makes such an objection will probably go on to point out how cannily such an approach evades the claim, of which so much has been made in this chapter and elsewhere, to the effect that reference and singling out must stretch all the way back to the first moments of a thing and arbitrarily far forward, however proleptically, towards its last.

My response is this: the view cited by the objector seems to be all of a piece with the widespread idea that first, and supposedly unproblematically (however singular terms are to be construed), there is synchronic identity, as in '$3 + 3 = 6$', 'The Dome of the Rock is the Dome of the Rock' or (falsely) 'Paris is Rome'; and then, differently and/or more problematically, there is diachronic identity, as in 'the man in front of me is the same person as the boy I shared a locker with at school' or (?) 'Hesperus is Phosphorus'. It would be good, though, to know the rationale for this differentiation. Is it founded in the claim that, insofar as we refer and refer deictically at *t*, nothing can be involved in the deixis that is not actually there and present at *t*?[30] If that is the idea, then (rather than object, as in fact I do, by protesting that this is an untenable doctrine of reference, that bare words at a time cannot of themselves fix their intended interpretation, that the formulation itself of the doctrine is radically unstable, etc), I shall say it leads into three doubts or difficulties.

'My candidate for the analysis of personal identity . . . is the unity relation for persons, that relation which obtains between two stages if and only if there is a person of which both are stages' (p. 71).

I note for the record that this is not the account of these matters given nowadays by the opponents of the substantialist position that I occupy. For this, see David Lewis, *op. cit.* below at note 32. In Lewis's version, it is far from clear that the position now called perdurantism would be at all exercised to deny my claim that singling out reaches all the way back to the first moments of a thing or arbitrarily far forward towards its last. For that is what a *sum* of horse-stages precisely does. As regards Lewis, however, I do question the reason that Lewis gives for importing talk of stages (see note 32 already cited). Moreover, the second part of the third objection against Perry raises serious questions about the coherence of the very idea that horse-stages could play the role Lewis supposes that they play in predication or individuation.

[30] The Doctrine (Specious) of the Deictic Indispensability of the Deictically Present?

First, one wonders about the status of a horse-stage concatenation as itself a potential object of reference. Is this not a continuant?[31]

Secondly, one wants to protest that, in English, for which sameness is just sameness, where time-specifications cling to verbs or qualifications not to nouns, there is no trace whatever of any bifurcation among the senses of 'is' or 'is the same as'.

Thirdly, one objects that these occurrences/parts/instances/stages/ phases, etc., seem *multiply* problematic. For instance, not everything that looks for a moment or behaves for a moment as if it were a horse *is* a horse. See Chapter Three, §1. Can anyone truly imagine the business of recasting into stage-talk the sorts of explication invoked there in connexion with natural kind substantives? The criterion for being a horse is essentially dispositional and diachronic. If horse-stages made sense at all, it would be easier to go from horses to horse-stages than to go, as the objector wishes, from horse-stages to horses. Nor is there any single recipe one can imagine for transposing the normal range of attributions to horses into attributions to horse-stages or horse-occurrences. (There is no recipe the mastery of which could be plausibly attributed to a thinker versed in the language of substances and their states, dispositions, etc.) Indeed, the whole resolve to postulate horse-stages and deploy them in complication of the truth-conditions of identity-sentences can only remind one of the conceptualist excesses criticized in the preceding section.

I should say that, in this province of inquiry, reasoned persuasion is relatively rare. But let me set out an argument once put forward against substantialist positions like mine by D. Gabbay and J. M. Moravcsik.[32]

---

[31] Two possible Answers: (1) The concatenation belongs to a different system of ideas from that of continuants. (See discussion later.) (2) One could indeed refer to a concatenation of horse-stages, but such a reference would not be *properly* deictic. As regards (2), I would ask: why can one not refer, whether 'deictically' or not, to the person who as a boy shared a locker with me and is now at such and such a spot in December 1998? If one *can* do this, then what objection can the theory of reference provide against an ontology of continuants that makes no provision for stages?

[32] See 'Sameness and Individuation', *Journal of Philosophy*, 70.16 (1973). A quite different kind of argument has now been put forward by David Lewis in *On the Plurality of Worlds* (Oxford, 1986), pp. 202–4, and in 'Is there a problem about persistence?' *Proceedings of the Aristotelian Society*, Supp. Vol. 61 (1987). Lewis's argument is answered by Mark Johnston (*ibid.*) – also by Aristotle (in effect). Aristotle's reaction to it is given in my 'Substance' (1996), §4:10. (See also, for a different overall account, Peter Simons in 'On Being Spread out in Time: temporal parts and the problem of change', in Wolfgang, Spohn *et al.* (eds.), *Existence and Explanation* (Kluwer, 1991).) The Aristotelian answer should not however be seen as a response to Lewis that *accepts* his problem and then resolves it. Rather, it defuses the problem. It puts us into a position to say: if an object is straight now but will soon be bent, what is the problem about that? Only a misunderstanding of the ontology of times that temporal adverbs like 'now' and 'soon' make possible can turn familiar facts like this one into some problem about 'straight' and 'bent' turning into relation words.

Their discussion has the further merit, over and above that of present-
ing a recognizable argument, of avoiding the classic confusions that
haunt the subjects of identity and individuation.[33]

Gabbay and Moravcsik begin by inviting one to consider the sentence:

> (6) The young woman I met eight years ago turned into the senior lec-
> turer whom I met last year.

and its putative 'restatement'

> (8) The young woman I met eight years ago is the same as the senior lec-
> turer I met last year.

Then Gabbay and Moravcsik say:

'[If] they are equivalent, a substitution in one should have the same result as the
same substitution in the other. If we substitute in (6) on the right side the expression we have on the left ['The young woman I met eight years ago'], and if we
construe the expressions as simply referring to the woman, then we get

> (11) The young woman I met eight years ago turned into the young woman I
> met eight years ago,

which is false. . . . When we perform the same substitution in (8) to obtain:

> (12) The young woman I met eight years ago is the same as the young woman
> I met eight years ago,

the result fails to be equivalent to (11) . . . (12) taken naturally is a truism, but (
11) is not. This shows that the 'is the same as' in (8) has a sense distinct from
identity; it also shows the need for interpreting the referring expressions in (6)
and (8) as denoting stages of entities instead of the entities themselves. Of
course, once we construe the referents as stages, the sameness involved cannot
be identity.'

Taken just as it stands the argument arouses the suspicion of something
analogous to a cancelling out fallacy.[34] But we can run it through again
like this: 'Suppose (6) and (8) are both true. Then substituting identicals
within (6) in the way licensed by (8) we obtain (11). But (11) is false.
Therefore 'is the same as' in (8) must have a sense distinct from that of
identity, and the referring expressions in (6) and (8) must denote stages
of entities, not the entities themselves.'

Change is more primitive than any ontology of times. Let us not visit upon 'I shall soon be bald'
the problems that come to be perceived in 'For some *t*, I am [timeless] bald at *t* and *t* is not too
long after now.'

[33] For a classic dissolution of several classic confusions, see Vere Chappell (1960).

[34] 'We cannot infer that if two propositions verbally differ precisely in that one contains the expression E_1, and the other expression E_2, then if the total force of the two propositions is the same,
we may cancel out the identical parts and say that E_1 here means the same as E_2' (Geach (1962),
p. 61).

Everything in this argument depends in the first instance upon (6). Is (6) given in ordinary English? How then in ordinary English – or, if (6) is not in ordinary English, then how in philosophical English – are we to understand the mode of combination it exemplifies between the verb and its subject(s)?

The answer to the first question is that no dictionary that comes to hand, nor any current catalogue of phrasal verbs and their uses, cites any sentence that is like (6) in respect of the second position that (6) furnishes for a singular term ('the senior lecturer whom I met last year'). More typical of the sentences we find in English are these: 'caterpillars turn into butterflies', 'the experience has turned him into a sad and bitter man' (thus 'by this experience he has been turned into a sad and bitter man'), 'The witch turned the prince into a frog'. In itself, this is of no great consequence. (Though the finding can be strengthened further by consideration of examples with the verb 'become' and the oddities of 'become identical with'.) But it points towards the right answer to the second of the two questions just posed.

Consider the sentence:

Following a not altogether credible tradition, the chroniclers represent that, in his youth, Prince Hal was a dissipated roysterer who was suddenly changed into a model king.[35]

The first thing to remark here is that we shall have no difficulty with the substitution that is made possible by the truth that Prince Hal is the same man as Henry V of England. If Prince Hal was in his youth a dissipated roysterer who was suddenly changed into a model king, then Henry V was in his youth a dissipated roysterer who was suddenly changed into a model king. But then the example suggests, as do all the others, that, in order to give a sense to (6), we need to identify some new state or form or condition that was assumed by the young woman whom Gabbay or Moravcsik met in 1965, or a property she came to exemplify. Let this be the property of being a senior lecturer. Why not see (6) like this then? It says that the young woman whom Gabbay met in 1965 came to have the property $(\lambda x)(x$ is a senior lecturer$)$, the very property exemplified by the woman he met in 1973, or else it says that the young woman Gabbay met in 1965 came to have the property $(\lambda x)(x$ is a senior lecturer and Gabbay meets x in 1972$)$. It does not matter very much which you say.

---

[35] Cf. Frederick W. Moorman, *The First Part of Henry the Fourth* (London and Glasgow, undated), p. xxx.

Back to (8). All that (8) and the intersubstitutivity of identicals now gives us is that the senior lecturer Gabbay met in 1972 came at some time (when?) to have the property exemplified by the senior lecturer he met in 1972 (or the property simply of being a senior lecturer he met in 1972). The senior lecturer in question wasn't, in other words, born that way. The new sentence is not false – just trivial.

There are other possible construals of (6) – too many in fact. If (6) were an ordinary sentence of ordinary English, I should be greatly embarrassed by the arbitrariness attaching to the choice. But, as things are, (6) needs to have a sense conferred upon it. Still less can the truth of (6) make mandatory for us any business of transposing (6) or (8) into the language of occurrences and stages. The positive case for such transposition still needs to be made. (See further below.)

In the here and now, pending fresh argument, let us cease to resist the appearances – the appearance, I mean, that identity is just identity and need not be divided up between synchronic and diachronic, and the appearance that, with 'Hesperus is Phosphorus', 'Mary Ann Evans is George Eliot' or 'the man before me is the same person as the boy I shared a locker with at school', matters are just as they seem. Each of these statements is true if and only if the persisting thing mentioned on the left is one and the same as the persisting thing mentioned on the right. Let us make sense of such identities without invoking either object-stages or the so-called unity relation. My plea is made in full awareness of the widespread assumption that, in the end, all questions of identity and persistence should be transposed to a four-dimensional framework. Let me now demonstrate that awareness by breaking for one moment my long silence about that assumption.

The assumption comes in two forms, which it is helpful to distinguish carefully. In its first form, the contention is that questions about continuants are transposable into problems about scientifically palpable items that are there to be discovered at (more or less) the same addresses in space and time. In this form, the assumption is usually inarticulate. It is part of a world view that has a powerful appeal. But no principles have ever been provided by reference to which the fidelity of such transpositions could be judged.[36] I think it has been assumed that such principles are not needed because everything that lies at a given location in space and time must be one and the same. This assumption is unwise, however, as will appear to anyone who pays attention to the full variety of

---

[36] Compare the complaint made by Woodger in the citation given in the last footnote of Chapter Five.

adjectival or substantial predications applicable to things discoverable at a given location.[37]

The second form in which we find the assumption in favour of the four-dimensional framework goes like this: the time has come for us to *abandon completely* the attempt to operate the old discredited Aristotelian ontology of everyday thinking. The time has come to stop trying to apply modern physics to ordinary continuants by means of *ad hoc* mereological improvisations. Instead, let us apply the language of modern physics directly to that which we encounter in experience.

On this second view, the theory of identity is simply one case among hundreds where we should make the effort to see the world as a scientist officially does – and a case where the scientist himself, in the laboratory that he so frequently describes in lamentably unofficial or Aristotelian terms, should try to follow through his own discoveries. If only we will *all* do this, it may be said, then we shall usually find, entirely satisfyingly, that the question we wanted to answer disappears of its own accord.

One cannot help but admire the honesty of so fresh and engaging a proposal. If I do not concur with it, that is only for two reasons: first because, in practice, it seems almost impossible to find again in the new framework either the things or the properties that our philosophical and everyday concerns and questions involve us with. In this new framework, one might well find events – for the category of event is common to the four-dimensional and the everyday frameworks – but scarcely the events articulated by our own ways of individuating or characterizing events. As for the counterparts of the things, properties and substances that are close to human life or that force us into the philosophy of identity, these will not be discoverable at all. Solving problems by making them disappear can be an excellent strategy in philosophy. But it cannot minister to all needs or the great generality of questions. Indeed it is tempting to predict that any sincere and prolonged attempt to arrive at a four-dimensional reformulation of every legitimate question or concern that exercises us and every predicate that is indispensable to us would only fortify the conclusion towards which common sense already beckons, namely that the everyday scheme and the four-dimensional scheme are complementary not competing schemes of thought, each with its own strengths and limitations.[38]

---

[37] See my note 'On Being in the Same Place' (1968); and see Frederick C. Doepke (1982).

[38] On all these matters, see Peter Simons (1987), p. 125, and, more generally, pp. 123–7; also D. H. Mellor, *Real Time* (Cambridge, 1981).

10. MORE ABOUT THE RELATION OF IDENTITY

Identity is an equivalence relation, a congruence relation, a determinate relation, an absolute relation, or so we have concluded. But can it be reduced somehow to other properties and relations? Philosophers rarely or never avow the explicit belief that it has to be so reducible. But I venture to think that some such belief must have been at work when, a long time ago, Jaakko Hintikka was moved to rule[39] that

Each possible world contains a number of individuals with certain properties and with certain relations to each other. We have to use these properties and relations to decide which member (if any) of a given possible world is identical with a given member of another possible world.

If Hintikka is right, then *strictly* one cannot specify world one by saying that in world one Alcibiades is blue-eyed and specify world two by saying, without more ado, that in world two Alcibiades, the same man, is green-eyed. If nobody is moved to say something analogous to this about other basic properties or relations than the identity relation – if no problem is held to exist about saying that in world one all swans are *white* and in world two all swans are *black* – then why is the claim so perennially attractive where identity is concerned?

Perhaps the relevant thought is that the special thing about identity is that it is unobservable, and unobservable because it's somehow consequential on something else. But can one not see directly (albeit fallibly) that it is one's brother, not one's uncle, who has come to call on one?

Perhaps the relevant thought is that, even allowing for the point just registered, identity is inscrutable *except* as resemblance (its 'vanishing point', etc.) and that resemblance can only be a matter of properties and relations. But it hardly takes deep philosophy to reflect that resemblance is neither sufficient for identity nor necessary. It is only necessary in so far as, at any given time, *x* must exactly resemble *x*.

But maybe brisk philosophical exchanges of this sort will only deepen the apparent mystery about identity and strengthen the resolve of a certain sort of empiricist to account for our mastery of it in terms of whatever is cognitively less taxing. Since we work so happily with identity (he whispers), how can it help but ride on the back of something that is more manifestly manageable?

---

[39] See 'The Semantics of Modal Notions', *Synthèse*, 21 (1970), pp. 408–24. For further comment on these questions, see Chapter Four, §3 *ad fin.*, §5, §7.

Within technical philosophy, some have seen hope of such a quasi-reduction in the 'elimination' of identity for which Hilbert and Bernays first gave the recipe and which Quine describes as follows:

'Still nothing has been said [in *Word and Object*] as to the make-up of the admissible vocabulary of unanalysed general terms. But of this particular we may be sure: [the predicate] '=' will in effect be present, whether as an unanalysed general term or in complex paraphrase, at least provided that the vocabulary of unanalysed general terms is finite. For, write 'if Fx then Fy' and vice-versa with each of the absolute general terms of the vocabulary in place of 'F'; also write '(z) (if Fxz then Fyz)' and '(z) (if Fzx then Fzy)' and vice versa, with each of the dyadic relative terms in place of F; and so on to '(z) (w) (if Fxzw then Fyzw)', etc. The conjunction of all these formulae is coextensive with 'x = y' if any formula constructible from the given vocabulary is; and otherwise we can without conflict adopt that conjunction as our version of identity. In so doing we impose a certain identification of indiscernibles, but only in a mild way.'[40]

Wherever such eliminations are possible (I suppose the thought runs), there is a clear sense in which the predicate 'is the same as' is indeed reducible. Thus 'x is the same as y' is reducible by being replaceable by another and longer open sentence in x and y, an open sentence that is bound to have the same extension. How better or more satisfyingly could the whole mystery be dissipated of identity and our grasp of identity?

Chapter Two, §1, has committed me to be suspicious of this claim. Congruence should indeed flow from identity, but congruence as such will scarcely encapsulate the whole of identity. (Unless identity is already incorporated within congruence. See also Chapter Three, note 27.)

The first thing to remark is that the recipe Quine has given for the elimination of identity from a first level quantificational theory is indeed one recipe. But the results of the application of this recipe do scant justice to the evident univocity of 'x is the same as y'. Suppose that, for each of several languages unlike English in having a clearly delimited set of predicates and different from one another in respect of primitive vocabulary, we frame by exhaustion its surrogate identity predicate. Suppose we then replace the extant '=' predicate of the language by the surrogate predicate. What do the surrogates framed for these various languages have in common? Each expresses a certain congruence with respect to the predicates of the particular language into which it is introduced. But, so long as we restrict ourselves carefully to that which can be expressed in first level terms and we are confined to that which can register *within* Quine's first level definitions of 'x = y', we cannot express

---

[40] Quine (1960), p. 230.

what it is that constitutes each surrogate an identity or congruence predicate. For Quine's method makes whatever sense it makes for us by its surreptitious allusion to and dependence upon an idea which is essentially second level. The second level idea is that identity is the relation whose holding between *a* and *b* ensures that every property of *a* is a property of *b* and *vice versa*. The trouble with a second level account of identity, however, is that it involves quantifying over all first level properties, including reconstructed identity and countless other properties that latently involve identity. It might be replied that this does not matter so long as there is for *each* language some surrogate identity predicate. Such a defence would raise difficult questions about how it is that speakers with different active vocabularies, determining different surrogates, understand one another – unless on the basis of a second level conception of identity. But let us not dwell on this here. For there is a further and more specific reservation.

John Wallace points out that Quine's method of reducing '=' yields rather stranger results than any that Quine himself has countenanced explicitly.[41] Applied to a theory or language with just three unanalysed predicates '*x* is a forest', '*x* is a tree' and '*x* grows in *y*', Quine's proposal forces the truth-value false upon the sentence 'In every forest there grows more than one tree'. Of course the defender of the method may claim that such troubles will disappear so soon as we consider first-order theories with an expressive power more closely approximating to that of English. Wallace suggests that the claim of eliminability would need to be rephrased as follows: if a theory has a finite number of unanalysed predicates, then a finite number of predicates can be added to the theory, so that in the resulting expanded theory what we usually intend by identity is eliminable by the prescribed method. But now – at least for the purposes of the evaluation of the idea that identity can be reduced or explained in this way – everything is seen to depend on what predicates *are* added in order to force the desired truth-value upon the sentences involving the constructed predicate that is to be introduced in lieu of '='. Suppose the appearances can only be saved if monadic and polyadic predicates presupposing identity or place–time individuation or thing-individuation are supplied. If so, it is upon the presence of these that the success of the elimination recipe will depend.

---

[41] See John Wallace, *Philosophical Grammar*, Stanford University Ph.D., 1964, published by University Microfilms Ltd, Ann Arbor, Michigan, 1969. See pp. 8off. In order to clear identity from Wallace's sentence, Williamson proposes that his argument be recast as relating to the sentence 'In every forest there grow many trees', deploying a 'many' quantifier taken as primitive.

Here we are left with at least one question, namely the question of which predicates are really and truly identity-free. And pending that's being settled, I suppose that the hope will still persist that I am trying to dissipate. I can imagine my notional opponent's saying this: 'Maybe it was a mistake for me to get involved in questions about reduction and quasi-reduction. The thing that I want to hold out for may amount to less than that. My thought is that, if identity is to be empirically tractable, then it must be that in any given situation and any given context, all the identities of things involved are fixed or fastened down from some arbitrarily large sufficiency of information about all the various other predicates and relations that are instantiated there. Is not the fixation of identity by other properties and relations the condition of *significance* and of *workability* for the idea of identity? Whatever questions remain open about the reducibility of identity or the elimination of Quine's elimination recipe, identity must *supervene* on other properties and relations.'

That is what my opponent says. Let it be clear, however, that in doubting, as I do, whether there is any interesting sense in which identity supervenes on other properties and relations, I do not take myself to doubt that, in a given context with given object or objects, the identity relation must rub shoulders with and have relations of compossibility or incompossibility with other properties and relations. That is the normal condition of properties from different ranges converging upon a given object or objects. The controversial claim to which the reductionist/supervenientist is now committed is rather this: even if there is no one way in which identities are to be read off the not identity-involving properties and relations of the entities that are involved in a given set-up, there is, for each and every set-up, some way of determining, from a sufficiency of information about the not identity-involving properties and relations of the entities participating in the set-up, the identity of each thing involved.

How is this idea to be evaluated? My opponent speaks of other properties and relations fixing identities, fastening them down, or being the basis for ascertaining identities. But these may not be exactly the same. Think of a case where in a detective story (say), an identity is determined in a striking and unexpected way from some narrative about a whole group of entities. Is it this sort of thing that the empiricist has in mind? If it is, then the obvious objection seems to be that all that is in question there is a deductive reconstruction from an incomplete narrative of a fuller narrative. This is the recovery of a narrative in which things have an identity already determined. Epistemically speaking, there is here a triumph. But there is no model here for the *constitutive* determination of identity out of properties and relations that do not include identity.

Let this obvious finding be the occasion to reflect that the idea of supervenience is often said by those who set store by it to be this: that properties from a certain range of higher level properties should supervene on some other range of more explanatorily basic properties. But, if supervenience is some relationship between classes of properties, then is not the identity of the *subjects* of such properties treated as something taken already for granted? The supervenientists themselves seem to suggest this when they say (e.g.) that 'it is not possible that two things be indiscernible in respect of their lower level properties without also being indiscernible in respect of their upper level properties'. On this account of the matter, identity itself lies well outside the intended area of supervenience.

To defuse this objection, the empiricist might want to explore the following suggestion: *facts about* the identity of objects supervene on *facts about* the exemplification of properties and relations other than the identity of objects. When the claim is put in this way, it is left open what the exemplification of the other properties and relations comes to. Maybe these exemplifications are given in feature placing or quasi-pointillist style without any particular commitment to any particular ontology. Maybe matters of ontology and identity supervene *simultaneously* on matters about the distribution of *features*.

There are things here that are difficult to understand. But this may not matter. For my opponent has now committed himself to something very strong and highly questionable, something equivalent to the Identity of Indiscernibles, first mooted in Chapter Two. In that chapter it was pointed out how strong a principle Leibniz's Principle *eadem sunt quorum unum alteri substitui potest salva veritate* becomes as soon as possession of all the same properties is interpreted as sufficient for identity and the properties in question are strictly confined to the pure properties that do not presuppose the individuation of particular times, things or places. Wittgenstein noted that any such restriction would exclude a universe consisting only of two exactly similar spheres. Later, Strawson pointed out, in opposing the Identity of Indiscernibles, that

'It is necessary only to imagine the universe in question being repetitive or symmetrical in certain ways in order to see that there might be numerically different points of view from which scenes presented [to an individual monad] would be qualitatively indistinguishable, even though they comprehended the entire universe. . . . A very simple illustration will serve.

'Think of a chess-board . . . The problem is to provide individuating descriptions of each square, and to do so in terms of the view of the rest of the board obtainable from each square . . . The problem cannot be solved even if the view from each square is allowed to comprehend the entire board.' ((1959), pp. 122–3)

When faced with such examples, some people will not flinch from the thought that it is no less than a *presupposition* of our individuative practices that we do not live in such worlds as Strawson and Wittgenstein have described. Because the presupposition is *global*, they believe it can be lived with – pragmatically, say, and/or as a 'framework principle'. But matters are even worse than they suppose.

Is it also a presupposition of our individuative practices, or a framework principle for it, that there are no fully symmetrical objects? (A symmetrical object with exactly matching top half and bottom half has parts that are indiscernible. It is reduced effectively to half of itself by the Identity of Indiscernibles as strictly construed. Moreover, an object that is symmetrical about all planes which bisect it seems to be precluded altogether. For not only would the top half of such an object be indiscernible from its bottom half. The left side of the bottom half would be indiscernible from the right side of the bottom half. And as regards the residual eighth . . . We are eventually left with nothing but a line and then, at the limit, a geometrical point.) Are we to believe that it is a 'framework principle' that no object is symmetrical about all planes which bisect it?

In the face of these difficulties, no interesting thesis of supervenience seems defensible. Of course, it is a crucially important fact about identity, it is of the essence of identity, that it rubs shoulders with other properties and relations. But that is not enough for supervenience. Identity is just identity. It cannot be confected from other properties and relations.

11. MIGHT IT EVER BE TRUE TO SAY THAT *a* WAS ALMOST *b*, THAT *a* WAS ALMOST NUMERICALLY IDENTICAL WITH *b*?

Maybe identity is, as we have claimed, autonomous, determinate, irreducible, non-supervenient, primitive, not a matter of degree, all or nothing. But, despite all that, it may appear that a question remains: is it possible for *a* to be almost (numerically) the same as *b*? Again, where *a* is not *b*, someone would ask: *might a almost have been b*? In matters of identity, can sense be made of what is still called in post-World War parlance 'a near miss'? This question is still open. The fact that identity is all or nothing does not close it. Consider. Being tall enough to be a guardsman is all or nothing. Let six foot be the first acceptable height for a guardsman and let there be no last unacceptable height. By this ruling, one could say that being tall enough for a guardsman is all or nothing. Nevertheless the height of 5ft 11½in is a near miss. (Would it be better to call this a near hit?) If you really want to be a guardsman and you stand 5ft 11½in, you must grow. But you do not have very far to grow. If you fail, then this will have been a near miss.

For identity could there be anything similar? There is a case that interested the Roman jurists, who subsumed it under their doctrine of *accessio*. Let us state it and then adapt it:

Pictura. A paints a picture upon B's tablet. The picture is here considered the principal thing, the test ... being its value, and the tablet is considered the accessory. So the result belongs to A. But if B is in possession, A must pay compensation for the tablet, or be defeated by the *exceptio doli*. If A is in possession, B may bring an *actio utilis* for the tablet, but he must be prepared to pay for the picture, or himself be defeated by the *exceptio*; that is, if A got the tablet honestly. If A stole it, B has the *actio furti*.[42]

Here is the case to consider: on Monday, A comes upon B's tablet and discovers that there is a sketch painted on it, a landscape with farm buildings, trees and mountains indicated in the distance. Because it appears that, in one place, the picture must have been smudged before the paint dried, A gets out his paint box and retouches the passage. On Tuesday, A looks again at the tablet, approves his own restorations, but then itches to improve things further. He lightly retouches several other passages. On Wednesday, he looks again. Suddenly, he is moved to introduce into the scene the figures of human beings and animals, at the same time painting into the sky the sullen indications of an impending storm. On Thursday, B discovers the loss of the sketch painted on the tablet and makes inquiries about the whereabouts of his property. On Friday, he brings an action for the recovery of the tablet on which A's picture is painted. Meanwhile A enters the claim that the picture itself is his. Persisting in this claim, he has to offer compensation to B for the tablet on which he, A, is ruled to have painted a picture that is not B's property.

We may leave to the jurists most of the questions that arise here. Our sole concern is with one preparatory question, and one supplementary question arising from the answer to the preparatory question. Suppose

---

[42] *Roman Private Law founded on the Institutes of Gaius and Justinian*, by R. W. Leage, 2nd edn by C. H. Ziegler (London, 1932).

the magistrate determined in favour of A's plea to retain the picture, on the grounds that Wednesday evening's picture is not the same work as the sketch belonging to B that A discovered on Monday morning. Suppose everyone agrees that too much has happened on the tablet between Monday afternoon and Wednesday evening for any other finding. Suppose it has been ruled that Monday's work was restoration and Tuesday's mere meddling. The meddling has changed the original's appearance a little, there has been significant qualitative change, but on Tuesday the original still exists (albeit 'improved', A says). Obviously then, the moment when Monday's picture ceased to exist occurred on Wednesday. Suppose that the crucial changes that A made to the picture, though begun earlier in the day, were not fully in progress until 2.00 pm. Now consider this identity claim: 'The original sketch, the sketch that was visible on Monday, on Tuesday, and on Wednesday morning, is identical with Wednesday evening's picture.' That claim is certainly false (or so we are supposing). Yet is not the following remark, made by a witness Caecilia, true? – 'The picture that was on the tablet at 2.50 pm on Wednesday was *almost* the same picture as the picture belonging to B that A discovered on B's tablet on Monday. Indeed, if A had been attempting less, if A had not taken it into his head to impose his own conception of the scene depicted, then the picture to be found on the tablet at 2.50 pm on Wednesday would indeed have been the same picture as that which A discovered on the tablet on Monday.' (Cf. Chapter Four, §12.)

Let it be conceded immediately that, given the finding of non-identity between the original sketch belonging to B and A's finished work, this could well be a sensible, non-pointless and true thing to say. The question is whether the proper interpretation of the claim involves identity *itself's* holding either almost or not quite. What I should say is that, when she offers the commentary last quoted, Caecilia has no need at all to commit herself to that idea. For when she stated that the Wednesday 2.50 pm picture was almost the same as the original discovered on Monday, she can be interpreted faithfully as saying that the former picture has a strong qualitative resemblance to the latter. Caecilia can also be interpreted as expressing the thought that it was *almost the case* that there was on the tablet at 2.50 pm, Wednesday, a picture that was one and the same picture as the picture discovered on the tablet on Monday. If such and such hadn't happened, or if someone had dissuaded A from following his impulse, then the picture on the tablet at 2.50 pm would have been the same. But here the definite description 'the picture on the tablet at 2.50 pm on Wednesday' must have the sense of 'whatever picture it was/would have been'. (That is an entirely normal use, on some views a standard use, of a definite description.)

Nothing then forces this issue. One could accept Caecilia's remark entirely verbatim without having any use for the idea that *a* can be almost identical with *b* (in the numerical sense of identity) or could almost have been *b*. But why should one resist the idea?

If I resist, it is on the strength of the following thought. The aspirant who reaches a height of 5ft 11½in either goes on to 6ft or he doesn't. But whichever he does, whether he succeeds or he fails, he is there and he makes it or he doesn't make it to 6ft. It is he who lives through his good or bad luck. It is not so similarly easy to make sense of there *being throughout* something that would or would not count, on Wednesday at 2.50 pm, as numerically identical with the Monday picture. We could of course say, for the case of a variant on the actual history in which someone restrains A on Wednesday morning, that the picture of Monday was almost destroyed on that Wednesday, but escaped. But *in any scenario* that Monday picture can't have been almost identical with the actual Wednesday 2.50 pm picture. In the actual scenario, the Monday picture was obliterated or effaced some time on Wednesday before 2.50 pm. In the variant where A is restrained, the Monday picture is still on B's tablet on Wednesday at 2.50 pm. It is there, not almost there, even if it almost suffered the fate of being painted out.

In our putative example, there is indeed, in both variants, *something* that is there all along, namely the tablet that belonged to B. But B's tablet is not identical with either the original sketch or the new painting that A made out of that sketch. (Here Roman Law and the doctrine of individuation agree.) The tablet with B's picture on it can indeed become by degrees a tablet that supports the new picture that is A's property (even while it, the tablet, remains B's). It is not of course to be denied that the picture B owned can become *more like* the picture that will be ascribed to A. Under A's earlier restorative attentions, the picture that B owned can indeed, in this sense, creep up on the status of A's picture. But it cannot creep up on being the same picture as A's picture and either fail, or just fail, or just succeed or easily succeed in being that very picture. It is no easier for it to be almost the very same picture as A's picture than it is for it to be in part numerically identical with that picture.

Conclusion: When Caecilia comments, plausibly enough, that the 2.50 pm Wednesday picture is almost the original Monday sketch, or vice versa, she is not charitably or sensibly interpreted as saying anything at all that would entail that *this very picture*, even though it is just coming into being under the care of A, is almost numerically the same as the picture which, on Monday, A discovered on a tablet belonging to B. (Nor is the converse claim at all promising.) If this is right, then it supports the thought that identity itself is not only all or nothing. It actively excludes (or so it now appears) the ideas of just making it, almost making it, or a near miss.

Those who want always to be sure there is some formal demonstration in the offing may see the doubts I have just rehearsed about the idea of an entity a's being almost identical with an entity b (and my reading of Caecilia's claim as altogether innocent of that idea) as furnishing an advance commentary on the following derivation:

(i) $a = b$ (Hypothesis)
(ii) a is not almost identical with a and is not almost distinct from a
(iii) a is not almost identical with b and is not almost distinct from b
(iv) $(a = b) \rightarrow (a$ is not almost identical with b and is not almost distinct from $b)$
(v) $(a$ is almost identical with b or a is almost distinct from $b) \rightarrow a \neq b$.

Commentary. (v) is the contraposition of (iv). (iv) is arrived at by conditional proof from (iii) and (i), discharging (i). (iii) comes from (ii) and Leibniz's Law. (ii) is a substantive claim about a's identity with a. In (ii), the 'not almost' is read twice over in one natural way. This is the same as the way in which it is read in (iv). (ii) itself reflects one special thing about identity. It reflects the same thing that organizes the persuasive efforts of all the preceding paragraphs of this section. Moreover, (ii) is true.

12. CONCLUSION

In this chapter there is just one rash claim about identity (and singling out) that I have held back from entering. I have not said that findings of identity are uncontentious. All or nothing, no near misses, determinate, and all the rest – that is one thing. *Uncontentious* is another thing altogether. Identity can be all or nothing, determinate, exclude degree, exclude near misses . . . *and* be contentious. But the theory of identity that allows findings of identity to be contentious – *this* I have aspired to render less contentious. Once sober conceptualism comes to the aid of ordinary common sense, philosophy has no need (I declare) to supplant the common sense conception according to which identity is utterly special and unique.

Personal identity

You would not find out the bounds of the soul, though you traversed every path: so deep is its logos.

Heraclitus

The human body is the best picture of the human soul.
Wittgenstein, *Philosophical Investigations*, p. 178 (trans. Anscombe).

PART ONE

I. AN EXPEDITIOUS IF PRECIPITATE ANSWER TO THE QUESTION OF PERSONAL IDENTITY

If the thesis of the Sortal Dependency of Identity (**D**) is correct, then a simple expectation arises: namely that, in the case where A and B are persons, the content of the sentence 'A is the same as B' may be elucidated, through the equivalence of 'A = B' and 'A is the same something as B', as requiring for its truth that A should coincide with B under the concept *person*. This can scarcely be wrong. But, since the question that it pushes into immediate prominence, of what sort of thing persons are, leads into a thicket of philosophy, anyone who has been once through the thicket may wonder whether it can be skirted.

One way round seems to be to reflect that, if A and B are the kind of creature that we take ourselves to be – the kind of creatures writing or reading this book, I mean – then an equally good answer to the *same what?* question ought to be 'human beings'. For if A and B are persons and human beings, then A could never be the same person as B and not the same human being as B; or the same human being as B and not the same person. (Cf. Chapter One, §2 following.) So, *given* the human beinghood of A and B, this furnishes a perfectly good covering concept for the identity 'A is the same as B'. 'Person' and 'human being' differ in sense. They may even differ in their extension. But that is immaterial.[1] What matters is that here, in so far as they assign any, the concepts *person* and *human being* assign the same underlying principle of individuation to A and to B, and that that principle, the *human being* principle, is the one that we have to consult in order to move towards the determination of the truth or falsehood of the judgment that A is B.

Human beings, endowed as they are with a distinctive mode of activity of their own, are substances in the rich sense of 'substance' that has been built up in the preceding chapters.[2] Their mode of activity is nothing unknown to us. So one might well wonder how questions of identity covered by the *human being* concept could fail to find the notion of identity at its most straightforward and unproblematical best. By admitting of answers that are principled, such questions ought to exclude the risk (and even the risk of the risk) of indeterminacy. See Chapter Six. Ought it not to be safe then, in any case where it is not doubtful that A and B are determinately identified, to see the apparent non-determinacy of truth-value residing in a claim 'A = B' as entailing that A is actually not B? On this view, the difficulty of undecided questions of personal identity ought to derive either from faulty formulation or from ignorance. Or else, if *human being* is metaphysically troublesome (which need not be very surprising), then we must attend again, at need, to the question of what human beings are (cf. §16) in order that we be better placed to apply to the problem of their individuation the principled ingenuity and vigilance that ought to be promoted by any adequate dialectic of sameness and otherness.

2. DOUBTS, AND ANSWERS TO DOUBTS: SUBJECTS OF CONSCIOUSNESS

If, as some declare, these expectations (of determinacy and the rest) are not in practice borne out, why is this? It may be said that the reason is that the proposal just made will be deeply controversial so soon as it is applied to sentences of the form 'I am . . .', as in 'I am

---

[1] That they are not synonymous makes easier the expression of certain truths that it would be a pity for us to dispense with. Or so I aver at pp. 69–70 of Wiggins (1987b) and again at pp. 244–8 of Lovibond and Williams (1996).

   How may sortal predicates differ in extension but impose the same principle of individuation? Here is one model: 'tinker', 'tailor', 'soldier', 'sailor' all impose the principle *man/human being*. This is not the only model.

[2] More precisely – and imprecision is dangerous here – 'substance' has been shown to stand for a determinable whose particular determinations, *human being, ilex, mouse*, . . . must be expected to be rich, copious and exigent in what they require of things that answer to them.

Lohengrin', or 'I am thy father's spirit'. 'Such expectations were bound to fail' it may be said, 'because they have so little regard for the fact that, first and foremost, human beings experience themselves as subjects of consciousness.'

As a diagnosis of why personal identity is an issue that will not easily go away, this is plausible. But it is unclear, I should say, how much further regard, beyond that already accorded to it, a philosophical account of personal identity needs to have for the fact of our experiencing ourselves as subjects of consciousness. In advance of philosophy's magnifying or distorting things, what else is there here but this: that we experience our-selves as embodied and changeable substances among other human or non-human substances; that, even as we perceive things or do things or undergo things done to us, we experience ourselves as human beings interacting with other animate or inanimate beings (and can experience ourselves as experiencing ourselves so)? But, if this is what things come down to, it carries us back to the human being conception, to the phil-osophically familiar idea of a person as possessor of P-predicates *and* M-predicates,[3] and then to the question of how human beings do in fact get the idea of the distinction between that which is themselves and that which is other than themselves or grasp therewith the moral significance of that distinction.

At this point, various objectors will complain that too much that is bluntly empirical has been built too soon into the claim that we experi-ence ourselves as subjects of consciousness; that the whole tenor of the explication just given falsifies, as if deliberately, the real depth and diffi-culty of the original finding that we conceive ourselves as subjects of consciousness or as conscious selves.

In the face of such a complaint, there is a temptation for a *human being* theorist such as myself to find fault with the way in which the determinable 'conscious subject' has now been transformed into a fully fledged philosophical substantive of a non-empirical kind. Such a

---

[3] See P. F. Strawson (1959), Chapter Three. In the argument of that chapter, I should like to recon-strue P-predicates as predicates standing for properties of a person that are directly or indirectly consciousness-involving and M-predicates as predicates standing for properties of a person that are directly or indirectly body-involving. Physicalists can say then that, so far from being disjoint, all P-predicates are M-predicates (but not of course vice versa).

  Other works that have left their mark on the contentions of this chapter are Chapter One of Stuart Hampshire, *Thought and Action* (London, 1959); Lev Vygotsky, *Thought and Language* (Cambridge, Mass., 1986), revised translation edited by A. Kozulin – see especially the last chapter; Lev Vygotsky, *Mind in Society: The Development of Higher Psychological Processes*, ed. and trans. M. Cole, V. John-Steiner, S. Scribner, E. Souberman (Cambridge, Mass., 1978); David Bakhurst, *Consciousness and Revolution* (Cambridge, 1991), see Chapter Three.

theorist will say that he is reminded of the way in which the determinable 'substance' is misunderstood (and then welcomed or turned away, on all the wrong sorts of ground) as purporting to stand for a special and specific kind of thing. He will protest bitterly at the way in which, rather than see the dummy sortal or determinable predicate, 'subject', as the first fix by which one fumbles to subsume X (in this case some conscious thing) under a more specific and informative sortal specification, philosophers have come to think of a conscious subject as a peculiar kind of thing reached by a special kind of abstraction. One can only be amazed (he will say) that a mode of abstraction so dangerously similar to the procedures of creative definition[4] should come to be seen as legitimating, without further ado, a whole new branch of philosophical thinking.[5]

The matter cannot be so simply wound up, however, by warnings about the provenance and credentials of the term 'subject'. For the *human being* theory will still appear to do insufficient justice to a line of reflection still prompted by John Locke's account of these things: what I am in the present ('my present self') always lies under the cognitive and affective influence of what I remember having been or having done or undergone in the past, no less than of that which I intend or am striving to make real in the present or the future. But if it is the nature of persons to be remembering beings whose conception of what they themselves are is all of a piece with their experiential memory, then some constitutive connexion ought to be expected (it will be said) between their experiential memory and their identity. But, in that case (it will be asked), how can one be content in the simple expectation announced at the beginning, namely that personal identity for creatures such as A and B should amount to no more than the identity of the human beings A and B? So soon as the Lockean insight is developed in the direction of the theory of personal identity that it suggests, namely that person A is person B if and only if A's consciousness (or the subject self that A is) corresponds to B's consciousness (or the subject self that B is), it will prove that our judgments of personal identity can diverge in indefinitely many cases from those enforced by the human being account. Or so it will be objected.

---

[4] On creative definition, see still Patrick Suppes, *Introduction to Logic* (Princeton, N.J., 1957), Chapter Eight.

[5] The defensibility of the stand I take here is much enhanced by Quassim Cassam's painstaking and maybe exhaustive enumeration and critique of subject theories of the kind I am opposing. See *Self and World* (Oxford, 1997). See my (1987) and "Replies" in Lovibond and Williams (1996), cited at note 1 above.

3. THE LOCKEAN CONCEPTION; AND BUTLER'S CRITICISMS OF SUCH CONCEPTIONS

Familiar though it is, the reflection just rehearsed needs to be set out more historically and in a little more detail, if its force is to be measured and the response to it is to be fully clear.

Locke thought that it was among the defining marks of a person to be able to consider oneself the same thinking being in different times and places. (See *Essay Concerning Human Understanding* II.xxvii.9: 'A person is a thinking, intelligent being, that has reason and reflection, and can consider itself as itself, the same thing, in different times and places.') In Locke's account, identity of person is distinguished from identity of man. The apparent divergence of Locke's conception of personal identity – which is avowedly both subjective (inner) and (he says) 'forensic' – from the human being conception of personal identity, which I advocate, comes to light most clearly in cases where the human being theorists would say that B had completely forgotten what A had done. (The example that follows is drawn from Reid's *Essays on the Intellectual Powers of Man*.) The general has forgotten the exploits of the boy. He has forgotten stealing apples on some distant occasion that was at the time noteworthy in his life. For a human being theorist, as for one who believes in the unitary persistence of the soul, such forgetting is not constitutively relevant to the question of personal identity. For the Lockean, on the other hand, it is a challenge to reflection that ought not to be impatiently foreclosed.

Among the earliest critics of Locke's account of personal identity was Bishop Butler, the guardian at once of common sense and the substantial soul. In his polemic against the peculiarities of the divided account that Locke had been drawn into offering, Butler continued with a logical objection:

'though consciousness of what is past does thus ascertain our personal identity to ourselves, yet to say it makes personal identity, or is necessary to our being the same persons, is to say that a person has not existed a single moment nor done one action but what he can remember; indeed none but what he reflects upon. And one should really think it self-evident, that consciousness of personal identity presupposes, and therefore cannot constitute, personal identity, any more than knowledge, in any other case, can constitute truth which it presupposes.' (*First Dissertation* to the *Analogy of Religion*. (Compare Samuel Clarke, *Works*, III, p. 787 – a reference I owe to Mr Dewey Ducharme.))

One might wonder why this passage of Butler has not been permitted to settle the whole matter once and for all in favour of a substance account, either a human being account or else a soul account. Not only does it seem obvious that the general is the same person and the same subject as the boy. To one content to work within the framework which we owe to miscellaneous insights of P. F. Strawson (see especially Chapter Three of his *Individuals*) and of Donald Davidson, it will appear plainly that the most interesting point in the case sustaining Locke's insight could have been readily accommodated within the human being view. Let us see how.

Par excellence, a person is not simply one of us or a proper object of our reciprocity,[6] but a subject also of interpretation, a being that both interprets and is interpreted. In making sense of others and of ourselves in the business of interpretation, we cannot, however, make do with the bare idea of 'a subject of interpretation'. We need some further notion, however rough and ready, of what sort of thing is to count, empirically or operationally speaking, as a subject of interpretation. The grammatical substantive 'interpreter' lies too close to being a mere determinable to serve the purposes of individuation. If 'subject' or 'interpreter' is to play any properly sortal rôle at all here, if sense is to be made of how subjects of interpretation find other subjects of interpretation, there is need for some further determination. As we find our feet in the world and learn to adjust to others' expectations, as we begin to understand what we mean by the words we have learned already to utter, as we extend our capacity to interact with others and participate or co-operate with them, what stereotype of personhood do we have to catch onto, clearly if not distinctly, and learn to elaborate?[7] In its individuative and recognitional non-effectiveness, the conception furnished by John Locke is not very much better than the bare idea of 'interpreter'. Even here, however, we may be able to make a new beginning from the materials that Locke provided. People are *animate beings* (we may revise his declaration to say) – or *palpably substantial souls*, if you prefer – *bearers of* P-*predicates and* M-*predicates*, who not only *think things, but do things and undergo things*, beings who reason, reflect, perceive, feel, imagine, desire, intend and have experiential memory . . . are happy or miserable . . . conceive

---

[6] For the thought that 'us' has an essential occurrence in this claim, see *op. cit.* at note 1 above.

[7] *Pace* Peter Winch's presidential address, 'Eine Einstellung zur Seele', *Proceedings of the Aristotelian Society* (1980–1), the question does *not* presuppose that we find our feet in the world by procedures analogous to those that the philosophers of semantic interpretation have described. It only presupposes that, beginning and proceeding however we do, participatively and interactively no doubt, we reach some point where we know roughly what a person is. In catching on, we grasp the stereotype, clearly though indistinctly. For my use of the word 'stereotype' here, see Chapter Three, note 2, last paragraph. For clear and indistinct knowledge, see Chapter Three, footnote 6.

of themselves thus (as above) . . . who have and conceive of themselves as having a past accessible in experiential memory and a future accessible in intention. . . . Is it not by virtue of our grasping practically and following through some such stereotype, is it not by virtue of our perfecting our application of it in the perceptible world, that the marks of personhood come home to us, and are available to be elaborated in philosophy? More soberly, let us say that in this way the marks are assembled of persons *as we know them* from the only case we shall ever become familiar with, namely that of persons who are human beings. Finally, at the last step, the position of experiential memory comes to the fore. If experiential memory is a mark of personhood, and persons need to conceive of this faculty as essential to their own way of being, then that secures its full significance to our expectation that, when people do or suffer something, this will impress itself on their mind, extend their information, colour their experience and influence their future responses. In the absence of that expectation, few if any of our finer-grained interpretations of people or the practices these expectations support could ever be sustained.

If so much is correct, then, because of its central role in interpretation, experiential memory plays a special part in the full picture of personhood. But that finding (I insist) does not imply that experiential memory will impinge on the necessary (or sufficient) conditions of the *survival* of persons or play any role in the statement of sufficient conditions of survival. (Still less is memory put at the service of a construction of some self that is distinct from the human being.) Locke can be right about remembering as central among the marks of personhood without Locke's or the neo-Lockeans' being right about personal identity.

Neo-Lockeans have ignored such partial accommodations and distracted attention from them. Human being theorists may justly complain of that. But there are at least two other reasons why Butler's criticism of Locke's theory of personal identity has been found inconclusive. The first is that so many of Butler's admirers have appeared to overlook the possibility (the bare theoretical possibility, I mean, but it is one much prized by neo-Lockeans) that the act of experientially remembering (remembering 'from the inside') planting a fig tree (say) might be modelled (logico-grammatically speaking) on such acts as conceiving or imagining or visualizing planting a fig tree.[8] For the notable point about

---

[8] These are acts where the mental content imagined, visualized or conceived does not call for the subject of the act, the planter, to be specified. *A fortiori*, the subject need not be specified as the same as the conceiver, imaginer or visualizer. On these and related matters, see Bernard

acts such as these is that they do not make the kind of reference back to the self which invited Butler's charge against Locke. Taken by themselves, the would-be truisms adduced by the Butlerians are not enough to vindicate Butler's criticisms. And so much must be admitted by human being theorists.

In the second place, friends of Butler and human being theorists have sometimes overlooked how easily the boy whose exploits the general has forgotten can be reunited by the neo-Lockean view with the general himself. Lockeans were well within their rights to be irritated when Butlerians represented that there was an easy objection against Locke to be found in this quarter. The Lockean's point is worth making more explicit – not so much because it is decisive in Locke's or anyone else's favour as for the sake of a fairer recapitulation of some of the saner or more durable preoccupations of the philosophy of personal identity. In the absence of such a recapitulation, Butler's central insight will continue to be obscured, or its real significance will not be appreciated.

4. A NEO-LOCKEAN IDENTITY-CONDITION

Consider the relation that holds between person Q and person P when, for some sufficiency of things actually done, witnessed, experienced . . . by person P, person Q has at a time after the doing, witnessing, experiencing, some sufficient real[9] recollection of doing, witnessing, experiencing . . . them.[10] Let us call this relation (suitably tidied up with more about 'sufficiency', and glossed somehow to allow for sleep and other forms of inattention) the relation of *strong co-consciousness*. Then anyone bent on grasping the nerve of Locke's conception of person will see that the identity-condition he really has to consider is one that begins with

footnote 8 (*cont.*)

Williams, 'Imagination and the Self', in Williams (1973), especially p. 43 and thereabouts; David Wiggins, 'Locke, Butler and the Stream of Consciousness: and Men as a Natural Kind', *Philosophy*, 51 (1976), especially the second section (to which the present chapter is, of course, a necessary correction and supplement); David Velleman, 'Self to Self', *Philosophical Review*, 105, 1 (January 1996).

[9] The question will soon arise whether the words 'or apparent' should be inserted between 'real' and 'recollection'. My view is that it must not. See the end of §5 below.

[10] The notion of sufficiency figures twice in the definition. There is a great deal to be supplied here from the basis of ordinary norms and expectations relating to memory. At any given time one expects a person to remember fairly well his relatively recent past; and remembering one's very recent past involves being able to muster a rather detailed and complete narrative. Where t_k is much later than t_j, slightly less may be expected. The objections we shall urge against the Lockean account of personal identity are not very sensitive to how these details are supplied. But 'sufficiently' is to be glossed realistically, not in such a way that anything whatever qualifies as remembering provided the event is distant enough.

the idea that, so long as one persists, one normally remembers at least from one time to the next what one was doing or witnessing or suffering at the earlier time. Making use of that relation, one who wants to devise a Lockean identity-condition could first define a new relation C by disjoining co-consciousness with its converse (that is with the relation P has to Q if P is strongly co-conscious with Q) and then introduce the ancestral *C of that relation. (Compare Locke's own use of the word 'extend' at *Essay* II, xxvii, 9.)

With a view to stating the Lockean identity-condition explicitly, let us say then that, if Q remembers at t' doing, witnessing or experiencing a sufficiency of what P did or witnessed or experienced at t, then the ordered pair $\langle Q, t' \rangle$ stands in the strong co-consciousness relation to $\langle P, t \rangle$. Letting C stand for the disjunction of that relation with its converse, we have the relation

$$\langle P, t \rangle \; C \; \langle Q, t' \rangle.$$

Then, as promised, we define a new relation *C that an ordered pair of person and time may have to another ordered pair. Thus

$$\langle X, t_i \rangle \; {}^*C \; \langle Y, t_m \rangle \text{ is true just in case}$$
$$\text{either } \langle X, t_i \rangle \; C \; \langle Y, t_m \rangle$$
$$\text{or else, for some } \langle W, t_j \rangle,$$
$$\langle X, t_i \rangle \; C \; \langle W, t_j \rangle \text{ and } \langle W, t_j \rangle \; C \; \langle Y, t_m \rangle$$
$$\text{or else, for some } \langle W, t_j \rangle \text{ and some } \langle Z, t_k \rangle,$$
$$\langle X, t_i \rangle \; C \; \langle W, t_j \rangle \text{ and } \langle W, t_j \rangle \; C \; \langle Z, t_k \rangle \text{ and } \langle Z, t_k \rangle \; C \; \langle Y, t_m \rangle$$
$$\text{or else for some } \langle W, t_j \rangle, \langle Z, t_k \rangle, \ldots$$

Note that, in the absence of doctrine about personal identity or the semantics of 'recollect' or 'remember', it is simply not stipulated whether C itself is a transitive relation. But *C, introducing a chain of pairs consisting of persons and times at which they remember, and requiring for its satisfaction only membership of such a chain, gives a simple co-consciousness relation that is transitive by definition. It makes possible the following amended neo-Lockean equivalence:

$$I_p: \text{P is the same person as Q}$$
$$\text{iff} \, (\exists t, t') \, (t < t') \text{ and } \langle P, t \rangle \; {}^*C \; \langle Q, t' \rangle.$$

A Lockean who is not too discontent with this formulation of his intentions may be expected to insist that the 'P' and 'Q' here hold places for designations of persisting things or continuants that 'consider themselves as themselves at different times and places'. I could only applaud that insistence (however unclear I find the phrase just quoted). The strategy with the boy, his stealing the apples at t, and the general is that, if the general doesn't in 1700, when he's a general, remember stealing the apples in 1660, because he doesn't have sufficient recollection of any sufficiency of what he did in 1660, then we must look for someone (don't say someone *else*, say *someone*), a lieutenant in the Hussars, say, and an intermediate time, 1680, such that (a) that lieutenant's doings, witnessings and experiences as a Hussar are ones the general still remembers in 1700 and (b) the lieutenant remembers well enough in 1680 stealing the apples in 1660.

Let it be clear that there is nothing in these explanations of C and *C that Locke or his followers will want to see as committing them to abandon the ontology of mental continuants.[11] Let it be clear too that, if the definition of C is read just as we stated it and that of C* is understood conformably with that, then the full strength of the right-hand side of I_p may be brought out by drawing at need upon the causal conditions of remembering and/or real recollecting that are transferred more or less unexamined into the definition of C. For that reason, I_p is better than it at first appears. But this is no guarantee that it amounts to a faithful elucidation of personal identity or even to a formally satisfactory proposal.

I_p is a theory that the Butlerians will want to criticize. But it will be noted that, once the ancestral of C is deployed and C's full import is noted and enforced, the number of apparent divergences between the neo-Lockean account of personal identity and the *human being* account appears to be immensely reduced. For the general and the boy do figure together within the extent of a *C chain of paired persons and times. On the other hand, no deluded empathizer who has read my diary will become a candidate to stand in such a *C chain with me just by virtue of being in the state of seeming vividly and completely to remember most of what I did when I came home to find the kitchen in flames. The chief disagreements that remain will seem to turn on cases that many philosophers will find problematic in their own right. These are cases such as that of a person knocked down in a road accident, who never recovers consciousness at all even though (as a human being theorist would say) he lies in hospital for many months afterwards, still alive; or the person who recovers consciousness but has entirely forgotten (as I

---

[11] Fixing on the particular times t, t', of an experience and the recollection of it, nothing prevents the Lockeans from isolating the two-place relation holding for t, t' between the experiencer and the rememberer as follows: $\lambda x y \left(\langle x, t \rangle \text{ *C } \langle y, t' \rangle \right)$.

should say) who he is and everything else about himself. Such cases remain in dispute. But they are a poor locus for a decisive engagement over personal identity.

Here then is an interim report on the state of the argument. There is the human being theory (in purely logical alliance with Butler and with Reid) and there is the neo-Lockean theory. The fundamental disagreement is over whether experiential memory is in some way constitutive of personal identity over time. The human being theorist denies that it is so constitutive, even though he ranks the capacity for memory as one part of personhood. The Lockean persists in maintaining that experiential memory is constitutive of personal identity over time. This disagreement is important. Yet it is remarkable how closely, once we adjust the Lockean position in all the obvious ways that have issued in the proposal I_p, the two positions can apparently be aligned with regard to normal cases. The scene is now clear for a more decisive attempt to resolve the disagreement.

5. BUTLER'S CENTRAL INSIGHT

It is not hard to reconstruct Butler's comment on I_p. Consider the case where we do not know yet if B is A, but we think we may be able to establish whether now B is co-conscious with A. Suppose that we know that, probably inadvertently, A once (in August 1990) caused a fire in the library-stack in the library of the Chigwell College of Commerce. It may seem we should simply ask: does B remember anything of causing such a fire? It seems a fair test for whether B is A. (It is not the sort of thing people readily forget having done. Nor are many others likely to have done the very same act.) So we arrange for the question to arise somehow, but in a manner that does not make B jump to the conclusion that he is about to be handed over to the police (or yet that he is due to receive a medal). Suppose that it appears in due course that B does remember this, so that (for practical purposes) we seem very close to establishing the identity. What then?

In this case, I_p may appear for one moment to be an effective and plausible principle of identity. But how does it work? Well, B's seeming to remember setting fire to the book stack suggests to the inquirer, in the context of his knowledge that there was this fire in which A was involved, that B can indeed remember causing that fire in the book stack. Does the inquirer's new finding not come close enough to establishing that B is strongly co-conscious with A?

One might agree that the finding narrows the gap. But one can still ask how exactly the investigator argues from B's appearing to remember to B's actually remembering this incendiary activity. After all, B is only the same person as A if his seeming to remember is his really and truly remembering setting fire to the book stack. The answer will probably be that B can rehearse the act of setting fire to the book stack as if from the point of the view of the perpetrator and it seems to be the best explanation of B's ability to rehearse these things/events as if from the point of view of the perpetrator that B was there and did do the act.

All right. But now, on behalf of Butler and his doubt against Locke, it must be inquired what the foregoing argument takes for granted. The answer is that the argument takes for granted some understanding of *what it is* for someone to do such an act at a place and a time, survive, move on to other places and times, and remember later the earlier act, place and time. So it appears to take for granted the possibility of an account of identity other than I_p. Or (as I should say, deploying the terminology of this book) it takes for granted a criterion constitutively determining that for which all sorts of things can count as tests (tests the favourable outcome of which can count as evidence). What *is* this other account of identity? Even if it is consistent with I_p (which it may be or may not be) or even if it subsumes I_p, this other account can scarcely be I_p itself. For I_p presupposes the concept of real experiential memory, and, once we see that that presupposes the idea of someone's doing something and *then* correctly remembering doing it, we are reminded how exactly experiential memory presupposes identity. *Where someone appears to remember starting that fire, they can't be right unless they were indeed there at the fire.*[12] Pending the production of some other account of the identities of subjects, one that is anterior to I_p, the only visible candidate is the sort of account that is offered by the *human being* theorist.

---

[12] This way of explicating Butler is indebted to Bernard Williams (1956–7) and to A. J. Ayer's *The Problem of Knowledge* (Harmondsworth, Middx., 1956), p. 196. For an earlier critique of Locke, see A. G. N. Flew (1951) – to which I have come to see that the 1980 chapter, which the present chapter replaces, was culpably unjust.

Here is another fix on the same underlying point that I want to urge against Locke. Locke writes (II.xxvii.17), 'That with which the *consciousness* of this present thinking thing can join itself, makes the same *Person*, and is one *self* with it and with nothing else; and so attributes to it *self* and owns all the Actions of that thing as its own as far as that consciousness reaches.' The thinking thing that owns Actions as its own (acknowledges them, etc) needs to have got itself somehow some conception of itself *as* the thing that thinks etc. So soon as it follows through its conception of that thing, however, it must know that it is neither necessary nor sufficient for an Action's being that thing's that the thing should be prepared to 'join itself' to that Action. Apart from the case of forgetfulness, the said conception needs to take account of the cases of shame, delusion, confusion. . . .

Here the verdict must go to Bishop Butler, or so I conclude, or to his latter-day followers. It goes to him, not for the sake of his positive account of personal identity,[13] but for the sake of the thing that is validated as telling in his objection to John Locke's account.

At this point, the friends of John Locke may be tempted to try to escape Butler's point by experimenting with the definition of C and *C. They may weaken the right-hand side, for instance, so that it shall only require that one who is a candidate to be in some relation C to P should have sufficient real *or apparent* recollection of doing, witnessing, experiencing whatever P did witness/experience.[14] Their mistake hitherto was to be insufficiently bold in adjusting the idea of experiential memory, the Lockeans might say; perhaps they have been too timid in facing up to the potentially radical ontological consequences of their original insight.

There is no formal difficulty in the weakening manoeuvre, however questionable its philosophical motivation. But it should be noted that the price exacted will be a further diminution in the plausibility of I_p, and an altogether new kind of mismatch, a serious mismatch, with the common sense conception's verdicts on cases – as with the verdicts of the human being conception. The neo-Lockean must do much less or much more than tinker with the definitions of C and *C. (See below, §10.)

Let us call the relation to be aimed at in all future attempts by the neo-Lockeans the relation R.[15] As for *C itself, defined as we first defined it in the most ordinary terms of ordinary language, let us not modify it, but leave it just where we first had it, namely as part of one possible explication of the idea (almost certainly identity-involving, in fact, but that is a part of the philosophy of the matter, and nothing to be settled straight off by definition or stipulation) of the philosophical notion of co-consciousness. If C and *C have any interest, it will transcend that of the formulation I_p.

6. A NEO-LOCKEAN CONCEPTION

To the friends of Butler, that might seem to be the end of the matter. But it is notorious that the neo-Lockeans have not wanted to give up. No

---

[13] Butler's own account of identity is imperfect and at some points confused. In fact, it comes as a relief that he unreasonably refuses to elucidate a notion so simple, so final and so spiritual as that of identity of person. For the best statement of something that is closer to what Butler, given his beliefs and preoccupations, really ought to have said, see Thomas Reid (1785), II, §4.

[14] Of course, *some* strength might be restored to the right-hand side by reimporting (somehow) any causal components that are lost by inserting 'or apparent'. See below, §6 following. But the considerations urged in the next paragraph will still apply.

[15] I call it R because Derek Parfit calls it R. Let not the relation R be confused with the thesis **R** of the relativity of identity, denied in Chapter One; or C with **C**, denied at p. 75.

doubt there have been bad reasons for this – blind perseverance allied with the inertia of misplaced ingenuity, phenomenological (would-be phenomenological) overdrive, a hypostatization of the conscious subject (which prepares some of us to reject the conscious subject as so characterized) or the misunderstanding of the traditional idea of a substance (allied, no doubt, with an unacknowledged residual attachment to it or dependence upon it). But perhaps there have been good reasons, as well.

In a book published thirty-seven years ago and devoted in part to the diagnosis of a mistake that was far commoner then than it is now (in 1999/2000) – namely that of supposing that ordinary claims of experiential memory have to represent themselves as claims of identity (rather than as importing the presupposition of it) – Sydney Shoemaker proposed a striking thought experiment:

'Suppose that medical science has developed a technique whereby a surgeon can completely remove a person's brain from his head, examine or operate on it, and then put it back in his skull (regrafting the nerves, blood-vessels, and so forth) without causing death or permanent injury. . . . One day a surgeon discovers that an assistant has made a horrible mistake. Two men, a Mr Brown and a Mr Robinson, had been operated on for brain tumours, and brain extractions had been performed on both of them. At the end of the operations, however, the assistant inadvertently put Brown's brain in Robinson's head, and Robinson's brain in Brown's head. One of these men immediately dies, but the other, the one with Robinson's body and Brown's brain, eventually regains consciousness. Let us call the latter 'Brownson' . . . He recognizes Brown's wife and family (whom Robinson had never met), and is able to describe in detail events in Brown's life, always describing them as events in his own life. Of Robinson's past life he evidences no knowledge at all. Over a period of time he is observed to display all of the personality traits, mannerisms, interests, likes and dislikes, and so on that had previously characterized Brown, and to act and talk in ways completely alien to the old Robinson.

What would we say if such a thing happened? There is little question that many of us would be inclined, and rather strongly inclined, to say that while Brownson has Robinson's body he is actually Brown. But if we did say this we certainly would not be using bodily identity as our criterion of personal identity. To be sure, we are supposing Brownson to have *part* of Brown's body, namely his brain. But it would be absurd to suggest that brain identity is our criterion of personal identity.'[16]

At the time when Shoemaker's book appeared, and along with almost everyone else, I was extremely impressed by this example. Yet I see now that we were not all impressed for the same reason. Some were

---

[16] (1963), pp. 23–4. (See also pp. 20, 30, 193–4, 231, 245–71.)

impressed by the simple thought that, if the brain transfer were performed with preternatural dexterity, then Brownson's experience would
be a subjectively seamless continuation of Brown's. Others, a smaller
group perhaps, but the group to which I belonged and would have
avowed loyalty (this is not only hindsight), would have preferred to say
that the special thing about Brownson was that he was the functional
inheritor and continuator of all of Brown's vital faculties. *This* was the
reason why Brownson counted as the unique inheritor of the title to be
Brown, the reason why Brownson was Brown, that very substance.
Neither Brown nor Robinson nor Brownson *was* a brain. But the brain,
being the seat of memory and consciousness, was not just any old part
of the body among others.[17] It was the essential nucleus of a person (of
a human being) – or so we were wont to maintain. Moreover, experiential memory was more than a mere potentiality. It was a shaped and
developed capacity, conspicuous among all the vital functions of personhood and coeval (in persons as they are known to us) with our developed
faculties for sentience, locomotion, desire, cognition, . . . etc.[18] Why then
should not the embodied faculty for experiential memory enter into the
whole *principle of activity* of persons conceived as we conceive them? (See
D(v), Chapter Two, §7.) Why should it not enter into some plausible
emendation of the serviceable principle suggested by a misappropriation of Locke's own words 'the identity of the same *man* consists in
nothing but a participation of the same continued life, by constantly
fleeting particles of matter, in succession vitally united to the same organized body'? Why not let the emendation that is needed for the sake of
the Brown–Brownson case, considered as a case of personal identity,
require for the persistence of a person the operation of the same principle of activity and/or the participation of the same continued life
'vitally united to the same vehicle' or 'vitally united to the same seat of
vital functions'?

[17] See my (1967), p. 45, para. 2. (See also p. 246 of the second item cited at note 1.) There was
nothing to prevent one from being impressed by both kinds of consideration. I must have had
some regard to the other kind when, a little later, I wrote 'we should scarcely allow a criminal to
escape the penalty due to the unique doer of a criminal act by contriving his own fission'. See
'Locke, Butler and the Stream of Consciousness: and Men as a Natural Kind', *op. cit.* note 8
above, the precursor of the chapter that the present chapter replaces. But this kind of consideration was secondary.

[18] Even if Brownson had taken some time to settle down after the operation to get used to his body,
to exercise its neural connexions and resume Brown's life – and philosophers are still apt to under-
estimate the preternatural dexterity and knowledge that the imaginary surgeon and his equally
imaginary team of anaesthetists, suturists, radiographers, laser-technicians, physiotherapists,
psychotherapists, counsellors and the rest, would have to bring to bear – , the need for such a
convalescence might not have made any essential difference to that which then impressed one.

7. UNFINISHED BUSINESS

In 1965–6, when I first came across Shoemaker's example and was drawn into this response, I ought to have been much more troubled by the point that, even if Brownson could talk like Brown (which would not in itself have been easy – if it was required off-stage as well as on-stage, so to speak), he could scarcely have stood and walked and run and jumped and smiled and sulked and earnestly entreated and frowned and laughed like Brown. But the chief thing that then concerned me was the realization that, because of the doubleness of the brain itself, my response to Shoemaker's example threatened to reintroduce the same kind of reduplication problem that had already given me so much trouble with the case, which I had recently disinterred from Hobbes's *De Corpore*, of Theseus' ship.[19] What if Brown's brain was *itself* divided before multiple transplantation? It was with reduplication in mind that I drafted the personal identity condition that I defended in 1967 to require the vital functions of a person who persisted through time and change to be 'subserved by a single organized parcel of matter'.

For several reasons, this was not a stable resting point. About the connexion between accepting the Shoemaker example and being a Lockean in matters of personal identity, the reader was left with the vague (and I should now say wrong and confused) impression that *either* one must reconsider one's positive response to Shoemaker *or else*, persisting in the positive response, one must subscribe to the neo-Lockean idea that memory is constitutive of identity. In the case where Brown's brain was divided and each half was supplied to the body of one or other of two twin Robinsons, the question was whether Brownson (1) and Brownson (2) were the same person as Brown. Admittedly, given the transitivity of identity, the answer was no. They could not be the same because Brownson (1) was not identical with Brownson (2). But could nothing more be said? More was certainly needed. But three years later, the 'one parcel' stipulation and the universal–particular distinction[20] accounted for most of what I had in store to block the very different conclusion that Derek Parfit was shortly going to arrive at in his 'Personal Identity' (*Philosophical Review*, 80 (1971)).[21] Parfit's conclusion was that, since

---

[19] See Wiggins (1967), pp. 33, 37, 50–2. Cf. Derek Parfit (1984), p. 254.
[20] See Williams (1956–7), (1960), (1970), and Mrinal Miri (1973).
[21] I place on record here one not insignificant reminder that I mentioned in 1967 but did not emphasize. Not only does the full performance of all sorts of ordinary perceptual tasks require both halves of a brain. The two halves are not in fact equipollent. Moreover, one should hesitate before pronouncing it to be an unremarkable contingency that they are not. The halves are

Brownson (1) and Brownson (2) were not the same yet each had 'the relation to Brown that matters in normal cases of personal identity', identity itself was not what mattered in survival. He concluded that that which mattered in survival was the relation *C, or rather the new relation, still to be elucidated, that we are calling R.

From a defender of the 1967 account that I defended, which Parfit was going to upstage, the chief thing that was really needed at that time was for the defender to show how naturally and inevitably the 'one parcel' condition arose from the exigencies of understanding better what kind of thing a person or human being is. Further philosophical reflection was badly needed to explain, and explain on the basis of the sort of thing a person is or a human being is, what distinguished the relation Brownson bore to Brown, if that case was to be allowed as an identity and a true survival, from the relation that the splinters Brownson (1) and Brownson (2) bore to Brown. That is what this chapter must provide.

First, though, before entering into any of that, it will be good to make as plain as possible on what terms an adherent of Bishop Butler's criticism of John Locke might reasonably prepare to accept Sydney Shoemaker's case. It needs to be clear that, on the neo-Butlerian view, the intuitive (however provisional) willingness to allow the Shoemaker case as a case of identity creates no presumption at all in favour of I_p or any criterion like it. In concurring with Shoemaker about the case, we are not undertaking to wait for the idea of co-consciousness to be clarified or replaced by some better notion (of quasi-memory, for instance) which can figure in a condition like I_p. Nor yet are we preparing to dispense with the ontology of persons. Well or badly, we are simply thinking through our *existing* conception of the principle of activity for a human being. It is not to be denied that, if Brownson is Brown, his life story will be in one respect strange. But, on the still provisional terms

unequal because of the specialization of certain functions and most notably perhaps because one side of the brain has been colonized by structures that subserve the singular and extraordinary capacity of human beings to produce and understand syntactically ordered speech. If this capacity is as intimately connected as it appears to be with our capacity to keep track of the past, to direct our attention to our own perceptual and motor activity, to turn from the task in hand in order to think discursively, or in order to reason about what we are doing with a prospect of lighting on something else that needs to be adduced or compared, then the very thing that renders brains asymmetrical is *not* accidentally connected with that which renders the idea of a conscious self so interesting to us – and so productive of illusion. Perhaps it is almost as plausible now as it was when Aristotle wrote the first sentence of *Politics* that Nature (however much she does in vain) does nothing with no purpose. (The metaphor, as it has to be, will need to be unpacked, of course. But I shall exercise the right to be as lazy about disintentionalizing it as numerous present-day evolutionists are about the teleological language they themselves employ.)

now contemplated, it need not count as ontologically or metaphysically or epistemologically strange. For, as interpreted within the scope of our decision about Shoemaker's original case, Brownson's cognitive states need to be fully answerable in the ordinary way to all the norms by which we standardly regulate the ideas of memory, experiential memory, testimony and the rest. If Brownson claims to have planted a fig tree or scaled Vesuvius or seen the Aurora Borealis from a fishing boat off Orkney, he can only count as remembering such acts if he (Brown and Brownson) really did these things. Moreover, if he *thinks* he remembers, then that must create for him the normal if defeasible presumption that he did indeed do this planting or scaling or was indeed there in the fishing boat; and he must take responsibility for his account of what these experiences were and were like, etc.

This picture may usefully be filled out a little more. Suppose that, in a variation of Shoemaker's example, we are keeping track, eagerly and anxiously, of Brown's survival, Brown being a valued friend and colleague, mortally sick. Like every other substance, Brown is a *this such*. (This is Aristotelian jargon, but usefully resonant here.) In our watching over him tenderly and vigilantly, the *such* is taken care of by virtue of our remembering who and what it is, with what principle of activity and what particular determination of that principle, that we are to keep watch over. The *this* is subsumed by the focused specificity of the *such* that trains our concern onto the particular patient who is Brown. Here the mode of activity that is Brown's is one that is marked out, as I have said already, not merely by his possession of the standard human capacities but by his particular adaptation, development and realization of these capacities. The special and recognizable shapes and forms that he will have given at any point to the standard capacities will not of course be indelible or permanent. But, if we seek to cherish Brown and prolong *his* life, then in our concern for his particular realization of such potentialities we cannot help but feel a very special concern for the physiologically vital foundation of these things, namely the brain and/or the nervous system. Suppose then that, in some dreadful turn of events, it is planned that this foundation, the brain, should be somehow transposed to a new body. Then, in so far as we can still make sense of what is happening and keep track of it determinately (these are not conditions to take lightly) and in so far as we can regard the attempt as in any way appropriate or in keeping (a condition to be linked with the first, and not taken lightly, see below, §§15–16), our continuing concern must be for the transfer of the plurality of specialized and refined faculties and capacities[22] that are supported by *that* brain/nervous system. But, in the Shoemaker case, that *was* attended to – or so it seemed to those as impressed by the case as I was. Nor is that all. It is remarkable, once one thinks through the implications of the decision in favour of Brownson and we see the Shoemaker case in the way I am recommending, that absolutely everything that Bishop Butler could want *logically speaking* is already conceded to his objection (leaving on one side, I am saying, Butler's metaphysical conception of the soul itself). In order for the case to be seen like this, I_p is not required, nor is anything else that is very distinctive of neo-Lockeanism.[23]

8. THE THESES TO BE ARGUED IN THIS CHAPTER

The conclusion to be defended in the next phase of this chapter is that Shoemaker's case marks a turning point. *If* Shoemaker's case preserves identity (and the interim answer is that it does), then it must seem to be the *ne plus ultra* of identity and survival. In so far as further thought-experiments are to be taken seriously as conceivable thought-experiments (viz. the transplanting of split brains, their carbon copying, their pantographic reproduction, the putative teletransportation of human beings . . .), I claim that the creatures or artefacts that these further developments offer to our speculations will need to be seen as analogous to clones, copies, reproductions, models – as all of a piece with things that approximate to their originals, or simply behave *as if* they were their originals. No doubt clones or models are more impressive in their own way than were any pretenders to a royal throne who were drilled and counselled in the role that they were to feign, then let loose, so prepared, upon the world. But, however that may be, there ought to be no temptation to think that clones, copies, reproductions, etc., *are* their originals – even if those charged with managing the relevant part of reality are bold enough to invite a clone to take the place of the original (just as a bereaved spouse may, without confusion of any kind, be urged in some cultures to marry the brother or sister of their

---

[22] These are 'part of his identity', as ordinary people like to say. Or, as I might say in the language of this book, these things figure in the specific determination of the determinable principle of activity to be invoked in making judgments of identity through time between our colleague and the person the doctors or surgeons will finally confront us with.

[23] In disclaiming this affinity between the neo-Lockean view and the considerations that incline one towards the positive view of the Brown–Brownson case, I want to emphasize that I read the real John Locke's chapter as containing certain insights that every sane view of personhood and every sane view of identity will accept as such. See below, for instance, §§16–17. See also McDowell (1997).

deceased spouse).[24] They not only fail the 'same human being' test, by the passing of which it seems Brownson counts as Brown. And they not only fail it for Butler's reason. They also fall short of attaining to that which 'matters' in survival – or so, for reasons that will complement and extend Butler's objection, I shall aver. Finally, though, if so much can be established with any sufficiency of generality, the moment will come at last to return to a lingering doubt and the main topic of Part Two of the chapter, the doubt whether the way in which Shoemaker has Brown pass into Brownson really does preserve Brown himself or constitute Brownson the full and proper continuator of Brown. See, in due course, §15.

9. CO-CONSCIOUSNESS AGAIN, AND QUASI-MEMORY

So much for the plan and the question whether there are possibilities that exceed the Brown–Brownson case. Let us go back now to where we were before we registered the *prima facie* persuasive force of Sydney Shoemaker's example. Let us return to the version of Butler's objection that was set out in §5.

Having found nothing helpful in C or C* as they were originally defined for purposes of the formulation of I_p, and seeing no future in a version of C that made do with 'sufficient real *or apparent* recollection', the defender of Parfit's view of the splinters Brownsons (1) and (2) (contrast the view stated in §7 above) now needs to invoke some mental state or capacity that closely resembles plenary or identity-involving experiential memory, yet is neutral with respect to identity. It will be this that has to make survival conceivable without identity. At the same time, though, the defender's account of this state or capacity will have to resemble the account of ordinary memory (or so it was claimed at §5, penultimate paragraph) in *disallowing* all sorts of specious or apparent memories as not really memories (of any sort).

This task was first begun by Sydney Shoemaker (however unnecessarily, according to my opinion, so far as the Brownson case is concerned)

---

[24] Note in passing the ambiguity of 'clone': it may mean one of a group of almost exactly similar things, but it may mean the whole group or type – a highly unpromising model for those who want to count some unique clone of Brown as Brown himself. And under the first head, one may mean a genetic clone or (as here) a more or less exact copy (of the same maturity and all the rest as the originating being).

I have wondered who first imported the word 'clone' into present-day philosophy. My 1967 use of it was prompted, I think, by that of G. C. Stead. See 'ΟΜΟΟΥΣΙΟΣ ΤΩΙ ΠΑΤΡΙ', *Studia Patristica*, 3, 78 (1961).

in continuation of the work I have cited.[25] But many stages beyond that, the best version of R now on offer would appear to be that of Derek Parfit. His latest version appears in a passage of his *Reasons and Persons* where he is replying to an objection against his kind of account of the phenomena that we normally describe in terms of personal memory and personal identity.

Parfit writes as follows:

The objection would be this: 'It is part of our concept of memory that we remember only *our own* experiences. The continuity of memory therefore presupposes personal identity. The same is therefore true of your Relation R [of weak co-consciousness, which is the relation that our *C first set out to be]. You claim that personal identity just consists in the holding of Relation R. This must be false if Relation R itself presupposes personal identity.'

To answer this objection, we can define a wider concept, *quasi-memory*. I have an accurate quasi-memory of a past experience if (1) I seem to remember having an experience, (2) *someone* did have this experience and (3) my apparent memory is causally dependent, in the right way, on the past experience.

On this definition, ordinary memories are a sub-class of quasi-memories. They are quasi-memories of our own past experiences. . . . [p. 220]

We do not quasi-remember other people's past experiences. But we might begin to do so. . . . Jane has agreed to have created in her brain copies of some of Paul's memory-traces. . . . One apparent memory is very clear. She seems to remember looking across the water to an island where a white Palladian church stood out brilliantly against a dark thundercloud.

Even if [Jane's] apparent memories are presented *in the first-person mode,* Jane need not assume that, if they are not delusions, they must be memories of her *own* experiences. Even if she seems to remember herself seeing forked lightning, she could justifiably conclude that she is quasi-remembering one of Paul's experiences. . . . Jane might have to work out whether it was she or Paul who had some past experience. And this might sometimes be impossible. She might have to say, 'I do vividly seem to remember hearing that tune. But I do not know whether it was I or Paul who heard that tune.' [p. 221]

Confronting the definition furnished at the beginning of this citation,[26] reading Parfit's condition (1) as saying that there is an experience (an

---

[25] See Shoemaker (1970), pp. 269–85.

[26] I call it a definition not only because Parfit does but because a definition is needed. 'Quasi-memory' is a technical term. Technical terms in philosophy are rarely scrutinized with the same care that is devoted to such questions in mathematics or logic. Yet, as logicians will point out, apparently small faults in definition can give rise in that area – and why only there? – to large and unexpected, or even paradoxical, consequences. Consider the paradoxes of Russell and Grelling – or indeed those of Richard and Berry relating to the idea of definition itself. If unexamined definitions can issue in antinomy within the sphere of logic, is there not a comparable danger that faulty definitions will sever connections in metaphysics or issue in disabled conceptions of our active and cognitive faculties in the theory of knowledge?

action or event consciously participated in) that I seem to remember, and reading his condition (2) as saying that that experience was indeed someone's or happened to someone (for other interpretations seem obviously incorrect), we ought to begin, I think, by entering onto the record the first question it invites. What is it for me, the rememberer, to remember or seem to remember *that* experience which was indeed someone's? Close similarity between how things were with the experience itself, supposing that to be independently identifiable, and how the rememberer rehearses it to himself as having been is obviously not sufficient. Countless similar but distinct events are similarly remembered. Nor yet is it necessary. Some remembering of an experience (perhaps most remembering, really) is impressionistic and inaccurate in the extreme, without being inaccurate enough to be disqualified from counting as really remembering the experience. What is it then for someone to recall *that* very experience? Can the question be answered otherwise than by a condition of the following kind: the rememberer recalls experience x if and only if the recollection putatively of x recovers to the rememberer some sufficiency of the actual details of x and enables the rememberer to place x as an event in his, the rememberer's, life and . . . ?[27] This sort of suggestion cannot be welcome, however, because it reimports a requirement of identity and depends on our using the rememberer's own life to identify x.

10. A SECOND AND THIRD QUESTION ABOUT PARFIT'S DEFINITION OF 'Q-REMEMBER'

The second question we must enter onto the record is this: ordinary memories are stipulated by Parfit to count as quasi-memories, but need quasi-memories as such, defined as Parfit defines them, partake at all of the nature of memory? Either that matters or it doesn't. If it doesn't

---

[27] Well, that is how it needs to be normally (and there needs to be a 'normally'). Abnormally (and necessarily marginally), no doubt there is recollection of events the rememberer *cannot place at all.* The 'and . . .' holds a place for any further condition of a causal or explanatory kind.

For fear of seeming to disagree with absolutely everything, I have acquiesced in the grammatical forms deployed in Parfit's proposal. But I should prefer to see them as condensations of constructions more along these lines: I quasi-remember climbing the spiral stairs of Big Ben on my sixteenth birthday just if (1) I seem to remember climbing Big Ben on my sixteenth birthday; (2) someone did climb Big Ben on their sixteenth birthday; (3) my seeming to remember climbing Big Ben on my sixteenth birthday is dependent in the right way on the event that consisted in someone's climbing Big Ben on their sixteenth birthday. Adapting the first question to this reformulation, one obtains the following: What is it for my remembering, as in (1), to relate to an independently identifiable event e in virtue of whose occurrence (2) holds true? What is it for my remembering, as in (1), to rehearse the details of some particular event whose occurrence makes (2) true?

matter, then Parfit loses hold of any non-accidental link between the neo-Lockean conception and the ordinary memory that is conceived in an ordinary factive manner (and whose presence in John Locke's account of these things made it persuasive). If it does matter, though, then we must worry about the following. Surely I can seem to remember some experience that happened to someone, but without actually remembering it at all. For instance, George IV was sincerely convinced, having internalized and embraced imaginatively countless well-founded reports of the battle, that he had been at Waterloo.[28] If so, then he could have rehearsed many of the details of the battle accurately enough and as if from a first person or combatant point of view. But George IV had better not count, simply on this basis, as quasi-remembering Waterloo.

Such questions as this are bound to collect the reply that all issues of this kind are taken care of by Parfit's requirement (3) that the apparent memory be dependent *in the right way* on the experience apparently remembered. That reply gives rise to the next doubt, however.

The next doubt is whether quasi-memory, having been vindicated as memory by virtue of being causally explainable 'in the right way', i.e. the way proper to ordinary experiential memory, can then fall short of implying the identity of experiencer and rememberer. If the memory state has to stand to the experience that it is a recollection of as the right sort of effect, then the next question is how to give an explication of 'the right sort of effect', 'the right sort of cause' or dependence in 'the right way' that will place quasi-memory in the required proximity to memory as ordinarily conceived *and* permit that non-identity. That is the third question to be put on the record. (It generates a supplementary question, but that is the subject of §12.)

One way in which a follower of Parfit might try to answer that question and manage all these doubts is to invite us to grasp the right sort of way by examples, examples that he can exhibit. But here there is a challenge. Either the examples are normal cases, in which case there is identity, and we have already seen in §5 how intimately identity is involved in the ordinary point of making a memory-claim; or else they are abnormal. If they are abnormal and there is no identity of experiencer and rememberer, then it will be inherently controversial how much they have in common with normal cases so far as remembering is concerned.[29]

---

[28] As Anthony Flew points out. See the article cited at note 12.

[29] In 'The Causal Theory of Perception', *Proceedings of the Aristotelian Society*, 35 (1961), H. P. Grice gave a new authority to 'by-examples' methods of explication; but this was without any guarantee of the effectiveness of the method in cases where favour was to be gained at the same

A defender of Parfit may say that in the normal case we see an event befall someone and we take note of their capacity to recall the event afterwards. Well, in the abnormal case, this defender will say, it's just like that again *except that*, after the initial transaction that impresses itself on someone's memory, the ability to recall it is *transferred*. For instance, it may be transferred to two splinters of the original experiencer. In what manner then (we ask) is it transferred? Transferred in the right sort of way (the reply must go), and that is a way *sufficiently like* the way in which the capacity to remember is carried forward by the person who is involved in the normal way. Is it not obvious (the reply goes on) that, at least in the Brownson (1) and Brownson (2) case, what happens *is* sufficiently like? 'Surely, for one prima facie disposed to allow the Brown–Brownson case, *that* is not very controversial.'

Here and in response to the last claim, however, rather than dispute whether the Brownsons (1) and (2) case is controversial (for that is itself controversial, or so any follower of Butler will say) or insist again upon the apparent normality (for theory of knowledge purposes) of the Brown–Brownson case, I think one must make the defender stick to the point. A stipulation *de novo* was being offered of 'quasi-remember'. That stipulation brought with it the commitment to say something general about what 'the right way' was. The answer proposed was 'a way sufficiently like the way that is manifest in the normal case'. But, so far, this has only been explicated or justified on the basis of one or two cases. Our difficulty was that the normal case is the identity-involving case. What was needed then were *general* reasons, not reasons relating to one or two (or even three) particular cases, why identity of experiencer and rememberer was irrelevant to normality. Either that was needed or else (much better and more correctly) we needed a general explanation of 'right way' that was both plausible and identity free.

How then is one to move forward? No progress seems to be possible here until theorists of quasi-memory and the R-relation that it is meant

footnote 29 (*cont.*)

  time for a reconstrual of the phenomenon being explicated. Look towards the end of the citation from Parfit given in §9. Ask whether one could pick up from putatively paradigmatic cases
  of Jane's sort (where memories of an event may seem rather like pieces of shrapnel left over from
  an explosion) the mode of dependence on its associated event or experience that is required of
  a mental state that is to count as partaking of the nature of memory. What ideas will be at our
  disposal for us to focus on the relevant and requisite aspects of such examples if they are included
  among the paradigms intended to fix the extension and intention of 'causally depends in the
  right way'? Well, evidently, the ideas of *experience, having an experience* and *seeming to remember*. But
  in availing ourselves of the last we must of course prescind from all elements of *remember* itself
  that the definition of Q-memory will seek to dispense with. 'By examples' is not the straightforward business it is often taken for. It is certainly not straightforward here.

to define – I shall sometimes call them the Q-theorists – measure up to the requirements of full generality in definition-giving. Equally, though, and by parity, let it be conceded that no progress seems possible until those who are as sceptical as I am about these definitional efforts furnish a better account of our own reading of the semantical and epistemological *point* of attributions of experiential memory. We must clarify the connexion between this point and questions of identity.

II. DIGRESSION: AN ALTERNATIVE METHOD OF DEFINITION, REVEALING BY ITS INADEQUACY THE SEMANTICAL POINT OF THE ATTRIBUTION OF EXPERIENTIAL MEMORY

On the terms that I propose, there are various ways in which the Q-theorists might advance. I should need to shadow all of them. But at this stage in the argument, a digression may prove to be a short-cut. We shall understand better the utility and role of Parfit's definition *and*, as a bonus, approach closer to the semantical point of the attribution of experiential memory if we ask why Parfit did not offer a simpler proposal. The simpler proposal is that X quasi-remembers walking from St Paul's to Trafalgar Square (say) just if it is for X exactly as if he remembered walking so *except that* it may not have been X who did the walking in question. Or (better) X quasi-remembers walking from St Paul's to Trafalgar Square just if there holds, under the headings of causality and whatever else, everything that is required for X to remember walking from St Paul's to Trafalgar Square *except possibly this*: X's being identical with the person who did the walking.

Under this proposal, the idea would be that quasi-remembering ϕ-ing is X's remembering ϕ-ing *less* X's being identical with one who ϕ-ed. Quasi-remembering is remembering with or without identity of experiencer and rememberer. Of course, if (as most people suppose) one's in the ordinary way remembering walking from St Paul's to Trafalgar Square entails that one did walk so oneself, then the remainder that results from the subtraction from ordinary memory must not be reckoned under the scheme of X's remembering ϕ-ing and X's *not* being identical with the one who did this ϕ-ing. But we have already seen an obvious alternative, namely to say that everything is for X as if he remembered walking from St Paul's to Trafalgar Square *except* that, in so far as that remembering is held to require X's identity with the walker, X may fall short of what is required.

To show that this will not do, a critic on my side of the argument will begin by protesting how easily this kind of 'except in so far as' can have the effect of producing a description that is indeterminate for sense. Let the Q-theorist consider the near vacuity of 'It's as if there were a thunderstorm in progress except, maybe, in so far as that requires something to be happening in the sky', offered as a definition of 'quasi-thunderstorm'.

Here a Q-theorist who saw some future in the simple proposal that Parfit didn't offer would surely retort with the challenge to prove that this was a *fair* parody of his definition of 'quasi-remember'.[30] What then? Before rising to the challenge to prove anything, I think the critic should point out that one could never demonstrate in the way by which Parfit's defender insists it be demonstrated that 'quasi-remember' is like 'quasi-thunderstorm' *or* that it is unlike. For suppose, as is usually the case with real words for non-artificial kinds or acts, there exists no analytic definition at all of 'remember'.[31] Then any faultiness (vacuity, indeterminacy etc) in 'quasi-remember' might not be demonstrable by a strictly analytical procedure – just as its soundness would not either. But not only that, the critic ought to say. If there *is* no definition of 'remember', then there is no future in the project of defining 'quasi-remember' by subtraction from 'remember'. For, in the absence of an analytical definition, there is no question of arriving at the thing needed by a procedure of deletion.[32]

[30] Another thing he might do is to claim that, as defined, a quasi-thunderstorm might be blamed for turning the milk sour. But this scarcely restores 'quasi-thunderstorm' to any parity with 'thunderstorm', e.g. as the name of a causal-cum-explanatory kind.

[31] In *Tractatus Logico-Philosophicus* (see especially 5.451), Wittgenstein sees it as a precondition of the definiteness of the sense of an expression that it should have some unique exhaustive decomposition into semantically independent indefinables. Wittgenstein assumes that among senses there operates something analogous to the Axiom of Regularity (*Fundierungsaxiom*), which excludes in the world of sets the existence of an endless downward sequence from a given set A in the form: ... (D∈C), (C∈B), (B∈A). But against that one will want to object, with the later Wittgenstein, that grasping the sense of an expression cannot, in the normal or basic case, be the learning of a definition – or the as-if learning of one.

[32] This is the only serious thing that could be meant by the project of subtracting the concept of identity from that of experiential memory. If someone *starts on* the process of definition, someone else can, it is true, start on the process of deletion/subtraction. But how can the person deleting be sure he has finished? How can one ever say the new definition is completed?

Someone might say that 'swift' (the bird) has no definition but, all the same, one could define a new term 'martlet' by saying that a martlet was a swift without any feet. What would be wrong? Well as a recipe for painting heraldic devices, that would be all right. But as the definition of a possibly non-imaginary bird? Even in the case of a bird like the swift, indefinitely many real things about it may *presuppose* feet. Even if the martlet mated on the wing, could it hatch or feed its young on the wing? If not, how does the martlet perpetuate itself? Is the martlet in the heraldic image a well-defined kind of bird at all then? The grammatical correctness of 'X is a kind of swift that lacks feet' or 'X remembers Y's experience except that X may not be identical with Y' proves nothing.

In his inaugural lecture 'Meaning and Truth', *Logico-Linguistic Papers* (London, 1971), P. F. Strawson spoke of the 'bogus arithmetic of concepts'. For a development of that thought, see §3 of Jennifer Hornsby, 'Feminism in Philosophy of Language', in *The Cambridge Companion to Feminism in Philosophy*, ed. M. Fricker and J. Hornsby (Cambridge, 2000).

Defining a new term by the deleting of all uses of the identity concept from the definition of an old term would be an honest and straightforward enough method of introducing the new term. But there is no question of making such deletions from a definition whose actual text can never be submitted to the blue pencil.

This response to his defensive challenge will encourage the Q-theorist to issue another. If there is no lexical definition of 'remember', then how *does* 'remember' have its semantic identity and how are we to be assured of its soundness? Will the critic please explain himself?

The critic's reply must be that 'remember' has meaning in the way in which most non-technical words do – not by virtue of introducing a concept built up from simpler or more transparent concepts, but by virtue of use. 'Remember' has its meaning (he may say) by standing for a concept with a distinctive place in a whole skein of coeval concepts that came of age together, developed together and now work together to some present purpose. The work of these concepts in the case of memory is to make it possible for us to undertake the familiar but multiple operations and transactions by which we sustain and extend the economy of knowledge and awareness. What is more, that work progresses. Given this picture and given that there is no question of laying out the definition of 'remember' and scoring out every component that imports '=', the whole question between definer and critic must shift (according to the critic) to a different and more interesting place: *could* a species of memory that was identity free play the role that is played in the epistemic economy by ordinary memory?

One major role of experiential memory, the critic will now say, is that it supplies unmediated (albeit fallible) information that *one can take oneself to have got on the basis of one's own experience in the past*. (Is not the role of experience analogous to that which was assigned to gold or silver in older pictures of the real economy?) If no way is manifest for quasi-memory to do that, then the attempt to define 'quasi-remember' by 'everything is as if . . . except possibly in so far as . . .' will inevitably subvert the very thing that sustains the signification and point of a concept such as that of memory. Any serviceable or intelligible notion of quasi-memory that depends on the given meaning of 'remember' needs to respect the links that connect experience with knowledge. And these involve identity.[33]

Parfit's own proposal is still pending, still held in reserve, remember.

---

[33] 'Des expressions et formes qui ont un sens dans l'action vraie, sont excitées et employées hors de leur domaine – et perdent pied. Mais le philosophe ne s'en aperçoit pas': Paul Valéry, *Cahiers I*, ed. J. Robinson (Paris, 1973), p. 753.

But, since a real difficulty appears to lurk here for all accounts of quasi-memory, it will be best for the critic's line of argument to be filled out before we return to Parfit's proposal.

Suppose that our use of 'remember' depends on our participation in the living use of the verb phrase 'X remembers (–)ing'. If it is among the expectations conditioning this use of the word that the epistemological role of experiential remembering should be to help provide us with a starting place for the attempt (by further inquiry, in partial reliance on the testimony of others, etc) to extend our knowledge about how things are in the world,[34] then the starting place need not be something philosophically indubitable or infallible. The real charm of epistemological foundationalism, once we forget considerations about immunity from error, was rather this: that it saw that, if there is to be knowledge, there have to be some *unmediated* starting points. Among these there must surely be states of perceiving and remembering, including personal or experiential remembering. But if that is right, then the first thing that matters for the theory of knowledge is that perceptions and memories should be accorded by that theory their full presumptive title to count as the place from whence, however fallibly or defeasibly, we begin. For purposes of the pretensions of quasi-memory to play a role analogous to memory, it matters that quasi-memory should be a state of mind or faculty that not merely permits an exercise of it to count as a direct source of knowledge but *constitutes* it as a place to begin. But how is that possible (one wonders) if there are doubts about how Q-memory places the experiences it relates to, or if quasi-memory does not make the rememberer himself responsible either for the correctness of the recollection of the experience that is to be a starting point or for the reliability of the perceptions made at the time of the experience? (Q-theorists may appeal at this point to testimony. But our handling of testimony depends on our proper deployment of our own experience. Nor would

---

[34] The same goes for the role of direct perception and one's memory of what one believes. In the argument of these pages, I follow the argument of my article, 'Remembering Directly' (1992). That argument, I should record, is an attempt to develop in one particular direction one of the points made by Evans, *The Varieties of Reference* (Oxford, 1984), pp. 241ff. (I cannot understand Parfit's answer to Evans, given in his (1984), p. 516.) How dare I, having (in effect) criticized Q-memory theorists for not demonstrating the soundness of their definitions, offer non-conclusive arguments, all founded in the suspicion that the sense of the word 'remember' is at once indefinable and *sound*? I only dare because the dialectical positions are not *exactly* symmetrical. First, we scarcely know of any correct analytical definitions. So the most we have is the *prospect* of a correct definition of Q-memory. Secondly, 'Q-remember' is the neologism. We ought to refuse to use it till it is given a determinate use. In the case of 'remember' it has a determinate use. The conviction is at once defeasible and indispensable to us.

testimony itself be exactly what it now is once quasi-memory was counted among the sources of the testimony of others.)

Suppose it has started to rain and I need to be sure that, if I am going to go out later, then I shall not get wet. Then I need to be able to take it as a perceptual datum that I see that it is raining, and as a memory datum that I have an umbrella. If the question arises in my mind 'Am I sure I still have an umbrella?', then I need to be able to summon another memory, such as the recollection of having seen it very recently hanging on a peg. I need to be able to say from personal memory not only 'there are pegs in the hall and by the back door' but also 'I remember seeing the umbrella there yesterday night.' From perception and memory and memory of coming in last night, etc., I need to be able to say: 'I'm at home. This is the back door through which I entered. So the umbrella must now be hanging in the corridor at the back.'

The trouble with such a train of thoughts in the form in which it would need to be redeployed under the Q-modified conception of memory is that the idea of an umbrella-check effortlessly organized by someone's idea of his own single-tracked unitary life becomes problematic in a quite new way – precisely as we see it doing in the long citation from Parfit given in §9. We can dispense with infallibility. What we cannot dispense with is the organization of such thoughts by starting points consisting of the unmediated presentations of memory and perception and the accreditation of such presentations by their provenance *as* unmediated. That is not all. To know how to start upon any future collation of evidences I shall need to know which findings had that direct provenance. If I am remembering in the normal fashion and I can expect to *place* that which I remember, then I shall know, as and when I need, what explanation to seek of the relevant perceptual and memory findings, both the correct ones and the mistaken. I can weigh how compelling each such finding is and try to put a body of them together into a coherent narrative that accommodates together and explains together their several verisimilitudes or falsisimilitudes. But how else can they be placed so *except in a partial narrative of my life*? For thoughts such as these, identity is *not* eliminable.

The quasi-memory theorist may react to these difficulties by suggesting that the normal truth-condition for remembering be modified in such a way that all I need to be able to claim is 'someone in an R-relation to me saw the umbrella hanging on a peg'. If the Q-theorist is sticking to his brief, however, then he has no title to that explanation. Even if he can whitewash the 'me', he cannot appeal to the relation R in the explanation of 'quasi-remember'. For quasi-memory is one of the things he needs to use in order to *construct* the definition of R.

12. MORE ABOUT 'DEPENDENT IN THE RIGHT WAY'

That is the end of the digression. I hope it helps to discharge my obligations under the accord proposed at the end of §10. From the considerations rehearsed one has a lively sense of how wise it was for Parfit to define 'quasi-remember' positively and outright rather than by an attempt at subtraction. One sees how wise it was for him to invoke ordinary 'remember' itself (in the existing sense) only obliquely (as in his condition (1)). But one has some sense too, augmenting one's awareness of the open questions still left on the record (§§9–10), of the difficulty to be surmounted in any definition of quasi-memory that will respect the linkage we need to assume between experience, memory and empirical knowledge. At this point then, in advance of drawing any further conclusion, let us draw breath, and recapitulate the state of the argument about Parfit's definition of 'quasi-remember'.

In §§8–9, after it seemed that an identity-free concept of 'remember' was needed and it was furnished by Parfit, two questions were raised about the definition of quasi-memory quoted from *Reasons and Persons*; a third then arose concerning the phrase 'in the right way' as that figures in Parfit's condition (3). Condition (3) reads 'my apparent memory is causally dependent, in the right way, on that past experience'. In §11, the suspicion was voiced that identity of rememberer and experiencer, so far from being cancellable, is in fact integral to experiential remembering – as integral as it is to knowing *what* you're remembering. This last is something you normally do by exercising your presumptive right to place the experience apparently remembered within your own life.[35] It seems to presuppose the very thing that is still in question.

The time has come to advance to something new, if only to a new sort of question about Parfit's positive proposal. Here is the new question.

---

[35] A Parfitian might respond to these difficulties by allowing that I have given a correct account of how things must be subjectively speaking with the one who remembers. The Parfitian might allow that the rememberer's thoughts must indeed be as I have said. But that does not mean that experiential memory as such requires it. My reply to this would be multiple and would ramify, no doubt, in reply to the Q-theorist's replies to my replies. But the first point is that there is nothing as yet in the definition of quasi-memory that answers to the need for one who is remembering and seeking knowledge to organize his thoughts in the sequence suggested at the end of §11. For it is not obvious that anything in the Q-memorist's conception of memory can furnish the requisite materials for starting points that can be fortified as starting points by being addressed back to the course of the rememberer's life.

Does Parfit's condition (3) seek to discharge a responsibility to say how memory is to be distinguished (as indeed it needs to be distinguished) from the other mental states such as conceiving or fancy or imagination or hope or intention . . . which present objects or events to us? If so, does 'right way' require the operation of a certain distinctive mode of mental functioning? Or does (3) address a normative question, one also needing attention if quasi-memory is to subserve the growth of knowledge in the way in which memory does, a question about the goodness or badness of the fit between how the experience really was and how the recollection presents the experience as having been?

Interpreted exclusively in either of these ways, as concerned either with mode of functioning or with norm, condition (3) appears to be insufficient to constitute quasi-memory with the very same nature, epistemologically speaking, as normal memory. It seems likely then that condition (3) is intended to address both issues at once. Perhaps the thought behind condition (3) is that what quasi-remembering requires is that quasi-rehearsing a thing depend causally on some mode of mental functioning or a mechanism, but a mode or mechanism which *itself* satisfies some sort of normative requirement. Perhaps the normative requirement is this: that, for a wide variety of ϕ, the mode or mechanism should bring it about that the experience is presented afterwards as having been ϕ if and only if it really was ϕ. For instance, the mechanism should bring it about that my memory of climbing the spiral stairs of Big Ben is of a climbing, is of a climbing in the heat, is of a climbing something vertiginous, if and only if the experience itself was one of climbing, in the heat, something vertiginous . . . etc.

Read along these lines (let us not pause to make the choices needed in order to complete the task), Parfit's condition (3) certainly comes to life. But how well does the condition then provide for anything analogous to the distinction between better and worse (normal, identity-involving) experiential memory? There is no escape from the worry that the normative question of how *well or badly* someone's memory mode or mechanism has functioned or functions needs to be distinguished from the question of how satisfactorily the mode or mechanism involved approximates to a *memory* mechanism. Can condition (3) admit *incomplete* or *imperfect* or *partially wrong* or *oddly produced* memories as quasi-memories? If quasi-memory and memory are to be generically related, it needs to accommodate all of these. If the putative relation is to have any of the properties that first motivated the search for something like quasi-memory, then the question is important.

At this point we will turn again to Parfit's definition as it lies on the page, and then at last (with a start perhaps) we must wake up. The thing we see that Parfit presents there, once we attend properly to the passage I have quoted in §9, is not a definition of 'quasi-remember' or 'quasi-memory' at all. It's a definition (he himself announces that it is a definition) of 'have an accurate quasi-memory'. Inaccurate quasi-memory is not provided for.

This is not a tiny oversight, but the trace of a major philosophical difficulty. Nor is it hard to guess how the definition in front of us came into being. Putting together the two distinct issues of mode of mental functioning or mechanism and of norms of correctness, but being aware of the extent to which his condition (3) screwed things down too tightly, Parfit must have seen that he had to 'balance' his proposed equation (equivalence). Then he found (or so I surmise) that the only way of doing that was to add something to the left-hand side, rather than to remove an unwanted surplus on the right. So the definiendum was changed in the way we see in front of us.

Here one cannot help but sympathize. For it is simply not obvious how to lighten the right-hand side, or what to remove. The trouble is, though, that, as a technical term newly defined, 'accurate-quasi-memory' has now to be seen as a (so to speak) *fused* term. The components appear to have independent meanings, but, when they are taken as combining to mint a new technical term, no separate meaning has been given to them. Under this mode of definition, nothing Q-analogous to inaccurate ordinary memory *could* be provided for.

To dwell, as we do so often, on examples of highly accurate and otherwise perfectly ordinary remembering tempts us (I conclude) into elision. Such examples distract our attention from the difference between questions of mental mode/mechanism and questions of correctness.[36] So soon as these issues are allowed to coalesce, as they seem to have done in Parfit's definition, quasi-memory leaves the epistemological economy with a marked deficit.

In the first place, if quasi-memory excludes inaccurate memory and/or excludes variants on the actual mental modes or mechanisms of memory, there is already a serious problem. For the growth of knowledge by criticism, refinement and correction really cannot dispense with

---

[36] It may seem that I believe I have shown anti-naturalistically that these questions are utterly independent. No. The mechanism is no doubt selected as one for which there *can* be a norm. The operation of the norm is conditioned by the mechanism for which it *is* the norm. None of this is denied by one who simply insists as I am doing on the distinctness of distinct questions.

either of these possibilities. The relation R that Q-theorists want to define will not then be built on memory at all.

In the second place, if quasi-memory is to be akin to memory at all or to count as a direct source of knowledge about that to which it pertains, then there needs to be room for the whole purport of a given act of quasi-recollection – room for its pretensions qua memory state *as well as* room for that which it purports to present and room for how it presents that thing as having been – to be determinable independently of questions of the accuracy of the recollection and the goodness of its fit with the experience. Condition (3), taken as it stands, makes this separation problematical for Q-epistemology.

It may seem that the difficulties that arise from the conflation I allege of questions of mode or mechanism and questions of correctness are imported by the contingent particularities of Parfit's definition. But that style of definition arose out of his need to purify the memory concept of identity. It was indispensable to the campaign to show that identity was irrelevant to the thing which mattered constitutively in Brown's survival in the shape of Brownson.[37]

PART TWO

13. AS IT NOW APPEARS, THE STATE OF THE WHOLE ARGUMENT TO DATE

Here is a summation of what has been claimed so far in this chapter: for personhood as we know it, the identity of persons coincides (I began by

---

[37] There is a special difficulty in disentangling memory from identity. Unlike a perception, whose occurrence ties it to what was there to be perceived and whose correctness can in principle be regulated from other investigations of what was there to be perceived at the time and place of the perceiving, and unlike a portrait whose title and original provenance ties it to some sitter to whose appearance it is answerable, the act of recollecting an experience, the event *e* to which the recollection is answerable for its correctness, does not permit the identification of its content or referent, namely *e*, to be made on the simple basis of the place or time of the occurrence of the act of recollection. The place and time of doing the act of recollection afford no indication whatever.

On the inner view of memory, the importance of this comes out in the need (already mentioned) for the rememberer to *place* the thing remembered, the experience, and thereby signal the correctness condition of the memory-state in question, by reference to something in the sequence of his own life. He can only do this sort of placing or fixing of *e* by engaging in the kind of thought that the definition of quasi-memory does nothing to make sense of and that is problematic for Brownsons (1) and (2).

On the outer view of memory, the same point comes out first in the need to ascertain from the subject what memory presents to him (see the inner view) and secondly in the need to identify *by reference to the outer life of the rememberer* the very experience – wherever there is one – to which the recollective act or memory state is answerable for its correctness.

suggesting) with the identity of human beings. Human beings are substances possessed of a specific principle of activity to which, in the course of a life, each one of us gives his own yet more specific, more and more distinctive, determination. Prominent among the specifically human activities is our exercise of the cognitive faculties. Faced with Sydney Shoemaker's Brown–Brownson case, our provisional first finding was in favour of the identity of Brown and Brownson, because Brownson appeared to be the determinately traceable functional continuator of Brown (we said) and Brownson seemed to inherit (in the manner in which any ordinary person who has suffered no such adventures is constantly inheriting from himself) the perfected epistemic and other capacities of Brown. He carries these forward through time, together (we assumed) with Brown's other skills and abilities. Moreover, we found on further examination that the judgment that Brownson is Brown lies well outside the reach of Butler's objection to Locke. If there are difficulties with the Brown–Brownson case, they do not reside here. Neither for purposes of Brownson's thoughts, nor yet for the purposes of describing in third person mode (or in philosophical mode) the set-up that includes those Brownson thoughts, is there the slightest need to try to construct the identity free notion of experiential memory. Nothing appears to prevent us from thinking of Brownson as having full cognitive responsibility for the claims that he makes from direct personal memory.

That summarizes only what happened up to §8. Now for the rest. Consider the case where we have not Shoemaker's Brownson but two splinters, Brownson (1) and Brownson (2), resulting from the transplanting of the two halves of Brownson's brain into bodies of twin Robinsons (each found available, we are to suppose, in debrained condition). Here, we allowed that we may want to say that it is *as if* Brownson (1) and Brownson (2) remember. But we declared that, on the terrain lying beyond the case Shoemaker introduced, no stronger claim ought to be allowed than *it's as if*. For neither Brownson (1) nor Brownson (2) is the same as Brown, and there is no newly minted, properly defined *remembering-of-experiences* relation (or so it was argued) in which Brownsons (1) and (2) can stand to Brown. (That was the conclusion of §§9–12.) No new memory concept that was modelled on the notion of memory that once commended Locke's discussion to us ought to try to make room for personal or experiential remembering in the case of Brownsons (1) and (2). Friends of quasi-remembering seek to improve on the finding that in various ways it is for Brownsons (1) and (2) as if each of them were

Brown. But in so far as quasi-remembering gets us beyond that anodyne judgment into something that is stateable *without* the use of the 'as if', it brings nothing but conceptual disruption.[38] 'Quasi-remember' is ill-defined; and in its application to Brownsons (1) and (2), a confluence appears of two things that scarcely mix, the idea of a person as a singular thing with an individual biography and the idea of a person as a quasi-universal, susceptible of multiple instantiation.

14. PARTICIPATION IN THE GROWTH OF KNOWLEDGE

The force of the considerations mustered so far would be blunted if there were some way to contend that Brownsons (1) and (2) might after all participate in the ordinary processes by which empirical knowledge is expanded. Before we go further it needs to be enquired (even at risk of doing again work done already) what prospects there are of its being shown that, despite the fact that their 'earlier lives' are shared, Brownsons (1) and (2) could *in their own way* keep track of things they live through, mark 'memories' by their provenance, and place the experiences that 'memories' record by the position these experiences once occupied in their lives, etc.

I begin on this by saying that the whole case for examining this possibility may seem to depend upon the prospective availability of something like the relation R. If so, let us note how easily and unthinkingly we can relapse into the supposition that R is available already. Perhaps this is because we are bewitched (as I have said) by the putatively sufficient condition that is given such prominence by the hackneyed, familiar but special examples where the norm and mode/mechanism constraints are perfectly and simultaneously satisfied. These happy cases furnish no understanding of the necessary conditions of the presence of the R relation. All we really know about R we learn from purported cases of it and the role that R is meant to play – in philosophy. But that measure of understanding cannot (I have claimed) assure us that there really is a relation that will both perform that office *and* be independent of identity. Indeed, the rationale began to appear some sections ago for insisting upon some residue of the 'one parcel' condition mentioned in §7.

---

[38] At this point in the argument it may be desirable to point out that, for one who agrees to discuss these thought experiments but is drawn to the line I am still taking at this point in the argument, it is not at all necessary to deny that the splinters Brownson (1) and Brownson (2) *have mental states*. It is not even necessary to deny that any of the respect owed to Brown should be extended, where they actually exist, to Brownsons (1) and (2), however pathetic they seem. They are after all repositories of a kind. See §14.

In the second place, it is worth trying to think further about the epistemological condition of splinters such as Brownsons (1) and (2). In so far as they proceed as if they were direct rememberers, and in so far as they take their experiential memories as direct presentations to them of their own past, they must become party (we have said) to indefinite quantities of error. Each of them says that he remembers a momentous one-to-one dialogue with Isabel (say) or a confidential man-to-man transaction with Stephen. But there are two Brownsons and neither of them is the same as the substance that was there in converse with Isabel or Stephen. Each survivor thinks of himself as a single person with cognitive faculties, and a life altogether of his own, but such thoughts are just wrong. Again, each of the Brownsons thinks that he is a person who lives a life, a substance. He cannot be what he thinks he is. Moreover, if experiential memory is to work as it must work for purposes of cognition, there is no thinkable alternative but for it to induce in Brownsons (1) and (2) the sorts of beliefs that unsplintered people have. Nevertheless, the beliefs that Brownsons (1) and (2) need to have are beliefs that *cannot* all be true. For the sake of arranging for all this to seem possible, why on earth should anyone want to pretend that R is well defined when it is not?

Paul Snowdon has helped me to answer this question. The point is that, even after issuing all these denials about Brownsons (1) and (2) and their supposed experiential memories of Brown's life, the human being theorist is still faced with some impressive *apparent* memories. Whatever else one says, it is hard to deny that each Brownson represents a repository of memory traces or traces of memory traces relating to events that took place before either of them existed. So be it. We can and maybe we must treat them as repositories. It is as if they had each been there. There is no more one should say, however. In Parfit's example, Jane might be the sole remaining repository of information about the appearance of the portico of some remote island church destroyed, since Paul's death, by flood. Nevertheless, despite any gratitude we may feel for the existence of this vestige, let us be clear that Jane's state of being such a repository falls far short of the cognitive condition of one who displays her memories in cognitive engagement, takes responsibility for them, places them, and exercises an option to accord them the status of ordinary direct memory. For the same reason, the attainment of repository status by Brownsons (1) and (2) falls short of that which would have mattered in the survival of Brown.

A third remark. By practice, or even without practice, one can fall readily into the frame of mind where, having been impressed by the Brown–Brownson case, one finds it impossible to think that the Brownsons (1) and (2) case represents the *passing away* of Brown. The explanation is not far to seek. At this point in the supposed history of Brown, one very easily falls into thinking of Brown as a thing that persists in Brownson (1) *and* Brownson (2). One conceives of Brown as a thing that persists in its/his instantiations, a thing that is wherever they are – just as the sail that lies over you, over me, and over a friend of ours, is where I am, where you are, *and* where he is. (See Plato, *Parmenides*, 131b.) In short, one thinks of Brown as a concrete universal. Nothing need be wrong with that. Indeed it is very likely that, with a little care, one could invent a contradiction-free way of speaking of such a corporate being, not merely as a thing with a past but as one with a future. One could index the thoughts that are ascribed to the corporate being by reference to the members or constituents that give local hospitality to the thought, even as other members or constituents lack it or have another, possibly conflicting, thought. Under the new convention, the corporate being Brown will be large, but within him he may safely embrace contradictions. Moreover, if we are careful, we shall be able to say this as theorists without ourselves contradicting ourselves. Nevertheless, Brown reconceived as such a concrete universal is not the sort of thing whose survival was to have been described in the case of Brownsons (1) and (2). Nor is this how we conceive of subjects of experience when posing the question of personal identity. The problem relates to subjects who have lives of their own, to potential authors of autobiographies, who can say 'I think. . . .', rather than 'In respect of member *m*, I think. . . .'

Let it be clear that the difficulty here is not that metaphysics needs to look askance at corporate beings. Perhaps departments of physics or psychology or philosophy could conceive of themselves as such. By an effort of imagination or of memory, one might find even now some way of thinking of such departments as participating not merely in power or glory (high ratings) but in the growth of knowledge or understanding. But there is an important difference here from the sort of thing which Parfitians might think of as surviving or quasi-surviving. For, as we have said, Brown thinks of himself not as corporate and *not* as composed of splinters. If a concrete universal Brown thought of himself in (Shoemaker's) Brown's way, he would be wrong. Departments of physics, on the other hand, considered as cognitive beings that do not need to conceive of themselves as *not* having members or as *not* multiple, rather thinking of themselves as pursuing the truth about physics along the multiple paths pursued by different individuals or teams, must see it as their business to push physics forward by promoting individuals' and teams' constant effort, in seminars, in the laboratory or the canteen, to explain anomaly and transcend inconsistency. A department of physics has no need to suffer from the delusion that it is itself an individual person seeking after truth. Its corporate thought had better be that it is what it is, namely a corporate thing in search of the truth about physics by dint of the efforts of its members. Not only that. A corporate being such as this can offer a perfectly ordinary account of what sort of thing its members are. Suppose a correspondingly corporate notion of Brown were confected, what then? Then corporate Brown would be conceived as a person with members which could see itself as a person with members – and could say what sort of thing any one of its members was. Corporate Brown is not then the sort of thing to figure in an autobiography, a story of itself as one individual person. Parfit's account of survival is not, however, designed as an account of the survival of a corporate sort of thing. It is an account of the survival of things on the ontological level not of corporate Brown but of the *members* of corporate Brown.[39]

Epistemology has long needed to engage with the collective nature of our cognitive labours, with knowledge by hearsay, with the role of testimony, with the conditions for the accumulation and collective criticism and emendation of knowledge. Yes. But no sane enthusiasts for these tasks will seek to dispense with the hard-won insights of the empiricist epistemology of experience, eyewitness and recollection by individuals with lives and histories of their own. Not even an underlabourer can be a splinter like Brownson (1) or (2). The charm of neo-Lockeanism was that it seemed to engage with our given notion of memory – of personal memory, that is. When defended by all the necessary philosophical refinements, it gradually disengages with that notion and puts into question the only account we know how to give of the evidential fabric of our knowledge. Not only does its revised conception of memory denature memory. It has now put itself in danger of disengaging altogether with the idea of an individual 'self' which was its starting point.

---

[39] If a Parfitian person were corporate, what account would it offer of its own members? Does each member itself have members? In case there is a reader who wants to pursue this question and in case that may be useful, he will find an informal statement of the *Fundierungsaxiom* in note 31.

15. THE PENULTIMATE PROBLEM AND A VERDICT UPON IT, ALL LEADING IN DUE COURSE TO A REASSESSMENT OF THE ORIGINAL SHOEMAKER CASE[40]

In the philosophical transition that will carry us slowly back to our starting point, viz. the Shoemaker case in its original state, there remains one other case I have to comment upon, namely the case where the brain of Brown is split but only one of the two portions is successfully transplanted into a Robinson twin. The other dies, we may suppose. Let us call the survivor of these events Brownson Sole. In the circumstances (it will be asked), how can we refuse to treat Brownson Sole as Brown himself? If Brownson Sole claims to have seen the Aurora Borealis from a fishing boat off Orkney on which he was the only US national, if he gets the numerous details of Brown's adventure right and this is no fluke or accident, then how can we help but treat Brownson Sole as one who was indeed there? It may seem that the only thing that is left to ask is how well he remembers seeing the Aurora Borealis.

We can go as far as we like with the *as if* (I reply) and we can take the *as if* as lightly or as seriously as we wish to take it. Indeed we can take the *as if* fully seriously enough to experiment with questions put to a being that we count only as a 'repository' or the carrier of traces of some event they were not present at. When someone devises a whole philosophy of *als ob*, that can be taken seriously too. But consider the judgment that Brownson Sole is the same as Brown. If it is true, it ought to depend only upon Brown and Brownson Sole. It ought not to depend on an assurance about the existence or non-existence of another thing altogether besides Brown and Brownson Sole. It cannot depend *ad hoc* on the accomplished death or destruction or non-viability of the other half-brain that was poised to animate some rival to Brownson Sole. Any verdict about Brown and Brownson Sole issued in such dependence would infringe the *Only a and b* rule, **D**(x) of Chapter Three, §4, which is founded on **D**(vi) of Chapter Two, §7 (*ad fin.*) and the sortalist cum conceptualist argument for **D**(vi). The argument there was all of a piece, moreover, with our commitment to the distinction between a particular and a universal. (See above, §14, the paragraph beginning with the words, 'A third remark'.)

At this point, it is easy to imagine that someone may say that the *Only a and b* rule looks plausible enough as an abstract logical requirement,

---

[40] Readers following the suggestion in the Preface that §13 following should stand as a conclusion for the book will probably be familiar enough with present philosophical trends in thinking about personal identity to guess immediately what has been in progress here. If not, §1 and §6 of this chapter, with or without §8, will supplement §13.

but ask how the normal theory and practice of individuation as we have described it could ever underwrite its satisfaction: 'In practice, in the actual business of making identity judgments, the *Only a and b* rule is unworkable.' My answer to that runs as follows: if Brownson Sole were the same as Brown, where Brown is a human being and thereby a cognitive being, then Brownson would have to be the same human being and the same cognitive being as Brown. But Brownson Sole came into being from Brown *not* in a manner constitutively sufficient to preserve the transitivity of identity or to perpetuate the activity of a human being as a cognitive being. (See §9 following.) On *these* terms, there is no question of Brownson Sole's being the same as Brown. The *Only a and b* rule is not unworkable at all. It asks no more of us than that, when we address questions of identity, we should persist in a way of thinking that preserves the distinctiveness of identity and marks the difference between singular and universal. If identity itself is a matter of indifference to you, of course you can ignore the rule. (Cf. Chapter Three, §4, paragraph 9.) In that case, your judgments will not differentiate identity from resembling, succeeding, going proxy for, being a replica of . . ., and you don't care. If you do care, don't ignore the rule.

16. BROWN–BROWNSON RECONSIDERED

There is a point here which, if it deserves anything at all, deserves to be followed through completely. The principle we have just invoked is that, since our judgments of identity need to be informed by consideration of the kind of things that are in question and thus by the principle of activity of these, our positive judgments of sameness are answerable (by their nature) to a norm that requires anyone who makes a judgment of identity through change to assure himself whether the change is one that preserves this principle of activity – and *equally* requires him to withhold the verdict of identity in any case where the change that is in question would, in *other* cases that exemplified the same process, *fail* to preserve that principle of activity.

Once such a principle is announced, it will seem that in our application of it the question ought constantly and repeatedly to arise: 'what counts here and in this or that connexion as the same process?' One will expect that a constant need to engage with such questions will make us party to an elaborate system of casuistry by which the specifics of each ongoing process can be interrogated in the light of the formal properties of the identity relation and of the character of the thing-kind whose members are subject to the process. One will expect then that anyone making judgments of identity will have to put himself constantly into the frame of mind of a common law barrister, as if testing his every thought against previous rulings or precedents. But as an expectation relating to the world that we know, doesn't this seem extraordinarily implausible?

If there is a mystery here, I think it will disappear with the reflection that the individuative norms by which we normally proceed so effortlessly (but which it seems we have such difficulty in rendering articulate to ourselves) are incorporated already, en masse, within the grasp of thing-kind conceptions by which we find our way about the world. These conceptions are effective – in Leibniz's sense clear. They are not necessarily explicit or distinct. By reflection and practice we can make them more distinct (cf. Chapter Three, footnote 6). In so far as we have mastered these conceptions at all, however, they not only enforce for us the *Only a and b* rule that is disregarded in the proposal that Brownson Sole be ruled identical with Brown. They mark for us the distinction between singulars/particulars, which are not things instantiated, and universals which are. (Cf. Chapter Two, **D**(vi), Chapter Three, §4.) Normally we do not need to think about what we do. When we do need to think, we may have to struggle. (Philosophy is no sure ally here. Rather the reverse perhaps.) But none of this need count against the principle recently identified, the principle stated at the end of §15 and resumed in the paragraph before last.

In the light of that principle, the time has come to look once more at Shoemaker's version of the Brown–Brownson case. In pursuit of the enthusiasms of yesteryear, we allowed that case. Then we disallowed all the cases that followed on after it. But as soon as I announced (§8) that I would mark such a frontier, many philosophers will have wondered how much difference I could insist that there is between the process by which a whole brain is transplanted into a body ready and suitable to receive it, that by which one half of a brain is transplanted into a body ready and suitable to receive it and the process by which the second act is done twice over. If the second and third cannot yield identity, can the first?

Taken neat, this question is hard to answer, or even to see straight. But fending off the thought that questions of this sort ought to be reduced without residue to questions about the individuation and differentiation of surgical processes (questions for which I have just allowed we are ill prepared), why do we not remind ourselves yet again of our method and say, 'Well, here as everywhere it all depends on what sort of thing we take ourselves to be'? If we take that question more fully seriously, maybe we can recover a wiser norm of judgment than any that we exercised in §§6–7. So let us go back to that point and everything that led up to it.

At the beginning we organized our inquiry around the sortal concept *human being* and bracketed the concept *person*. But the aim was not to let go of the idea of personhood, still less to place the question of what we are under the alien direction of physiologists, biologists, evolutionists or others who are expert in matters relating to *organisms*. The aim was only to fight free of the philosophical conceptions criticized in §2 following, then to force upon ourselves and other persons the question of what, in thinking of ourselves as human beings and human persons, we have undertaken to think of ourselves as being. No doubt, the answer must be discursive and draw on our inexplicit knowledge. No doubt it will be essentially contestable too. But what should I say?

The answer I give begins from yet another misappropriation of Locke's thoughts. It proposes that we apply equally to the concepts *human person* and *human being* that which Locke said of *self* and of *person*:

> Wherever a man finds what he calls *himself*, there I think another may say is the same person. It is a Forensick Term appropriating Actions and their Merit and so belongs only to intelligent Agents capable of a Law, and Happiness and Misery. This personality extends it *self* beyond present Existence to what is past only by consciousness, whereby it becomes concerned and accountable, owns and imputes to it *self* past Actions, just upon the same ground, and for the same reason, that it does the present. (*Essay* II, xxvii, §26, punctuation modernized.)

If a term is truly forensic, it surely needs a palpable and public use – a use that is intelligible in the *forum*. But then the term's use in connexion with questions of praise and blame needs to be all of a piece with its other uses in the *interpersonal sphere* – and not least with all the uses to which P. F. Strawson drew attention when he showed how intimately our ideas of agency and responsibility depend on human beings' reactive and participative attitudes towards other human beings.[41] Because such attitudes depend on the reality of human presence, that directs us to find out the connexion between these questions and Strawson's earlier insistence on the indispensability to the metaphysics and epistemology of personhood of the idea that a person is the bearer of both P- and M-predicates. How a human being stands or walks or frowns or smiles or laughs or sulks or earnestly entreats, or how he fries an egg, this *is* one part of what he is – no less than is the sort of thing ('more mentally') he chooses to say to this or that conversant, how musically he plays the

---

[41] See 'Freedom and Resentment', *Proceedings of the British Academy*, 48 (1962), pp. 1–25.

violin (if he does), or how calmly or wildly, how sensibly or recklessly or obsessively, how magnanimously or ignobly (in a manner he is held responsible for) he responds day by day to the predicaments of ordinary life. Human beings' dispositions and capacities are gradually but constantly shaped and reshaped. In the process, the particular ways in which they come in due course to do whatever they do will become distinctive of what they have then become and *can be responded* to as having become.[42] If so, then P-predicates, properly understood, are a subset of M-predicates. Unless they are, unless physiognomy and the particularities of a person's physical presence and being find their way into the story, Strawson's account of reactive and participative attitudes is hard to follow through. But is enough room left for all these things by the acceptance of Shoemaker's thought experiment? Surely the character of a person is not independent of his or her physiognomy, and this physiognomy can scarcely be independent of the body.

Consider the same matter from another point of view, which is complementary to the foregoing. In the Brown–Brownson case, after all the events that Shoemaker describes, it seems that Robinson still walks. But Robinson *is no more* (or so we were prompted to decide). We must get used to this. It seemed that Brown was dead, but that isn't right either (or so it has been decided). Where Robinson seems to be, there is Brown. We must inhibit then the affective responses we once trained upon Robinson, and redirect our affective responses for Brown onto the person who looks like Robinson but is Brownson. We must look into the face of Robinson and try to see there, try to find there, Brown. Meanwhile Brown himself, wearing Robinson's face, must come to terms with the difficulty that we have in finding him there. These are among the things to be made sense of in the Brown–Brownson experiment. Can they really be made sense of?

In considering the characteristically human modes of activity that appeared to be preserved in the Shoemaker case and not preserved in the cases that go beyond it, there was much to learn about the cognitive

---

[42] As one speaks of these things, the phrase that may come to one's lips is 'his doing such and such an act in this or that particular way is a part of his identity'. When we speak at *t*, each of us, of 'our identity', what are we concerned with? Surely we are concerned with the fullest determination *as of t* of that which we are or have by the time *t* become. But this involves us with the so far shaped principle of activity which permits certain judgments of identity over certain imaginable transformations but disallows other judgments of identity over all sorts of other apparently imaginable possibilities. These other possibilities are thought of, however contentiously and by whatever admixture of bluff, as bringing with them the end or virtual end of the subject who undergoes them (if not necessarily of the subject's memory traces or the traces of those memory traces).

faculties and the conditions of their operation. But on the properly forensic view of human being-hood, why did not considerations of physiognomy (etc) that are familiar to us prompt, at the outset, all sorts of other doubts or hesitations about the Brown–Brownson case? How can the present author have been persuaded by the contingencies of current controversy to devote six long sections of this chapter to C, *C and R, but have allowed so fundamental an objection against most or all of these thought-experiments to lie fallow? It was strange, just because Brownson seemed in some ways to perpetuate Brown, for us to ignore the developed faculties of Brown which Brownson does *not* inherit and pay so little attention to all the implications of brain transfers of the kind that were described by Shoemaker. The high quality of the actors and mimics one sees on the stage should not lead one to think that the question of the fit of the brain to the physiognomy of the new body which is to receive it is as relatively simple as the transposition of music from one instrument to another.[43] But now that the Brown–Brownson Sole case and the potentially multiple output of the process by which Brownson Sole emerges as Brown alert us at last to further doubts, let us take them more seriously.

17. ONE LAST VARIANT – AND THE PHILOSOPHICAL MORAL OF SAME. FINALLY, HUMAN PERSONS AS ARTEFACTS?

At this point, the position must be considered of a philosopher who was not at all convinced by that which I said about the case of Brown and Brownson Sole (§15) but is suddenly persuaded that there is a serious case to answer concerning physiognomy and the Brown–Brownson case. The difficulty posed by physiognomy impresses him. Nevertheless, after further reflection, we may imagine that this philosopher insists that even the point that he has allowed casts no doubt on a case where Brown's brain is transferred to *the body of a Robinson who is an identical twin of Brown*. We may suppose that the philosopher also insists, with a fervour characteristic of present-day controversy (if not yet of science fiction New Comedy), that the point he accepts about physiognomy casts no doubt at all on a complicated situation where Brownson Sole emerges from the transplant of half of Brown's brain to the body of a Robinson who was one of four quadruplets. Let the first be Brown himself, a long lost son with a name given by foster parents; let the second be the Robinson

---

[43] Cf. Williams (1956–7).

whose body is animated by half of Brown's brain; let the third be a Robinson in whom it happens that the other half of Brown's brain dies; let the fourth be long since dead.

In the first of these two cases, as newly conceived, the body of Brownson Sole is for all relevant purposes indistinguishable (my adversary will say) from the body of Brown. In the second case too, anything Brown can do with his body Brownson can do with his, etc. 'As for the process by which Brownson Sole comes to be from Brown [this philosopher may say], let that be characterized as the process by which *a person x is perpetuated in matter qualitatively indistinguishable from x's and as the sole inheritor of x's particular faculties and physiognomy*. If such a thing were demanded [he will add], then a guarantee could certainly accompany the process just characterized. For, *as thus characterized*, this process can be guaranteed not to create multiple candidates for identity with *x*. It can also be guaranteed not to collide with any of the cognitive considerations adduced in the endless chapter on this subject by David Wiggins. It is all very well for the purist of identity to claim that he is coming to terms with the forensic marks of our concept of human being. It is time for the purist to come to terms with the forensic character of our disputations about identity. Provided that we slightly redescribe the Brown–Brownson case and all its successors, these cases can still show everything they were intended to show.'

My preliminary reply to this philosopher will be to voice my doubt whether making Brownson's face *very like* Brown's face can fully overcome the disquiet that attaches to the very idea of 'wearing' a face. Off stage, one does not wear a face, only an expression of the face.

My second point of reply is that the guarantee my opponent proffers for Brownson Sole is entirely empty if the guarantee now given for the said process's not delivering multiple candidates only consists in the fact that, if it did do so, then we shouldn't *call* the process in question 'the process by which a person *x* is perpetuated in matter qualitatively indistinguishable from *x*'s own and as the sole inheritor of *x*'s . . . particular faculties and physiognomy'. Within our given ontology of processes, with going standards (however local, inscrutable or challenging to theory) of identity and difference, a separation of the kind that my opponent is attempting simply cannot be achieved by putting a special label upon one part of one variety of one of them. (Compare Aristotle, *Metaphysics*, vii, 1030[a 1] ff.) New nomenclature cannot undo the obvious truth that, by the processes he is deploying and the means he is using to perpetuate Brown in Brownson, a surgeon skilled in such techniques (namely transplanting brains or half-brains into bodies matching exactly the bodies they come from *or else*, for this involves the same things, into the bodies within which they will be viable) could produce multiples, and might indeed produce all sorts of further outcomes for which we are even worse prepared.[44]

The third point of reply relates to the idea of a guarantee. This is an idea my opponent wants to cut down to size, to mock and belittle. Let us strive harder to make sense of it. A genuine guarantee relating to this or that process must relate to the nature of the process itself rather than a mere description of it. Moreover, genuine guarantees exist. However you describe it, the process of jam-making can be guaranteed not to produce heavy water out of ordinary water. The now standard process by which a stone is removed from the gall-bladder or is broken up there can be guaranteed not to remove the appendix. Another process that comes with a certain guarantee is the natural process, sustained by the operation of numerous laws of biochemistry, physiology and the rest, by which a human being comes into existence, matures and eventually ceases to be, by 'natural death'. That process is *not* of course guaranteed to save a human being from murder or from premature death by asbestosis, say, or irradiation. But it is certainly guaranteed not to produce multiples, not to transplant brains or half-brains, and not (if that were the better way to think of Brownson) to furnish new bodies to living, continuing brains. That is what makes this familiar process and the principle of activity associated with it one part of the basis for the making of judgments of *identity*. It is the lawful dependability of this process that entitles one whose judgments are shaped by that principle of activity to claim that his practice is answerable to the *Only a and b* rule. If the practice is answerable to that rule and it sees itself as reliant on dependable processes of this sort, then the practice will properly differentiate judgments of identity from judgments to the effect that the object *b* is the

---

[44] 'When Parties in a State are violent, he offered a wonderful Contrivance to reconcile them. The Method is this. You take a Hundred Leaders of each Party; you dispose them into Couples of such whose Heads are nearest of a Size; then let two nice Operators saw off the *Occiput* of each Couple at the same Time, in such a Manner that the Brain may be equally divided. Let the *Occiputs* thus cut off be interchanged, applying each to the Head of his opposite Party-man. It seems indeed to be a Work that requireth some Exactness; but the Professor assured us, that if it were dextrously performed, the Cure would be infallible. For he argued thus; that the two half Brains being left to debate the Matter between themselves within the Space of one Scull, would soon come to a good Understanding, and produce that Moderation as well as Regularity of Thinking, so much to be wished for in the Heads of those, who imagine they came into the World only to watch and govern its Motion: And as to the Difference of Brains in Quantity or Quality, among those who are Directors in Faction; the Doctor assured us from his own Knowledge, that it was a perfect Trifle' (Jonathan Swift, *Gulliver's Travels*: Book III, *A Voyage to Laputa*).

proper replacement/surrogate/proxy for object *a*, or of *a* ('is one of the *a*'s'). No doubt, as I have already allowed, the distinctiveness of identity may in some connections be unimportant. But those cases are a poor basis on which to engage in rhetoric about the 'forensic character of our actual disputations about identity'.

This threefold reply is likely to stir up at least two counter-objections. The first will consist of a challenge to apply the positive account that I have given of the human principle of activity to the case of the human zygote. Normally, the zygote becomes the embryo, but sometimes it divides and becomes twin embryos. What do I say about that? I am committed to react to this fact with a general ruling to the effect that the human being dates from a time after the zygote finally splits or settles down to develop in unitary fashion. The human being, the human person, dates from the point whenceforth it is nomologically excluded that its zygote will divide. I am happy, however, to be committed to say that.[45] An advantage of this decision, which entails that the fertilization of the egg is one part of the assemblage and further preparation of the materials from which the fetus develops, is that it has the effect of blocking the unwelcome suggestion that the fetus is the particular egg that the sperm activated. (If we concurred in that unwelcome suggestion, the fetus might even be accounted as just as old as the egg itself. What will explain better than the ruling that I have proposed why nobody wants to say that the fetus is as old as the egg itself?)

The second objection to what I have claimed concerns the guarantees on which the ordinary business of individuation normally relies. It may be expected to arise from the fact that such guarantees fall far short of any *logical* exclusion of the sort of events that figure in cases that reach beyond Shoemaker's example: 'These guarantees are logically insufficient. But it would be foolish [I shall be told], on the part of those who are so enamoured of their theory that they will put their shirt on guarantees of the kind that you mention, to seek to strengthen these guarantees. For then these enthusiasts will find they have excluded the

---

[45] I find that, years ago, intuitively and in its own way, by a route not wholly dissimilar from that followed in the text, the Committee of Enquiry into Human Fertilization and Embryology (1982) chaired by Baroness Warnock came to substantially the same conclusion. (See Lords Hansard, 7 December 1989.) On 'become' see p. 73, note 14.

If one is moved by moral arguments to adopt a certain conception of the person and one correctly deploys this conception upon some question of identity and difference, must the decision about identity and difference then qualify automatically as a 'moral decision'? I am uncertain, if only because of uncertainty concerning the terms of the question. Leaving that uncertainty on one side, let us not forget that seeing a moral reality can be the reminder of a metaphysical reality.

interventions of orthodox medicine and dentistry from 'proper' or 'admissible' application to human beings as such.'

To this I should reply that it is not my concern, either here or anywhere else, to represent judgments of strict identity as resting on justificatory premises that culminate in the deduction of an identity or that bring among their logical consequences the satisfaction of the **D** principles given in Chapters Two and Three. That is not how the strictness of the relation of identity is to be marked or vindicated. We have long since rejected the deductive conception of identity-judgment. See Chapter Three, §5. (See also Chapter Six, §10, where I found myself reminding the reader of the familiar fact that one can see directly, however fallibly, that it is one's brother not one's uncle who has come to call on one.) The thing which really matters, where someone makes a responsible (however fallible) judgment of identity between the individual objects a and b, is that the various things the person judging has regard for in arriving at it should be the right things for a judgment of identity – that they be things appropriate for a type of judgment which, by its nature, goes well beyond the weaker claim that b instantiates a, that b inherits the role of a, or that b is interchangeable or interfungible with a. One who makes the judgement that a is b deploys an understanding which is all of a piece with the business of subsuming object a under some kind that is associated with a principle of activity (or way of behaving) that things of a's kind exemplify. His understanding must be all of a piece with knowing how to keep track of such things, with grasping things' natures well enough to chronicle what they do or undergo, etc. (See Chapter Two and the various **D** principles that are assembled and paraded there. See also the Preface, last paragraph but six, for the description I see as consequential upon conceiving thus of identity and individuation.) For any genuine object, there is some right way of keeping track of it and this must track it *as a particular*. Cf. Chapter Two, §6. It is from this simple truism that the whole business of making of judgments of identity extrapolates.

What remains then of the difficulty about splitting (etc)? The real difficulty that the theory of individuation must have from cases of splitting, medical intervention, transplantation and the rest (or so I conclude) is not that such occurrences breach the limited and specific guarantees at which the objector is sneering (and which are all that are needed to sustain the relevant way of thinking of something's being securely singled out), but that they *add complications* to the picture we have held out of a substance coasting along (as it were) autonomously or under its own steam. (Which does *not* mean that, even in this picture, it interacts with nothing else.) In coming to terms with these complications, quasi-casu-istically so to speak, without much generality but in ready appreciation of the universality of the commitments that one creates by deciding in one way rather than another, we need constantly to refer the issues that arise back to our conception of the sort of thing that we are dealing with. Minor interventions (medical, dental, orthopaedic, osteopathic . . .) in a human being's pattern of being and acting confront us with no concep-tual difficulties at all. In acquiescing in these, we do not prejudice our understanding of such a pattern. The substance's organic independence can still be conceived as undiminished. There is no problem of persis-tence. (We do not commit ourselves to allow anything on the scale of the Brown–Brownson case.) At the other extreme, however, in the so far imaginary cases where it seems a human being is simply treated as a tem-plate for the production of copies, it is manifest (it ought not to be con-troversial) that ideas are changed almost out of recognition. That is what I should say about Parfit's teletransportation, a fictional process which can as readily carbon-copy me twice (or thrice, or the number of times it takes to make a regiment) as once. In so far as these cases are taken as amounting to the perpetuation of the person Brown, we have lost hold altogether of the notions we began with of what Brown is. The judg-ment that the singular being Brown persists thereby is unsustainable.

Everything depends then on that which lies between the unproble-matic cases and the cases that are out of the question. In these interme-diate cases, where massive transplanting of organs or constant interchange of parts is contemplated, as well as constant fine-tuning of a human being by such expedients as gene therapy, the newly emerging conception under which we subsume a human substance will still be the conception of an individual thing or substance with a destiny of its own. Nevertheless, as we proceed along the road indicated, the conception of a human person will diverge further and further from that of a self-moving, animate living being exercising its capacity to determine, within a framework not of its own choosing and replete with meanings that are larger than it is, its own direct and indirect ends. The conception will converge more and more closely upon the conception of something like an artefact – of something not so much to be encountered in the world as putatively made or produced by us, something that it is really up to us (individually or collectively) not merely to heal or care for or protect but also to repair, to reshape, to reconstruct . . . even to reconceive.

This new or emerging conception of what a person is will perplex us not only with philosophical variants on the problem of artefact identity but with practical questions. At the beginning, it may seem these questions will be easy enough. Later on, when less and less seems to be excluded by the then prevalent conception of human beinghood, they may bewilder us. I speculate that this bewilderment can only grow as that conception is progressively adjusted to the thought that little or nothing that a human being might more than idly wish needs to be out of the question or excluded by our human limitations. Will not bewilderment then turn to total *aporia* as our conception of human personhood is adjusted to the further thought that it is not merely our destiny that is (in large part) up to us, or our ethical identity, but even the kind of thing it is that we are? In the here and now, at a point well short of this limit, there has, of course, been a huge increment in the sum of human well-being. Why deny that? But before extrapolating this gain mindlessly into the open future, or simply rejoicing in the technological freedom that geneticists and medical scientists have been encouraged to create for us, there are questions to answer.

Here is one of them. If we cannot recognize our own given natures and the natural world as setting any limit at all upon the desires that we contemplate taking seriously; if we will not listen to the anticipations and suspicions of the artefactual conception of human beings that sound in half-forgotten moral denunciations of the impulse to see people or human beings as things, as tools, as bearers of military numerals, as cannon-fodder, or as fungibles; if we are not ready to scrutinize with any hesitation or perplexity at all the conviction (as passionate as it is groundless, surely, for no larger conception is available that could validate it) that everything in the world is in principle ours or there for the taking; then what will befall us? Will a new disquiet assail our desires themselves, in a world no less denuded of meaning by our sense of our own omnipotence than ravaged by our self-righteous insatiability?[46]

I frame the question and, having formed it, I grave it here. But a book such as this is not the place in which to enlarge upon it, to answer it, or to speculate about the mental consequences of our available energies being diverted from the gradual discovery and enhancement, within the limits set by our animate nature, of more sustaining human ends – and the further consequences of these energies being progressively redirected to the endless elaboration of the means to ends that are less and less often explored in thought or feeling. This book is not the place nor

---

[46] As the book goes to press, I find a perceptive account of some related misgivings in Harry G. Frankfurt, *Necessity, Volition, and Love* (Cambridge University Press, 1999), pp. 108ff.

is its author the philosopher or moralist to hold up to human beings the image of the insatiability by which they relentlessly simplify the given ecology of the earth and change out of all recognition the given framework of human life. In a treatise on identity and individuation, it is enough and more than enough to point to the conceptual tie that links together these issues of life's framework and meaning, of individuation, and of the way in which we conceive of a human being.

In this work, the chief thing that needs to be made clear is that no freedom that the theory of individuation leaves it open to us to exercise in how we think of ourselves could ever liberate us from the constraints laid down in Chapter One. Whatever it may amount to, our freedom to remake the idea of personhood (to remake it by our pursuits and our choices) could not entail that it would be up to us, once it was determinate what a and b were, whether a certain identity judgment $a = b$ was true or false. For it is impossible on the level of reference and truth-value for there to be such freedom. As soon as it is determinate what a or b is, the result of Chapter One, §10, is inescapable. Moreover, once an identity question is construed in a definite way, it must be determinate what the question turns on. Nothing is left to stipulate. Only at the level of sense is there any room for conceptual invention to enter. At that level, I do not deny, there is freedom to reformulate bit by bit the answer that we commit ourselves to give to the *what are we?* question. It is a freedom we cannot really escape. It is cognate with the conceptualist (residually idealist) insight we expounded in Chapter Six and linked there with our miscellaneous capacities to come to terms with the exigency of the identity relation. But we should think much harder how we exercise it. We should think harder then about the choices that commit us to think of personhood in one way rather than another. These questions are essentially contestable. But from that it does not follow that they permit of more than one answer.

Apart from the logic of individuation, what ought to constrain us in how we think of human beinghood? Only the power of discursive reflection. How wise is it then to allow the goal of attaining the perfect state of material and bodily well-being to fly constantly before us like the rainbow or a will o' the wisp? How wise is it for those who have almost everything to project limitlessly into an open future their opportunities to reconstruct and reconceive themselves in order to have yet more? Where once angels feared to tread, how far will we go? If Schopenhauer had conceived how elusive and difficult the question was going to be found of what conception we should make for ourselves of ourselves; if he had conceived how difficult it would be found by the very substances who exemplify the thing-kind whose nature has come into question; if he had known what kind of commotion the question would occasion or how sensitive the answer would be to the stability or instability of the expectations that still prevail about the world in which we still hope to find meaning and have our engagement; then I wonder whether he would have wanted to persist in his optimistic declaration that 'Just as the boatman sits in his little boat . . . so in the midst of a world of suffering the individual man calmly sits, supported by and trusting the *principium individuationis*' (*World as Will and Idea*, §63).

Select bibliography

For the basis of selection, see Preface, ad fin.

Anscombe, G. E. M., 1953. 'The Principle of Individuation', *Proceedings of the Aristotelian Society*, Supp. Vol. 27, 83–96.

Aristotle, *Categories*, especially Chs. 1–5.

Physics, Bk I, Chs. 7–9; Bk II, Chs. 1–3.

De Anima, Bk II, Chs. 1–4.

Metaphysics, e.g. Bk V, Chs. 6, 7; Bks VII, VIII, X.

Topics, 103a6ff. and 103a23–31.

De Generatione et Corruptione, 318bff.

Politics, 1276 a34–b13.

Ayer, A. J., 1954. *Philosophical Essays* (London: Macmillan), Ch. 2, 'The Identity of Indiscernibles'.

Ayers, Michael R., 1974. 'Individuals Without Sortals', *Canadian Journal of Philosophy*, 4, 113–48.

1992. *John Locke* (London: Routledge), Vol. II, Parts One and Three.

Barcan Marcus, Ruth, 1947. 'The Identity of Individuals in a Strict Functional Calculus of First Order', *Journal of Symbolic Logic*, 12, 12–15.

Black, Max, 1952. 'The Identity of Indiscernibles', *Mind*, 61, 153–64.

Burge, Tyler, 1975. 'Mass Terms, Count Nouns and Change', *Synthèse*, 31.

1977. 'A Theory of Aggregates', *Nous*, 11.

Butler, Joseph, 1736. *First Dissertation* to the *Analogy of Religion Natural and Revealed to the Constitution of Nature*.

Cartwright, Helen M., 1965. 'Heraclitus and the Bath Water', *Philosophical Review*, 74, 466–85.

1970. 'Quantities', *Philosophical Review*, 79, 25–42.

Cartwright, Richard, 1971. 'Identity and Substitutivity', in Milton K. Munitz (ed.), *Identity and Individuation* (New York University Press), 119–33.

1979. 'Indiscernibility Principles', *Midwest Studies in Philosophy*, 4, 293–306.

1987. 'On the Logical Problem of the Trinity', in *Philosophical Essays* (Cambridge, Mass.: MIT).

Chappell, V. C., 1960. 'Sameness and Change', *Philosophical Review*, 69, 351–62.

Chisholm, R. M., 1970. 'Identity Through Time', in Howard E. Kiefer and Milton K. Munitz (eds.), *Language, Belief, and Metaphysics* (Albany: State University of New York Press), 163–82.

1976. *Person and Object* (London: Allen and Unwin), especially Ch. III, Apps. A and B.

Coburn, R., 1976. 'The Persistence of Bodies', *American Philosophical Quarterly*, 13.

Doepke, Frederick, 1982. 'Spatially Coinciding Objects', *Ratio*, 24, 45–60.

Dummett, M. A. E., 1973. *Frege: Philosophy of Language* (London: Duckworth), especially pp. 130–1 and Ch. 16.

1980. 'Does Quantification involve Identity?', in Harry Lewis (ed.), *Peter Geach: A Profile* (Dordrecht: Reidel).

Evans, Gareth, 1975. 'Identity and Predication', *Journal of Philosophy*, 72.

1978. 'Can there be Vague Objects', *Analysis*, 38.

Flew, Anthony, 1951. 'Locke and the Problem of Personal Identity', *Philosophy*, 26.

Fraassen, Bas C. van, 1977–8. 'Essence and Existence', *American Philosophical Quarterly Monograph*.

Frede, Michael, 1987. 'Individuals in Aristotle', in *Essays in Ancient Philosophy* (Oxford University Press), 49–71.

Frege, Gottlob, 1950. *The Foundations of Arithmetic*, trans. J. L. Austin (Oxford: Blackwell), sect. 62.

1952. 'On Sense and Reference' and 'Concept and Object', in P. T. Geach and M. Black (ed. and trans.), *Translations from the Philosophical Writings of Gottlob Frege* (Oxford: Blackwell).

1979. 'Comments on Sense and Reference', in Hermes, Kambartel and Kaulbach (eds.), *Posthumous Writings*, trans. Peter Long and Roger White (Oxford: Blackwell).

1980. 'Letter to Husserl', dated 24 May 1891, in Gottfried, Hermes, Kambartel, Thiel and Veraart (eds.), *Philosophical and Mathematical Correspondence*, abridged for the English edition by Brian McGuiness, trans. Hans Kaal (Oxford: Blackwell).

Geach, P. T., 1962. *Reference and Generality* (Ithaca: Cornell University Press), especially sections 31–4. In the third edition (1980), see especially p. 215.

1965. 'Some Problems About Time', *Proceedings of the British Academy*, 51.

1972. *Logic Matters* (Oxford: Blackwell), pp. 238–49, 302–17.

1973. 'Ontological Relativity and Relative Identity', in Milton K. Munitz (ed.), *Logic and Ontology* (New York University Press).

Goodman, Nelson, 1972. *Problems and Projects* (Indianapolis: Bobbs Merrill), Pt IV. See also under Leonard, Henry S.

Griffin, Nicholas and Routley, R., 1979. 'Towards a logic of relative identity', *Logique et Analyse*.

Hacker, P. M. S., 1979. 'Substance: The Constitution of Reality', *Midwest Studies in Philosophy*, 4, 239–61.

Hacking, Ian, 1972. 'Individual Substances', in Harry G. Frankfurt (ed.), *Leibniz: A Collection of Critical Essays* (New York: Doubleday).

1975. 'All Kinds of Possibility', *Philosophical Review*, 76.

Hampshire, Stuart, 1956. 'Identification and Existence', in H. D. Lewis (ed.), *Contemporary British Philosophy* (London: Allen and Unwin), 3rd series, pp. 191–208.

Heraclitus, 1951. Diels fragments B1, B12, B47, B91, B125, in H. Diels and W. Kranz, *Die Fragmente der Vorsokratiker* (Berlin).

Hobbes, Thomas, *De Corpore*, Pt II, Ch. II, in W. Molesworth (ed.), *The English Works of Thomas Hobbes* (London: John Bohn, 1839–45), Vol. I.

Ishiguro, H., 1972a. 'Leibniz and the Idea of Sensible Qualities', in S. Brown and G. Vesey (eds.), *Reason and Reality* (London: Macmillan).

    1972b. *Leibniz's Philosophy of Logic and Language* (London: Duckworth, and 2nd edn Cambridge University Press, 1990), especially Chs. II, IV.

Johnston, Mark, 1987. 'Human Beings', *Journal of Philosophy*, 84.

Kripke, S., 1971. 'Identity and Necessity', in Milton K. Munitz (ed.), *Identity and Individuation* (New York University Press).

    1972. 'Naming and Necessity', in G. Harman and D. Davidson (eds.), *Semantics of Natural Languages* (Dordrecht: Reidel).

    1980. *Naming and Necessity*, revised text (Oxford: Blackwell).

Leibniz, G. W., *Nouveaux Essais sur l'Entendement Humain*, especially Bk II, Chs. 23, 27; Bk III, Chs. 6, 10, 11, translated as *New Essays on Human Understanding* by Peter Remnant and Jonathan Bennett (Cambridge University Press, 1981).

    Discourse of Metaphysics, Gerhardt IV, pp. 427–63. See next entry.

    Die Philosophischen Schriften von G. W. Leibniz, ed. C. I. Gerhardt, Berlin, 1875–90.

    Correspondence with Clarke, Gerhardt II, Leibniz's fifth paper, sections 21–6.

    'Meditationes de Cognitione, Veritate et Ideis', Gerhardt IV, pp. 422–6.

    Correspondence with De Volder, Gerhardt II. See L. E. Loemker (ed.), *Philosophical Papers and Letters* (Dordrecht: Reidel, 1969), pp. 515–39.

Leonard, Henry S., and Goodman, Nelson, 1940. 'The Calculus of Individuals and its Uses', *Journal of Symbolic Logic*, 5, 45–55.

Lewis, David, 1976. 'Survival and Identity', in A. Rorty (ed.), *The Identities of Persons* (Berkeley: University of California Press).

Locke, John, *Essay Concerning Human Understanding*. II, xxvii.

    Reply to the Bishop of Worcester's Answer to his letter, especially *ad fin*.

Lovibond, Sabina and Williams, S. G., 1996. *Identity, Truth and Value: Essays for David Wiggins*, Aristotelian Society Series, Vol. 16 (Oxford: Blackwell).

Lowe, E. J., 1997. 'Objects and Criteria of Identity', in Bob Hale and Crispin Wright (eds.), *A Companion to the Philosophy of Language* (Oxford: Blackwell).

MacIntyre, Alasdair, 1967. 'Essence and Existence', in Paul Edwards (ed.), *Encyclopaedia of Philosophy* (New York: Macmillan), Vol. III, pp. 59–61.

Mackie, Penelope, 1994. 'Sortal Concepts and Essential Properties', *Philosophical Quarterly*, 44, 311–27.

    1998. 'Identity, Time and Necessity', *Proceedings of the Aristotelian Society*, 98.

McDowell, John, 1977. 'On the Sense and Reference of a Proper Name', *Mind*.

    1997. 'Reductionism and the First Person', in J. Dancy (ed.), *Reading Parfit* (Oxford: Blackwell).

Miri, Mrinal, 1973. 'Memory and Personal Identity', *Mind*, 82.

Noonan, H., 1976. 'Wiggins on Identity', *Mind*, 85.

    1978. 'Sortal Concepts and Identity', *Mind*, 87.

1985. 'The Only X and Y Principle', *Analysis*, 46.

1996. 'Absolute and Relative Identity', in Lovibond and Williams (eds.).

Parfit, Derek, 1971. 'Personal Identity', *Philosophical Review*, 80, 3–27.

1984. *Reasons and Persons* (Oxford University Press), Pt Three.

Pellettier, J. F., 1975. 'A Bibliography of Recent Work on Mass Terms', *Synthèse*, 31.

Perry, John R., 1970. 'The Same *F*', *Philosophical Review*, 79, 181–200.

Plutarch, 'On Common Conceptions' 1083A–1084A, quoted with other materials in Long and Sedley (eds.), *The Hellenistic Philosophers* (Cambridge, 1987).

Popper, K. R., 1953. 'The Principle of Individuation', *Proceedings of the Aristotelian Society*, Suppl. Vol. 27.

Pratt, Vernon, 1972. 'Biological Classification', *British Journal for the Philosophy of Science*, 23, 305–27.

Prior, A., 1960. 'Identifiable Individuals', *Review of Metaphysics*, 13.

1968. 'Time, Existence and Identity', in *Papers on Time and Tense* (Oxford: Clarendon Press), pp. 78–87.

1976. 'Things and Stuff', in *Papers in Logic and Ethics* (London: Duckworth), pp. 181–6.

Putnam, Hilary, 1970. 'Is Semantics Possible?', *Metaphilosophy*, 3; also in *Mind, Language and Reality*, Philosophical Papers, Vol. 2 (Cambridge University Press, 1975).

Quine, W. V. O., 1953. *From a Logical Point of View* (Cambridge, Mass.: Harvard University Press), especially pp. 65–79 ('Identity, Ostension and Hypostasis') and pp. 139–59 ('Reference and Modality').

1960. *Word and Object* (Cambridge, Mass.: MIT Press).

1963. *Set Theory and its Logic* (Cambridge, Mass.: Harvard University Press), Chapter One, §1.

1964. Review of Geach, P. T., *Reference and Generality*, in *Philosophical Review*, 73, 100–4.

1966. 'Three Grades of Modal Involvement', in *The Ways of Paradox and Other Essays* (Cambridge, Mass.: Harvard University Press).

1969. 'Natural Kinds', in N. Rescher (ed.), *Essays in Honour of C. G. Hempel* (Dordrecht: Reidel).

1972. Review of Milton K. Munitz (ed.), *Identity and Individuation*, in *Journal of Philosophy*, 69, 488–9.

1976. 'Worlds Away', *Journal of Philosophy*, 73.

1977. 'Intensions Revisited', *Midwest Studies in Philosophy*, II.

Quinton, A., 1972. *The Nature of Things* (London: Routledge and Kegan Paul), Pt I.

Rea, Michael 1997. (ed.), *Material Constitution: A Reader* (Lowham, Md.: Rowman and Littlefield).

Reid, Thomas, *Essays on the Intellectual Powers of Man* (Edinburgh: John Bell, 1785), Essay III, especially Chs. 4 and 6.

Salmon, N., 1981. *Reference and Essence* (Princeton University Press), pp. 219–29.

Shoemaker, Sydney, 1963. *Self-Knowledge and Self-Identity* (Ithaca: Cornell University Press).

1970. 'Persons and Their Pasts', *American Philosophical Quarterly*, 7, 269–85.

1970. 'Wiggins on Identity', *Philosophical Review*, 79.

1984. 'Identity, Properties and Causality', in *Identity, Cause and Mind* (Cambridge University Press), 234–60.

Shwayder, David, 1963. 'Man and Mechanism', *Australasian Journal of Philosophy*, 41.

Simons, Peter, 1987. *Parts: A Study in Ontology* (Oxford University Press).

Sloman, Aaron, 1965. 'Functions and Rogators', in J. N. Crossley and M. A. E. Dummett (eds.), *Formal Systems and Recursive Functions* (Amsterdam: North Holland Publishing Co.), pp. 155–74.

Smullyan, A. F., 1948. 'Modality and Description', *Journal of Symbolic Logic*, 13, 31–7.

Snowdon, Paul, 1996. 'Persons and Personal Identity', in Lovibond and Williams (eds.).

Stevenson, Leslie, 1972. 'Relative Identity and Leibniz's Law', *Philosophical Quarterly*, 22, 155–8.

1975. 'A Formal Theory of Sortal Quantification', *Notre Dame Journal of Formal Logic*, 16, 185–207.

Strawson, P. F., 1959. *Individuals* (London: Methuen), especially Chs. Three and Four.

1970. 'Chisholm on Identity Through Time', in H. E. Kiefer and Milton K. Munitz (eds.), *Language, Belief, and Metaphysics* (Albany: State University of New York Press), 183–6.

1976. 'Entity and Identity', in H. D. Lewis (ed.), *British Contemporary Philosophy* (London: Allen and Unwin), Vol. IV.

1979. 'May Bes and Might Have Beens', in A. Margalit (ed.), *Meaning and Use* (Dordrecht: Reidel).

Tarski, Alfred, 1956. 'Foundation of the Geometry of Solids', in *Logic, Semantics, and Metamathematics* (Oxford University Press), pp. 24–9. See also under Woodger, J. H.

Wallace, John R., 1964. *Philosophical Grammar*, Stanford University Ph.D., pp. 80–3. Published by University Microfilms Ltd, Ann Arbor, Michigan, 1969.

Wiggins, David, 1967. *Identity and Spatio-Temporal Continuity* (Oxford: Blackwell).

1968. 'On Being in the Same Place at the Same Time', *Philosophical Review*, 77, 90–5.

1974. 'Identity, Continuity and Essentialism', *Synthèse*, 23.

1975. 'Identity, Designation, Essentialism and Physicalism', *Philosophia*, 5, 1–30.

1978. 'Are the Criteria of Identity that hold for a Work of Art in the Different Arts Aesthetically Relevant? Reply to Richard Wollheim', *Ratio*, 20, 52–68.

1979. 'The Concern to Survive', *Midwest Studies in Philosophy*, 4, 417–22.

1982. 'Heraclitus' Conceptions of Flux, Fire, and Material Persistence', in M. Nussbaum and M. Schofield (eds.) *Language and Logos: Essay for G. E. L. Owen* (Cambridge University Press).

1984. 'The Sense and Reference of Predicates: A Running Repair to Frege's Doctrine and Plea for the Copula', *Philosophical Quarterly*, 34, 311–28.

1987a. '"The Concept of the Subject contains the Concept of the Predicate": Leibniz on Reason, Truth and Contingency', in J. J. Thompson (ed.), *On Being and Saying: Essays for Richard Cartwright* (Cambridge, Mass.: MIT Press); reprinted in Roger Woolhouse (ed.), *Leibniz: Critical Assessments* (London: Routledge, 1994), Vol. II, pp. 141–63.

1987b. 'The Person as Object of Science, as Subject of Experience, and as Locus of Value', in A. Peacocke and G. Gillett (eds.), *Persons and Personality* (Oxford: Blackwell).

1992. 'Remembering Directly', in J. Hopkins and A. Savile (eds.), *Psychoanalysis, Mind and Art: Essays for Richard Wollheim* (Oxford: Blackwell).

1993. 'Putnam's Doctrine of Natural Kind Words and Frege's Doctrines of Sense, Reference and Extension. Can they Cohere?', in A. W. Moore (ed.), *Meaning and Reference* (Oxford University Press)

1995. 'Substance', in A. C. Grayling (ed.), *Philosophy: A Guide through the Subject* (Oxford University Press).

1997a. 'Sortal Concepts: a Reply to Fei Xu', *Mind and Language*, 12, 413–21.

1997b. 'Natural Languages as Social Objects', *Philosophy*, 72, 499–524.

Williams, B. A. O., 1956–7. 'Personal Identity and Individuation', *Proceedings of the Aristotelian Society*, 57.

1960. 'Bodily Continuity and Personal Identity', *Analysis*, 21.

1970. 'The Self and the Future', *Philosophical Review*, 79, 161–80.

1973. *Problems of the Self* (Cambridge University Press), papers 1–5.

Williamson, Timothy, 1995. *Vagueness* (London: Routledge).

1996. 'The Necessity and Determinacy of Distinctness', in Lovibond and Williams (eds.).

Woodger, J. H., 1937. *The Axiomatic Method in Biology* (Cambridge University Press), Ch. III, p. 1, and Appendix E (by Tarski), p. 16.

Woods, M. J., 1959. 'Substance and Quality' (B.Phil., Oxford).

1963. 'The Individuation of Things and Places', *Proceedings of the Aristotelian Society*, Supp. Vol. 37, pp. 203–16.

1965. 'Identity and Individuation', in R. J. Butler (ed.), *Analytical Philosophy* (Oxford: Blackwell), 2nd series, pp. 120–30.

Index of names of persons cited or mentioned
See also the Select bibliography

Index of content (themes, theses, examples, etc)

See also Table of contents and Preface pp. xii–xvii